"Captures some of the evenings' most intimate and secret moments."
—*J. Jaronczyk Hawthorne*, *Playboy* (three-bunny review)

"Only one journalist has ever been given long-term complete access to the Oscar telecast, and the great news is that it's Steve Pond. A masterful writer, Pond gives you the wonderful feeling that you're along for the ride as his exclusive guest. He whisks readers backstage, behind the curtain, and into the inner sanctums, taking you through the laughably pretentious moments, the quiet sadnesses, and the humor, preparation, anxiety, glory, and aftermath of the biggest show around."
—*Cameron Crowe*, Oscar-winning writer/director of *Almost Famous* and *Jerry Maguire*

"Surely [Pond's] got superhuman powers of time-space travel . . . The *Premiere* vet appears to have overheard *everything* during fifteen years of total access behind the scenes at the Academy Awards, and he reports it all, too, with the concentration and devotion to minutiae of a true Oscar nerd. (That's a compliment.)" —*Lisa Schwarzbaum*, *Entertainment Weekly*

"Loaded with scandalous backstage Oscar tidbits . . . Oscar's never sounded so wild!" —*David Caplan*, *Star* (three-star review)

"Required reading for the annual extravaganza." —*Vancouver Sun*

"Pond appears to be everywhere at once: in production meetings, onstage at rehearsals, backstage and in the lobby during shows . . . I kept wondering why, say, Steven Spielberg didn't blurt out, 'Who the hell is this guy, and why is he listening in on my conversations?'"
—*John DiLeo*, *The Washington Post*

"After nearly a decade of amazing access, Steve Pond tells all in a deeply dishy, always engaging look at What It Takes to put together everyone's favorite Hollywood extravaganza. Nobody can take you behind the scenes of Oscar night like Steve Pond, which is why *The Big Show* is a must-read for any Oscar fan . . . and any Oscar winner."

—*Chris Connelly*, five-time Oscar pre-show host
and red-carpet fixture

"Pond knows this backstabbing territory well, and fans of Hollywood gossip will find plenty of colorful new material."   —*Publishers Weekly*

"Steve Pond has long been the hardest-working pop-culture writer around, and *The Big Show* proves it. This backstage journey through the last decade of Academy Award specials adds up to way more than the sum of the de rigueur gossip, glamour, and glitz—though there's plenty of that. Based on years of his own behind-the-scenes reporting, Pond delves deep into a closely held world that the public never gets to see, and brings back an all-access-pass portrayal of the stars and of the star-making machinery that makes sure the show must go on. If the Academy awarded Oscars for books about their annual festivities, *The Big Show* would have no competition."

—*David Rensin*, author of *The Mailroom:
Hollywood History from the Bottom Up*

"Anyone who's been around show business comes to realize that often the show behind the show is the most entertaining and intriguing. Steve Pond has taken full advantage of his unique, fly-on-the-wall perspective on the Oscars. The winning result is a compelling, insightful, and revealing look into the glamorous engine room of Hollywood's biggest night."

—*David Wild*, author of *The Showrunners: A Season Inside
the Billion-Dollar, Death-Defying, Madcap World of Television's Real Stars*

Steve Pond

The Big Show

Steve Pond has been writing about popular culture and the entertainment industry for more than twenty-five years at such publications as *Premiere*, the *Los Angeles Times*, *Rolling Stone*, and *The Washington Post*. He lives in Los Angeles.

The Big Show

The Big

SHOW

HIGH TIMES

and

Dirty Dealings

BACKSTAGE

at the

ACADEMY AWARDS®

STEVE POND

*Photographs by Art Streiber,
Lara Jo Regan, David Strick,
and Antonin Kratochvil*

Faber and Faber, Inc.

An affiliate of Farrar, Straus and Giroux / New York

This book is not affiliated with the Academy of Motion Picture Arts and Sciences.

Faber and Faber, Inc.

An affiliate of Farrar, Straus and Giroux

19 Union Square West, New York 10003

The Library of Congress has cataloged the hardcover edition as follows:

Pond, Steve.

The big show : high times and dirty dealings backstage at the Academy Awards / Steve
Pond.— 1st ed.

p.   cm.

Includes index.

ISBN-13: 978-0-571-21193-7

ISBN-10: 0-571-21193-3 (alk. paper)

1. Academy Awards (Motion pictures)   I. Title.

PN1993.92.P66 2005

791.43'079—dc22

2004013294

Paperback ISBN-13: 978-0-571-21190-6

Paperback ISBN-10: 0-571-21190-9

Designed by Abby Kagan

www.fsgbooks.com

1   3   5   7   9   10   8   6   4   2

Contents

Contents

The Big Show

Prologue

A True Tragedy

THEY COULD ALWAYS HEAR HIM COMING. A big man with a bum hip, Allan Carr walked slowly through the rooms of Hillhaven Lodge, his sprawling brick mansion down a private road in Benedict Canyon, a mile north of the Beverly Hills Hotel. His feet dragged a little, and his cane squeaked, then thwacked into the hardwood floors. The house was dimly lit, quiet, and warm, with a gleam from the fireplace reflecting off the polished floor. In the winter of 1989, staff members for the 61st Academy Awards often sat in the study waiting for Carr, and they heard him a couple of rooms away: the shuffle of his feet, but mostly the sound of the cane skidding on the floor, then slamming down. Creak . . . *whap*. Creak . . . *whap*. Creak . . . *whap*. He arrived in his robe and in pain, but the man knew how to make an entrance.

Everybody said the same thing about Allan Carr: he was a *showman*. Carr was short and rotund, swathed in custom caftans when he wasn't wrapped in a robe or a smoking jacket; his baby face was topped with a tousled blond mop and framed by oversized designer glasses. At fifty-one, he had been a manager, a publicist, a producer, and a master promoter, self-

and otherwise. He'd had a hit movie, *Grease*, and a Broadway smash, *La Cage aux Folles*. He knew how to make a fuss, how to attract the press, and especially how to throw a party. In fact, he'd installed a fully functioning disco in the basement of Hillhaven Lodge, which had been a more sedate estate in the hands of its former owner, actress Ingrid Bergman.

But the history was beside the point, because Carr, in the early months of 1989, was producing the Academy Awards. Friends said he looked at it as the pinnacle of his career, as his crowning achievement. In interview after interview, he promised that it would be the biggest, the most glamorous, the most beautiful, the most star-studded, the most *fabulous* Oscars ever.

Carr had been dying to tackle the Oscar assignment ever since he'd put on a particularly festive Governors Ball after the fiftieth-anniversary show in 1978. Expecting a call back then, he was disappointed when it didn't come; a decade later, though, he eagerly took the unpaid job when it was offered to him by Richard Kahn, the president of the Academy of Motion Picture Arts and Sciences. Kahn had originally offered the job to director Gilbert Cates, but when he and Cates couldn't agree on a direction for the show, he turned to the more flamboyant Carr. "Allan was a showman of the first degree, and I wanted to invest our show with the kind of excitement he brought to everything he did," says Kahn. "And we got a lot of excitement, much of which we did not expect."

The new producer was not always in the best of moods: between the hip replacement surgery he'd had in October and the torn knee cartilage he suffered in mid-February, he hurt and he was often cranky. He was overly protective of the stars he considered his friends, and sometimes seemed not to trust anybody but himself to deal with them. He seldom appeared at the dingy, windowless, drab green production office on La Cienega Boulevard, preferring to hold court at Hillhaven, where he'd installed a six-foot Oscar statue by the front door. On the occasions when he left the house on Oscar business, associate producer Michael Seligman drove him around. Carr was a heavy, rough passenger: when the show was over, Seligman had to replace the front seat in his Mercedes SLC.

Carr thought fast, talked fast, made decisions instantly. Some of his staffers were inspired and invigorated by his energy and creativity, but he also kept people off-balance, ill at ease, and wary of slipping and setting off his volcanic temper. Douglass M. Stewart, who put together film clips for the show, was reminded of the character played by William Castle in *The Day of the Locust*, the 1975 film based on Nathanael West's novel about the excesses of Hollywood. "Allan was a flamboyant producer the likes of which are often depicted on-screen," Stewart says. "He was the colorful, charismatic figure screaming from the top of a crane before the whole thing came crashing down around him."

What Carr wanted in an Oscar show was old-fashioned, fabulous glamour. "I remember going with him for our first survey of the Shrine," says Jeff Margolis, the director of that show, which was held at the aging Shrine Auditorium in downtown Los Angeles. "He walked in, and I remember him saying, 'I'm not doing the show here unless they redo all the bathrooms. I want the bathrooms redone, and I want all the hallways and the lobby painted. I want it to smell like it's brand-new.' " Carr got his renovations, whereupon he had a million tulips flown in from the Netherlands and fifty thousand glass beads affixed to the Shrine's curtain. There were names for production designer Ray Klausen's elaborate sets, names that captured the elegance Carr envisioned: "Stars and Diamonds," "Tiffany Jewels with Crystal Beads and Chiffon Swags," "Beaded Victorian Flowers," and "The Grand Drape" among them.

Off the stage, occupying a corner of the adjoining Shrine Exhibition Hall, was perhaps the grandest space of all. The green room at previous Oscar shows had usually been a utilitarian area where stars could relax during the show; Carr dubbed his version Club Oscar and turned it into the most elaborate green room anybody had ever seen. "You never would have known that you were backstage in a theater," says Margolis. "It was like you were in some highfalutin club in West Hollywood or New York City."

Some crew members wondered about the producer's fanatical attention to Club Oscar. "Everybody felt he was more concerned about the green room than the show itself," says stage manager Dency Nelson. "We thought, The guy knows how to throw parties, but does he really know how to produce an awards show?"

But Carr was determined to take care of his stars. He was proud of the people he'd attracted, and proud of the way he was putting them together as part of an overall theme: couples, costars, companions, and compadres.

Sure, not all of his plans worked out: Warren Beatty and Jack Nicholson declined his offer to be presenters, Paul Newman and Joanne Woodward didn't want to fly, Brigitte Bardot would do it only if she could talk about animal rights, Loretta Young only if she could give out best picture by herself. But Demi Moore and Bruce Willis said yes, as did Michael Caine and Sean Connery and Roger Moore, Kim Novak and Jimmy Stewart, Melanie Griffith and Don Johnson, Bob Hope and Lucille Ball.

To kick off this fabulous assemblage, Carr knew he needed a particularly fabulous opening—something to get 'em talking the next day, to announce that these were *his* Academy Awards. Lavish production numbers had long been an Oscar staple, but in recent years they'd been heavy on technical flash and high-tech trickery. "He wanted to simplify it a little bit," says Margolis. "He wanted the production numbers to be big and grand like the old Hollywood movie musicals, without laser beams or smoke and mirrors."

The answer, Carr decided, lay 350 miles to the north in San Francisco, where the satirical, campy musical revue *Beach Blanket Babylon* had been a hit for fifteen years. Simultaneously spoofing and celebrating pop culture, creator Steve Silver threw dozens of pop icons together in a deliriously silly extravaganza. Carr persuaded Silver to adapt the show for the Oscars— whereupon, says Seligman, "that hellacious opening number just grew and grew."

The number became a trip through old Hollywood as taken by a wide-eyed Snow White, a central character in the San Francisco show. She started by speaking with *Variety* columnist and Oscar greeter Army Archerd, visited the legendary Cocoanut Grove nightclub, went on a "blind date" with the young star Rob Lowe, and wound up surrounded by dancing usherettes at Grauman's Chinese Theatre. "Steve kept expanding it, and Allan did not take charge and tell him when to stop," says Seligman. "He brought in Merv Griffin, he brought in Rob Lowe . . . I told him he had to shorten the number, but Allan let it go." Silver's widow, Jo Schuman Silver, remembers it differently. "Steve wanted it to be five or six minutes long at the most," she says, "but Allan got nervous and threw in everything but the kitchen sink."

For the Cocoanut Grove section, Carr lined up several tables full of classic stars, including Doris Day, Dorothy Lamour, Cyd Charisse, Vincent Price, and Roy Rogers and Dale Evans. But his biggest coup was to cast the ultimate Oscar-night host, Irving "Swifty" Lazar, as himself. The reticent Lazar agreed to leave Spago, where he traditionally hosted the hottest Oscar party in town, to table-hop in the number.

At the Shrine, though, even Carr eventually had to face the fact that Silver's production was too big. "It ended up way, *way* too long," says Margolis. "It became a special in itself. We had to cut it, because we knew you could only push the envelope so far in terms of length and style." Some of those who'd watched rehearsals thought the cuts hurt the number and made it more confusing. Late in the game, Swifty Lazar changed his mind and opted not to leave his own Spago soiree.

By the day of the show, the theater was gleaming and Carr was ready. Elaborately costumed and coiffed dancers from Steve Silver's number filled the aisles as the broadcast began. "I sat down at the Shrine, and the curtain was a dazzling, shimmering, huge piece of sequins and velvet," says Douglass Stewart. "Then these *characters* filled up the aisles. The whole house was just so intrigued, so curious, so excited about what was going to happen."

Bruce Davis, who would soon assume the post of executive director of the Academy, sat nearby not knowing what to expect. "He wanted it to all be a surprise, not only to the audience but to us," says Davis. "And when I saw Snow White walk down the aisle and kind of brush by me, I thought, Oh, my God, I wonder if anybody's cleared that. I knew there were some things you have to do some checking around on."

The squeaky-voiced princess, played by a twenty-two-year-old actress named Eileen Bowman, greeted stars in the orchestra section, then sauntered onstage to sing what quickly became an infamous duet with Rob Lowe, who looked shell-shocked as he butchered a rewritten version of the Creedence Clearwater Revival rocker "Proud Mary." "Used to work a lot for Walt Disney / Starring in cartoons every night and day," Bowman warbled, and then Lowe picked up the story: "But you said good-bye to Doc and Sleepy / Left the dwarf behind, came to town to stay . . ." The impossibly cheesy number, which went on for an agonizing twelve minutes, also included dancing tables, a high-kicking chorus line of ushers, and Merv Griffin singing "I've Got a Lovely Bunch of Coconuts" in front of a batch of legendary stars sprinkled across the stage like so much window dressing. "His mistake was having that first number go on for so long," says Gilbert

Cates, who would in subsequent years produce the Oscar show himself. "When you see something that doesn't work, by four minutes it's terrible, by five minutes it's outrageous, by eight minutes it's the kiss of death, and by twelve minutes it's the worst thing you've ever seen in your life."

Not long after the opening number, Carr visited the press tent behind the Shrine. "How's the food?" he asked the reporters, some of whom were simultaneously trying to watch the show on monitors, interview winners and presenters, and grab sandwiches from a modest buffet. When asked his opinion of the show so far, Carr beamed. "We couldn't be happier."

Midway through the evening, another fifteen-minute production number showcased twenty "stars of tomorrow" singing a regrettable anthem entitled "I Wanna Be an Oscar Winner." (A "super-trouper, super-duper Oscar winner," no less.) The youngsters included Corey Feldman doing a Michael Jackson impersonation, Christian Slater sword fighting with Tyrone Power, Jr., Patrick Dempsey undertaking a soft shoe, Chad Lowe emoting ("I'm a thespian in the classic sense!"), fifteen-year-old Savion Glover tap-dancing (one bit of actual talent on display), and other offerings from Blair Underwood, Holly Robinson, Joely Fisher, Keith Coogan, Patrick O'Neal, Carrie Hamilton, Ricki Lake, Tricia Leigh Fisher, Corey Parker, Tracy Nelson, D. A. Pawley, Tracy Edwards, Melora Hardin, and Matt Lattanzi, most of whom looked vaguely embarrassed. For the record, none of the twenty have come close to winning an Academy Award in the ensuing years, though Christian Slater won an MTV Movie Award for "most desirable male" and Chad Lowe watched his wife, Hilary Swank, pick up Oscars for *Boys Don't Cry* and *Million Dollar Baby*.

Elsewhere on Carr's show, the chitchat between his carefully matched presenters was cutesy and interminable. The best-picture award was entrusted not to Loretta Young but to the less legendary but (to Carr's mind) more fabulous Cher, who dressed for the occasion in a fringed, strapless mini. Reading from the TelePrompTer and addressing his wife, Geena Davis, Jeff Goldblum could have been speaking for most of the participants when he asked, "Have we lost our sense of dignity . . . here?"

Still, many of those present were swept up in the sheer exuberance of the producer's outlandish vision. When the show ended and the credits began to roll, it was quiet in Club Oscar until Carr's name appeared on the screen.

Then Bruce Willis began to applaud, quickly joined by most of the stars in the room. At the Governors Ball, remembers Margolis, "Everybody was flying high. There was a buzz in the room, people were talking about how different it was.

Yet as he left the Governors Ball that night, Carr knew his brash style had alienated people. "We were driving to Spago for Swifty's party," remembers Bruce Vilanch, "and Allan turned to me and said, 'I burned a lot of bridges on this one.'"

The trouble began early, as Academy president Richard Kahn was sitting at his desk. "I was basking in the terrific ratings and the reaction we'd gotten," remembers Kahn. "And at about 9:15 I took another phone call, which I thought would be somebody else telling me what a great show it was." The caller was Frank Wells, the president of the Walt Disney Company and one of the most respected executives in Hollywood. "I think we have a real problem," Wells said.

Carr had not cleared the use of Snow White, and Wells wanted a formal apology. By midday, Disney lawyers were threatening to sue for copyright infringement; by the end of the day, they'd carried out the threat. Kahn drafted an apology that was delivered at a press conference eleven days later. Carr attended the press conference, and then the devastated producer called Jeff Margolis in tears.

Critics savaged his show: "one of the most grotesque television broadcasts in recent memory," said film critic David Ehrenstein in the *Los Angeles Herald-Examiner*. Gregory Peck wrote Kahn a letter saying "it looked like the Photoplay Awards," a reference to a tacky show put on by the now-defunct movie magazine, and threatening to give back his two Academy Awards if subsequent shows were going to look like Carr's. Seventeen Academy members, including Peck, Paul Newman, Billy Wilder, and Julie Andrews, wrote an open letter calling the show "an embarrassment to both the Academy and the motion picture industry"—although Kahn says, "I collared the people one by one, and most of them expressed no recollection of putting their names on that letter."

Carr never knew what hit him. He briefly tried to come to his own defense, claiming that former president Ronald Reagan called it "the best television show I've ever seen," and showing *Los Angeles Times* reporter

Charles Champlin a stack of laudatory letters and telegrams. One came from agent Michael Ovitz, for whom the night had been a particular triumph: the movie Ovitz had shepherded through years of adversity, *Rain Man*, had been the big winner. "You brought show business back to the movie business," Ovitz wrote.

But the complaints overwhelmed the kudos, and Carr sank into a depression that gripped him for years. "He was blindsided completely, and it devastated him," said Seligman. "His biggest mistake was to tell everybody beforehand that he was going to do a show better than any other producer, because that set every previous producer against him. And when he failed, he completely lost respect in the community. He never got over that."

Gil Cates sympathizes with his predecessor as well. "I think Allan got a bad rap, and I think it hurt him beyond measure," says Cates. "Had that first number been three minutes long, Allan Carr might still be alive and still be producing the show."

Years later, Carr briefly surfaced for the twentieth-anniversary rerelease of *Grease*. Otherwise, he stayed out of sight. He died ten years after his Oscar show, without having done much in the interim. The cause of death was liver cancer, but some thought that other factors contributed.

"It's a true tragedy," says Seligman. "It killed him. Frankly, I think, more than anything else, the reaction to that show really killed him."

IF IT WAS A DISASTER ON MANY LEVELS, Allan Carr's show shaped the modern Academy Awards in more ways than the producer could have realized. Much of what has happened to the Oscars since then has been a reaction against the Carr show: the Academy convened a panel to figure out what went wrong and how to keep it from happening again, and then hired the man who headed that panel, Cates, to produce eleven of the next fifteen shows. Carr's show caused a backlash that restored dignity to the Oscar show . . . if you can call David Letterman's Top Ten List or Whoopi Goldberg's double entendres dignified. It doomed large-scale production numbers . . . but only until Debbie Allen and Paula Abdul began choreographing battalions of dancing fish, genies, and lions. It did away with cute chat between presenters . . . briefly, if at all. Carr's, in fact, was a night whose excesses weren't all that far removed from some of the excesses seen on shows produced by the guy who was hired to be the anti-Carr, or the others who followed him.

"He brought the show into the new era," insists Richard Kahn, "and did things that had never been done before but are now tradition." Carr was the one who replaced the phrase "and the winner is . . ." with the less exclusionary "and the Oscar goes to . . ." He was the first to hire a fashion coordinator and stage an Oscar Fashion Show, the first to hand out Oscar nominee sweatshirts, the first to take the crucial step of finding corporate partners for promotional tie-ins. He was the first to turn the green room into a glamorous sanctuary for stars. He was the first producer to hire writer Bruce Vilanch, who has been the chief comic voice of the show ever since.

"That was widely felt to be a disastrous show, both inside and outside the Academy, but it's amazing how many of the innovations that Mr. Carr introduced are still with us today," says Bruce Davis. "He was selected because he was a showman, and by God, he did some things that were fun. It's hard to change the Oscars, but he was an energizing force."

Jeff Margolis defends the show even more avidly. "There was a sameness to the shows before that, and Allan really turned it on its ass," he says. "People were walking out of there going, 'What the hell just happened?' which was great. Allan was just what the show needed."

"To me, there is no question that Allan Carr's show paved the way for what has happened since then," says Chuck Workman, an Oscar winner who has made short films for most of the shows since 1988. "Often, I think that it takes a terrible disaster to let people see what is possible. You see that in politics: at Kent State, four students got killed, but that was the point where the hippies won. And you see that in popular culture all the time. Something is totally disastrous, somebody went too far, but the next person senses what is possible. We have to give Allan Carr his due for that."

THE PAST FIFTEEN YEARS have been a period in popular culture in which Allan Carr, under different circumstances, would have felt at home. The flamboyant, outsized producer, enamored of glamour and excess and celebrity, had embraced the hedonistic indulgences of the disco era and the shiny consumption of the eighties; had he been a participant rather than a broken man during the nineties, he could have enjoyed the pace of an era in which the media and the public eagerly built up, knocked down, embraced, and discarded celebrities and wannabees with astonishing speed.

The show that helped destroy Carr has been a significant part of the process. From the rise of the independent film to the decline of the major television networks, from the success of brain-dead blockbusters to the burgeoning of movie marketing as a contact sport—over the past fifteen years, the Academy Awards have been a battleground in which the themes running through the entire entertainment industry have played out.

At stake is the most widely recognized symbol of excellence in the entertainment industry—and also, clearly, one of the most potent marketing tools ever created. The monetary value of an Academy Award varies widely from film to film—generally speaking, the more successful a movie is before winning an Oscar, the less it benefits—but in most cases it reaches into the tens of millions of dollars. For the city of Los Angeles, the state of California, the movie industry in general, the value of the show is even harder to quantify, though the *Los Angeles Times* once estimated the figure at nearly $650 million, factoring in everything from the cost of trade advertisements to the money spent on pre- and postshow parties.

Advertising during the Oscar show alone brings ABC more than $75 million, of which as much as half goes to the Academy for broadcast rights. The Academy of Motion Picture Arts and Sciences pays for the production of the show, which costs more than $10 million; events surrounding the show add many more millions to the cost. What's left from ABC's fee is enough to cover virtually all of the Academy's annual operating budget.

The Academy has other sources of income: its membership dues bring in more than $1 million each year, while the organization built up an endowment worth tens of millions through fund-raising efforts that began in the early 1990s. But just as the Oscar show brings in the lion's share of the Academy's income, so has it become to most people the public face of the organization, and of Hollywood. The Academy operates a world-class film archive, awards screenwriting fellowships, and runs year-round screenings, exhibitions, and lectures—but to the public, it has a singular identity as the group that hands out Academy Awards.

The irony here—that an organization devoted to motion pictures supports itself by selling the rights to a TV show—is not lost on Academy officials. But they've embraced it, making sure that the Oscar show is always designed with TV viewers rather than the theater audience in mind.

Most years, the Oscars attract more of those viewers than any other nonsports program on television. The best-picture winner is usually seen by far more people on the Oscar show than in theaters; in recent years, only *Forrest Gump*, *Titanic*, and *The Lord of the Rings: The Return of the King* have boasted the kind of attendance figures that might rival their Oscar-night audiences. The party line that the Oscars are watched by a billion people is a lie, as the Academy will admit when pressed—but viewers still number well into the hundreds of millions, making the show a rival of the Super Bowl as the most watched telecast around the world.

"The Super Bowl kills us in the United States, and we don't have accurate figures for the rest of the world," concedes Bruce Davis. "But if you think about it, what's more popular around the world—American movies, or American football? I think we catch up to them in other countries."

Particularly over the past ten years, scrutiny of the event has increased on nearly every level. Dozens of magazines and nearly as many television shows are devoted to the lifestyles, foibles, and missteps of the rich and famous, and to them the Oscars are the main event. No other night is quite so resplendent with the top echelon of stardom, quite so grand a showcase for celebrity in all its finery and its absurdity. But in a culture highly attuned to competition, as witnessed in everything from the Super Bowl to *American Idol*, the Oscars are also irresistible in the way they ruthlessly turn the stars into haves and have-nots, supplying far more of the latter than the former. When those five boxes appear on the screen showing the faces of the nominees as the envelope is opened, who doesn't want to catch the losers in that moment of disappointment that proves impossible to hide? The show also fits neatly into the desire to track celebrities through every predictable moment of the *Behind the Music* or *True Hollywood Story* arc: Winona's down, Nicole's back, Whitney's heading for a fall . . . The Oscars can serve equally well as the moment of redemption, or as the pride that goeth before the fall.

The Academy Awards also reflect, more and more fully, the vicious side of Hollywood. In the 1980s, as the post–*Star Wars* blockbuster mentality firmly took control of Hollywood's major studios, the Oscars were one time of year when the studios could tell themselves it wasn't all about money. Even if studios were desperate for the next *Top Gun* or *Rambo*, Hollywood could point to Academy Awards for smaller films like *Kiss of the Spider Woman* or *Tender Mercies* as proof that the business was still about art *and* commerce.

But a business accustomed to the cutthroat pursuit of money could easily adapt to the cutthroat pursuit of gold statuettes. Over the past fifteen years, Oscar campaigns have displayed a nearly unprecedented ferocity. Ironically, more than a few of the campaign tricks came straight from Allan Carr's strategy for landing *The Deer Hunter* a best-picture win in 1979. Carr persuaded EMI and Universal to open the movie late in the year, building the buzz through special screenings and making it the movie of the moment precisely at the time when Oscar ballots would be in the mail. A decade later, this would be a strategy frequently used to great effect by Miramax as the company revolutionized Oscar campaigning.

But the strategy of opening late was only a start. Ad campaigns relying solely on genteel "for your consideration" ads in the Hollywood trade papers became a rarity, replaced by multifront campaigns encompassing parties, talk shows, celebrity endorsements, and the use of occasional underhanded tactics that ranged from artfully obscuring the true nature of your film to quietly bad-mouthing an opponent's entry.

The Academy finds the very thought of Oscar campaigns to be distasteful, along with the idea that those campaigns have any influence on voters. The organization is well aware that the importance and significance of the Academy Awards is tied to the perception that they genuinely are awarded for merit. When Halle Berry broke down sobbing after winning the best-actress Oscar in 2002, she was not doing so because her win meant another $20 million in box-office grosses and video sales for *Monster's Ball*, or because her asking price had just gone up; the numbers that affected her were the 6,000 voters who'd chosen her as the best, rather than the 600 million viewers who watched it happen. To safeguard that prestige, the Academy had spent much of the last decade fine-tuning its regulations that relate to campaigning, reacting as studios have violated the letter and the spirit of the law, and punishing the most serious transgressions.

At this point, though, even the Academy would not pretend that its annual awards are, or ever were, an artistic oasis unsullied by the mercenary zeal of the movie business. Oscar statuettes are the most valuable prizes to be accumulated by companies determined to accumulate both money and prizes by any means necessary.

At the center of these questions about intention and competition is the Academy Awards show itself. Whether you celebrate the Oscars as a sincere effort to honor artistry, or condemn them as a symptom of all that is wrong with Hollywood, the show is often irresistible television. It's a glitzy, glamorous, frequently god-awful display of fashion; it's a variety show, an increasingly rare commodity on TV, in which big stars sing songs you probably don't recognize; it's a chance to watch rich and famous people attempt to act pleased when somebody else wins an award. For three and a half or four hours, Hollywood's (and, often as not, a handful of the world's) brightest, most beautiful, and occasionally best get all dressed up, parade in front of cameras, and then pretend to be pleased as 80 percent of them go home losers.

In the last decade and a half, the Academy Awards broadcast has reached record lengths on three separate occasions, while battling a trend of declining ratings for network television. It has showcased five different hosts, and served as a sometimes eager, sometimes reluctant vehicle for the coronation of such outsized egos as James Cameron and Harvey Weinstein. At times, it has seemed irrelevant to the battles waged elsewhere in Hollywood; other times it has been a perfect case study in those battles. It is still the grandest, wildest celebration, dogfight, fashion show, and circus ever staged by the movie business. And just as in Allan Carr's day, dance numbers are still roundly panned, viewers still go to the refrigerator during the endless procession of technical awards, and presenters still look lost when they try to talk to each other.

IN EARLY 1994, the Academy agreed to give *Premiere* magazine unprecedented access to production meetings and rehearsals for that year's Oscar show, as well as backstage access during the show itself. While the rest of the massive Oscar press corps was invited to staged events and sequestered in the press room during the show, I was allowed to cover the event from the inside. Although the arrangement was initially envisioned as one time only, the Academy and the producers of the Oscar shows continued to allow me access in ensuing years. The degree of that access has varied slightly, but for the most part I have been allowed near-total entrée into an event that receives saturation coverage, but only from the outside; that draws intense scrutiny for about two months, then fades.

"It has the most glorious short life of any enterprise that I've ever been involved with," said Gil Cates, the most frequent producer of Oscar shows over the past fifteen years. "When you finish shooting a movie, you have to edit it, and afterward there's a life on television, on cable, on tape, in foreign markets. If you do a play, even if it closes there's the potential of an afterlife somewhere. The Academy Awards show lives gloriously in over a hundred countries for three and a half hours, and then it's gone. And I guess the reason I keep coming back to the well is that the process just astonishes me."

The goal of this book is to look inside that process, at the unseen, unguarded side of the Oscars. In studying the negotiations and machinations, the politics, the compromises, and the excesses of a strange, extraordinary event, I also hope to sketch a portrait of fifteen years of shifting currents, adjustments, and upheaval in the motion picture industry.

A NOTE ON DATES: The Academy refers to Oscar shows by the year during which the eligible movies were released. The show that takes place in February 2005, for instance, is officially the 2004 Oscars. I have tried to avoid that labeling as often as possible, because I'm dealing more with the Oscar shows themselves than with the movies under consideration. Thus, if I mention the seventy-fifth Oscar show, which took place in March 2003, I've tried to call it "the Oscars in 2003" rather than "the 2002 Oscars." I know that's not how the Academy likes to identify its shows, but I find it less confusing.

Introduction

History Is Made at Night

IT DIDN'T LOOK LIKE MUCH ON PAPER. Tucked away in the middle of a statement of aims drafted by the newly formed Academy of Motion Picture Arts and Sciences was a modest suggestion, almost an afterthought. The organization, it suggested, should encourage its young industry in a variety of ways, including handing out "awards of merit for distinctive achievement."

Awards weren't the point of the new Academy, which was formed in 1927 in large part to consolidate power in the hands of Hollywood studios and producers, and by doing so to stem the tide of unionization by workers in the fledgling industry. The document drafted by the group's thirty-six founders, which emphasized the noble more than the practical, put the emphasis on ideals like promoting harmony among movie professionals, protecting "the honor and good repute" of the industry, and "meeting outside attacks" from both church and state. In fact, the idea of awards wasn't even pursued until a year after the organization's founding, during which time the Academy had already intervened in a looming labor dispute, raised

$35,000 for victims of floods along the Mississippi River, and begun a library of material related to motion pictures.

Initially, Academy Awards were given out in a dozen categories: actor, actress, director, comedy direction, cinematography, interior decoration, the catchall engineering effects, three writing awards (adaptation, original story, and title writing), and the confusing tandem of best production and artistic quality of production. The winners were chosen by a committee of five, one from each of the Academy's branches. The committee was overseen by MGM chief Louis B. Mayer, hardly a disinterested observer.

Mayer, the driving force behind the formation of the Academy, was an autocratic boss who ran the most influential of Hollywood's studios, and by extension much of the town as well. Born in Russia but raised in Canada, the conservative and moralistic Mayer controlled the contracts of an enormous collection of stars, painting himself as a father figure while keeping a tight hand on the purse strings. The idea of the Academy had been floated during a small dinner at Mayer's home, and while he stayed out of the limelight (the actor Douglas Fairbanks, the organization's first president, having been deemed a better public face for the Academy), Mayer was known to cajole, argue, and otherwise pull strings behind the scenes.

The first Academy Awards took place on May 16, 1929, in the Blossom Room of the Hollywood Roosevelt Hotel. The midsized banquet room, which sits across the street and less than a block west of the current site of the Oscars, the Kodak Theatre, hosted less than three hundred Academy members and guests, who partook of dinner and dancing before Fairbanks handed out statuettes to the winners and scrolls to the runners-up. The only recipient to make a speech was Darryl F. Zanuck, who accepted a special award for *The Jazz Singer*—which, as a talking picture, had been ruled ineligible for the regular awards. Another special award—and, in a way, another consolation prize—went to Charlie Chaplin, who'd failed to be nominated after writing, directing, producing, and acting in *The Circus*.

At that first ceremony, there had been no attempt to create suspense: the winners had all been announced three months before the banquet, and two of those winners—best actor Emil Jannings and Paramount head Adolph Zukor, accepting the best-production award for *Wings*—had already been given their statuettes.

Slowly, though, the awards and the presentation underwent a metamorphosis. The second year, the Academy tried to clear up the problems caused by two de facto best-picture awards, consolidating best-production and artistic quality of production categories into a single best-picture award. The engineering award was eliminated, the three writing awards reduced to one, and the two directing awards to one. Four of the seven awards went to founding members of the Academy, including one to art director Cedric Gibbons, the man who also designed the statuette. Mary Pickford was named best actress for *Coquette*, a movie that had not been well received, intensifying criticism of the committee system. After the ceremony, the Academy decided that all its members would henceforth be allowed to vote.

But raising the number of voters from five to four hundred did not end complaints about the results, or about the pervasive influence of studio bosses. The following year, Greta Garbo's acclaimed performance in *Anna Christie* was overlooked for best actress in favor of Norma Shearer, the wife of MGM executive Irving Thalberg. Rumors flew that the studio, which released both Garbo's and Shearer's films, had urged all its employees in the Academy to vote for the latter. "What do you expect?" snapped Joan Crawford of Shearer's win. "She sleeps with the boss."

Throughout much of the 1930s, the Academy Awards remained a collegial event, designed more for the industry pals who filled banquet rooms than for the general public. Although a local radio station broadcast segments of the show beginning in its second year, postdinner entertainment usually consisted of nothing livelier than protracted speechmaking. In 1931, in fact, so many notables got up to talk—beginning with the vice president of the United States, Charles Curtis—that the awards weren't handed out until after midnight. By the time Marie Dressler was named best actress for *Min and Bill*, ten-year-old nominee Jackie Coogan had fallen asleep on her shoulder. Dressler had to gently dislodge him before accepting her award.

Over the next few years, the Academy saw its award grow in stature and importance, and also acquire the nickname of Oscar—though it's still uncertain whether the moniker came from Academy librarian Margaret Herrick, actress Bette Davis, or gossip columnist Sidney Skolsky, all of whom claimed responsibility. Those years also produced the show's first dead heat (Fredric March won the 1932 best-actor race by a single vote over Wallace

Beery, but Academy rules considered anything closer than three votes a tie) and the only write-in winner in its history, cinematographer Hal Mohr for *A Midsummer Night's Dream.*

Mohr had not been nominated, he believed, because of the ill will caused by his activism in the labor disputes that threatened Hollywood in the mid-1930s. The Screenwriters Guild and the Screen Actors Guild, both formed in 1933, were initially populated by writers and actors who'd quit the Academy, angry at its tacit support of Depression-era regulations that would have imposed salary ceilings and restricted the ability of actors to switch studios after fulfilling their contracts. The Screen Directors Guild was formed three years later, and like the other guilds encouraged its members to skip the Oscar ceremony. When the major studios followed by withdrawing their financial support of the floundering Academy, it fell to new president Frank Capra to right the sinking ship.

Capra, the thirty-eight-year-old, Sicilian-born director of *It Happened One Night* and *Mr. Deeds Goes to Town,* had gotten off to a rough start with the Academy. He'd first been nominated for best director for his 1933 movie *Lady for a Day,* and had attended the ceremony badly wanting to win. That night's emcee, Will Rogers, had a folksy, conversational way of announcing the winners, and when he got to Capra's category he rambled for a bit before announcing, "Come on up and get it, Frank!" In his autobiography, Capra said he got to his feet and was halfway to the stage before realizing, to his enduring embarrassment, that Rogers had been addressing *Cavalcade* director Frank Lloyd. But Capra made the walk for real the following year, when *It Happened One Night* won Oscars for best picture, actor, actress, adapted screenplay, and director.

After rewarding his movie with that unprecedented sweep of the top categories, the Academy made Capra its president during the stormiest time in the organization's brief history. In an attempt to save the show in 1936, Capra turned the evening into a tribute to film pioneer D. W. Griffith, attracting stars who might otherwise have boycotted. He also moved to ensure the integrity of the voting process by hiring Price Waterhouse & Co. to collect and tabulate the votes.

In order to meet the deadlines for late newspaper editions, though, the Academy continued to give the results to the press at the beginning of the festivities. In 1937, this allowed an impatient best-actress nominee, Gladys George, to stroll through the press room and learn she'd lost to Luise Rainer; a disconsolate George headed for the ladies' room, where she shared the bad news with fellow nominee Carole Lombard. Three years later, after the *Los Angeles Times* published the results in its 8:45 p.m. edition, which was carried into the show by late-arriving guests, the Academy decreed that envelopes would henceforth remain sealed until they were opened onstage.

Since the ninth Oscar show in 1937, those envelopes had included the new categories of supporting actor and actress. Character actor Walter Brennan won three of the first five supporting-actor Oscars, a record attributed in part to the fact that in 1938 the Academy had opened voting to members of all Hollywood guilds—including the populous Screen Extras Guild, whose members liked to honor those who, like Brennan, had come up through their ranks. The extras were also instrumental in the best-picture win for *Casablanca* in 1944. *The Song of Bernadette* had more nominations and was the odds-on favorite coming into the awards—but in an unusual if not unprecedented attempt to make it a prestige picture, 20th Century-Fox limited *Bernadette* to a few theaters in Los Angeles and New York, with tickets priced significantly higher than the nationwide average of 29 cents. After the Oscars, a survey of the Screen Extras Guild members, not the most well-heeled group of voters, showed that only one in four had even seen *Bernadette*, while almost all had seen *Casablanca*.

The show at which *Casablanca* won was also the first to be held in a theater rather than a banquet room, an expensive dinner dance having been deemed unseemly in wartime. Oscar winners during World War II received plaster statuettes, which were replaced with the gold-plated metal ones after the war ended. (Since 1941, the statuettes had carried a stipulation that still stands: winners were forbidden from reselling them without first offering them back to the Academy for ten dollars.)

As the war ended, another battleground heated up. Returning to prominence with the title role in *Mildred Pierce* after nearly a decade of lackluster, largely unsuccessful movies, actress Joan Crawford hired press agent Henry Rogers, who masterminded what might have been the first true Oscar campaign. While open solicitation of votes had proved fruitless when MGM became the first company to take out trade ads on behalf of the Eugene

O'Neill drama *Ah, Wilderness* in 1935, Rogers's style was subtler. Planting items in gossip columns, calling friends at the studios, and making sure Crawford was available and cooperative with anyone who wanted to talk about her maturation, by Oscar night he'd turned his client into the odds-on favorite—at which point a terrified Crawford refused to attend the show because, she said, she knew she was going to lose.

Undaunted, Rogers notified the press that his client was in bed with a 104-degree fever, while dispatching a hairdresser and makeup man to her house, just in case. Crawford won and director Michael Curtiz accepted on her behalf; back home in Brentwood, the actress managed to get out of bed, don an appropriately photogenic negligee, and sit with her groomers. When Rogers delivered her Oscar after the ceremony, Crawford was ready for her close-up. Said the admiring publicist later, "The photo of her in bed clutching the Oscar pushed all the other winners off the front page."

The following year, members of the actors, writers, directors, and extras guilds were removed from the voting rolls. The guilds were still invited to participate in the nominations, but only Academy members made the final choices. Even with an influx of new members that more than doubled the size of the Academy, to sixteen hundred plus, the electorate was far smaller than the previous year's total of more than nine thousand. With fewer voters to influence, campaigning by the studios picked up. That year, Rosalind Russell was the prohibitive best-actress favorite for *Mourning Becomes Electra*, but when Fredric March opened the envelope and read the name of Loretta Young, the audience was shocked—none more so than Russell, who'd already begun to rise from her seat in anticipation of a triumphant walk to the stage. Thinking quickly, Russell simply stayed on her feet and started clapping, appearing to graciously lead the standing ovation for her opponent.

Within two months of that ceremony, the five major Hollywood studios were dealt a blow by the Supreme Court, which ruled that it was a violation of antitrust laws to own both movie studios and theater chains. The studios became desperate to cut costs after the loss of what had been as much as 50 percent of their income, so they decided they could no longer underwrite the Oscar ceremony. Faced with canceling the show in 1949 for lack of funds, the Academy instead downsized, moving from the 6,000-seat Shrine

Auditorium to the 985-seat screening room in its Melrose Avenue headquarters. That night, in a move that some saw as payback for Hollywood's stinginess, six awards went to British films, including best picture to *Hamlet* and best actor to Laurence Olivier. The following year, the studios restored their financial support and the show moved to the ornate, twenty-eight-hundred-seat Pantages Theater in Hollywood.

The post–World War II years were rough ones for the movie business, battered not only by the court's ruling but also by a substantial slump in movie attendance largely attributed to the new medium of television. Unwilling to aid the enemy, the Academy had always resisted the idea of televising its show—but by 1953 it had little choice. In the face of uncertain support from the studios, a $100,000 offer from the National Broadcasting Company was irresistible. Men were warned that white shirts didn't photograph well under TV lights, women were told that pale colors worked best, and many stars took the easy way out and stayed home. Still, the likes of Mary Pickford, Jimmy Stewart, Ginger Rogers, and Olivia de Havilland appeared, and the bond between the Academy and the young medium was cemented when the ratings came in. The show had drawn the biggest audience in the five-year history of commercial television.

The move to television also marked the return to the Oscars of Bob Hope, who'd hosted all or part of five shows before his own television show had briefly rendered him unacceptable to the Academy. With the organization now committed to TV, Hope would return to host thirteen more times over the next twenty-five years. Over that time, Hope would perfect a standard shtick made up of mild political and movie-industry gags and countless jokes about how he'd never won an Academy Award (never mentioning that he'd been given five honorary awards).

Another milestone came with the best-picture winner *Marty* in 1956: the low-key drama, which began life as a television play, became the first film whose production cost ($340,000) was less than the price of its Oscar campaign ($400,000). With extensive prerelease screenings to foster word of mouth; ads bearing endorsements from actors such as Charlton Heston, Dean Martin, and Jane Russell; nonstop personal appearances by the film's likable star, Ernest Borgnine; and an unprecedented offer to send a 16-millimeter print of the movie to the home of any Academy member, the film's promotional blitz netted it four Oscars, including best picture and best actor.

By the end of the decade, the alliance between the Oscar show and television was becoming a comfortable one. The Hollywood studios even agreed to buy all the advertising for three years running, from 1958 through 1960. Still, adapting to the new medium was not entirely smooth: Bette Davis, for instance, fumed in 1958 when the network cut away before she handed out five honorary awards. The following year, emcee Jerry Lewis ran into the opposite problem: the show was twenty minutes ahead of schedule when it went into its final number, a rendition of "There's No Business Like Show Business" sung by actress Mitzi Gaynor. Lewis shouted "Another twenty times!" and desperately mugged for the cameras until NBC mercifully ended the broadcast early.

Beginning in 1961, the Oscars headed for the beach for seven years, to the Santa Monica Civic Auditorium. One of the few larger venues that could give the Academy enough setup time, the three-thousand-seat Civic was the first Oscar venue well outside the Hollywood–downtown Los Angeles axis. The inaugural show there was notable for the first public appearance of Elizabeth Taylor following an illness that had caused her to undergo a tracheotomy in London. Taylor had been nominated for her role in *Butterfield 8*, a seamy potboiler in which she hadn't wanted to appear—and though she continued to insist that she hated the movie, the sympathy vote helped win her the best-actress trophy over Shirley MacLaine in *The Apartment*. That film's director, Billy Wilder, sent MacLaine a telegram that read, YOU MAY NOT HAVE A HOLE IN YOUR WINDPIPE BUT WE LOVE YOU ANYWAY.

The controversy over Taylor's win was minor compared to the flap that surrounded John Wayne's three-and-a-half-hour epic *The Alamo*. To support his expensive, flag-waving film, Wayne mounted one of the most excessive Oscar campaigns in history, with ads essentially suggesting that it would be unpatriotic not to vote for his film. His campaign resulted in six nominations—including one for supporting actor Chill Wills, who proceeded to outstrip his costar with a campaign of unparalleled tastelessness. One Wills ad purported to name every Oscar winner for which the actor had ever voted; another listed every single Academy member and said, "Win, lose or draw, you're all my cousins and I love you all." Groucho

Marx couldn't resist the setup: the comedian took out his own ad, which read, "Dear Mr. Wills, I am delighted to be your cousin, but I'm still voting for Sal Mineo." The last straw, though, was an ad that pictured the cast of *The Alamo* and suggested that they were praying for a Wills victory "harder than the real Texans prayed for their lives at the Alamo." Wayne blasted Wills, press agent W. S. "Bow-Wow" Wojciechowicz took the rap, and in the end *The Alamo* won only a single Oscar, for sound.

The following year, the Academy's board of governors was forced to issue its first major statement on Oscar campaigning. Condemning what it called "outright, excessive and vulgar solicitation of votes," the board urged that nominees eschew ad practices "which are irrelevant to the honest evaluation of artistic and technical accomplishments." It declined, however, to set specific guidelines, leaving that to "the good conscience of the nominees."

George C. Scott, a supporting-actor nominee for *The Hustler* the following year, also claimed to be repulsed by the nature of the Oscar races. "I take the position that actors shouldn't be forced to out-advertise and out-stab each other," he said, asking the Academy to withdraw his nomination. The organization refused, and others pointed out that Scott's distaste for the Oscars came only after he'd been nominated for *Anatomy of a Murder* in 1960 but lost—unjustly, many felt—to Hugh Griffith from *Ben-Hur*, which set a new record that night by winning eleven awards. Scott lost again in 1962, this time to George Chakiris from *West Side Story*, on a night when Stan Berman, the self-described "world's greatest gate-crasher," managed to sneak onstage and hand presenter Shelley Winters a homemade award for Bob Hope.

To some, another unwelcome visitor to the Santa Monica Civic stage was Joan Crawford, who in 1962 costarred with longtime rival Bette Davis in the melodrama *Whatever Happened to Baby Jane?* Davis had been nominated for best actress, while Crawford was overlooked. While all involved denied any friction, Crawford immediately wrote congratulatory notes to the other four nominees, gallantly offering to accept the Oscar in the event they couldn't attend. The night of the show in 1963, Davis stood in the wings, confident she'd go home with the third statuette of her career; instead, the absent Anne Bancroft won for *The Miracle Worker*, and Crawford accepted on her behalf. It was, Davis said later, "despicable."

For all the backstage strife, the Academy Awards managed to ignore the battles being waged in the streets and in popular culture for much of the 1960s. Rock 'n' roll was never seen on the show; civil rights consisted of Sammy Davis, Jr., joking about calling the NAACP when he was mistakenly given the wrong envelope. In 1967, though, the show was almost canceled by a strike of the American Federation of Television and Radio Artists, which was settled only three hours before showtime. The following year, the fortieth Oscar show was postponed for two days after the assassination of Dr. Martin Luther King, Jr. That night, the big winner was a drama about race relations, *In the Heat of the Night*.

It wasn't until the end of the decade, 1969, that a serious attempt was made to overhaul and update the Oscar show. Gregory Peck, the president of the Academy, brought in Broadway director and choreographer Gower Champion, who'd made his name with shows like *Hello, Dolly!* and *Bye Bye Birdie*. The show was moved to the newer, more elegant Dorothy Chandler Pavilion in downtown Los Angeles; Champion tried, but failed, to eliminate the bleachers full of fans. He also gave Bob Hope the boot as host in favor of ten "friends of Oscar," including Jane Fonda, Sidney Poitier, Diahann Carroll, Frank Sinatra, and Natalie Wood. He couldn't do anything about the voting, though: the best-picture winner was the distinctly old-fashioned musical *Oliver!* while the riskier likes of *2001: A Space Odyssey*, *Rosemary's Baby*, and *Belle du Jour* weren't even nominated. Bob Hope, meanwhile, got a standing ovation when he showed up to present the Jean Hersholt Humanitarian Award to Martha Raye.

The following year, the voters managed to walk an artful middle ground: they gave John Wayne his first Oscar for *True Grit*, a genuine career-achievement gift to one of the old guard, but then handed the best-picture trophy to the edgy, X-rated *Midnight Cowboy*. The 1971 ceremony got another jolt courtesy of George C. Scott, who again tried to decline a nomination for *Patton*, and this time had to decline the Oscar statuette as well. Marlon Brando refused his Oscar for *The Godfather* two years later, but Brando sent along an actress named Maria Cruz to decline on his behalf. Claiming to be a Native American named Sacheen Littlefeather, Cruz lectured the audience about the shameful "treatment of American Indians today by the film industry . . . and on television in movie reruns."

By this point, politics had infused much of the Oscar show. When Charlie Chaplin was coaxed into receiving an honorary Academy Award in 1972, his acceptance became one of the most emotional moments in Oscar history partly because the eighty-two-year-old actor hadn't been in the United States for twenty years, dogged by criticism over his neutrality in World War II and his nonpayment of U.S. taxes. Three years later, open warfare spilled onto the stage after producer Bert Schneider, who won for his Vietnam documentary *Hearts and Minds*, read a telegram offering the thanks of the Viet Cong delegation to the ongoing Paris Peace Talks. Backstage, Bob Hope was incensed that Schneider had proffered greetings from the group U.S. forces had been fighting. Hope persuaded cohost Frank Sinatra to read a statement apologizing for "any political references made on the program." But Sinatra's apology infuriated a third cohost, Shirley MacLaine, who proceeded to berate Sinatra in the wings. "I'm a member of the Academy," she raged, "and you didn't ask me!"

In the early 1970s, a pair of executives began long stints at the helm of the Oscar show: Howard W. Koch produced the first of his eight shows in 1972, while director Marty Pasetta began a seventeen-year run the same year. Koch had a real sense of glamour, while Pasetta was determined to always use the latest, most advanced technology on every show. But neither Koch nor the show's other producers seemed to know what to do about Oscar hosts: the first eight shows of the decade all had multiple hosts, from a low of four to a high of thirty-two. Those who took a turn onstage ranged from Helen Hayes to Goldie Hawn, Fred Astaire to Burt Reynolds, Myrna Loy to Richard Pryor.

Of the seventy-four stars who tried the gig during those years, the best moment probably belonged to British actor David Niven, who in 1974 had the wit—or, some insisted, the script—to respond to the sight of a streaker with the line, "Isn't it fascinating to think that probably the only laugh that man will ever get in his life is by stripping off his clothes and showing his shortcomings?"*

---

*The streaker, thirty-three-year-old Robert Opal, made some TV appearances, was hired by Allan Carr to streak a party for Rudolph Nureyev, tried to make it as a stand-up comedian, and five years later was murdered in a San Francisco sex shop.

Between 1977 and 1979, a trio of Oscar telecasts revealed deep divisions between approaches to the show. The first of those years, film director William Friedkin was persuaded to produce the show. Friedkin was notoriously difficult to work with in those days, and his films—among them *The French Connection*, *The Exorcist*, and *Cruising*—were notably lacking in sentimentality. As might have been expected, he proved to be a hard-nosed, jaundiced overseer: he brought in Richard Pryor, Warren Beatty, Jane Fonda, and Ellen Burstyn to host, and vetoed a plan for Loretta Young to salute the recently deceased Rosalind Russell. He also asked *Network* writer Paddy Chayevsky to accept the Oscar should the late actor Peter Finch win for best actor; the last thing he wanted, he told the writer, was to have a weeping widow on his stage. But Chayevsky double-crossed Friedkin when Finch won, immediately summoning Elthea Finch to the stage.

Friedkin's show drew the lowest TV ratings of any Oscar telecast, and the director wasn't invited back. The following year, the job went once more to Koch, who produced a fiftieth-anniversary show long on tradition and sentiment. Bob Hope was back as emcee, while legends like Fred Astaire, Bette Davis, Greer Garson, and William Holden also participated— as did past Oscar winners Ernest Borgnine, Dorothy Malone, and Burl Ives, among others unfortunately lumped into an awkward opening sequence. And while actress Vanessa Redgrave caused another furor with a speech that included a condemnation of "Zionist hoodlums" in Israel, the Academy was able to shrug off the controversy when the ratings came in: the show had drawn the largest television audience of any Oscar show.

The following year, the Academy began its sixth decade with a new approach—or, to be more specific, a new host. Unlike most emcees, Johnny Carson was not a movie star, but the host of *The Tonight Show*. He had an easygoing manner that had been pleasing the television audience for more than fifteen years. The Academy found a style and sensibility in the fifty-two-year-old Carson that was comfortable to the public; he had enough of an edge to separate his material from the predictable patter of a Bob Hope, but he didn't make the Academy nervous the way the likes of Richard Pryor did. (The first line of Pryor's monologue the year he hosted the show had been, "I'm here to explain why black people will never be nominated for anything.")

Still, Carson had a tendency that did not endear him to all the branches of the Academy: he'd tell the home audience "this might be a good time to make some dip" before the reading of the rules, and even worse, he wasn't shy about mocking the occasional nominee or winner in the technical categories. For instance, when the recipient of the sound effects editing award for *The Black Stallion* couldn't make it in 1980, Carson seized the moment. "It always happens," he said. "First George C. Scott doesn't show, then Marlon Brando, and now Alan Splet."

The branches always bristled at that kind of belittlement, but Carson kept it up. To make matters worse, his first turn as host included a medley entitled "Oscar's Only Human," which was designed to showcase great movie songs that hadn't been nominated for Academy Awards.

When members of the music branch heard about the medley, they tried to convince producer Jack Haley, Jr., to drop it. It had been a rough few years for the branch: in 1976, after Diana Ross's hit song "Theme from *Mahogany* (Do You Know Where You're Going To)" failed to win a nod from the special committee that picked the best-song nominees, the outrage had been so widespread that the branch changed the rules, threw out the committee's choices, and had all its members quickly vote a new slate of nominees. (The Ross song made the cut.) Two years later, similar howls ensued when not a single song from the Bee Gees' landmark *Saturday Night Fever* soundtrack was nominated; this time, though, the branch had no real recourse but to endure the complaints. But when the members learned of plans to make an Oscar-night medley of their most notable errors in judgment, they immediately cried foul. Haley branded the music branch "thin-skinned," threatened to quit and take Carson with him, and got his medley, one of the best-received moments of that particular show.

Carson brought a steady voice and a stability to the show during the five years he hosted between 1979 and 1984. Those years included a one-day postponement of the show in 1981, after an attempt on the life of President Ronald Reagan, as well as a sillier contretemps two years later when Polish director Zbigniew Rybczynski, a winner in the best animated short category, stepped outside the Chandler for a smoke, then couldn't talk his way past an overzealous security guard to get back in. Rybczynski kicked the guard, who promptly had him arrested and carted off to jail; there, the director called the only American lawyer whose name he knew, celebrity divorce specialist Marvin Mitchelson.

During the Carson years, Academy membership crept toward the five thousand mark, and the length of the Oscar show crept toward, and past, the three-and-a-half-hour mark. When Carson walked away from the gig, producers struggled to find the right tone. Actor Jack Lemmon opted for brevity in 1985, the year of Sally Field's famous "You like me, you really like me" speech, while legendary musical director Stanley Donen booked the mismatched host trio of Robin Williams, Jane Fonda, and Alan Alda the following year, and stumbled with an elaborate production number featuring actress Teri Garr and a crew of wing-walking high-steppers. By 1987, producer Samuel Goldwyn, Jr., was forced to face the fact that the Oscars were no longer considered a prestige booking: he wanted to open the show with a version of the *Guys and Dolls* standard "Fugue for Tinhorns," but got turned down by everyone from Frank Sinatra and Dean Martin to Steve Martin and Rodney Dangerfield. In the end, he settled for the distinctly bargain-basement threesome of TV's Kojak, Telly Savalas, *The Karate Kid*'s Pat Morita, and rotund comic actor Dom DeLuise.

Goldwyn, who loved producing the Oscars, was one of several producers to tackle the show during this era. (Another, film director Norman Jewison, told friends he hated the job.) The one constant, though, was Marty Pasetta. The director and the highest-ranking paid employee on the production staff, Pasetta was responsible for many of the procedures that Oscar staffers—and those who worked on all other awards shows—would come to take for granted. "Seat-fillers, stand-ins, picture cards, camera techniques— a lot of the ways awards shows are now done started with Marty," said Danette Herman, who worked closely with Pasetta for several years.

"He had this great kind of bigger-than-life feeling of what a ringmaster should do," said Michael Seligman, who began working with Pasetta on the fiftieth Oscar show in 1978. But Pasetta also had a temper. "No no no no no," he'd snap if an underling did something he didn't like. "*Wrong*. Nonononono. *Wrong*." When the day of the show rolled around, Pasetta rarely had a voice left.

By 1988, Pasetta had directed seventeen consecutive Oscar broadcasts, and according to many who worked on the shows, he often acted as if he alone were running the show. That year, though, the director overstepped his bounds for the last time. Pasetta loved to stage elaborate musical numbers, and started the show with a routine set to a song from the musical *A Chorus Line*. Producer Samuel Goldwyn, Jr., hired Michael Kidd, a legendary Broadway choreographer who'd also worked on films including *Seven Brides for Seven Brothers* and *Hello Dolly!* But Pasetta and Kidd had some disagreements about how the number should be staged. Kidd pleaded his case to Academy president Robert Wise, for whom he'd choreographed sequences in the 1968 film *Star!* On one of the final days of rehearsal, in an incident still legendary within Academy and production circles, Wise approached Pasetta on Kidd's behalf—and Pasetta dismissed the president of the Academy with a curt, "I think we can take it from here, Bob."

"It's not like Bob didn't have any credentials to sit in on a music discussion," said one Academy official of Wise, the Oscar-winning director of *West Side Story* and *The Sound of Music*. "And he was the president of the goddamn Academy. When the story went around, that was that. The board was just appalled." Howard Koch continued to hold out hopes that the board might someday relent, but Pasetta's run at the helm of the Oscar show was over.

At that point, the Academy Awards were long and glitzy, by turns glamorous and silly, occasionally ponderous and sometimes almost elephantine. At a time when MTV was revolutionizing the look of music and entertainment on television, the Oscars were determinedly old-fashioned. Ratings were still good, but the trend was downward, not upward; stars, especially younger ones, were not as easy to corral for the show as they had once been.

Richard Kahn, who took over as Academy president from Wise, knew the institution needed an infusion of energy. He brought in Allan Carr. A year later Carr was a bad memory, Gilbert Cates was in charge, Billy Crystal was on board, and the modern Oscars had begun.

1

Putting It Together

The 66th Academy Awards

"THE PELLET with the poison's in the flagon with the dragon," Chuck Warn muttered to nobody in particular as he walked down a long central hallway in the Academy Awards production office. "The vessel with the pestle has the brew that is true." Dressed all in black and cutting an imposing figure at well over six feet and three hundred pounds, the bearded, longhaired publicist for the show's producer paused, then picked up the pace. "The pellet with the poison's in the flagon with the dragon, the vessel with the pestle has the brew that is true . . ."

The lines, first uttered by actor/comic Danny Kaye in the 1956 comedy *The Court Jester*, had nothing to do with the 66th Academy Awards, which would take place in six weeks. Most of those weeks would be filled with steady, sometimes frantic activity: yet to come was flash and furor and spectacle beyond anyone's control, the Oscar carnival in all its finery and silliness. For the moment, though, on the third floor of a nondescript high-rise office building on Wilshire Boulevard in West Los Angeles, things were calm enough that staffers who wanted to spend a few minutes declaiming Danny Kaye dialogue could do so.

Inside the largest of the offices that lined the hallway Warn was pacing, Gilbert Cates sat behind his desk and looked out the window, across Westwood Village and toward the UCLA campus. "I've always been a fan of the circus," he announced. "And this is the greatest circus." He returned his gaze to the room, where pages of schedules, notes, and numbers sat on the desk. Behind him, over his right shoulder, a shiny metal gong hung within reach so that he could notify staffers of each new booking with an appropriately dramatic flourish. Across the room, a bulletin board, protected from unauthorized eyes by a set of white miniblinds, broke down the show and sported the names of presenters and performers, some already booked and others merely coveted. "This show presents great opportunities, great highs and great lows," he said. "It requires a tremendous effort, but it's a lot of fun." Cates paused, allowing a small grin to crease the corners of his mouth. "And I use that word *fun* carefully."

The spectacle was a familiar one to Cates, who had produced every Oscar show since Allan Carr's momentous mess of five years earlier. "I think Gil totally saved the Oscar show," said Chuck Workman. "It was moribund. And he was the perfect man at the perfect time. He was able to make it a much more modern show, keep it very much about Hollywood but also catch up with the rest of entertainment."

A member of the Academy's board of governors for eight years, as well as a two-term past president of the Directors Guild of America, the fifty-nine-year-old Cates had started his career in 1955, after graduating from Syracuse University. Originally a premed student at Syracuse, Cates became fascinated with the theater almost by accident: a member of the school's fencing team, he'd been drafted to teach the actors in a campus production of *Richard III* how to wield swords. He switched his major to theater, stage-managed on Broadway after graduation, and then worked on a string of largely forgotten TV game shows (*Haggis Baggis*, *Picture This*, *Camouflage*) during the 1950s and early '60s. Cates broke into the movie business in his midthirties with the circus-themed 1966 film *Rings Around the World*. He continued to move between theater, television, and film; in that last arena, his most notable successes were a pair of Oscar-nominated early '70s dramas, *I Never Sang for My Father* and *Summer Wishes, Winter Dreams*.

Cates's film career cooled off after those movies, and he turned largely to television, where he was allowed to make the kind of socially themed movies in which he was most interested. While directing TV movies about mental illness, domestic abuse, and the like, he remained active in Academy affairs. In 1989, after six years on the board of governors, he was asked to head the Awards Presentation Review Committee formed to scrutinize Allan Carr's show.

Cates's committee recommended using a single host whenever possible, relying more on film clip packages than on production numbers, and booking single presenters to prevent awkward chit-chat. In many ways the most dramatic suggestion, though, was to pay the producer of the Oscar show. "The idea that we didn't need to pay because the producer's job was a great honor was a double-edged sword," said Bruce Davis, who assumed the executive director position the year after the Carr show. "It *is* a great honor, and only the top directors and producers in town had ever been asked to do it— but if you ask a guy to put that kind of time into a project and don't pay him, you almost lose your ability to rein him in. We would frequently get the reaction, 'Look, I'm doing this for free and now you guys are gonna nickel-dime me?' To pay the producer put the show on more of a business footing."

The first year, the job carried an honorarium of $150,000. New Academy president Karl Malden, also a member of the review committee, figured that the man who chaired the panel ought to do the job (and pocket the paycheck) himself. Cates took his share of ribbing as both the man who recommended the producer be paid, and the man to benefit from that recommendation—but four years later, with four Oscar shows under his belt, he was still the only man who'd ever been paid to produce the Academy Awards. "It's embarrassing, being the first producer to be paid," Cates said at his first board of governors meeting after taking the job. "I can only say that had I known it was going to be me, I would have said the pay should be much higher."

As a producer, Cates had certain tendencies: he felt that each show should open with a film clip, but he also loved staging those oft-maligned dance numbers (though he subscribed to the theory that each individual element should last no longer than three minutes). He liked to give themes to his Oscar shows, and he was fond of surprise appearances by both people and animals. But despite his penchant for dogs and horses and Debbie Allen, Cates was also a steadying, calming influence—particularly when compared with the likes of Carr. As befitted a college dean and an occasional teacher, Cates had a professorial manner. But when the mood struck him, the generally soft-spoken producer delighted in sprinkling his speech with expletives.

On the slow Monday morning in early February, Cates conferred briefly with Chuck Warn, then walked back down the hall toward his own office. Outside the door, he stopped to look over the schedule kept by his assistant, Debbie Olchick.

"Oh, this is a very important meeting that demands all my attention," he said as he ducked back into his office. "It's hard work, figuring out if the fucking jackets and hats should be red or black."

THE PAST FOUR YEARS had been a smooth stretch for the Academy Awards. When he took over on the heels of Allan Carr's show, Cates tried to streamline the operation and unify the staff. Where previous producers had often worked in separate offices from much of the production staff, he brought everyone together in one office.

He also had a different sensibility, one formed by a background that included theater, film, and live television. "Gil had produced television and produced motion pictures and directed television and directed motion pictures, and he had some Broadway experience as a producer and director," said Jeff Margolis, who returned to direct his second show. "He also had a whole different philosophy from Allan. He wanted to do it bigger and better, but he knew the limitations of television. He knew we weren't making a movie, we were doing a television show, and that was a whole different way of approaching the show."

His first year on the job, Cates took the crucial step of lining up Billy Crystal to host. Crystal's brief routine had been one of the best-liked moments of the Carr show; the comic had a stand-up background, but movies like *When Harry Met Sally* had also given him a cachet in the movie business.

Initially, Crystal had been enamored by the gig, but reluctant to commit. To make his pitch, Cates took Crystal to lunch at the Friar's Club in Beverly Hills—where the producer received an unexpected assist from the eighty-one-year-old comedian Milton Berle, who dropped by their booth to say hello and, when he learned why the men were meeting, launched into an enthusiastic monologue about why Crystal simply *had* to take the job.

Although Cates had heard from some naysayers who felt that Crystal's humor might be too ethnic for Middle America, the comic immediately found the right tone. At his first show, in 1990, his monologue was filled with Hollywood jokes that were inside enough for the audience at the Chandler, but broad enough for the millions at home. His first line, though, alluded directly to the previous year. "Is that for me," he said as the audience applauded, "or are you just glad I'm not Snow White?"

In fact, Ms. White had already made an appearance on the show, which had opened with a breakneck montage of famous movie clips put together by Chuck Workman. Among the more than three hundred scenes crammed into five minutes was an entirely deliberate shot of the Disney heroine. "I asked, 'Do you think this will offend anybody?' " said Workman, "and Gil said, 'Fuck 'em, it's good.' "

Cates was determined to make his Oscars a classy one—and since the Cold War had essentially ended in 1989 and the Iron Curtain had come down across Europe, an international event as well. He sent crews to London, Moscow, Sydney, Tokyo, and Buenos Aires, enormously complicating the technical side of the production.

"Nothing like that had ever really been attempted before, and we went on the air not knowing if we were ever going to have any sound coming from Russia," said Margolis. "During all the setup and all the rehearsals, we never got the audio and video together at the same time. I thought, poor Jack Lemmon. We've shipped him all the way to Moscow, and now nobody will be able to hear him. But it worked. I loved it."

Cates's initial show was well received, both within the Academy and outside it. "We could do no wrong that year, because we were following Allan Carr," said Roy Christopher, the production designer for the show in 1990. "It was much more what the Academy, and the public, seemed to want." The show was nominated for five Emmy Awards, with Christopher winning; over the next three years, Cates's shows would secure twenty-six nominations and six more wins.

During those years, the producer continued to trot out variations on his Oscar formula. Each year he gave the show a theme ("100 Years at the Movies" in 1991, "The Pure Joy of the Movies" the following year, "Women and the Movies" in 1993), and each year he used Crystal as host, relied heavily on film montages, but also threw in dance numbers, often as not choreographed by Debbie Allen.

Some of those numbers were gruesome (including a 1991 opening that purported to trace the history of film and involved lots of people jumping back and forth through screens), and sometimes the real world intruded on the relatively smooth machine Cates was running. In 1991, the recent Gulf War caused security to be far tighter than usual, as for the first time Oscar guests (with the exception of Bob Hope) were run through metal detectors on their way to the red carpet.

Cates initially figured he'd produce no more than three shows, but by 1994 he was on something of a roll. "It's very hard to conceive of a producer agreeing to do it again while he's in the throes of it, or within a month or two afterwards," said Bruce Davis. "But when they calm down and relax, you can sometimes talk them into doing it again. And considering that Gil had done the show before and done it well, that he'd actually succeeded in cranking up the ratings little bit, and that ABC embraced him, the talk within the Academy was along the lines of, 'Do you think we can talk him into doing it again?' "

ABOUT FOUR MILES EAST of the production office, it looked as if a hurricane had hit the Beverly Hills headquarters of the Academy of Motion Picture Arts and Sciences. In fact, the disarray—missing ceiling panels, soiled carpeting, dented furniture—had come from a 6.7 magnitude earthquake that hit Los Angeles just after 4 a.m. on Martin Luther King Day, January 17, 1994. Throughout the seven-story building, bookcases had been toppled and the emergency sprinkler system had drenched desks. In subsequent days, the closet in Bruce Davis's office filled with Oscar statuettes that were returned to the Academy for repair (or, more often, replacement) after the quake: Oliver Stone's Oscar for *Platoon* was bent at the base, while Jack Nicholson's for *One Flew Over the Cuckoo's Nest* had been dented when it fell on its head.

Amid fallout from the temblor, bookcases and tables were piled high with boxes of publicity photographs, slides, bios, and press kits. In preparation for the next morning's announcement of Oscar nominations, studios had sent over promotional materials for all who had a shot at a nomination, and some who didn't: near a stack of bios of Holly Hunter, considered a lock for a best-actress nomination for *The Piano*, was a box that Touchstone Pictures had supplied in the unlikely event that Kathy Najimy won a supporting-actress nod for *Sister Act 2: Back in the Habit*.

For most of the day, a team from the accounting firm of Price Waterhouse had locked itself in the sixth-floor copy room, where they compiled lists of the nominees, copied those lists, and double-checked spellings and punctuation with Academy staffers. Of course, they couldn't just come out and ask, "How do you spell *Spielberg*?" So they'd pass Academy officials a list of several names to be checked; one name would belong to a true nominee, while the others would be decoys.

Just after 6 p.m., the building was cleared of all but essential personnel, and the switchboard was shut down. At the same time, the Price Waterhouse reps came into Davis's office and officially presented him with the list of nominees. In a ceremony whose formality was at least partly tongue in cheek, the executive director thanked the accountants for doing another meticulous job of counting, whereupon his staff descended upon the lists of nominees and tore through them.

The list contained the names of thirty-seven feature films and thirteen shorts, eighteen different actors and actresses, and close to 150 other nominees. To the surprise of no one, the film with the most nominations was Steven Spielberg's *Schindler's List*, the Holocaust-themed drama that had been considered the Oscar front-runner since its December release.

Spielberg had a troubled history with the Academy, which sometimes seemed mistrustful of the kind of zestful popular entertainment in which the director specialized. In 1975, his film *Jaws* became the top-grossing movie ever made, and the twenty-nine-year-old wunderkind was considered such a strong candidate for a best-director nomination that a TV crew went to Spielberg's home to record his reaction when the nominations were announced. But there is often a discrepancy between the five films nominated for best picture by the Academy's entire membership and the five directors nominated by the smaller directors' branch—and more often than not, that discrepancy manifests itself when a director responsible for a successful popcorn movie is bypassed in favor of an artier auteur. Such was Spielberg's fate: as the film crew watched, he found that *Jaws* was up for best picture, but he had been left out in favor of Italian legend Federico Fellini, whose autobiographical *Amarcord* had won the Oscar for best foreign film the previous year but was eligible in other categories in 1975. "I can't believe it," said Spielberg, head in hands. "They went for Fellini instead of me."

Spielberg had other reasons to complain in subsequent years. He was nominated for *Close Encounters of the Third Kind*, *Raiders of the Lost Ark*, and *E.T.*, but lost to Woody Allen (*Annie Hall*), Warren Beatty (*Reds*), and Richard Attenborough (*Gandhi*); his 1985 film *The Color Purple* won eleven nominations, including best picture, but was passed over in the best-director race. The following year, the board of governors' decision to give Spielberg the Irving Thalberg Award carried the unmistakable air of an apology.

But with *Schindler's List*, the feeling was that Spielberg had finally made a movie the Academy could not help but embrace wholeheartedly, whatever reservations it may have had about the director's youth, commercial success, and populist instincts. Competing with *Schindler* for best picture was director Jane Campion's austere but erotic *The Piano*; *The Remains of the Day*, from the high-toned Merchant Ivory team; *In the Name of the Father*, director Jim Sheridan's fact-based story about a young Belfast man falsely accused of being a terrorist; and the action film *The Fugitive*, inspired by the '60s TV series. Campion became only the second woman to receive a nomination for best director (following the Italian director Lina Wertmuller in 1976), while eleven-year-old supporting-actress nominee Anna Paquin was the youngest performer to be nominated since eight-year-old Justin Henry fourteen years earlier.

Final voting for the Academy Awards was conducted in a simple, straightforward manner. But the nominations were arrived at in a far more complex way, through a method known most commonly as the preferential system.

The system had been recommended to the Academy by Price Waterhouse in the 1940s, after the accounting firm had studied the pitfalls of alternatives. Academy members were asked to vote for five nominees, in order of preference, in each of their branch's categories, plus the best-picture category. Initially, a small group of Price Waterhouse employees, working at a location the firm kept secret, separated the ballots into stacks based on the film listed first. Nominations automatically went to films receiving first-place votes on one-sixth of the ballots, plus one; with five nominations in a category, it would be impossible for five other films to receive more votes.

Films that received no first-place votes were eliminated from contention, while the ballots of voters whose first-place choices received the smallest number of votes were redistributed into the remaining piles based on their second choices. (If a voter's second choice was no longer in the running, the third, fourth, or fifth pick would be used.) The process was repeated, with the films drawing the least support eliminated in each subsequent round, until only five piles remained.

To complicate matters, if a film received far more first-place votes than it needed to secure a nomination, all of the ballots in its pile were redistributed into the other piles, with the second choices listed on those ballots given a fractional value based on the percentage of that member's vote required to ensure the first choice a nomination. (For instance, if *Schindler's List* received twice as many first-place votes as it needed, it earned a nomination and the second choice of all *Schindler* voters counted as half a vote.)

The idea was to allow each member to vote for favorite films without second-guessing or worrying about electability. "The problem with the usual weighted system," said Davis, "is that the two points you give to a guy lower on your ballot might be just enough to push him past the guy you really want at the top of your ballot. It leads to a certain amount of game playing, because if you're afraid of other candidates you might put them way down." Under the preferential system, a member didn't have to worry about a third or fourth choice hurting a film listed higher on the ballot—because the third choice can't be counted unless the voter's first choice is either out of the running or already assured a nomination. "I don't think a very high percentage of members could describe exactly how it works," conceded Davis. "When I hear them talking about it, I can tell that they don't understand."

ON FEBRUARY 17, the week after the nominations were announced and five weeks before the Oscar show, Cates convened a production meeting in a conference room across the hall from his office. Sitting around the long table were the core members of the Oscar team. Director Jeff Margolis was a barrel-chested veteran of five Oscar shows and dozens of variety telecasts. Danette Herman, the show's executive in charge of talent and in Cates's words "the heart and conscience of the show," was a soft-spoken woman who nonetheless was known to quietly exercise steely control over her province, which ranged from booking performers and presenters to making sure that the stars on the show were well treated. Associate producer Michael Seligman, short and sharp, was the money man. Production designer Roy Christopher had designed three of the past five Oscar sets, between his day job as the art director of TV series like *Frasier* and *Murphy Brown*. Composer and conductor Bill Conti, Cates's usual choice to head the Oscar orchestra and an Oscar winner himself, was a slight, sardonic man who invariably played his best-known composition, "Gonna Fly Now (The Theme from *Rocky*)," at least once during every show. Chuck Workman was the master of fast-paced montages of film clips—one of which, *Precious Images*, had won him an Oscar in 1987. Costume designer Ray Aghayan, diminutive and deeply tanned, was one of the oldest (and during production meetings, quietest) members of the Oscar crew.

As aides brought in a modest selection of sandwiches and soft drinks, Cates went over the show's musical numbers. The songs were always a key part of the Oscar show, and one over which the producer had no control: whatever the music branch nominated had to be performed. Since he took over, Cates had gone out of his way to book the original performers on the show; he knew that viewers had cringed in the past when the songs were handed over to less suitable interpreters.

This time, three of the five nominations had gone to major stars in the fields of rock and pop music: Bruce Springsteen and Neil Young for "Streets of Philadelphia" and "Philadelphia," respectively, both from Jonathan Demme's film *Philadelphia*; and Janet Jackson for "Again" from *Poetic Justice*, a film by director John Singleton. The final two nominations went to the light pop tune "A Wink and a Smile" from *Sleepless in Seattle*, which was sung in the film by the popular jazz-pop singer and pianist Harry Connick, Jr., and to the formula love song "The Day I Fell in Love," a duet by country diva Dolly Parton and soul crooner James Ingram from the comedy *Beethoven's Second*. With one exception, the original performers had already agreed to appear—and the one who declined to do the song was the demanding Connick, whose absence had caused no great dismay in the production office. Conspicuously missing from the nominees was anything from an animated Disney movie, although that studio had recently dominated the category, winning seven nominations and three Oscars in four years.

"Janet Jackson is going to do her song," Cates said, looking at the first item on his agenda. "She also wants to do it on the *Jackson Family Honors* television show, which is coming up before us, so we're trying to discourage that." Cates then summed up a conversation he'd had with Rene Elizondo, who directed many of Jackson's videos and was her husband of three years, although the couple had kept the marriage secret. "Rene says he and Janet want to do it with five violins, very simply, and with candles," Cates said. "Armani's going to dress her. He said they have a sense of it being *bluish*."

"Got it," said Christopher. "Five blue candles playing violin."

Margolis had worked with Jackson many times before. "She's sweet as can be," he said, "but fairly inflexible. Rene is sweet as can be, but he's a killer also."

Bill Conti frowned. "We're not gonna have another rehearsal like Madonna pulled, are we?" he asked, remembering a 1991 run-through of legendary difficulty.

"I hope not, Bill," said Cates calmly. "The thing to remember with them is that they're guests on our show. Give them all the courtesy we can."

Conti grimaced. "Okay," he muttered.

"Next up is 'Philadelphia,' " Cates said. "Neil Young's going to do it. He wants to do it with an acoustic piano, by himself."

"As opposed to the way he does it on the record?" asked Conti.

"I guess so."

"I wonder if he wants to use that funky, incredibly bad piano he uses on the record," mused Conti.

"Well, they told me he's bringing down his own piano from Northern California, so that's probably the one," said Cates. "Now, Roy, I think we want to keep this pretty straightforward. Nothing too fancy on the stage behind him."

"I'll come up with a simple, strong look," said Christopher. "Do you want to contact him about clothes? That could be a sensitive issue."

"I don't think he'll listen," said Aghayan.

Herman shook her head. "Let's not tell Neil Young how to dress," she suggested.

After dealing with "The Day I Fell in Love" and "A Wink and a Smile," Cates got to the final song. "Last but not least," he said, "is Bruce. He does what he does. He has four people. I'm expecting that he wants to do it just like he did it at the AIDS Project L.A. show last month, which was great. It's a very powerful song. I'm very excited about it, and his people say he's really thrilled to be doing the show."

"So what do we have to do about it?" asked Conti.

"Nothing, for the moment," said Cates.

"No dancers in any of these?" asked Christopher.

"No," said Cates. "We only have two dance elements on the show this year, the opening number and the ballet."

Conti frowned. "Ballet?" he said. "What's that?"

Cates looked incredulous. "You're not aware of that?"

"No."

"Oh, what a hole in the loop." Cates explained that Allen was choreographing a ballet to accompany selections from the five nominated scores, to be performed by pairs of dancers from several of the world's leading ballet companies.

This was Herman's territory. "The biggest problem," she said, "is logistics. The Africans speak French, the Chinese barely speak English. Twelve dancers come into town on February 28, but six of them leave on March 6 and don't come back until the seventeenth or eighteenth. The Shanghai dancers arrive on the twelfth, the Paris ballet not until the eighteenth. The

Cubans, the Central Ballet of China, and the Africans will be in town the whole time."

"This has to be very organized," said Cates. "It can't be last minute."

"And it's going to be a hard number to design," said Aghayan. "I can't just load it up with sequins and send it out there."

The last musical number on the agenda was the first one in the show: an opening sequence set to Stephen Sondheim's "Putting It Together" and sung by Broadway star Bernadette Peters. "Bernadette will be arriving in L.A. next Monday," Cates told the staff. "And as is her custom, her assistant will be driving her around in a sedan without a phone."

The song would be recorded the following Tuesday night; later in the week, Workman would shoot a movie that would introduce, incorporate, and illustrate the song. "One thing to remember, though, is that it's a little too long now," Cates said. "We might want to cut some of it. But if we see things we think need to be changed, we need to let Bernadette and Sondheim know at the same time. They're best friends, and they talk on the phone constantly, so we don't want one of them feeling left out if the other knows something first."

WHEN IT WAS FIRST HELD IN 1982, the nominees' luncheon was designed to be little more than another photo op. "Somebody thought there was a lull in the publicity between the nominations announcements and the show itself," said Bruce Davis as he waited to greet nominees near the entrance to the ballroom at the Beverly Hilton Hotel. "It was originally proposed, I think, out of fairly cynical motivations. But it was such an immediate hit among the nominees that we realized, Jesus, everybody says it's a great honor to be nominated, but the only time we ever bring the people together is on this terrible night when four out of five of them will walk away feeling like they've lost something."

Enter the luncheon, which had become a supposed respite from the competitive air and frayed nerves of Oscar season. Nominees, their guests, Oscar staffers, Academy officials, and members of the board of governors were spread out across two dozen tables on three levels of the same ballroom that had hosted the Golden Globe Awards six weeks earlier. The seating chart was drawn up so that no nominee sat at a table with anyone else nominated in the same category, or anyone else who worked on the same film.

The crux of the lunch came just after the appetizers were served, when Academy president Arthur Hiller officially welcomed everyone. "It's unfortunate," he added, "that in less than two weeks, 80 percent of you are going to, how shall we say, perceive yourselves as losers when your name isn't called." The nominees were asked to stand on a riser that curved around a huge Oscar statue. When they'd jostled into place, the annual group photo was taken, after which the nominees came to the stage in alphabetical order to receive a certificate of nomination and an official Oscar nominee sweatshirt.

The shirt was another innovation of Allan Carr's, though he'd insisted that each shirt be personalized with the name of the nominee. A couple of years' worth of inevitable omissions and misspellings later, Bruce Davis prevailed upon Cates to hand out generic sweatshirts, in this case gray ones sporting a small gold Academy Award and the inscription OSCAR NOMINEE.

After lunch was served, Cates gave a short speech. "Veterans of this lunch know that this is the time when I get to talk to you nominees about your speeches," he said. "I've had my fantasies: a trapdoor behind the podium, or a treadmill going from one side of the stage to the other, thirty-five seconds and you're out . . ." But those remedies, he said, shouldn't be necessary. "Forty-five seconds is a long time, ladies and gentlemen. You can do a lot of things in forty-five seconds."

In the press room at the luncheon, composer Marc Shaiman, who'd been nominated for writing the song "A Wink and a Smile," needed less time than that to cause a minor furor. Shaiman had been annoyed when Harry Connick, Jr., declined to perform the song on the Oscar show, and frustrated at how long it had taken to secure a replacement. He'd spoken to David Bowie, who'd briefly entertained the idea, and watched while the likes of Bob Hope and George Burns were approached. He was happy when Tony Bennett agreed to perform the song, then irked when Bennett suddenly cited a prior commitment.

At the luncheon, Shaiman had just learned that actor/singer Keith Carradine would be performing the song. The composer knew Carradine's voice was well suited for the light, bouncy tune, but he was also smarting after a couple of weeks that had left him feeling, he said, "like such category-filler." When the publicist he'd hired plopped him in front of the assembled press, Shaiman figured they didn't care what he had to say—especially when he looked toward the door and saw Steven Spielberg and Tom Hanks waiting their turns at the microphone.

"I was like the kid in school who wants to make the bullies laugh," he said. "So when someone with a real edge in his voice said, 'How come Harry Connick isn't singing your song?' I said, 'Well, he's busy recording, and he has social commitments, and he's a schmuck.' "

Having gotten his laugh, Shaiman didn't think anything of it until the following evening, when the phone in his hilltop Los Angeles home began ringing off the hook. "I finally turned up the volume on the answering machine and heard a musician in New York going, 'Good for you, Shaiman! Tell it like it is!' It had already been on *Entertainment Tonight*: 'Songwriter gets into Yiddish name-calling with pop star!' " Suitably embarrassed, Shaiman apologized to Connick in a letter that, he said, "should be studied as an example of self-effacement."

THE AFTERNOON of the nominees' luncheon, a new schedule was distributed to the production staff. A running joke had been added to what was normally a dry, straightforward document. Under the heading SATURDAY MARCH 19, there was a new entry for 8:00 a.m.: TUNE NEIL YOUNG'S PIANO."

A little later, at 12:30 p.m.: TUNE NEIL YOUNG'S PIANO.

Sunday March 20, 8:00 a.m.: TUNE NEIL YOUNG'S PIANO.

Sunday, noon: TUNE NEIL YOUNG'S PIANO.

Monday, March 21, 8:00 a.m.: TUNE NEIL YOUNG'S PIANO.

Monday, 9:00 p.m.: STRIKE NEIL YOUNG'S PIANO.

"THEY'D SAVE a *fortune*," said Douglass M. Stewart, Jr., "if they knew who the winners were ahead of time."

For more than a decade, Stewart and his company, DMS, had been responsible for most of the short film clips that ran throughout Oscar shows—

and for the more numerous clips that were prepared but never shown. DMS assembled the clips of nominated films and performances, the brief montages used to explicate categories like costume design, makeup, and visual effects, and the footage that was shown on-screen while some winners (i.e., the lesser-known ones, whose trips to the stage were not of intrinsic interest to most viewers) walked to the podium. Every time one of those last clips was shown, it meant four others went unused.

Stewart also prepared a reel of historical footage about the Academy Award and the Oscar show, which was kept on hand in case something disastrous happened and the producer needed to cut away from the stage. Though the emergency reel had never been used, it was reworked and updated every year, in order that it could fit as seamlessly as possible into each new show.

With less than three weeks to go before the show, Stewart called the DMS staff into his office at a nondescript two-story complex south of Beverly Hills. To begin the meeting, he showed a montage of dog clips designed for an interlude in the Dolly Parton–James Ingram duet from *Beethoven's Second*. "We spent a month looking at seventy to eighty dog films," he said, "and started with a list of forty dogs we wanted to include. But finally, I think we've got a lock on it." He cued up a montage that included only six celebrated canines: Toto from *The Wizard of Oz*, Asta from the *Thin Man* movies, Sandy from *Annie*, and from the films that bore their names, Lassie, Old Yeller, and Benji. "Gil thinks that Old Yeller ought to be last," said Stewart. "Does anybody think that Old Yeller has more emotion than Benji?"

"No, Benji's much more recognizable," said Stephanie Sperling, a DMS film coordinator. Around the room, the other staffers nodded.

"I like it the way it is, too," said Stewart. "So we'll keep it this way." He paused. "If we can use it."

"Is Disney still a problem?" asked one staffer.

"Yeah," said Stewart. This wasn't a surprise: famously protective of its properties, as the Academy had learned when Allan Carr didn't get permission to use Snow White, Disney had declined to make any of its footage available for a montage celebrating the history of film animation unless the piece showcased nothing *but* Disney animation. Now the company was making similar dog demands. "They say they don't want Old Yeller and Benji to be included in a bit honoring another studio's dog," said Stewart. "We told them it's about famous dogs, and there are no shots of Beethoven in it. It's on approval."

He paused. "We didn't mention that Beethoven's going to be onstage."

Stewart looked at a five-page list that included the status of all the film clips needed on the show, and brought up a litany of problems. ABC wouldn't allow a scene from *In the Line of Fire* in which John Malkovich put his mouth around a gun barrel . . . They needed better footage from the making of *The Piano*, which had such a small budget that there wasn't enough money for the usual behind-the-scenes crew . . . They were still waiting for Steven Spielberg's okay to use footage from *Jurassic Park* for the sound effects editing category . . . And they had no access at all to any footage from *Schindler's List*, but were simply waiting for the director to assemble his own clips from the suggestions they'd given him.

"We're getting close," said Stewart as the meeting wound down. "Until the next train wreck happens."

After the meeting, Stewart called a staffer at Miramax, which had released *The Piano*. The independent studio, notoriously aggressive when it came to campaigning for Academy Awards, had scored ten nominations—two for the Chinese film *Farewell My Concubine* and eight for *The Piano*, including crucial nods in the best-picture, best-director, best-actress, and best supporting actress categories. But as zealously as Miramax campaigned, the company was difficult to work with when it came to supplying film clips. Miramax worked slowly, and worse than that it tended to offer the same scenes that had already been seen in every ad or on every talk show.

"We're running out of time, and I need a ten-second shot for cinematography," Stewart said into the phone. "Pick the most beautiful shot in the movie, and give me ten seconds. It's better with stars in it, if you've got it."

"LOOK!" said Cates, pointing to the call sheet in his hand. "I'm listed as *talent*. All my life I've wanted to be listed as talent."

The producer was standing in a small television studio located on the outskirts of Culver City, south of Beverly Hills and only a few blocks away from the old MGM studio lot, now home to Sony Pictures. He'd arrived at the complex at 6:15 a.m. for the domestic satellite press tour, in which he and actress Laura Dern would do short interviews with shows on eighteen different ABC affiliates around the country. Dern showed up fifteen minutes after Cates, fully made up and camera ready; this impressed staffers who remembered that for a similar press tour a week earlier, Nicole Kidman had arrived at 4:30 a.m. for two painstaking hours of primping.

Cates's priority was to sell the show, something he felt ABC hadn't been doing as effectively as usual. The network had long since sold all its Oscar ads, at a cost of $630,000 for each thirty-second spot, and the show did not carry a ratings guarantee—meaning if the viewership slumped, as it had for many recent awards shows, ABC would not have to make it up to advertisers. But nobody wanted to concede a ratings slump that in truth had been going on since the mid-1980s. The solution, the Academy's Public Relations Coordinating Committee had decided at a meeting two days earlier, was to use every opportunity to emphasize the heavyweight musical talent on the show.

Cates and Dern took their places in a small studio, one of several in the complex. Behind them was an Academy Awards backdrop; in front of them were several cameras and a group of placards listing the nominees in all major categories, lest they forget anybody.

The first interview was with a morning show in Cleveland. "What's the most distressing part of the awards for you?" asked the host. "When the stars go off on their own?"

Cates admitted he found that distressing, but in about thirty seconds he'd worked the conversation around to the musical performers. "Now, this year we've got Bruce Springsteen, Janet Jackson, Neil Young, Dolly Parton, and James Ingram . . ."

The questioner addressed Dern, who was nominated in 1989 for *Rambling Rose*. "What's it like as a nominee, Laura?" he said.

"It's great," she said. "Hopefully you can just concentrate on the event, and not worry about the competition . . ."

Then the next morning show came on the line, and the routine began again. Interviewers and cities changed, but some things remained constant:

Dern described what it was like to be nominated, and Cates turned the conversation to music.

Columbus, Ohio—*"Laura, you've been nominated. What goes through your mind waiting for the envelope?"*

Dern: "It's a great opportunity to enjoy a celebration of the work. Hopefully you can do that and not think about the competitive aspect of it . . ."

"How do you make sure two presenters don't wear the same dress?"

Cates: "If they're interested in finding out, they can call Fred Hayman. Oddly enough, sometimes it happens with singers. This year we have Bruce Springsteen and Janet Jackson and Neil Young . . ."

Houston, Texas—*"Laura, how do you make sure no two outfits are the same?"*

Dern: "Well, Fred Hayman is the fashion coordinator . . ."

"Gil, how's it going with Whoopi?"

Cates: "Okay. By the way, the question you asked Laura is interesting, because sometimes it happens with musicians. For instance, this year we have Bruce Springsteen and Janet Jackson and Neil Young . . ."

Buffalo, New York—*"Laura, what is it like to find out you're nominated?"*

Dern: "It was great, because I really cared about the movie . . ."

"But you didn't win."

Dern: "Guys!"

Cates: "You know, who wins is just caprice. For example, this year we have Bruce Springsteen and Janet Jackson and Neil Young . . ."

In the control booth, this transition—or, to be more accurate, this non sequitur—got big laughs. "He's taking that corner on two wheels," said Chuck Warn. Afterward, Cates and Dern took a short break, and Cates shook his head. "I feel like a used-car salesman," he said. "All I want to do is plug Bruce Springsteen."

A GRAY-HAIRED WOMAN who looked more like a suburban grandmother than a Hollywood insider, Bethlyn Hand spent more than eleven months out of each year working for the Motion Picture Association of America, the lobbying arm of the film industry. The MPAA and its chairman, Jack Valenti, were perhaps best known for creating, implementing, and zealously defending the movie rating system, which had been designed in the 1960s to keep legislators from trying to exercise control over the content of Hollywood movies.

The two most recognizable organizations serving the film industry, the Academy and the MPAA had a cozy relationship. The slick, dapper, pint-sized Valenti was almost always booked as a presenter on the Oscar show, and he was usually given the pleasure of copresenting with an attractive young actress. As for Hand, her MPAA duties included rating movie trailers—but come Oscar time, she was also in charge of Oscar escorts.

These were publicists, most of them recruited from the ranks of the major film studios, who led winners through the press rooms during the show. The job of an Oscar escort usually fell to young studio publicists; for more experienced flacks, the joys of hobnobbing with Oscar-toting celebs were more than outweighed by the grind of spending four hours dragging dazed winners through corridors and up and down elevators and stairs.

Inside the Dorothy Chandler Pavilion for an escort walk-through, Hand loaded two dozen publicists into two elevators for a trip to the fourth floor, where the press rooms were located. "This floor is where all the winners will be taken," Hand told them. "Near the end of the night, you may have a wife or spouse with you, because they're not going to want to wait in the hall after the show is over. If you do, make sure you know who you've got, because they won't have a badge." She laughed. "They almost threw out Larry Fortensky last year, until somebody realized that he was Elizabeth Taylor's husband."

Personal publicists, she added, were generally not allowed upstairs; neither were agents. "According to my memo," said the Academy's John Pavlik, "if Steven Spielberg wins, Mike Ovitz will be coming up here with him."

"I hope he's got a badge," said Hand.

"If he doesn't, I'm throwing him out," laughed Pavlik. "He's not *my* agent."

Hand led the group down a narrow hallway and into a tiny room with a small stage and a rudimentary set of bleachers. This was the room for deadline press, mostly newspaper and wire photographers who needed to file their work during the show. Behind a curtain was a larger room, with far more spacious bleachers facing another stage. "I lovingly call this my animal room," said Hand, "because it's a zillion photographers from all around the world, and they all act like animals."

In the two photo rooms, she explained, the winner and the presenter would be photographed together. "Photographers are not allowed to take pictures of the presenters without the winners. If Robin Williams comes in here with somebody who won for his short film, we can't have the winner being insulted because everybody just wants pictures of Robin." After leaving the photo rooms, she explained, the presenters would head back downstairs, leaving the winners to continue through the two interview rooms. This would spare lesser-known winners the humiliation of facing a battery of reporters interested only in their famous presenters.

The first of the two interview areas was a spacious room holding almost two dozen long tables for print and radio journalists. Beyond that was a final, smaller room for television reporters.

"If a winner isn't very well known," Hand added, "you'll send a runner ahead to the general press room to make sure that people want to interview them. If there's no interest, the runner will come back and tell you that, quietly I hope, so you can bypass the room. Obviously, we don't want the winner to know that nobody wants to interview them. You'll do that again for the television room—and in the television room, you most assuredly will have bypasses."

Before the escorts left to go downstairs, Hand offered a final instruction. "You've got to remember to stay with your winners," she said. "They are absolutely euphoric, or numb, so they'll follow you *anywhere*."

THE DOROTHY CHANDLER PAVILION sat on a hill in downtown Los Angeles, anchoring one end of a block that also contained the Ahmanson Theatre and the smaller Mark Taper Forum. The block was known as the Music Center—and it was there, home to the Los Angeles Philharmonic, the L.A. Opera, and the Center Theatre Group, that twenty-two Academy Awards shows had taken place in the last quarter century.

Built in the early 1960s, the Chandler was beginning to show its age. But for the Oscar production staff, it worked. It had dressing rooms downstairs, on the same level as the artists' entrance; it had a few offices on the stage level, along with enough extra space to erect a green room and a production office; and outside the building was enough room for a series of production trailers and trucks, most notably the command truck that would serve as Jeff Margolis's home base while he directed the show.

Four days to show time, Margolis sat in the truck and stared at a wall of monitors, which showed him the view from more than a dozen cameras inside the theater. To help him plot camera moves for each entrance, exit, and acceptance speech, a full complement of stand-ins waited for instructions from the show's stage managers. Most of the stand-ins, who covered a wide range of ages and looks, were hired from local theater companies; many returned to the Oscars in this capacity year after year, working for AFTRA scale of about twenty dollars an hour.

To make the rehearsal as real as possible, the stand-ins who subbed for presenters were given dummy Oscar envelopes to open. Inside each envelope was the name of a winner, along with one extra, and crucial, line of text: FOR THIS REHEARSAL ONLY. For the next four days, no one would announce an Oscar recipient without using that phrase. Other stand-ins were positioned in the audience, occupying the seats of that category's nominees. The "winner" would come to the stage, give an acceptance speech, and then exit into the wings.

By this point, large seat cards occupied the chairs of every nominee, presenter, and performer on the show. Block letters listed the names and categories of lesser-known nominees, while movie stars' cards sported black-and-white photos as well.

Virtually all the stars were seated in the first eight rows, the section located in front of the TelePrompTer and the only area of the audience that received significant on-screen exposure. Mixed in with the actors were a few agents and studio heads, plus blocks of seats for Cates, Hiller, host Whoopi Goldberg, and other Academy and show executives. Nominees were placed close to the side or center aisles, for easy exit in case they won. And along the side aisles beginning about eight rows back were the nominees in the less glamorous categories.

By placing all the nominees for the craft categories in one or two rows, Margolis only needed one handheld camera to cover all the possible winners—as opposed to the awards in the acting categories, where the nominees were spread out across the orchestra section and a different cameraman would be assigned to each.

Seating decisions were more difficult in years when the Oscars were held at the Chandler, as opposed to the show's less elegant but far more cavernous alternate home, the Shrine Auditorium. Though its stated capacity was on the high side of three thousand, camera placement and the needs of the production reduced the usable size to about two thousand eight hundred people, less than half the capacity of the Shrine. Around one thousand seats went to nominees, presenters, and guests of the Academy, including small blocks to sponsors of the television broadcast. Each nominee was officially given two seats, though some ended up with more. The rest were distributed by lottery to Academy members, who paid $50, $100, or $200, depending on the location. The lottery system was supposed to ensure that members who didn't get tickets one year were more likely to get them the next, but it invariably left plenty of disgruntled Academy members.

By this point, the seating chart had been eyed by Margolis for camera placement, and by Academy controller Otto Spoerri, who allocated tickets and seated the organization's guests around the nominees and presenters. Then Cates looked things over to avoid a different kind of problem. One year, he remembered, one nominee had in the audience his wife, his current girlfriend, and two former lovers, one of whom had remarried. "Sometimes, you just have to spread certain people out," he said with a laugh. "I think I get at least one of those phone calls warning me about that every year."

SATURDAY AFTERNOON, Whoopi Goldberg made her first appearance at the Chandler. She walked out of the wings accompanied by Cates and Bruce Vilanch, who had been writing for the Oscars since the Allan Carr show. Burly and frizzy-haired, Vilanch hitched up his pants and buckled his belt as he followed Goldberg to the podium, then took a seat in the front row alongside Cates, Seligman, Warn, Herman, and senior executive consultant Robert Z. Shapiro.

The houselights were darkened. Susan Futterman, an ABC director of broadcast standards for comedy and variety shows (or, in her own words,

"Madame Censor Lady"), sat a few rows farther back, a script in her lap and a pen in her hand. And then Goldberg sashayed onstage, a smug grin on her face, and delivered her entire opening monologue in a high-speed, falsetto mumble that rendered her jokes completely unintelligible, except when she slowed down for the last word of her punch lines: "Schindler!" "Nicholson!" "Tonya Harding!"

She went on to practice her intros and transitions, this time taking them at normal speed. "This next presenter," she read from the TelePrompTer, "was Madonna's friend in *A League of Their Own*, Meg Ryan's friend in *Sleepless in Seattle*, and my friend all the time." She stopped. "Rosie O'Donnell? I don't *know* her."

And so it went: Goldberg moved through her lines quickly, mocking most of them, adding her asides, eliminating lines, or rewriting them on the fly. When a few bars of "Help Me Make It Through the Night" inexplicably played over the sound system after she introduced Al Pacino, she stopped dead.

"If this mother comes out singing that song," she said, "I'm goin' home. Al Pacino doing country western? I couldn't handle it." Then she grinned again. "I know: you're just trying to see if you can throw me. Well, we'll see where the power is Monday night."

AFTER DINNER, the first thing the crew did was tune Neil Young's piano. For real.

It was a night for rock stars at the Chandler. First there was Young, who arrived in a 1954 Cadillac limousine and took his time onstage, virtually ignoring the needs of Margolis and his camera crew. Then Bruce Springsteen's band showed up for their own rehearsal—without their boss, who'd spent the day in New Jersey, at the wedding of his nephew. With a stand-in taking the place of Springsteen, the band set up and ran through the song "Streets of Philadelphia" a couple of times. Behind them on the stage were two enormous boxes, lit from the inside and shining brightly against the black backdrop.

Springsteen's manager, Jon Landau, didn't like the look of the set, but initially he decided to wait until the next day and let Springsteen himself decide. But as the band continued to rehearse, Landau watched closely on a monitor at the production table, shaking his head when the light boxes showed up on the screen. "I don't want Bruce's first impression of this show to be a set that he's not going to like," he said.

The manager told Margolis and Seligman that he'd rather Springsteen sang in front of a plain black backdrop. Christopher resisted. "That's one of the key looks of the whole show," he said.

Cates had gone home for the night, leaving no one with the authority to resolve the dispute. The next morning at 8 a.m., though, Landau received a phone call from Cates. "If you don't want a set," the producer said, "then we won't have a set."

THE FIRST DRESS REHEARSAL was always a moment of truth. The rehearsal took place the night before the real show, after a day that had been devoted to star presenters dropping by to rehearse their lines at fifteen-minute intervals. Until the dress, the show had been rehearsed mostly in bits and pieces, seldom for more than five minutes at a stretch. Calculations made in the production office gave an idea of how long the show might run, and past experiences suggested potential trouble spots—but much of the planning remained guesswork until the crew ran through the entire show in as close to real time as it could manage. It was the last time that significant changes could be made: a second full-show run-through would follow the next morning, but if anything major was still wrong at that point, it would likely remain wrong.

Dress rehearsal featured the host and the musical performers, with stand-ins taking the place of presenters and winners. But Goldberg was still determined to keep her jokes fresh, so she once again delivered her monologue in a high-speed mumble. Midway through, she grinned, "You know they're really sweating now."

The host did some sweating of her own a few minutes later, when stagehands took far too long resetting the stage for Janet Jackson. "They're asking me to stretch," Goldberg confessed after ad-libbing a few extra jokes. "They want me to do an act, basically." She looked into the audience, scanning the seat cards. "How cool is it that the Boss is here?" she said. A long pause. "So,

Bruce Vilanch," she said, turning and looking into the wings. "This could be the tampon bit." In the audience, Futterman laughed nervously.

Aside from the botched changeover and some sound problems with Neil Young, the rehearsal ran fairly smoothly. The show seemed long—though without a real audience or any gushing Oscar winners, it was hard to tell if the length would be a problem, or if the emotion of the evening would compensate.

Throughout the run-through, the "for this rehearsal only" winners were assigned randomly. But some crew members were making guesses—and plans—accordingly. While a stand-in for *In the Name of the Father* director Jim Sheridan made an acceptance speech after receiving the best-director award, a couple of cameramen huddled in the center aisle, mapping out their moves so they wouldn't block Steven Spielberg's walk to the stage the next night. "I'll drop back quickly and he can go around you this way," said one. "Does that sound okay?"

"THE WORLD SERIES. The Olympics. The Rose Bowl. None of them mean anything." Joseph DiSante stood in front of a room of 126 well-dressed men and women seated at long tables draped in white tablecloths. "Because *tonight* is the night. Let's go to the Oscars, folks."

At 10 a.m. on Oscar morning, DiSante was holding his yearly indoctrination of the Academy Awards' seat-fillers. These were volunteers deployed to make sure that when the cameras turned toward the audience, viewers would see smiling faces rather than empty seats. DiSante was ABC's head of guest relations, but for twenty years he had also selected and trained seat-fillers, choosing them from as many as 550 letters and 1,200 phone calls he'd received from those who aspired to the gig.

DiSante had already eyed each of the chosen as they entered a sound-stage at ABC Prospect, the network's lot on the eastern edge of Hollywood. Most were dressed well (and tastefully) enough to pass muster, though he'd sent home a fortyish blonde in a peach miniskirt, asking her to change into something more appropriate. (She came back sporting a floor-length lime number.) In lieu of actually being paid, the seat-fillers received Oscar hats, posters, and programs when they signed in.

Around the perimeter of the room, buffet tables were laden with chafing dishes of hot food, plus cookies, brownies, and beverages that included milk, water, and coffee, but nothing alcoholic. Red, white, and gold balloons decorated the room. A bus was parked outside, ready for a trip to the Music Center.

But first, DiSante picked up the microphone and delivered what was partly a pep talk, partly a lecture in the art of seat-filling. "It is a very tough, hard process, getting to be a seat-filler," he said. "You are hand-picked because I think you can look like you belong."

Wearing a gray Oscar sweatshirt, DiSante asked the seat-fillers to stand up, introduce themselves to each other, and compliment each other on how good they looked. "It's very important that you know one another," he said. "We're asking you to be part of our security. Through the course of the evening, there will be people who will try to sneak into your lines. We need you to spot them and point them out to us."

Then he outlined the logistics. A team of seat-fillers would be stationed on each side of the house. The team would include "sitters," who would fill the seats; "spotters," who'd point out the seats that were emptied at each commercial break; and "runners," who'd hustle the sitters into position. Their territory, he added, would include everything from the front row to the TelePrompTer, behind which the camera rarely ventured. Seat-fillers would be issued laminated passes, which they were not to remove. "But when you sit down," added DiSante, "you need to hide your badge so that the camera doesn't see it. Men, tuck your badge inside your tuxedo jacket. Women, turn it so it's hanging down your back."

Some of them, DiSante said, would wind up in a seat for the entire show. "If that happens, God bless you and enjoy the show." Some would be challenged by the people they sat next to. "Just tell them you're temporarily filling the seat for camera purposes." Those who filled a winner's seat, DiSante said, could count on about forty-five minutes before the winner finished the press run and returned.

"In the first seventeen or eighteen rows of the Dorothy Chandler Pavilion," he said, "the entire power structure of Hollywood is sitting. This is not your night. This is *their* night."

The two most veteran seat-fillers then demonstrated what DiSante called "the Groucho Marx walk," a quick, hunched gait designed to get people into seats unobtrusively, and "without stepping on people's feet or putting your lovely butt in their faces."

Then he covered the etiquette of sitting next to a movie star. "Let's talk about autographs," he said. "Absolutely not. No autographs. If they talk to you, knock yourself out. But do not initiate the conversation." A few seat-fillers groaned. "Sorry, but it has to be that way. Most of them will talk to you. And if you sit next to a nominee and feel the urge to wish them good luck, go ahead."

DiSante looked around the room. "Is anybody getting nervous?" he asked. A few people raised their hands, so he called one woman, Linda Sanderson, to the front of the room. "What are you nervous about?" he said.

"Being on television," Sanderson said. "Sitting next to Alec Baldwin."

"You're not gonna sit next to Alec Baldwin," he said.

"Why? You're not going to let me?"

"Kim is gonna sit next to Alec Baldwin."

"Maybe she'll go to the bathroom."

After suggesting that the seat-fillers help start standing ovations for the show's two honorary Oscar winners, Paul Newman and Deborah Kerr, DiSante issued a warning.

"If you're down there and any of the press want to talk to you, I consider that an unauthorized interview," he said. "You're gonna hear and see a lot of things that most people never hear or see. Please, don't embarrass yourself, don't embarrass the Academy or the talent. If you're interviewed, remember: what the press really wants to know is what did Clint Eastwood say when you were sitting next to him? He might have said, 'Jesus, it's so hot I can't wait to get outta here.' But that's not what you're gonna say. If you embarrass the Academy or any of the talent, it's going to be all over, and you're not going to be back next year.

"If somebody from the press gets ahold of you," he concluded, "remember: only positive, nice things."

AT THE MUSIC CENTER, the day underwent a slow metamorphosis. Jeans and T-shirts were commonplace when the morning rehearsal began, but as the day wore on more and more staffers showed up in gowns and tuxedos.

Security guards and Los Angeles Police Department officers began to survey the hallways and check the doors more frequently. During the lunch break that followed the end of the rehearsal, about 3:00, almost the entire staff vacated the area around the stage, the green room, and the production offices; when they returned, the women sported formal dresses or suits, the men tuxedos.

This was an ironclad rule at the Oscars: everyone working on the show was required to wear formal dress. It didn't matter if you'd be seen on camera, or if you were anywhere near a winner, nominee, or presenter. A wardrobe bank below the stage provided tuxedos for all who wanted them, depleting the supplies of several tux-rental shops around town.

By 3:30, traffic had been diverted on all the streets surrounding the Music Center, while fans in the bleachers outside grew more impatient as they awaited the first arrivals at the red carpet. A bus stop on Grand Avenue, near the artists' entrance, was taken out of service. An airplane flew overhead, towing a sign that contained a phone number and a promise: WORLD'S FUNNIEST SCRIPT. Lower in the sky, half a dozen police helicopters circled the block continuously. In front of the Chandler on Hope Street, an army of parking valets was ready to take cars to an underground garage beneath the Department of Water and Power building across the street.

The valets sprang to action when guests began arriving about 4:00. The bleacher crowd screeched for each new star, while emcee Army Archerd hauled as many of them as possible to his platform midway down the red carpet. Archerd coaxed a few words out of reluctant nominees, plugged *Variety* every chance he got, and asked a hundred variations on the question "How do you feel?" Sometimes, though, his job was easy: he simply stood back and watched when veteran actress and forty-nine-year-old blond bombshell Sally Kirkland, who'd received a best-actress nomination for *Anna* in 1988 after waging one of the most aggressive campaigns in memory, launched into an unprompted monologue about how it was the first year Hollywood was raising people's consciousness, and how her dress was designed by an African American designer, and how she was making a movie called *Wrestling Monty*.

———

6:00 P.M., PACIFIC DAYLIGHT TIME: *"From Los Angeles, it's the 66th annual Academy Awards."*

As the traditional montage of arriving celebrities began, Whoopi Goldberg left her dressing room and waited in the wings of the stage. Backstage, Tom Hanks emerged from the men's room.

In the lobby, the crowd of late arrivals included Kurt Russell and Goldie Hawn, Ralph Fiennes, Pete Postlethwaite, and Daniel Day-Lewis. Standing amid a crowd of unused seat-fillers, Fiennes, Postlethwaite, and Day-Lewis decided they weren't comfortable watching the first twenty minutes of the show from the lobby. They slipped through a nearby door and walked down a small corridor that led backstage. Seeing that things were even more chaotic there, they changed their minds and tried to get back into the lobby, inadvertently causing a huge traffic jam outside an office used by the show's writers.

"So, they gave me a live microphone for three hours," said Goldberg early in her monologue. "There haven't been so many showbiz executives so nervous, sweating over one woman since Heidi Fleiss, honey." Backstage, Al Pacino walked down a hallway muttering "One Mississippi, two Mississippi, three Mississippi . . ."

Twenty minutes into the show, Hanks presented the first Oscars of the night to the art director and set decorator for *Schindler's List*. After Allan Starski gave a fifteen-second speech, his partner Ewa Braun leaned to the microphone to say a few words of her own. Before she could speak, Cates gave the cue to Margolis, who instructed Conti's orchestra to cut her off. (Any time the producer was in the command trailer, he made the call to play off winners; during the infrequent occasions when he was elsewhere, the decision fell to the director.)

Cates kept Conti in check for the first big winner of the evening, Tommy Lee Jones, even though the supporting actor committed the unpardonable (to Cates) sin of reading his fifty-three-second speech off a piece of paper. To make matters worse, Jones kept his head down while doing so, giving the TV audience an unfettered view of his gleaming, nearly bald head, which had been shaved for his role in the film *Cobb*. "The only thing a man can say at a time like this is, 'I am not really bald,' " he explained. "I'm lucky enough to be working."

One floor above the stage, Janet Jackson left her dressing room. A beefy security guard watched her walk by, then sighed. "Me, being that close to Janet Jackson?" he said, grinning. "I'll get over this tomorrow."

During commercials, Goldberg huddled with Vilanch in her dressing room stage left, or in a small room lined with black curtains in the wings of the stage. Nearby were tables covered with Oscar statuettes. Two Price Waterhouse representatives stood in the wings, one on each side of the stage; each carried a full set of envelopes, and each had memorized the results and had orders to immediately interrupt the show if an incorrect winner was announced. One of the two "trophy ladies," models hired to carry statuettes onstage and escort winners off, waited by each table of Oscars. (Officially dubbed "trophy ladies," the women were nonetheless called "trophy girls" by virtually everyone involved with the show.)

A little more than an hour into the show, Gene Hackman gave the supporting actress award to the evening's most stunning, and stunned, winner: eleven-year-old Anna Paquin. The hyperventilating Paquin managed to blurt out a short speech, then ignored the trophy lady trying to steer her into the wings, instead fleeing down the stairs and back to her seat.

Outside the Chandler, the tiny foyer of Jeff Margolis's command truck contained a table laden with junk food: Baby Ruth bars, Pepperidge Farm Goldfish, Oreos, peanuts, rice cakes, M&M's, raisins, Fig Newtons, salsa, peanut butter, chips . . . Above the buffet, someone had pasted a cartoon of two surgeons. One was sweating and wiping his forehead, while the other said, "Relax, man, it's not television."

Watching monitors that showed the view from each of the more than a dozen cameras, Margolis yelled out the camera numbers: "Four! Now . . . Cue her! Cue her! Cue her!" As he made each command, he snapped his fingers, and assistant director Wendy Charles Acey yelled her own orders into her headset at exactly the same time. During Debbie Allen's dance number, Margolis dispensed with spoken commands almost entirely; when he wanted a camera move, he waved his hand at the screen, and Acey translated and ordered the appropriate cut or fade. At the end of the routine, Margolis broke his silence. "Roll playback," he said, "ba-bing!"

"Good job, boys," said Cates from his seat directly behind Margolis. "Good job."

On the other side of the building, Christian Slater stepped outside the Chandler for a smoke. Springsteen got a quick touch-up in the makeup chair, then headed for the green room muttering, "Nervous, nervous." As he walked away, Geena Davis took his place in front of a makeup mirror. She was so tall that she couldn't see her face in the mirror, but it wasn't her face she was interested in. Davis was instead eyeing her cleavage, carefully patting and adjusting the folds of her dress around it.

Two and a half hours into the show, Springsteen performed. Pages immediately rushed him back to his seat, and a few minutes later he won the Oscar for best song. "This is the first song I ever wrote for a movie," he said. "So I guess it's all downhill from here."

As soon as he walked off the stage, Springsteen was hustled into a crowded elevator, along with a group that also included Whitney Houston, who'd presented him with his award. In the elevator, a page asked Springsteen for an autograph. "I guess so," he muttered, looking dazed. "I'm a little excited right now."

Upstairs, Chuck Warn, acting on the orders of Springsteen's management, rushed the press-shy winner through the four media rooms as quickly as possible. As Springsteen left the last room and headed for the elevator, the film critic and TV personality Gene Siskel pursued him down the hallway, yelling, "Bruce! Congratulations! But I just want to ask you one question about the process. What comes first, the words or the music?"

Bruce stopped to consider the oldest and dumbest question in the book, while a security guard stationed in the corridor shouted at Siskel, "No interviews in the hallway!" Springsteen gave a tentative answer—"Well, it really depends on the song"—before he was rushed away. As he waited for an elevator, he heard from a nearby monitor that Tom Hanks had won the best-actor award for *Philadelphia*, the same movie for which Springsteen had written his song.

"Is there someplace we can go to see Tom's speech?" he asked. Knowing that the Chandler's elevators were notoriously slow, Warn quickly came up with an alternate route. "We can take these stairs," he said, pointing to a door. The men dashed down four flights of stairs, only to find that the first-floor doors that would lead them back to the green room were locked.

"Shit!" yelled Warn. "They told me that this door was going to be unlocked!" After pounding on the door to no avail, Warn ran up one flight; that door was locked, as well. Finally, he found an open door that led to a nearly empty corridor on the third floor. A lone man stood in a doorway at the end of the corridor. "Do you have a monitor down there?" yelled Warn.

"Yeah," yelled the man. Springsteen ducked into the room, a makeshift headquarters for staffers from Eastman Kodak, which was shooting each winner with a large-format instant camera in one of the upper balconies.

On the screen, Hanks was giving an emotional acceptance speech, which began with thanks to a high school classmate and a drama teacher, whom he identified as "two of the finest gay Americans" he'd ever met. "[T]he streets of heaven are too crowded with angels," he said. "They number a thousand for each of the red ribbons that we wear here tonight . . ."

In the doorway of the room, a Kodak staffer watched Springsteen rush by and take a seat on the couch. "Um, does that guy have an Academy Award?" he asked.

"Yes," said Warn.

A pause. "Who is he?"

When the Kodak employees finally figured out that they had an Oscar-winning rock star in their midst, they asked for autographs and photos. Springsteen finally made it back to the first floor right about the time that Holly Hunter picked up the best-actress award for *The Piano*, completing a sweep for that film's female stars—as well as its writer-director, Jane Campion, who won the Oscar for her original screenplay.

But Campion didn't walk away with the other prize for which she'd been nominated: to the surprise of nobody, Steven Spielberg continued what had been a very good night (five Oscars so far for *Schindler's List*, plus three for *Jurassic Park*) by winning the best-director award. "Am I allowed to say that I really wanted this?" Spielberg asked.

A few minutes later, *Schindler's List* won for best picture. In the backstage hallway, a large crowd clustered around a monitor to watch the speeches of Spielberg and producer Branko Lustig, himself a Holocaust survivor. "It's a long way from Auschwitz to this stage," said Lustig, as Neil Young walked through the crowd on his way out the back door.

"Well, that's Oscar sixty-six, baby," said Goldberg a minute later. Spielberg came offstage, Oscars in hand, and was herded toward the elevator. The director, famously wary of elevators, stopped. "Can we walk?" he said.

"Yeah," said his escort. "We can walk."

Most of the crowd had begun making its way toward the Governors Ball, but the bulk of the Oscar staff stuck around. On the side of the stage, Cates was approached by ABC's John Hamlin. "I think this Oscar show will go down in history," said Hamlin, who had supervised Oscar shows for more than two decades. "It wasn't a big, showbizzy, Broadway-type show. It was a great, emotional show."

Cates made a detour into the production office to thank his staff, then slipped into the Governors Ball by a back entrance. He quickly did a few interviews, telling the handful of reporters allowed inside the ball how delighted he was with the show. Then he left the tent the same way he came in, rejoined his wife, and made his grand entrance through the front.

Soon, the ball was crammed with people. Hanks and Spielberg spent more than an hour talking to the press; other winners and nominees dispersed to their tables. Bruce Springsteen stood at the bar, waiting without much luck for a bartender to notice him and take his order. "Ya win an Academy Award," he said with a grin, "and ya still can't get service at the bar."

MANY HOURS LATER, Springsteen, Spielberg, Hanks, and Goldberg were among those who ended up at a private party at Dani Janssen's Century City apartment. Janssen, the widow of actor David Janssen, attracted that crowd partly because the Oscar party scene was undergoing a seismic shift: Irving "Swifty" Lazar had died at the end of December, and Spago, the site of his legendary Oscar party, had closed for the night out of respect for the agent.

Janssen had stepped into the void with a small, private party, while other events made a more public play for the A-list. While Elton John had drawn a good crowd the year before with a Maple Drive party that benefited his own AIDS foundation, the most serious newcomer was *Vanity Fair* magazine, which cohosted a bash at Morton's restaurant with producer Steve

Tisch. The Academy, meanwhile, took notice of the absence of Spago on the scene, and took steps to increase attendance at its own soiree: it asked Spago's owner, Wolfgang Puck, to supervise the menu at the following year's Governors Ball.

The morning after the show, Cates read all the reviews, but he didn't pay them much heed. *The New York Times* wrote the show a love letter, the *Los Angeles Times* was lukewarm, others found the evening bland. "The first time I ever produced the show, I spoke to Samuel Goldwyn, and he told me something great," said Cates. "He said, 'It doesn't matter what kind of show you do. Some of the reviews are going to hate it, some of them are going to love it, and there's nothing you can do about it. So do the show *you* want to do, and forget about everybody else.' "

Ratings did not slide the way some had feared. In the months leading up to the Oscars, the Grammy Awards, People's Choice Awards, and American Music Awards had all scored their lowest ratings in years, but the Academy Awards show held its own, dropping off only slightly from the previous year and managing its second-highest rating in a decade. At three hours and eighteen minutes, it was also the shortest Oscar show in five years—a change that could be attributed in large part to Whoopi Goldberg, who spent considerably less time on her entrance and her monologue than Billy Crystal would have done.

One interested viewer of the show was writer Paul Rudnick, who wrote a satirical film review column for *Premiere* magazine under the name of Libby Gelman-Waxner. Under his own name, Rudnick had recently written the script for the comedy *Addams Family Values*, and he was struck by Tom Hanks's disclosure that his high school drama teacher was gay. Though Hanks did not, as some publications charged, "out" the teacher against his will—he'd called the retired, sixty-nine-year-old Rawley Farnsworth and asked permission a few days before the show—Rudnick was inspired to begin work on a script about a deeply closeted drama teacher who's outed by a former student at the Oscars. Three years later, that film, *In & Out*, would win an Oscar nomination for actress Joan Cusack.

2

≡

Restraint and Decorum

The 67th Academy Awards

AT FIRST, IT SEEMED LIKE A GOOD IDEA. Gil Cates had chosen "Comedy and the Movies" as the theme of the 67th Academy Awards show, and nobody doubted that David Letterman knew comedy. True, his comic sensibility was the sort that might have made him a long shot most years, and he might not have been a movie star the way Billy Crystal and Whoopi Goldberg were—but Letterman was funny and his late-night show was on a roll, so Cates won plaudits for making what many thought was a gutsy, inspired choice that might put a fresh spin on the Oscars.

To go with Letterman, Cates had to break his informal rule: usually, he looked for a host who was both a movie star and a live performer capable of working a room. Those qualifications essentially limited the pool to a handful of stand-up comics who'd gone on to have movie careers, though Cates's short list also included Tom Hanks, an actor with no stand-up experience.

Letterman was by no means a movie star: his film acting debut, such as it was, consisted of a tiny part in his friend Chris Elliott's disastrous 1994 comedy *Cabin Boy*. Still, Letterman's *Late Show* was the undisputed champion of late-night television, regularly trouncing Jay Leno's *Tonight Show* in the ratings and winning over critics with a sardonic and occasionally absurdist wit far sharper and smarter than Leno's market-tested gabfest. Letterman had badly wanted to host *The Tonight Show* himself following the retirement of its longtime host, Johnny Carson, but after much deliberation NBC went with the safer bet, Leno; Letterman, who'd been on NBC following Carson at 12:30 a.m., jumped to CBS and the 11:30 time slot, where in the eyes of many he'd been making NBC regret its decision.

The *Late Show*'s rating encouraged Cates that Letterman might well attract new viewers to the Oscars, and he also knew that there was ample precedent for handing the ceremony's reins to a talk-show host. The most successful host between the Bob Hope years, which ended in 1978, and the Billy Crystal stint that began a dozen years later was Johnny Carson, Letterman's idol and mentor.

Carson stayed away from his usual *Tonight Show* gags but retained the easygoing, self-deprecating charm he had on that show. He also liked to puncture the pomp of the event: his first monologue, in 1979, began with a classic line that called the Oscar show "two hours of sparkling entertainment . . . spread over a four-hour show." Carson hosted five times in six years, before walking away from the gig and resisting subsequent entreaties to return.

Letterman, the Oscar staff hoped, would follow the lead set by his hero fifteen years earlier. Still, some observers and insiders worried about the clash of cultures between Letterman and the Academy. NBC had opted for Leno largely because the network thought Letterman's humor was better suited to the 12:30 time slot. With his self-mocking wit, his perpetually sour expression, and stunts like his "stupid pet tricks," Letterman simultaneously hosted a talk show and mocked the entire enterprise. The Academy Awards, on the other hand, took themselves seriously. Comedy was fine, but propriety mattered.

Immediately, Letterman's presence changed a few things about the institution of the Oscars. Academy press releases were usually predictable documents, sporting the expected harmless plaudits that Cates could dish out with the best of them: "Whoopi Goldberg has all the qualities of a great Oscar host," "Jeff is a great television director," that sort of thing. The press release announcing Letterman, though, actually slipped in a bit of deadpan facetiousness, a commodity usually in short supply in Academy corridors. "David Letterman . . . is punctual, well groomed, and knows how to keep an audience awake," it quoted Cates as saying.

Added Letterman, "We're changing the format this year. The whole show will be forty minutes long, and I'll be giving away cars."

IN A WAY, the tension between the host and the event fit the tone of the Academy Awards race in 1995. The previous year had been a stormy one, one in which Kurt Cobain committed suicide, O. J. Simpson was charged with the brutal murders of his ex-wife and her friend, and Disney Studios chairman Jeffrey Katzenberg left the company on the heels of his biggest triumph, *The Lion King*, when CEO Michael Eisner refused to give him the job of president, which was left empty after longtime executive Frank Wells died in a helicopter crash.

While *The Lion King* was the top-grossing movie of the year, two other films dominated the Oscar race. One was the blockbuster hit *Forrest Gump*, a paean to blissful ignorance starring Tom Hanks and helmed by *Back to the Future* director Bob Zemeckis. The tale of a good-hearted southern-born simpleton who stumbles through many of the key events of the past forty years, *Forrest Gump* took pains to emphasize the personal and political destruction wrought by the sixties counterculture. Jenny, the free spirit played by Robin Wright and loved by Tom Hanks's title character, embraced the protest and hippie movements and paid for it with an early death, while Forrest Gump himself became an uncomprehending hero almost by accident.

The other film was the profane and bloody *Pulp Fiction*, the second feature from Quentin Tarantino, the young director of *Reservoir Dogs*. Tarantino reveled in the freedom to craft an entertaining movie out of staggeringly violent and offensive material. He and cowriter Roger Avary littered their screenplay with obscenities and vulgarities, gunfights and savage beatings, while never quite losing a sense of fun. *Pulp Fiction* became the first $100 million movie ever released by Miramax, and a milestone in the world of independent cinema.

When nominations were announced in February, the best-picture competition quickly boiled down to a race between *Gump* and *Pulp*—"Life is like a box of chocolates" in one corner, "Any of you fuckin' pricks move and I'll execute every motherfuckin' last one of ya" in the other.

Publicly, Zemeckis and Tarantino played nice, incredulously painting *Gump* and *Pulp* as films cut from the same cloth. "I don't see them as being drastically different," said Tarantino to Zemeckis in the *Los Angeles Times*. "I actually think [*Gump* is] a black comedy." (Away from tape recorders, meanwhile, Tarantino was known to be dismissive of much of *Gump*.)

With those two films battling it out, perhaps the Oscars were ready for a tougher, more sardonic host. Still, there were danger signs early on, caused largely by Letterman's independence and inaccessibility. Often, Cates couldn't even get Letterman to return his phone calls. "I remember Gil calling me," said stage manager Dency Nelson, who'd been the cue card man on Letterman's morning talk show in 1980 and had stayed in touch with the host ever since. "Gil said, 'I can't get through to him. He's an odd duck, isn't he?'"

At a production meeting in mid-March, Cates acknowledged that communications with his host had been sporadic at best. "I actually even spoke to Dave last week," Cates said to his staff, who responded with a round of knowing laughter. "So I'm real confident that he will be here."

FOR MIRAMAX PICTURES, the 67th Academy Awards were a milestone. The company, founded in 1979 by two brothers from Queens, Harvey and Bob Weinstein, had become a brazen, inescapable force in the world of independent film, and by far the most successful of the companies that distributed what were largely low-budget movies. The brothers, particularly the corpulent, flamboyant Harvey, were known for abusing staffers, bullying filmmakers, throwing tantrums, driving hard bargains, and a host of other sins both common and uncommon in the movie business—but they also pushed art films like *sex, lies and videotape*, *My Left Foot*, and *The Crying Game* into the mainstream.

By the early 1990s, Miramax was beginning to work its scorched-earth marketing techniques to perfection on the Academy Awards. They were one of the first companies to aggressively send out screener cassettes to Academy members, an area that had become one of the prime campaign battlegrounds of the time. "The advent of video distribution afforded studios the opportunity to do more than just send a video out in a cardboard mailer," said Richard Kahn, the former Academy president and member of the committee that oversaw campaigning. "Suddenly we were seeing studios spend enormous amounts of money packaging their videos and including fifty-, sixty-, seventy-dollar coffee table books." In 1994, Sony had enclosed eight of its videos in a black laminated wooden box that Kahn called "something any bride would be proud to put her dowry in." The Academy discussed instituting stricter rules about packaging, but in 1995 the likes of *The Lion King* were still going out in elaborate packages, with extra goodies thrown in.

Most of the studios sent out videos and included extras; Miramax distinguished itself by going further, by making sure their filmmakers were seen with the right people and at the right parties during Oscar season. They also hired consultants to spread the word about their movies—and, rivals always charged, to spread dirt about the competition. Among actors and filmmakers eager for the kind of exposure, cachet, and cash that comes with an Oscar, Miramax's stock rose every time another one of its films racked up the nominations: five for *My Left Foot* in 1990 (and a win for its leading actor, Daniel Day-Lewis), six for *The Crying Game* in 1993 (including best picture, best director, and two acting nominations), eight for *The Piano* in 1994 (with three wins, all in big categories).

By the time the Oscar nominations were announced in 1995, Miramax had been acquired by the Walt Disney Company, though it still operated with a large degree of autonomy. The nominations were a triumph for the Weinsteins: Miramax garnered twenty-two nominations, which was twelve more than its parent company and five more than Paramount, its closest rival. In two categories, supporting actress and original screenplay, Miramax had four out of the five nominations; in the best-director competition, the company had three out of five.

As Miramax celebrated, the Academy was dealing with a firestorm of criticism. One of the most acclaimed films of the year had been *Hoop*

Dreams, a three-hour documentary that followed two high school basketball players from inner-city Chicago, both of whom hoped to make it into the National Basketball Association. The film, directed by Steve James, received the kind of acclaim and mainstream attention rarely given to documentaries; Fine Line Features even mounted a campaign to win the movie a best-picture nomination, which the company knew was a long shot.

But not only did *Hoop Dreams* not win a best-picture nomination, it also wasn't chosen as one of the five nominees in the feature documentary category, where many observers had expected it to win easily. That was a category in which a special committee chose the nominations—but since the Academy did not have a documentary branch, the documentary screening committee was comprised of volunteers from all thirteen branches of the Academy.

With sixty-three movies in contention for nominations, committee members needed to be available every Tuesday and Thursday night for three months; the requirement skewed its membership toward the aging and retired. Bruce Davis called them "a very eccentric group of individuals" with strong opinions and unconventional manners. One woman, for instance, would routinely start crying during the discussions that followed screenings.

At those screenings, committee members were asked to "vote" with flashlights fifteen minutes after each documentary began. If three-quarters of them turned on their lights, the movie was stopped. If a documentary passed the fifteen-minute mark, a new vote was taken every ten minutes, and the power to stop the movie shifted to a simple majority.

"A lot of very good movies were turned off because people didn't want to spend the time," said Chuck Workman, a member of the committee. "These people were smart and they were dedicated, but their documentary experience was basically older films or films on PBS. There was a whole world of nonfiction film going on from about the late eighties, exciting stuff, that they just kind of missed."

The failure to nominate *Hoop Dreams* caused an uproar that dwarfed the outcry when the committee had previously overlooked commercially successful documentaries like *Woodstock*, *The Thin Blue Line*, and *Roger and Me*. Critics found it particularly disheartening that one of the nominations went to *Maya Lin: A Strong Clear Vision*, a documentary that won mediocre reviews but was directed by Freida Lee Mock, a past chairwoman of the documentary committee. (Mock had disqualified herself from voting because her film was in contention.) "Leaving out *Hoop Dreams* is like leaving out *Schindler's List*," Lianne Halfon, executive producer of the acclaimed but snubbed documentary *Crumb*, told the *Los Angeles Times*.

The day after the nominations were released, Arthur Hiller announced that he would take "a close, hard look at the procedures of the documentary committee." Bruce Davis followed by taking what was for him an unprecedented step. He called Price Waterhouse and asked to see the complete results of the voting. The accounting firm prepared a rundown for Davis that left out the names of the voters, but showed how each voter had scored every movie in contention.

In voting, members of the committee were asked to rate each documentary on a scale of zero to ten—a departure from other Oscar categories scored by committee, which used a scale of six to ten. "What I found," said Davis, "is that a small group of members gave zeros to every single movie except the five they wanted to see nominated. And they gave tens to those five, which completely skewed the voting."

Choosing his words carefully, Davis summed up the results. "There was one film that received more scores of ten than any other, but it wasn't nominated," he said. "It also got zeros from those few voters, and that was enough to push it to sixth place."

AFTER FIVE YEARS at the Dorothy Chandler Pavilion, the Oscars had returned to the Shrine Auditorium. The Shrine was a seventy-year-old theater that sat in a dodgy part of town just south of downtown Los Angeles, nestled next to the University of Southern California and across the street from the venerable Felix Chevrolet auto dealership.

Cates preferred the Chandler because it was more elegant and looked better on camera, but that twenty-eight-hundred-seat theater simply didn't have enough room for all the Academy members who wanted to attend the show. Moving to the six-thousand-seat Shrine allowed the Academy to clear its backlog of members who'd lost out in annual lotteries for seats at the Chandler.

Six days before the show, crew members worked to turn the cavernous building into a usable theater for the Oscars. Bleachers were erected and the red carpet laid in front of the Shrine; production trailers, trucks, and a huge press tent filled the parking lot behind the building. Inside the Shrine, tables were laid across seats in the orchestra section to create command posts for the producer, the network, the design crew, and the stage managers. Stage left and downstairs were dressing rooms. Through the wings stage right was the green room, nestled in a corner of the Shrine Exhibition Hall, which doubled as the site of the Governors Ball.

Seats near the stage sported seat cards that indicated who would be sitting where come Monday night. The front row contained Rene Russo, Samuel L. Jackson, Andie MacDowell, Hugh Grant, Annette Bening, Julia Ormond, John Travolta, Jeremy Irons, Arnold Schwarzenegger, Tom Hanks, Sharon Stone, Denzel Washington, Jodie Foster, Jack Nicholson, Holly Hunter, and Anthony Hopkins. Also Uma Thurman and Oprah Winfrey.

As work proceeded, the host of the Oscar show was nowhere to be seen. Letterman had arrived in Los Angeles, but he was spending his time with the twenty-odd *Late Show* staffers he'd brought with him. Occasionally, word of Letterman's doings filtered down to Oscar staffers, some of whom said they'd heard that the host really was planning to raffle off a car onstage, just as he'd promised in the initial press release. The raffle, of course, was to be rigged. "They wanted Jessica Tandy to win," said an Oscar staffer with ties to the Letterman camp. "They didn't realize that she died six months ago. So now they're looking for somebody else to give the car to."

Letterman was expected to make his first appearance at the Shrine the next day. In the meantime, the TelePrompTer he would use displayed a more philosophical bent: IF THERE ARE WORDS ON THE PROMPTER AND NO ONE READS THEM, it read, ARE THEY REALLY THERE?

THREE DAYS BEFORE THE SHOW, during a dinner break, Bruce Vilanch walked into the production office wearing a T-shirt that read: THANK YOU

FOR NOT BEING PERKY. Vilanch picked up a phone message that had been pinned to the board all day: "D. Letterman," it read, with a return number. "8:35 a.m." Vilanch laughed. "He called me at home at 8:36," he said. "I don't think I need to return this."

The frizzy-haired, three-hundred-pound, openly gay Vilanch had been a common sight (always in baggy pants and humorous T-shirts) at Hollywood awards shows for years. The former journalist began writing for Bette Midler's stage act in the early 1970s, spent some time on variety shows like *The Brady Bunch Hour*, and over the years had written material for the likes of Diana Ross, Lily Tomlin, Richard Pryor, and Joan Rivers. He had been writing for the Oscars since the Allan Carr show in 1989, mostly for the host but also on occasion for presenters.

"With Billy, we wrote material and refined it over weeks," Vilanch said as he tossed Letterman's phone message into the trash can beneath his desk. "With Whoopi, I wrote it and she said it. But Dave doesn't work like that. He wants *tons* of material. And then he goes off by himself, sifts through it all, and digests it on his own."

CATES USUALLY FELT that the Oscar show should begin with a piece of film rather than a production number, but he did make an occasional exception for a routine that mixed film and dancing. In 1991, for instance, he'd hired Debbie Allen for the first time, and she'd choreographed a frenetic number in which live dancers burst through a movie screen and danced onstage. In 1994, Allen and Chuck Workman had collaborated on another tricky routine, which found Bernadette Peters appearing both in film footage and, at the conclusion of the song, on the stage of the Dorothy Chandler Pavilion.

And in 1995, Workman and Allen were collaborating on an even more difficult blend of live action and film. Set to "Make 'Em Laugh," Donald O'Connor's tour de force from *Singin' in the Rain*, the production number featured a barrage of film clips illustrating the art of film comedy. Several singers and dancers, chief among them *Sister Act* actress Kathy Najimy, *Rocky Horror Picture Show* star Tim Curry, and the seven-year-old star of *Mrs. Doubtfire*, Mara Wilson, jumped in and out of a huge screen, which was slit to accommodate their entrances and exits. The three singers would be seen live onstage, but also in new footage, shot by Workman, which depicted them watching classic film comedies. Occasionally, they'd be inserted into those classic clips as well.

The live audience wouldn't be able to see the entire number; they'd be looking at the performers come and go through a large blank green screen. Only at home would viewers be able to fully appreciate the number—and then only if Margolis could find a way to shoot it without simply confusing the audience. "It was one of those openings that was *way* too difficult to do on a live show," said the director, "but it's the Oscars, so you push the envelope and do what you can. I had to keep cutting to the stage in a way that would remind the audience at home where we were."

From the start, the number had been a mess. Workman didn't want to use Najimy, and thought the actress was "only concerned with her own image." As he tried to make the piece work, the filmmaker grew more argumentative and difficult. At one point, he went to Cates and suggested dumping the number entirely. "No, keep working on it," the producer insisted. "It'll be okay."

On the stage of the Shrine, though, take after take got no closer to making the routine smooth, or even comprehensible. "The thing about the Oscars," said Workman later, "is that it's like turning around an aircraft carrier." On his own, the filmmaker was used to sitting in an editing room, trying out tricky cuts and juxtapositions, and quickly revising or jettisoning ideas that didn't work. But working within the context of an Oscar production number, where his film was only one part of a mammoth undertaking that also involved dancers, actors and their agents, a director, a choreographer, and many others who had to be alternately challenged, coddled, and consulted with, Workman found that he could no longer work as efficiently or effectively as usual; change came as slowly as if he were a Navy captain piloting an eleven-hundred-foot vessel. "And you can't blame it on the machinery," he said, "because if you work on that show you have to understand that you are on an aircraft carrier."

As staffers watched the performers struggle to sync their moves with the film clips, and Margolis fight to find the right camera angles and cuts, the intricacies of "Make 'Em Laugh" seemed overwhelming. "Man, if this thing works it'll be a miracle," said one viewer. "It's so friggin' complicated."

RANDY NEWMAN was a six-time Oscar nominee, but so far the prize had eluded him. Partly, that was because the songs he wrote for movies were rarely as distinctive—or, for that matter, as tough and as mean—as the work with which he'd made his name. The songs on Newman's pop albums, including the deceptively gorgeous anthem to slavery, "Sail Away," the nihilistic "God's Song," and the cracker anthem "Rednecks," were often barbed and cruel; his big pop hit had been "Short People," in which the six-foot Newman was presumably joking when he proclaimed, "Short people got no reason to live." By contrast, his movie tunes tended to be jaunty, even pleasant. His latest nominated song, "Make Up Your Mind," from the Ron Howard movie *The Paper*, was typical: bouncy, professional, and forgettable.

Still, Newman remained a formidable talent and intellect. He may not have had a pop hit since 1977, but he'd written some classic film scores and found a lucrative niche following in the footsteps of his uncles Alfred and Lionel, both notable film composers.

Newman arrived at the Shrine on Saturday afternoon to rehearse "Make Up Your Mind." Before sitting down at the piano, he walked over to his background singers and addressed them solemnly. "Remember," he said, "give me at least 64 percent."

"Hi, Randy," said Margolis over the P.A. system as Newman took his seat. "How are you?"

"Really good," said a characteristically deadpan Newman. "I've got my speech all ready in case *The Lion King* vote cancels itself out."

This was, of course, a long shot. After a year in which the song nominations had gone to the likes of Bruce Springsteen, Neil Young, and Janet Jackson, Disney had returned with a vengeance. Its blockbuster animated film *The Lion King* dominated the music categories: not only did composer Hans Zimmer win a nomination for his score, the film captured three of the five nominations for the best song. One of those nominations, Elton John's ballad "Can You Feel the Love Tonight," was the only hit among the nominees, and the odds-on favorite.

Sitting at the piano, Newman turned his gaze to the audience, scanning the seating cards until he spotted the star of *The Natural*, for which Newman wrote an acclaimed (and Oscar-nominated) score. "There's Robert Redford," Newman joked to no one in particular. "He belched his way through the movie I did with him."

Newman performed his nominated song once, then looked into the orchestra pit and located conductor Bill Conti. "That was a little faster than it should go," Newman told Conti, "but it was pretty good. And it was good enough, since I've lowered my standards so much."

After Newman left, Margolis prepared to rehearse another of the nominated songs, Patty Smyth's "Look What Love Has Done" from the Arnold Schwarzenegger comedy *Junior*. The director sat in his truck behind the Shrine, staring at a wall of some sixty-five different TV monitors. The three largest screens sat directly in front of Margolis's seat, where they showed him the camera being used at any given moment, along with the next two he was planning to use. Smaller screens surrounding those three featured the view from each of the sixteen cameras that would be used during the show. Beneath those screens were pieces of masking tape with the camera number and the name of the cameraman: CA-1 BILL . . . CA-2 HECTOR . . . CA-3 LARRY . . .

With a background in music and variety shows, including *The Gong Show*, the American Music Awards, and Dolly Parton's short-lived variety show, Margolis had first been hired after Marty Pasetta had proved too imperious for the Academy's taste. Margolis didn't have Pasetta's temper; he grinned a lot and kept quiet when things went wrong. His crews tended to like him, and not just because he'd hired his son as a stage manager and his father as a stand-in; even those who weren't related found him loose and open to outside ideas. Among the higher echelons of the Oscar staff, though, occasional doubts were raised about the director's agenda. It didn't help when Margolis's own press agent began to solicit the attention of the media, which was eager for any Oscar-related access.

Margolis was in his booth going over the plans for "Look What Love Has Done" when he got a call from stage manager Ken Stein. Patty Smyth, said Stein, didn't want to make her entrance by walking down a small stairway that had been placed on the stage.

"Why not?" asked Margolis.

"I don't know," said Stein. "I think it's a female thing, because we get it from all of them."

The woman who sat to Margolis's right in the truck, associate director Wendy Charles Acey, quickly chimed in. "Because she'll be wearing three-inch heels and she's afraid she'll trip in front of everybody, of course," said Acey.

Smyth was the coquettish former lead singer of the pop band Scandal, who had two small hits a decade earlier with "Goodbye to You" and "The Warrior." She'd already caused one problem by asking that her boyfriend be allowed to play guitar in her band on the show; the trouble was that her boyfriend was the temperamental tennis player John McEnroe. Cates nixed the request on the grounds that McEnroe's presence would be a distraction.

When Smyth said she didn't want to use the stairs, Margolis left the truck to speak to her. While he was gone, Bill Conti radioed the truck. "Does this girl cause as much commotion as Streisand, or what?" he asked.

"Yeah," said Acey. "I guess I should find out who she is."

Conti laughed. "*Exactly*," he said.

A few minutes later, Margolis returned to the truck. "Oh, boy," he sighed, sinking back into his chair.

Margolis had planned to begin the number with a slow pan to Smyth as she walked down the stairs. With that option gone, he watched her run through the song, shaking his head as he tried to figure out how to shoot it. None of the camera angles seemed interesting to him, nobody cared much for the song itself, and the director seemed defeated by how to make it work on-screen.

After the first take, Smyth leaned into the microphone. "It's really muddy up here," she said to the sound mixer.

"Okay, just give us a couple of minutes," Margolis told her over the P.A. system. Then he shut off his mike and leaned back in his chair. "A couple of minutes to find another song," he muttered.

"Another singer, maybe," added Conti, whose headset allowed him to hear conversations in the truck.

For the next fifteen minutes, Margolis studied the script in front of him, jotting down notations for each dissolve, cut, and camera move. Finally, he came up with a plan for the song. "Okay, here we go for rehearsal," he said into his microphone. "Thank you for your patience." Then he addressed his cameramen. "Guys," he said, "try to give me something here you didn't do on the other song."

But the next take was no better than the last, and Margolis stared back at his script. Smyth paced the stage, idly singing the Bobby Gentry hit "Ode to Billy Joe," then questioning the crew about when they'd be ready for her again.

"Kenny, you better go talk to her," said Margolis to Ken Stein. "She's getting really impatient, and I need some time here."

"What should I tell her?" asked Stein.

Margolis sunk his head in his hands. "Just tell her," he said wearily, "I'm redesigning the whole fuckin' thing because she wouldn't come down the stairs." He stopped. "No, just tell her to relax for a minute. Tell her we're lighting or something."

Unaware of the mood in the truck, Smyth stretched out her arms and did a little dance. "We have some choreography we'd like to show you next time through," she announced.

"Just as long as it starts with you walking down the stairs," said Margolis.

"*Falling* down the stairs is what I'll do," said Smyth, a notorious klutz who swore she once broke a rib putting on her bra. "But I'll try it if you want."

"No," said Margolis. "This'll be fine."

Slowly, Margolis puzzled it out. "Camera twelve's got the first shot, four's got the second, three's got the third . . ." They tried Margolis's new plan, but cameramen kept getting in each other's way. "Forget it boys, it's not working," said the director. "Let's try something else. If anybody's got a good shot, show it to me."

Over the next few takes, Margolis slowly found a handful of shots and camera moves he could live with. He clearly wasn't happy with the number, but neither was it a complete disaster. "If I stop after this one," he said to Acey at the beginning of one take, "am I on schedule?"

"No," she said. "But you're closer than you were."

"Okay," sighed Margolis when the take ended. "Thank you very much, Patty. Thank you, guys. Let's move on."

In the trailer, Acey shook her head. "Well," she said, "it's been a slow year for music."

"THE IRVING THALBERG AWARD," read Arnold Schwarzenegger, "is given to people who have devoted their lives to making movies of lasting value." The action star looked at the TelePrompTer, which displayed the lines he'd be using to present a special Oscar to Clint Eastwood. He started to laugh. "Heck," he ad-libbed, "I don't think they're going to be giving *me* that one."

Near the production table, Susan Futterman from ABC approached the show's senior executive consultant, Robert Z. Shapiro. Futterman had an open script in her hands. She pointed to the second page of the script. ITEM # 2, it read. OPENING COMMERCIAL BILLBOARDS. On it were the voiceovers that announcer Randy Thomas would read at the top of the show. Four companies had paid for plugs: Revlon, American Express, Chevrolet, and Coca-Cola. The problem, Futterman told Shapiro, was that while the first three companies had short plugs ("Revlon: Revolutionary products for revolutionary women . . . American Express: For life, for living . . ."), Coke had altogether too much copy.

"Look at it," she said, jabbing her finger toward the lines: "And Coca-Cola, in the genuine Coca-Cola bottle. Nothing looks like it. Nothing tastes like it. Because it's always Coca-Cola."

"It's more than five seconds," Futterman insisted. "It's seven."

"Is that really a problem?" asked Shapiro.

"Yes it is. You have to cut the line, 'in the genuine Coca-Cola bottle.' "

"Are you sure?"

"Yes," she said firmly. "Why should they get seven seconds, when we're selling everyone else five?"

WITH DAVID LETTERMAN and his staff on the premises, communication had improved between the host and the production team—though that's not to say that Dave and the Oscars were always on the same page. For one thing, Letterman wanted to wear a suit, while Cates insisted on the usual tuxedo. Letterman wanted his own drummer in the orchestra pit to punctuate his jokes with the kind of rim shots the Oscars had always done without. He wanted sound effects and slow motion and instant replays, all mainstays of his television show.

"We talked to him about a number of ideas we didn't feel were really appropriate," said Margolis, whose wrath Letterman had incurred by suggesting that Hal Gurnee, the director of *The Late Show*, would have been able to provide a slow-mo replay effect Margolis didn't want to use. A subsequent meeting in Letterman's trailer had ironed out some of the differences, but a gulf still existed between the Oscar staffers and their host. "A lot of the stuff that he does in the Ed Sullivan Theatre is brilliant there," said Margolis. "But it wasn't going to translate to the Shrine, to our audience."

On Friday afternoon, Letterman had breezed through a few introductions and gotten the feel of the stage (while his head writer, Rob Burnett, had taken note of the seat cards, particularly the ones that indicated where Uma Thurman and Oprah Winfrey would be sitting). At 8:30 p.m. on Saturday night, he took the stage once more; as if to show that this rehearsal was more serious, he entered to the strains of Richard Strauss's "Also Sprach Zarathustra," aka the theme from *2001: A Space Odyssey*, aka the portentous music with which Elvis Presley announced his arrival onstage for much of the last half-decade of his life.

Letterman wore jeans, a T-shirt, and a San Francisco Giants cap and jacket. He sported several days' growth of graying beard. Almost immediately, the rehearsal took on the look and feel of a *Late Show* broadcast—though not, it seemed, a particularly inspired *Late Show* broadcast. He showed a lackluster film package of New York City taxi drivers talking about the movies, and a funnier one of stars reinterpreting Letterman's line from *Cabin Boy*: "Would you like to buy a monkey?" His punch lines were punctuated by the sounds of breaking glass, and by drummer Anton Fig's rim shots. He read a Top Ten List, "Top Ten Surprises in Kato Kaelin's Testimony." (Word quickly spread among the crew that the list was from a recent Letterman show, and that he'd have a new, custom list ready for Oscar night.) He called Bill Conti "the world's most dangerous Oscar orchestra leader," a line borrowed from his traditional introduction of the band on his own show. He even did a Stupid Pet Trick, bringing out Sadie, The Dog That Spins When You Applaud. As the title suggested, the hyperkinetic German Shepherd spun madly in circles when the audience applauded.

And as he promised in the initial press release, Letterman held a raffle. "Some lucky nominee," he said, "could be driving Oscar home in a brand-new car." With Jessica Tandy out of the running, Letterman's writers had decided to give the vehicle to Sally Field instead. Margolis, Letterman, and *Late Show* producer Robert Morton spent a great deal of time trying to figure out how to drive the car onstage so that the winner could immediately get behind the driver's seat (the only solution was to back it on), and how to position the raffle cage from which one of the show's trophy ladies would pull the winning name.

As Letterman's rehearsal wound down, many of the Oscar staffers began repeating a line that would come to sound like a cross between a mantra and a plea: "Well, I'm sure he's saving his best stuff for Monday night."

Still, the rehearsal left more than a few people disappointed and disconcerted. "I'm a little surprised," confided Roy Christopher. "I had hoped that he wouldn't do so much of his usual stuff. Carson didn't do that, you know."

KEANU REEVES ducked into the green room, a script page in one hand and a motorcycle helmet in the other. Unlike most of the other stars due to rehearse on the afternoon before the show, Reeves hadn't come to the Shrine in a town car provided by the Academy. Instead, he rode his motorcycle there.

Army Archerd said hello to Reeves and then nodded at the script. "What are you doing?" he asked.

"One of the best-picture things," said Reeves, who had been given the plum task of introducing the film clip from *Pulp Fiction*.

"Oh, that's good."

"Is it?" asked Reeves. "I'm out there by myself. I wanted to give out an *award*, and be with a *girl*."

Reeves spotted Vilanch, whose T-shirt du jour read, MIGHTY MORPHIN FLOWER ARRANGERS. "You're one of the writers," he said to Vilanch, holding up his script. "In this line, 'This shocking, brutal, hilarious adventure is called *Pulp Fiction*,' can I say 'entitled' instead of 'called'?"

"I don't see why not," said Vilanch.

"Okay, good," said Reeves. "Also, don't they mention the names of the directors in these things?"

"In the clip intros?" asked Vilanch. "I don't think so. Quentin will be mentioned lots of other places."

With his concerns about the script assuaged, Reeves began pumping Vilanch for information about the show. "What's Dave been like?" he said.

Vilanch laughed. "Oh, you should see it," he said.

Reeves caught something in Vilanch's tone, and frowned. "He's not doing stuff like he does on his show, is he?" he asked.

"Well," admitted Vilanch, "there will be a Top Ten List."

"No."

"And he's got some of those film clips he does. There's one with taxi drivers."

"No!"

"And there is a Stupid Pet Trick."

"No! He *can't!*" said Reeves angrily. "Whatever happened to restraint and decorum?"

Before long, the green room was cluttered with stars who'd arrived for the rehearsal ritual that took place the day before every Oscar show. Sarah Jessica Parker was casual in black sweats and sneakers; Annette Bening was elegant in a maroon suit. Anna Paquin wore an oversized T-shirt; Sylvester Stallone jeans, sunglasses, and an open shirt. Radiant in pastels, Andie MacDowell carried her baby daughter, Sarah. Sharon Stone wore a long, filmy dress, causing (and to all appearances basking in) a huge commotion everywhere she went. Sigourney Weaver bemoaned the fact that she didn't bring high heels to wear as she rehearsed her walk across the stage. Tim Allen stopped to chat with the stagehands on his way off the stage, while Paul Newman charmed everyone he encountered. Everywhere Matt Dillon went, he was shadowed by his publicist. In fact, lots of the stars were shadowed by their publicists—which led to some tense scenes, since the past few months had seen an abnormal amount of publicist-switching among actors. At one point, a press rep for a small firm walked out of the green room, made a U-turn, and quickly came back in, shuddering and looking for refuge. "All of PMK's out there," she said, referring to the huge PR firm that, according to its chief, Pat Kingsley, had twenty clients on the show.

The action-film star Steven Seagal, whose last big hit movie had been *Under Siege* three years earlier, walked in the artists' entrance wearing black and looking serious. In his wake, many staffers were heard to mutter, "Why is *he* on the show?" Some suggested that the answer had to do with the fact that Seagal and Letterman shared the same agent, CAA's Michael Ovitz.

All afternoon, Vilanch and his fellow writers, Hal Kanter and Buz Kohan, had been hastily rewriting lines to suit the stars. For the most part, introductions were simplified, stripped of jokes, and shortened. Steve Martin's bit, though, was lengthened to include a routine about the power of movies. "I remember sitting in a darkened movie theater with seventeen-year-old Mary Jo Rasmussen, trying to get to second base," he said. "I even remember the name of the movie: *The Lion King*." The joke got big laughs—just as it had the first time he'd used it, a couple of months earlier on *The Tonight Show*.

"WELL, at least we're going to get a sense of timing," said Michael Seligman, standing in the aisle of the Shrine. "We're very long at this point."

With a few minutes to go until the first dress rehearsal, the length of the show was only one of a series of question marks. The theater was cleared of most guests, and then rehearsal began with a stand-in reading Arthur Hiller's welcoming speech and introducing the "Make 'Em Laugh" dance number. The singers and dancers slipped smoothly through the slit screen that stood center stage, and got through the song without any notable technical goofs. But the blend of live performances and filmed footage went by so quickly, and involved such a complex blend of media, that it remained confusing.

Still unshaven, Letterman made his appearance in a blue blazer, blue T-shirt, and tan slacks. His opening monologue was truncated and uninspired. "If life really is like a box of chocolates," he said, "I think it's safe to say that Dom DeLuise has eaten every one."

This time through, Letterman asked for Paul Newman's help with the Stupid Pet Trick; a stand-in subbing for Newman helped the host unroll the carpet on which Sadie spun. Letterman scrapped the car giveaway and delivered a new Top Ten List, "Top Ten Things Overheard at Last Night's Rehearsal." It included, "We'll just be ready in a couple of weeks," "According to my stopwatch, the running time of the show is exactly eight hours," "Margolis grabbed my ass," "Why don't they let that spinning dog be the host?" and "What does Gil Cates do?" Number one was, "Is it too late to call Billy Crystal?" Immediately, crew members asked if they could get the list printed on T-shirts.

Besides the inside jokes in that Top Ten List, though, Letterman's material did not go over particularly well. The phone in front of Cates rang more and more frequently. At one point Cates and Seligman huddled intently with Robert Morton. "For the first part," Cates told Morton, "it *has* to be a tuxedo."

Clearly, the Letterman camp was as anxious as the production staff. Midway through rehearsal, Vilanch walked to the production table, sat down near Cates, and turned on his laptop. "They're getting nervous," Cates said.

"I know," said Vilanch. "I was paged."

AT MIDNIGHT, Cates and Margolis met in the production truck. "Well, Jeff, you did a good job," sighed Cates, who always tried to keep his complaints to a minimum after the dress rehearsal, because there wasn't enough time to make major changes. "Very, very, very nice run-through, given everything."

Margolis nodded. "It's a good show," he said. "I don't know what Dave's gonna do tomorrow, but I love him."

"They may well come back tomorrow and change things," said Cates. "They may switch the order of the film bits."

"The way we just did it felt like the right way to do it to me," said Margolis.

"I don't feel that way," said Cates with a sigh. "But ultimately, it's their decision."

Bill Conti entered the truck, and Cates patted the conductor on the back. "Wonderful job," he said. "But Billy, if you ever do this again, you've got to change the music when people walk onstage." Cates hummed the familiar fanfare, and then grinned. "*I'm* at my wits' end," he said, shaking his head, "but I'm sure that you'll do this again."

Outside the truck, a few high-level staffers gathered to kibitz about the show, and to grumble about the aloof and difficult Letterman. "The man," said one high-level staffer, "is a major neurotic."

They looked toward the trailer where Letterman and his writers were watching a tape of the rehearsal. "Should I go over there, shake the trailer, and yell *'Earthquake'*?" asked one. The idea garnered significant support.

Meanwhile, a publicist for Tim Allen called the production office to ask how she could guarantee that Allen would be included in the montage of arriving stars that opened every show. "Be aware that traffic will be very heavy," Chuck Warn told her. "And get him here on time."

MONDAY DAWNED HOT AND BRIGHT. Letterman still hadn't shaved.

The second run-through was a little faster, a little funnier, than the first—though to cover a delay in resetting the stage for Elton John, Letterman resorted to an encore appearance by The Dog That Spins When You Applaud.

Rehearsal ended just after three o'clock. A few minutes later, Letterman walked across the stage with Rob Burnett, tossing a football back and forth. In an aisle near the side of the theater, Gil Cates looked around the nearly deserted theater.

"The playwright Robert Anderson had a great quote," he said quietly. "He said he feels best about a play when he's finished writing it, just before he sends it off to anybody. He's done it, but nobody's seen it so nobody can say anything about it, nobody can piss on it. I feel the same way. Right now the show is ready, and nothing has gone wrong yet. All we can do now is wait and see what happens."

An hour or so before show time, Dency Nelson dropped by dressing room number one, which sat just off the wings stage left. Letterman had shaved, but he was still wearing a T-shirt. He had a joke he wanted to try out on Nelson.

"What do you think, Dency?" Letterman asked. Pretending that he was onstage, the host looked toward an imaginary audience. Uma," he said, pointing toward the spot where Uma Thurman would be sitting. Then "Oprah," pointing toward Winfrey's seat. "Uma, Oprah," he repeated. "Oprah, Uma." He looked at Nelson. "Should I do it?"

Nelson thought the gag sounded like a typical David Letterman goof; it was dumb, but he loved how Letterman was unafraid to be dumb. "Yeah, I like it," he said, laughing. "You should do it."

In front of the Shrine, meanwhile, the storm had already begun. In the back, by the artists' entrance, crew members with walkie-talkies communicated with others out front, keeping track of precisely which nominees and presenters had arrived, which ones were on their way—and, most seriously, which were unaccounted for. With several walkie-talkies open, though, what emerged was confusing as often as it was clarifying.

"John Travolta is here."

"Thank you."

"Rene Russo."

"Thank you."

"Two of Patty Smyth's musicians are missing."

"Is Jamie Lee here?"

"Yes."

"Steven Seagal?"

"No."

"Do you read me?"

"David Alan Grier's limo is at Thirtieth and Figueroa in the limo line."

"Did anybody call Sharon Stone's car?"

"Sharon shut off her communication with us. We cannot reach her."

"Can you hear me, Danette?"

"Has Paul Newman arrived in back?"

"No, Danette, we have not seen him."

"Someone should try to reach Steve Martin."

"Danette, do you copy? Steve Martin is two minutes away."

"Hugh Grant, Denzel Washington, are those confirmed?"

"Yes."

"Arnold Schwarzenegger has arrived. Hugh Grant has arrived."

"I can't hear anything. Can you hear me?"

"What's the status on Steve Martin's car?"

"Danette, can you read me? Steve Martin's two minutes away."

"Winona Ryder has arrived."

"Winona? This is a new one."

"I know."

"Steve Martin . . . with Diane Keaton!"

"That's something to tell the seating people."

"Got it. Steve Martin and Diane Keaton."

"Has Helen Mirren arrived? She's the only nominee that we haven't heard from."

"Anybody we're missing, get on the phone and start calling those cars."

"Who are we missing?"

"Ellen Barkin, Tim Allen . . ."

"What?"

"Ellen Barkin's coming in."

"Thank you."

"Can you guys hear *any* of this?"

As this went on, Jack Nicholson strolled by the green room, a bottle of water in his hand and a platinum-blond Rebecca Broussard on his arm. Anthony Hopkins returned from the men's room, tucking his shirt beneath his cummerbund. Former teen actor Corey Feldman showed up at the back door in a ruffled shirt and velvet tux, with thick hair mousse and Michael Jackson–style makeup. Feldman, who didn't look too different than he had six years earlier, when he'd done a Jackson imitation as part of Allan Carr's "Stars of Tomorrow" number, had an animated conversation at the sign-in table for presenters and performers, though he was neither.

Nicholson walked by again, heading the other direction. "Just wandering around," he announced. "No logic to it."

A stagehand watched him pass. "He's so fucking cool," he said.

Paul Newman arrived and came down the steps on the arms of two young women. "We're carrying him," one of them announced. "He's weak." Newman grinned and let his legs buckle.

In the orchestra section of the Shrine, an elderly man grabbed anyone with a production pass. "Do you have anything to do with seating?" he asked, pointing to a large camera. "I'm not paying five hundred bucks to sit behind *that* fucking thing."

6:00 P.M., PACIFIC DAYLIGHT TIME: *"The Academy of Motion Picture Arts and Sciences presents the 67th annual Academy Awards."*

Oscar announcer Randy Thomas stood in her sound booth in a truck behind the Shrine. Thomas was one of the only women to have served as the voice of Oscar, which she'd done in 1993, Cates's year for saluting women in film. (Warned by ABC that sponsors would never accept a female announcer, Cates hired Thomas quietly and kept her hiring a secret; afterward, no one complained.) Thomas was also the voice of the Hooked on Phonics learning system, which Letterman often mocked on his show, and she'd been waiting all week for somebody to apprise Letterman of that fact. If Dave knew, Thomas was sure he'd make a joke about it. But either nobody told Letterman or he passed up the chance to mention it, because the host had yet to say a word about Thomas.

In her hands, Thomas held a stack of index cards with the names and brief descriptions of two dozen movie stars. These were the stars who had been filmed arriving at the Shrine and edited into the montage that would open the show. To the network, this opening was five of the most important minutes of the Academy Awards—because if viewers weren't drawn to the Oscar races themselves, they needed to be quickly reassured that they'd be seeing all their favorite stars over the course of the show.

Thomas couldn't watch her monitor and read the cards at the same time, so another staffer stood behind her, tapping her on the shoulder every time the picture on the screen changed. When Thomas felt the tap, she flipped to the next card and read the ID: "Nominee tonight for best actor, Hollywood legend John Travolta . . . nominee for best actress, double Oscar winner Jodie Foster . . . worldwide box-office favorite Arnold Schwarzenegger, with his wife, Maria Shriver . . ." Tim Allen was not included.

Out in the lobby of the Shrine, latecomers filled the lobby and rushed toward the doors, trying to get in before the cameras were turned on the audience. *Pulp Fiction* star Samuel L. Jackson, nominated for best supporting actor, was one of the last to make it in before the doors from the lobby to the theater were closed. "Samuel! Samuel!" yelled people in the lobby as ABC pages pulled him through the crowd. He turned, waved, and signed one quick autograph before making it into the hall and into his front-row seat.

In his truck, Margolis scanned the monitors in front of him as his cameramen roamed the audience, zeroing in on famous faces. Assistant directors and video technicians surrounded Margolis; behind him, sitting in a row of chairs at the rear of the truck, were Cates, Seligman, and Hamlin. Before Letterman's monologue got under way, Dency Nelson radioed Margolis. "Make sure you have cameras ready for Uma Thurman and Oprah Winfrey," Nelson warned the director.

"I've been dying to do something all day," said Letterman, "and I think maybe we can take care of this." He walked to his left and pointed into the audience. "Oprah." He walked to his right. "Uma. Uuuuma, Ooooprah." Inside the Shrine, the joke fell completely flat. Listening to the silence from his spot in the wings, Nelson grimaced and fervently hoped that he wasn't the only one who'd encouraged Letterman to use the gag.

Scanning his monitors during the monologue, Margolis looked for reaction shots. Susan Sarandon laughed. "Six!" he shouted. Jodie Foster grinned. "Four!" For much of the monologue, camera ten was fixed on Winona Ryder—but she wasn't laughing, so Margolis never called for her.

"Forrest Gump said, 'Life is like a box of chocolates—you never know what you're gonna get,' " continued Letterman. "Unless, of course, you're sitting next to Roger Ebert, and then you know you're not gonna get any." One of the cameras was aimed at Sally Field, who played Forrest Gump's mother. But Field just rolled her eyes, so Margolis chose not to go to her.

"Oprah, Uma. Uma, Oprah," said Letterman a minute later. "It's gonna be one of those things I won't be able to stop doing all night long." Next to Margolis, Acey scanned her script to identify the subjects of the next joke. "Schwarzenegger and Shriver are next," she said into her headset. Camera four went to them.

"One of the pictures nominated tonight for best foreign film is *Eat Drink*

Man Woman," said Letterman. "Coincidentally, as I understand it, this is also how Arnold Schwarzenegger asked Maria Shriver out on their first date." Margolis cut to camera four just in time to catch Schwarzenegger's good-natured laugh, and Shriver's considerably more exuberant one.

Almost half an hour into the show, Tommy Lee Jones handed out the first Oscar of the evening, for best supporting actress. The preshow favorite in most Oscar pools, Dianne Wiest in Woody Allen's *Bullets Over Broadway*, won. "You did good," said Cates, patting Margolis on the shoulder as the show broke for its first commercial. Cates then left the truck, followed quickly by an L.A.P.D. officer who'd been standing nearby and was assigned to shadow the producer during the show.

With the Stupid Pet Trick coming up in the next act, there was a brief moment of panic backstage. Letterman had been planning to ask for Paul Newman's help on the bit, but Newman was no longer in his seat. A stage manager was dispatched to the green room to find him, but Newman wasn't there either. (He was in the bar in the lobby of the Shrine.) Staffers scanned the crowd, looking for a star who was seated close to the stage and might be agreeable. Just before he took the stage, Letterman got his new assignment: "Pick Tom Hanks!"

Hanks looked shell-shocked when Letterman asked him for help, but he gamely played along, helping the host unroll a carpet before the dog came onstage. The audience clapped obediently, Sadie spun frantically, and Winona Ryder laughed and clapped her hands. "Ten!" shouted Margolis.

A few minutes later, Martin Landau won the best supporting actor award for *Ed Wood*. Thirty-one seconds into his speech, the sixty-three-year-old actor threw down a gauntlet of sorts. "Gil Cates, don't put music on," he warned. " 'Cause if it's the *Mission: Impossible* theme, I'll get very angry." Back in the truck, Cates immediately stood up; he knew that long speeches were most troubling early in the show, because they set a bad precedent.

Forging ahead, Landau thanked *Ed Wood* director Tim Burton, Disney, Johnny Depp, his makeup artists, the press . . .

"Come *on*," said Margolis urgently.

. . . his agents, his daughter, his best friend . . .

"Is the clock up?" asked an agitated Cates. Not only was Landau running long, but he was delivering the bane of any Oscar producer: the list of names. "Put the clock up." By this point, if Landau looked toward the TelePrompTer, he could see a flashing red background, and block letters that read PLEASE WRAP UP. But he went on, thanking his sister, then the entire Academy, then the actors' branch of the Academy.

Cates stepped forward, until he was right over Margolis's shoulder. There was an unspoken but undeniable double standard when it came to Oscar speeches: actors were always granted more leeway than unknowns. But this actor was showing no signs of stopping.

Two minutes and seven seconds into his speech, after plugging the NEA, Laudau stopped to take a breath.

"*Music!*" yelled Cates angrily. "Fuck him!" Margolis gave Conti the cue, and the music started.

Onstage, Landau yelled "*No!*" just as cameras cut to Matt Dillon, who stood on the other side of the stage and looked awkwardly toward Landau. Stage manager Jason Seligman cued Dillon to begin reading from the TelePrompTer.

In the doorway to Margolis's truck, the officer assigned to Cates quickly got on his walkie-talkie to a cop stationed inside the house. "Did he clear the stage?" he asked nervously. Told that Landau had finally gone into the wings, he relaxed. The Academy Awards had security measures designed to deal with gate-crashers and overzealous winners who wouldn't relinquish the stage—measures that began with blinding spotlights aimed at the stage and went as far as rubber bullets—but nobody wanted to use them on a sexagenarian Oscar winner. (In fact, none of the measures had ever been used.)

Ninety minutes into the show, Paul Newman surfaced to give the cinematography award to John Toll for *The Legends of the Fall*. On his way across the stage with Toll, with whom he was supposed to go to the press rooms, Newman suddenly stopped. He stared into the rafters above the stage, where Jamie Lee Curtis, clad in a short, impossibly tight black dress, hung from a prop helicopter, ready to make a dramatic entrance to present the sci-tech awards. As she was lowered to the stage in an homage to a scene from the movie *True Lies*, a grinning Newman ran back to catch up with Toll. "Sorry," he said. "Did I leave ya? I just had to see that. Now where do we go?"

A few minutes later, Cates left the truck and came into the wings in search of Tim Robbins and Susan Sarandon. The producer had booked them on the show despite his anger two years earlier when they'd departed from their script to plead the case of a boatload of HIV-positive Haitian refugees. Cates found the couple waiting to go onstage, and quietly urged them to stick to their script rather than mentioning any political causes.

Sitting in a small, curtained enclosure on the other side of the stage, Letterman was not enjoying himself. "Is it over yet?" he kept asking. To cheer him up, stage managers Dency Nelson and Debbie Williams began to approach every star who came through the wings, asking if they'd like to say hello to Dave. Steve Martin, Jack Nicholson, and almost everyone else did so; Sally Field declined, explaining that she had to focus on her job introducing the *Forrest Gump* film clip.

Letterman's Oscar Top Ten List turned out to be "Top Ten Signs the Movie You're Watching Will Not Win an Academy Award." The biggest hand was reserved for number six: "It's a beautifully made documentary about two kids in the inner city trying to realize their dream of playing professional basketball." Number one, "Four words: Dom DeLuise is Ghandi!" was not a particular favorite, and didn't even spell *Gandhi* correctly.

Backstage, tensions rose as Elton John's performance of "Can You Feel the Love Tonight" neared. Nobody wanted a reprise of the spinning dog, but not once during rehearsals had the crew been able to set up John's equipment quick enough to prevent that. But just before John was due to perform, the Russian film *Burnt by the Sun* won the Oscar for best foreign film. Its director, Nikita Mikhalkov, came to the stage accompanied by his daughter Nadezhda, one of the stars of the film. His speech was emotional but also long and rambling. Even after it hit the two-minute mark, though, Conti and his orchestra remained silent. For once, Cates and Margolis didn't mind a long speech, because every minute Mikhalkov spoke gave John's crew more time to finish its setup.

By the time Mikhalkov finished, John was ready. Sadie, who'd been led into the wings just in case, returned to her dressing room. In the press tent, meanwhile, Jack Nicholson broke with Oscar protocol: rather than accompanying honorary Oscar winner Michelangelo Antonioni only through the two photo rooms, Nicholson stuck with the eighty-two-year-old Italian director through the two interview rooms as well. There, he artfully deflected questions that dealt with Nicholson rather than Antonioni.

In a small space between the print and television rooms, Antonioni stopped to blow his nose. "God, he looks tremendous," said one onlooker.

Nicholson grinned slyly, and leaned toward the director. "Not as good as *me*," he whispered to Antonioni. "But tremendous."

Leaving the press area, Nicholson congratulated a dazed Elton John, who was carrying the best-song Oscar he'd just won for "Can You Feel the Love Tonight." Nearby, a security supervisor looked at the growing crowd outside the green room. "The exits are not secure, there are too many people here, and I'm not happy," he told his men.

At 8:45, Al Pacino and Robert DeNiro arrived together in a limo and made a beeline for the green room, where DeNiro huddled with Antonioni.

In the wings of the stage, Clint Eastwood waited for his cue. Letterman walked offstage. "Hi, Clint," he said.

"Hi," said Eastwood. "Hey, I know your people have been calling about getting me on the show."

"Yeah, I know we're always bugging you about that," said Letterman. He grimaced; it was bad enough that he was suffering through the Oscar show, but now he had to hear about his staff harassing famous people on his behalf.

"Well, I think it might be fun," Eastwood assured him.

Letterman shrugged. "I don't know if it'd be fun for you," he said, "but it'd sure be a thrill for *us*."

Eastwood chuckled and changed the subject. "How are you feeling?" he asked.

Dave sighed. "I feel like going home," he said.

Eastwood quickly looked over at the host. "*What*?"

"I feel," said Letterman quietly, "like I sort of want to go home."

Within forty minutes, it was mercifully over for Letterman. Tom Hanks presented the best-actress award to Jessica Lange for *Blue Sky*, then won the best-actor award himself for *Forrest Gump*. Robert Zemeckis won the best-director award for that same film, and then *Gump* completed its sweep over *Pulp Fiction* with a best-picture win. (The only category in which *Pulp* won, best original screenplay, was one in which *Gump* was not eligible.)

Onstage, Letterman looked into the audience one last time. "Ladies and gentlemen, congratulations to everyone," he said. "I've had a lovely evening, thank you very much for inviting me. Good night, folks."

As the credits ran to end the three-hour-and-thirty-two-minute show, an anxious Rob Burnett approached Seligman by the production trailers. "What'd you think?" he asked, frowning.

"What'd I think?" repeated Seligman. "I think you guys did great." A pause. "I'm being honest. I think you should be proud."

In his dressing room, Letterman was downcast. Debbie Williams and Dency Nelson stopped by and told him that he'd done a great job, but the host shook his head. "No, I didn't," he said.

"No, Dave, you were great," they insisted.

"Do you know what Gil said to me?" the famously insecure Letterman replied. "He walked by me after the show and said, 'See you sometime, somewhere.'"

At the Governors Ball, which for the first time was being catered by Wolfgang Puck, Arthur Hiller gave a speech. "I think this was the best Oscar show," he said, "since . . . last year." Stars schmoozed, ate, networked, and headed off to other parties around town. Letterman didn't show his face; instead of making an appearance at the ball, he headed for the airport to go on vacation.

By midnight, the party was emptying. On the steps outside the artists' entrance, Morgan Freeman sat with his wife and daughter, waiting for his limo, and waiting for somebody in charge to explain why his driver had been denied entrance to the parking lot.

There were no more than a dozen people standing around when Sadie, The Dog That Spins When You Applaud, was led out the door, down the steps, and along the red carpet. Seeing one of the stars of the Oscar show, the bystanders broke into a round of unthinking applause. And Sadie of course started spinning for all she was worth. The Oscars were history, the final strains of "Stardust" were drifting out from the party that was winding down inside—and out in the parking lot, a crazy dog twirled wildly as she headed down the red carpet and into the night.

JUDGING BY THE NUMBERS, the 67th Academy Awards show was a huge success. Curiosity over Letterman, together with the fact that a couple of big-grossing movies were in contention, helped give the show its best ratings in a dozen years. The audience was mostly male; in New York City, the ratings were huge.

This did not, however, mean that the show was an unqualified hit in other ways. Reviews for the show were mixed, as always, but generally unkind to Letterman. Even on the Internet, comments from the host's usual rabid fans ranged from "Well, that was painful to watch" to "I think his entire performance was an inspired breath of fresh air into an otherwise archaic and stodgy institution." From inside the Academy, though, the outcry was louder and more negative than at any time since the Allan Carr show.

And from the sound of things, Dave might even have agreed with his critics. A week after the Oscar show, Letterman did his first new *Late Night* broadcast. The Top Ten List was "Top Ten Complaints About the Academy Awards"; number one was "Letterman." By the end of the year, Letterman would regularly trail Jay Leno in the ratings. Leno's resurgence was often tied to the publicity he gained in June, when actor Hugh Grant used *The Tonight Show* for his first public appearance since his arrest for soliciting a prostitute in Los Angeles. Some observers, though, thought that Letterman's decline began with the Oscars.

More than a decade later, some show staffers were still baffled. "Letterman loved Carson, and Letterman wanted to be as good as Carson was on the show," said Seligman, who worked on all five of Carson's Oscar shows. "The difference is that Carson was the host of the Oscars. Letterman didn't do the Oscars, he did the Letterman show."

Added Chuck Workman, whose opening collaboration with Debbie Allen was always awkward and confusing, "The Letterman show was a mess for everybody. My piece didn't work, I was not at my best, and it's the only piece of mine that I regret doing."

The results of the 67th Oscar show also impacted the Academy in ways that had nothing to do with Letterman. Hans Zimmer's win for *The Lion King* in the best original score category was in many ways the final straw for the music branch. The win marked the fourth time in six years that an animated Disney film had won in both the expected category, best song, and also in the best-score category. (Disney didn't release major animated musicals the other two years.) While the wins in the song category could be defended, the branch found it harder to stomach the fact that legendary film composers like John Williams, Ennio Morricone, Jerry Goldsmith, and John Barry, along with hot newcomers like Elliot Goldenthal and Thomas Newman, were being beaten by the music used to link cartoon songs together.

The branch took one of its few available options: it split the award for best original score into two separate awards, one for musical or comedy score, the other for dramatic score. (Technically, the musical or comedy award replaced the Oscar for original song score, a category that hadn't been used in a decade.) The move put the music branch at odds with the rest of the Academy, which never separated categories by genre—but it was, perhaps, a more politic action than the alternative, which would have been to send the members guidelines that read, "Stop voting for animated movies with lots of songs in the original score category."

The Academy also added a new branch, Visual Effects, bringing to thirteen its number of branches.

The chief fallout from the show, though, had to do with the documentary branch of the Academy, and its failure to nominate *Hoop Dreams*. In June, after a three-month review of the documentary screening committee's procedures, the Academy revised its rules for the documentary feature category. The committee was split into two groups, one based in Los Angeles and the other in New York. Rather than a single committee screening sixty-five films, the eligible documentaries would be divided between the two; finalists selected by the L.A. committee would then be screened by the New Yorkers, and vice versa. No longer would a show of flashlights be enough to end a movie prematurely, and no longer would committee members be allowed to hold discussions before voting.

Just as crucially—though its importance was not apparent to those who didn't know that *Hoop Dreams* had lost a nomination largely because of a handful of zero scores—the scoring system was brought in line with other

Oscar categories. In the future, voters would score each documentary on a scale of six to ten, reducing the damage a small group of voters could do to any film. "I don't know," insisted Hiller, "that any of these changes would have made any difference at all in the outcome of nominations voting this year."

For Gil Cates, meanwhile, his sixth Oscar show had not been an easy one. Not only had Letterman proved to be a disappointment, but Cates had started to feel increasing interference from the Academy and the network. In the summer, after Arthur Hiller was reelected to his third term as the president of the Academy, Cates let Hiller know that he would not be available to produce the next Oscars.

3

A Change Is Gonna Come

The 68th Academy Awards

ON THE CALENDAR of Academy Awards–related events, the Oscar Fashion Show was one of the more useless entries. It was, essentially, a big photo opportunity designed to remind people that the show was coming. Models paraded through the lobby of the Academy's Beverly Hills offices wearing clothes that the show's official fashion coordinator, Beverly Hills clothier Fred Hayman, would like stars to wear on Oscar night. Hayman provided commentary, and a small audience clapped politely. No nominees or presenters showed up to get ideas; that battle was already being waged in private, as top designers courted nominees and presenters with phone calls, letters, freebies, and invitations to hotel suites where the latest, chicest creations were laid out.

At the Oscar Fashion Show, things were ceremonial. The press got to interview the show's producer, down some free coffee and bagels, ogle a few models. And the Academy got a quick, relatively inexpensive blast of publicity to keep itself in the news during the downtime between nominations announcement and the nominees' luncheon.

At least, that's the way it once was. Then came Quincy Jones, executive producer of the Academy Awards show in 1996.

Officially—and to a large extent truthfully—Gil Cates's decision not to return as producer was blamed on his schedule as the producing director of the Geffen Playhouse, a refurbished five-hundred-seat theater near the UCLA campus. With Cates out of the picture, Arthur Hiller opted for the sixty-three-year-old musician and producer Jones, the previous year's recipient of the Jean Hersholt Humanitarian Award. A jazz trumpeter who'd turned to record production and film composing in the 1960s, Jones had made his name, and his fortune, shepherding the likes of Michael Jackson, James Ingram, and Chaka Khan in the recording studio, winning multiple Grammy awards for albums like Jackson's *Thriller* and his own *The Dude*.

In the 1980s, Jones moved into film producing, helping to bring Alice Walker's book *The Color Purple* to the screen with director Steven Spielberg. That movie became one of the biggest losers in Oscar history in March 1986, when it won not a single one of its eleven nominations. (Eight years earlier, *The Turning Point* had attained the same 0-for-11 record.)

No sooner had Jones accepted the gig than he and his business partner of three years, David Salzman, announced that they planned to change *everything* about the Academy Awards. And on March 7, perhaps to persuade those who wondered just how much they could do within given the constraints of an Oscar broadcast, they turned the once-sedate fashion show into a statement of purpose.

For starters, the producers ran up a reported $40,000 tab installing a stage, a full sound system, a checkerboard runway, and a huge lighting rig in the lobby of the Academy building. They brought in choreographer Toni Basil (who, in another incarnation, had the 1980 pop hit "Mickey") to work with the models. They turned on a smoke machine, turned down the lights—and when the lobby was sufficiently dusky, Hayman intoned, "Let the show begin."

It did so not with the usual procession of Oscar-worthy gowns, but with a sultry male model, his black hair slicked back severely and his dark skin gleaming, tap dancing across the stage clad in the kind of outfit that might well get him turned away at the door of the Dorothy Chandler Pavilion: a white silk tuxedo shirt that was not only untucked but also wholly unbuttoned, its shirttails flapping freely around his thighs. When he dropped back into the shadows, a procession of models strode to the runaway and tried their best to look mysterious. They moved quickly, turned suddenly, glanced around the room furtively. They adjusted their shades and fingered their jewelry and conspiratorially struck poses. One strode down the runway leading a pair of Russian wolfhounds.

The music boomed around them: dramatic orchestral passages, hip-hop beats, Booker T and the MGs, flamenco, salsa, forbidding twentieth-century chamber music, Beethoven's Fifth. The outfits were insane. There was a Paco Rabane chain-mail jumpsuit, an Issaye Miyake dress that looked as if it could have been made of Saran wrap, and an iridescent silver shirt with a huge collar that would have looked at home on retro-rocker Lenny Kravitz. One model sported a tuxedo that resembled nothing so much as an electric blue version of the shiny gold lamé suit Elvis Presley wore on the cover of the 1957 album best known as *50,000,000 Elvis Fans Can't Be Wrong*.

In the audience, Bruce Davis looked on impassively. Jeff Margolis beamed. Danette Herman boogied in her seat.

Then Jones and Salzman strutted down the runaway clad in Versace and Donna Karan, respectively. "I bet you thought you were gonna see your usual pre-Oscar fashion show," Quincy said. "The many firsts you saw today were just a little preview of the many firsts you'll see at the show. The evening's story will still be the winners, but just wait until you see what else happens."

Near the rear of the room, longtime Oscar publicity staffer John Pavlik laughed and shook his head. "I'll be curious to see," he said, "if this generates more press than we used to get with a piano and sixty bucks."

IT HAD NOT been a good year for movies—at least, not for major studio movies that might reasonably be expected to compete for Oscars. The year's top-grossing films were *Batman Forever*, the third and definitely not the best of the recent Batman movies, and *Toy Story*, an animated picture made by a relatively young company called Pixar and released by Disney, which to its astonishment watched the entirely computer-animated film make its own large-scale animated effort, *Pocahontas*, look old-fashioned and bland.

A more typical Oscar entry was Mel Gibson's *Braveheart*. Released during the summer, the violent and rousing, if historically suspect, bio of Scottish freedom fighter William Wallace was greeted with respectful but mixed reviews, and only adequate business at the box office. Ron Howard's *Apollo 13*, a look at the ill-fated moon mission that nearly ended in tragedy in 1970, was one of the stronger candidates to come from the major studios, though again it prompted more respect than rapture from critics. And Chinese director Ang Lee, little known in the United States, turned to a quintessentially English story with surprisingly persuasive results when he filmed Jane Austen's *Sense and Sensibility* from a script by actress Emma Thompson.

The year's best-reviewed films, in many cases, came from smaller, independent companies: the harrowing *Leaving Las Vegas*, in which Nicolas Cage drank himself to death while a sympathetic hooker played by Elisabeth Shue watched; actor/director Tim Robbins's *Dead Man Walking*, a grim examination of murder, retribution, and the death penalty, with striking lead performances from Sean Penn and Susan Sarandon; and the Italian film *Il Postino*, the tale of a postman from a small village who's smitten by the power of verse while delivering mail to poet Pablo Neruda. Miramax had picked up this last film for distribution, and the company, always adept at Oscar campaigning, quickly played up the tragic true story behind the film: its star, Massimo Troisi, made the film while seriously ill with a heart condition, and died the day after his final scene.

When the nominations were announced, *Braveheart* and *Apollo 13* were the two leaders, with ten and nine nominations, respectively. *Sense and Sensibility*, *Il Postino*, and *Babe* were the other three best-picture nominees; *Leaving Las Vegas* and *Dead Man Walking* were left out of the top category, but each film scored acting nominations for its two leads, as well as best-director nods for Mike Figgis and Tim Robbins. To fit Figgis and Robbins on the ballot, Ron Howard and Ang Lee were passed over despite the fact that their movies were in the running for best picture.

"IT'S FAST-PACED, peppy, very very different," said Danette Herman. She managed a small smile. "It'll be a lot of fun."

A soft-spoken redhead who always knew more than she let on, Herman had been an Oscar regular for almost two decades. She worked her first show while still attending college in 1968, the year the Oscars were postponed for two days after the assassination of Martin Luther King, Jr. Several years later, Herman began a steady run on the show, booking and dealing with talent during a time when the grand old Hollywood stars gradually yielded to younger faces. "Those were shows that Cary Grant came to," she said, "and Katharine Hepburn and Gregory Peck, Burt Lancaster, Kirk Douglas, Audrey Hepburn. There's always a constant shift going on with the stars, but in the eighties the names were more consistent for a longer period of time. And they weren't asked to do fifty awards shows a year."

Herman still loved classic Hollywood—her favorite Oscar moments centered around names like Greer Garson, Luise Rainer, and Federico Fellini—but she also adored the likes of Liam Neeson, Emma Thompson, and John Travolta. She was known to be fiercely protective of the stars who came on her show: open and kind one moment, she could just as easily slip on a tight frown and assume a kind of tunnel vision, closing out all but the matter that occupied her at the moment. Chuck Warn called it "the Danette face."

As she sat in the production office on a Friday morning just a few days before the production team would move its offices to the Dorothy Chandler Pavilion, it wasn't yet time for the Danette face. Still, with ten days to go until the show, Herman was dealing with the usual myriad of small details and last-minute glitches. The publicist for best-song nominee Bruce Springsteen, for instance, called to ask if Springsteen could once again use Warn as his escort if he won and had to make the trip through the press rooms; Herman had to tell the publicist, Seth Cohen, that Warn worked for Gil Cates. "Chuck's not on the show this year," she told Cohen. "The escorts they have are all publicists from the studios."

No sooner had Herman hung up than she got a call from David Salzman's assistant, Mary Aymar, passing on a message about presenter Nicole Kidman. "She's approved her dialogue," Aymar said, "but she wants us to know that she's blind, so she needs it in really large print."

As she looked from her office window across the garden level of a new (and, except for the Oscar staff, completely unoccupied) office building in

Beverly Hills, Herman had another, bigger worry: the show had yet to be fully booked. "There are still a couple of slots to fill," she said, "which is very unusual for this time of year."

Those decisions were long overdue, but they couldn't be made without Jones, who hadn't yet appeared in the office. As the clock inched closer to 1 p.m., Herman got antsier; she was hoping to meet with Jones and get some answers before one, when she knew he was scheduled to sit for three hours of TV interviews.

As they'd promised, Jones and Salzman had tried to change countless aspects of the Oscar show. Rather than using clips from the nominated performances, they commissioned mini-filmographies incorporating three separate films from each of the acting nominees; when Doug Stewart suggested that they were ordering an enormous amount of work for a feature that might well be cut for time if the show was running long, Salzman insisted, "We're committed to this." But the producers did want to save time, and they hated how long it took for nominees to get to the stage in the craft categories. They floated the idea of moving each category's nominees into the front row when it came time for the category, or running the Oscar and a microphone into the audience so that winners could make speeches without leaving their seats. At one point, they considered putting all the nominees onstage before opening the envelope. "Some of their ideas were just . . . *amazing*," said one Oscar vet carefully.

"Change is good, adjustments are good, but you can't turn the Academy Awards into the MTV Music Awards," said Jeff Margolis. "Some of their ideas were just logistically impossible, and some were good ideas but not for the Academy Awards." Margolis felt that Jones was sensible while Salzman was too determined to change things, so he tried to deal mostly with Q, as everyone called the producer. Others grumbled that Margolis himself was making a power play by separating the two producers.

A few minutes before 1 p.m., Salzman emerged from his office with Alec Berg and Jeff Schaffer, a pair of writers from the *Seinfeld* TV show who'd been hired to punch up the script. "Were they good?" Aymar asked after Salzman showed the writers to the elevator. "I haven't seen that look on your face in a long time."

"Yeah, they were great," he said.

"Just let me ask you a couple of questions," she said.

"Okay, but ask me quick." Then he glanced toward the elevator, and saw that Jones had just arrived. "Wait just a minute," he told Aymar. "While Quincy's not talking, I've got to grab him."

The two men went into Salzman's office, where Herman quickly joined them. She walked over to the bulletin board where the show was laid out, pulled off a small card with the name Hugh Grant on it, and tore it in half. Salzman looked confused. "I thought he was dying to do it," he said.

"He was dying to do it," said Herman. "But he's doing a movie, and they can't change the schedule."

"Who else can we get?" said Salzman.

"Annette Bening?" suggested Herman. "Goldie Hawn? It would be good to get a woman in that slot."

"I prefer Annette Bening," said Salzman. "Now, have we figured out if we're getting Kevin Costner?"

"Quincy, you need to call him today," said Herman. "If we can't get him, I'll go to Jack Lemmon and Walter Matthau. Do we have any word from Dustin Hoffman?"

Jones shook his head. "I don't want to talk about people we don't know if we can get," he said. "I want names up there that we can really get."

Herman sighed. "We should have had this conversation at eight o'clock this morning," she said. "We have five slots open, and we need to fill them *today*."

Salzman looked at the board and frowned. "Is Schwarzenegger willing to introduce the best-picture clip for *Braveheart*?" he said. "Or is he going to insist on presenting an award?"

"We don't know yet," said Herman.

"If he has to give an award, we can give him editing and move Anthony Hopkins to screenplay."

"I'm trying to find out," Herman said, "but I haven't gotten an answer yet from his publicist."

"Forget that," said Jones. "I'll call Maria. Forget about all this other crap. If she likes the idea she'll *make* him do it."

"What about Steven Seagal?" asked Salzman. "He doesn't really want to give out sound. He's thinking about it, but he'd rather do best foreign film."

"Pretend he never existed," Jones snapped. "He was begging for a slot on the show, and then we give him one and he has to *think* about it?"

AS OSCAR NIGHT APPROACHED, the consensus in Hollywood was that the best-picture race was wide open and unpredictable. While even Harvey Weinstein had to realize that *Il Postino* probably fell into the it's-an-honor-just-to-be-nominated category, that didn't stop him from pulling out the stops: Miramax's mailing to Academy members included the video, a CD of celebrities reading the poems of Pablo Neruda, and the original novel by Antonio Skármeta. The Academy found the package unseemly, and took away two of Miramax's tickets to the show.

Meanwhile, cases could be made for any of the other four best-picture nominees. *Sense and Sensibility* was classy and high-toned and had won the Golden Globe for best drama, but Ang Lee's failure to be nominated for best director suggested that his film wasn't embraced by the entire Academy. *Apollo 13* was the kind of serious, inspirational mainstream movie often honored by the Academy, and the fact that director Ron Howard had also been overlooked was partly offset when the Directors Guild, usually a reliable indicator of Academy support, gave him its top award. *Braveheart* hadn't picked up any big critics or guild awards—but with actors making up by far the biggest branch of the Academy, it was foolish to underestimate the appeal of a big, rousing epic directed by an actor. (Kevin Costner's *Dances with Wolves*, after all, had beaten Martin Scorsese's *GoodFellas*, and a decade earlier Robert Redford's *Ordinary People* had beaten Scorsese's *Raging Bull*.)

Still, there was no question which of the nominated films garnered the most affection. As a sweet, funny fable about a talking pig, *Babe* may not have been typical Oscar fare, but its charm and ingenuity had won it a legion of admirers. As the show approached, sentiment began to shift. *Apollo 13* may have been a narrow favorite in the minds of most Oscar forecasters, with *Braveheart* in the running as well—but the momentum, it seemed, was with the little pig.

Jones and Salzman took note of the affection surrounding *Babe*, and decided to incorporate its star into their show. (It didn't hurt that the movie was also a particular favorite of their host, Whoopi Goldberg.) But Babe and the Oscars were an uneasy fit. Where the animators at Pixar eagerly got to work on a segment in which the *Toy Story* characters Woody and Buzz would interact with an Oscar statue (a *talking* Oscar statue—another first, as Salzman proudly pointed out), the creators of *Babe* were more cautious.

Jones and Salzman had decided to include a mock "satellite link" between Goldberg, on the stage of the Dorothy Chandler Pavilion, and Babe, back home on the farm. But the producers could only obtain an unused three-second clip of the piglet, so their plan was to incorporate another famous swine, Miss Piggy. "We have to somehow disguise the fact that we only have three seconds of Babe," said Daniel Salzman, who'd been hired by his father to oversee several segments of the show. "We're doing lots of cuts to Whoopi and to Miss Piggy, and we'll pretend that the satellite is going out." Frank Oz, who operated and supplied the voice for Miss Piggy, would be on hand to help the porcine diva do her bit live, while the voice of Babe, Christine Cavanaugh, would record new voiceovers.

But George Miller, a physician-turned-filmmaker who had directed *The Witches of Eastwick* and the three *Mad Max* movies before producing *Babe*, was fiercely protective of both the movie and the character. He agreed to participate and he supplied the three-second clip, but didn't like the initial script, in which his farm-bred hero evinced too much familiarity with things like box-office returns and Oscar acceptance speeches. "He wants something that preserves Babe's innocence and naïveté," said Daniel Salzman.

David Salzman sighed. "And our script doesn't? 'I'd like to thank all the little people, all of whom are bigger than me'?"

"His point," said Daniel, "is that Babe wouldn't know about acceptance speech clichés."

At 3 p.m., David Salzman picked up the phone and prepared to call Miller, who was working on a film in South Africa. "Okay," he said, "let's do the root canal." As he dialed, he shrugged. "George is a delightful guy and a great artist. He's just trying to protect his project." Daniel Salzman walked around the desk and took a position over his father's left shoulder, ready to listen in and offer suggestions.

"George, I hear that you have some questions and concerns, and I don't want you to have any," Salzman said when he reached Miller. "We just want to do a sweet piece."

Miller told Salzman that he didn't think the script was true to the essential innocence of his little pig, who wouldn't know anything about satellite hookups or the Academy Awards.

"I totally understand what you're saying, George," Salzman said. "This is still an innocent little piglet who's unaffected by all of this. We'll make changes to reflect that." He listened to Miller some more. "Yes, Miss Piggy does have a lot of lines," he said. "You're right about that." He paused. "Yeah, we'll probably cut out a joke or two of hers to tighten it up."

Daniel Salzman grinned. "He's coming around," he whispered.

Miller then suggested a new ending to the piece, one that replaced Babe's "acceptance speech" with a nod to actor James Cromwell, who played the kindly farmer who watches over (and profits from) the little pig.

"That's good, George," said Salzman. "That's good. That's a nice three-beat." Salzman hung up the phone and let out a relieved sigh. He read Miller's new lines to his son: "Babe will say, 'Give my regards to the boss,' and Whoopi will say, 'Oh, you're a Springsteen fan?' And he'll say, 'Farmer Hoggett, silly!' This is a great ending that he wrote for us."

At 3:30, Herman marched into Salzman's office, a determined look on her face. "Quincy's out of his interviews now," she said. "We have *got* to converse. The sun is going down, and we have to know who we're asking to do sound, who's doing screenplay . . ."

HOLLYWOOD BLACKOUT, read the headline on the March 18 issue of *People* magazine. The issue detailed what the magazine said was "a shocking level of minority exclusion" in the movie business. The article did not charge that the Academy Awards were in any way responsible for that exclusion, simply that the lack of African American nominees—only one, it said, out of 166—was a timely symptom of the problem.

Seizing on the magazine story, Jesse Jackson decided to use the scarcity of black Oscar nominees as the focal point of an organized protest by his Rainbow Coalition. Jones, who agreed with many of the points in the *People* article—though he thought the magazine was "thirty-five years too late"—tried to convince Jackson that it might be misguided to protest an Oscar ceremony produced by and hosted by African Americans, and one with a distinctly multiracial lineup of presenters and performers. In an attempt to avoid a swarm of protesters in front of the Chandler, Arthur Hiller contacted Jackson to work out a compromise.

While the Academy president worked that front, Quincy Jones walked into the Dorothy Chandler Pavilion. "The set is screamin'," he said, looking at the stage. "Screamin'."

The Chandler stage was dominated by massive white columns, by sail-shaped pieces hanging over the stage, and by video monitors in gold gilt frames. As production designer Ray Klausen directed placement of the columns and video screens, Jones stood in the aisle watching. "It's got so many looks," said Jones as he gazed at the stage. "The graphics are constantly changing, the Oscars are constantly moving, the screens come down with the names of the categories and the nominees on them . . ."

Backstage, reviews were less generous. Many of the same crew members worked on the show year after year, as well as on other awards shows; they were practical people who knew their jobs, did them well, and were neither starstruck nor dazzled by glitz. Some of them had to move the talent in and out quickly and efficiently; others had to make sure the set changes worked. They knew how to ignore the occasional odd sight backstage: Audrey Hepburn in her slip, ironing her own gown just before going onstage; an unconcerned but stark naked Sigourney Weaver undergoing a last-minute fitting in a dressing room just off the stage. And they knew that no matter how screamin' a set might be, its pieces needed to move in and out quickly and quietly.

On this last count, things were not gelling. "The set is overdesigned," said one. "It's too big, it's got too many moving parts, and it doesn't work. It's a nightmare."

For Jeff Margolis, the biggest problem was that when the set was in place, it left little room for presenters to make their entrances. "Ray Klausen is a brilliant production designer," he said. "But when we got to the theater, it wasn't the same as it was on paper. Whatever the hell happened, there were no entrances. Everybody just had to come around a corner, and that made me nuts."

The crew tried to make it work, a task that involved ditching parts of the set and rearranging others. As they did so, other technical tests continued.

Thursday morning, a stagehand read into Goldberg's microphone in order for the sound crew to set levels and balance the sound. Given the previous year's rocky Oscar show, his choice of reading material was nervy: a book of David Letterman's Top Ten Lists. "Top Ten ways the Dalai Lama is going to spend his Nobel Prize money," the stagehand read. The list included "New kitchen cabinets for Mrs. Lama," "Give Cadillacs to Sonny and Red," and "One seriously large order of McDonald's french fries," but the stagehand didn't get far enough into it to draw a laugh. No sooner had he read "one seriously large—" than stage manager David Wader walked to the podium and interrupted him.

"ABC/Cap Cities says you cannot read that," Wader announced. "You have to read this." He handed over a considerably drier text: "Health and Safety Standards for the Academy Awards."

BY THE MORNING OF SATURDAY, March 23, things were well behind schedule. Of the sixteen awards that were slated to have been rehearsed using stand-ins between 8:30 and 10:00, only six were completed; the others fell victim to unusually long set changes. At 10:15, with a long day of music rehearsals looming and no time to catch up, many of the stand-ins were sent home. "Am I going to see you tomorrow?" asked one stand-in to a friend who was packing up and heading for his car.

"I don't know," came the reply. "They haven't told me yet. I don't think they have any idea."

That afternoon, the stage was awash in dancers, some of them dressed in full flamenco gear, others a mixture of crop tops, spandex, and spike heels. Behind them was an elaborate set that reproduced a Spanish courtyard. In their midst was room for a rock band and for the thirty-six-year-old Canadian rock star Bryan Adams, the singer and one of the writers of "Have You Ever Really Loved a Woman." The film from which his song came, *Don Juan DeMarco*, was only modestly successful, but the lavish, romantic ballad was the biggest hit of the nominated songs, a number-one record for five weeks.

The Canadian singer had made his name as a derivative, commercial,

Springsteen-lite rock 'n' roller, but many of his biggest hits in recent years had been lush love songs drawn from movie soundtracks. His last real rock hit had come in 1987; since then, he'd scored with the hugely successful ballads "(Everything I Do) I Do It for You" from *Robin Hood: Prince of Thieves* and "All for Love" from *The Three Musketeers*. Adams always denied that he was bothered by the dichotomy between his hard-rocking roots and his treacly pop hits, but those close to the singer would occasionally admit that it rankled him.

The scene on the stage of the Chandler—the lavish courtyard setting, the dancers, and several new musicians in addition to Adams's usual band—was one that might also be expected to annoy Adams, who sometimes wore his tough-guy exterior as a badge of honor. But Adams wasn't there to complain: he'd skipped this rehearsal, and his stand-in was undoubtedly more patient than he would have been. "We hear that he's not thrilled with the idea of dancers," said Daniel Salzman as he watched. "But he didn't make it to rehearsal, so too bad."

Outside the theater, a rock star who did make it to rehearsal sat in his trailer waiting his turn. When he got the nomination for writing the title song to *Dead Man Walking*, Bruce Springsteen was just about to begin a solo acoustic tour of Europe—but he rescheduled dates at the Royal Albert Hall in London in order to come to the Oscars. "I just felt like if my song was going to be on the show, I should be the one singing it," he said.

When Springsteen took the stage to rehearse, Daniel Salzman, fresh from cadging an introduction to the Boss from his dad, plopped down between the seat cards for Mel Gibson and Tim Robbins. "I've never had front-row seats for a Bruce concert before," he said.

Springsteen ran through the song twice, while Margolis directed the cameramen to focus tightly on his face. Between takes, Springsteen's manager, Jon Landau, talked on the phone to the director. Though the song ended with a close-up far closer than you usually see on television, Landau wanted it even closer. The lighting was darker than usual for TV, but Landau wanted it darker still. As he'd done two years earlier when Springsteen had performed "Streets of Philadelphia," Landau pushed the crew to forget their usual ways of doing things.

"These are the best people at what they do," explained Landau afterward. "Jeff is the best television director anywhere. What we're trying to do is take the television out of him."

ALL DAY LONG, the mantra continued: *change, change, change* . . . "They told me," said one puzzled member of Springsteen's crew, "that the whole idea was to change every single thing about the show: the way nominees are announced, the way they give out awards in the smaller categories . . . I said, 'Well, Quincy, the statue looks the same.' And he said, 'We're *tryin'*, baby.' "

The biggest change was on display after dinner, when the parade of singers was interrupted by an invasion of six-foot, hundred-pound women with perfect cheekbones, and sculpted hunks with washboard abs and immaculate stubble. In an outgrowth of the Oscar Fashion Show, the producers had decided to showcase the clothing nominated for best costume design not with the traditional sketches or film clips, but with a mock fashion show. Supermodels would strut down a runway erected on the Oscar stage; they'd be surrounded by dancers portraying both photographers and rabid fans, and accompanied by loud music and a barrage of flashbulbs and strobe lights. Photographer Matthew Rolston directed the show, which was to be introduced by actor Pierce Brosnan, flanked by übermodels Claudia Schiffer and Naomi Campbell.

The original plan, though, had been to use a different star. "It was going to be Jack Nicholson with Claudia Schiffer on one arm and Naomi Campbell on the other," ABC's John Hamlin told a colleague in the audience. But Nicholson declined, so the current James Bond was deemed stylish enough for the gig. "Pierce Brosnan *looks* terrific," Hamlin said, "but you need somebody who really has a twinkle."

Loud, glitzy, and more than a little silly, the segment was slated to be the first award of the evening. And if that didn't make a clear enough statement, the copy written for Brosnan and crew spelled it out even further. Within the space of three sentences, it used the phrases "in a totally new way," "as you've never seen them before," and "trust me, as never before."

The rehearsal progressed in an old-fashioned way: slowly and with great difficulty. The models, who included Tyra Banks, Marcus Schenkenberg, Veronica Webb, and Tyson Beckford, didn't have a true runway on which to work; they were restricted to striking quick, pouty poses on a small ramp, most of them inexplicably sucking on lollipops as they did so.

For one take, the voiceover announcer, Les Marshak, was out of sync with the models when he introduced them as they took the stage. Before the next take, a female voice from behind the curtain yelled, "Say my name sexier, please." Stationed in a truck outside the Chandler, Marshak couldn't hear her.

Progress was painstaking, and changes were frequently made to tighten up the awkward segment. After a few run-throughs, Margolis announced, "We're taking a five-minute break here. Five minutes." Backstage, Schiffer went into Jones's and Salzman's office, followed a few minutes later by Campbell. Bruce Vilanch quickly grabbed his copy of the script and joined them, as did writer Stephen Pouliot. The office door closed; a minute later it opened, and David Salzman thrust a couple of script pages at production coordinator Benn Fleishman. "I need five copies, *quickly*," he said.

Danette Herman turned the corner, walking fast. "I need two bottles of water," she said. "How hard can that be?"

As the atmosphere grew tenser, supermodel Tyra Banks walked up the stairs, approached Jones's office door, and looked around. "Somebody said they had an extra burger," she said.

"An extra burger? I don't think they've arrived yet," a staffer told her.

Banks wasn't backing down. "They said there was an extra burger in Quincy's office," she insisted.

"Why don't you let us look into it?"

"Okay," she said. "I'll be sitting out there."

The door to Jones's office opened, and Vilanch walked out. "Welcome," he said, "to *Prêt-à-Porter*."

AT NOON ON SUNDAY, Jones and Salzman gave a press conference outside the Chandler. At least three-quarters of the questions dealt with Jesse Jackson, who had announced that he planned to lead a picket line during the Oscar show. (Out of respect for Jones, the protest would take place not at the Music Center, but at the ABC Prospect lot.) After a few minutes of facing questions about Jackson, Salzman got testy. "Too bad you didn't ask about the exciting races or the new things we're doing this year," he said. "We'd have a lot to say about it, but since you didn't ask, bye."

All afternoon, stars ran through their lines in front of an audience of friends, family, and a few Academy guests. When Sidney Poitier rehearsed his category, best picture, the winner (FOR THIS REHEARSAL ONLY, of course) was *Sense and Sensibility*. Immediately, ABC publicist Dan Doran phoned his sister Lindsay, the film's producer. "Just wanted to let you know that at rehearsal, you won," he told her. Writer Anthony Lane, who was allowed to observe part of the rehearsal for a story in *The New Yorker*, overheard Doran and decided that he was making a consolation call. Because a winner at rehearsal "bears no relation to the name of the eventual victor," he later wrote in an inexplicable leap of logic, the opening of a dummy envelope "therefore cuts one horse out of the field."

In fact, the rehearsal winners were chosen mostly at random. Price Waterhouse made five complete sets of rehearsal envelopes, including every possible winner in each category. Unless the crew needed to test a certain camera move, pure chance determined which films won. The envelopes opened were not, as Lane apparently assumed, the leftovers in a pile from which Price Waterhouse had already removed the true winners.

The atmosphere in and around the green room, where stars could socialize, snack, and watch monitors, was relaxed—though Sharon Stone spent a lot of time complaining about the press, and in particular about a recent *New Yorker* story that painted her as demanding and difficult. "It's always taken out of context, it's always distorted," she said. "I'd say that story was sixty percent fabricated. And the Mark Rydell quotes, he says he didn't say anything like that." She went on a while longer, then shook her head. "The thing to do," she announced, "is *never* do interviews. You just can't do them."

Stone spotted Angela Bassett and gave her a big hug. "How are you?" said Bassett. "Well, you know what it's like," sighed Stone. "I don't know how many dresses I've tried on this week, and they all suck."

In another corner of the room, Steven Seagal cornered Michael Seligman. "I feel like the TelePrompTer guy got a little bit lost when I ad-libbed," Seagal said. "So maybe if I tell him what I'm going to say, he can be ready for it. How would I do that?"

In one corner of the green room, five Oscar posters were laid across a table. Each star was asked to sign all five. The first four were earmarked for Jones, Salzman, Hiller, and Margolis; the fifth, explained a woman at the table, was for Christopher Reeve, who had yet to appear in public following a fall from a horse that had left him paralyzed ten months earlier. Most of the stars quickly autographed the first four, then stopped to write messages on Reeve's.

If the mood was largely good-natured around the green room, it was much tenser down the hall, outside the producers' offices. Jones's door remained shut, guarded by a longtime aide who kept his hand on the doorknob at all times. Occasionally Jones and Salzman emerged, always unsmiling, and hurried away. "They're getting harried," said Arnold Robinson, one of Jones's publicists. "They just want to get the show done."

Getting the show done, though, was proving to be complicated. The set was still causing problems, to the point where some crew members had begun suggesting alternative entrances to Margolis when the planned moves were impossible to implement. At one point, stagehands trying to move the enormous Spanish courtyard set out of the way inadvertently pushed it off the loading dock, where it crashed to the ground. Midafternoon on Sunday, Richard Dreyfuss was standing in the wings with stage manager Debbie Williams when they heard a crash from across the stage.

"What was that?" asked Dreyfuss.

"I don't know," said Williams. "But did you ever see *Naked Gun 33 1/3*?"

"Yeah," said the actor, who was familiar with the comedy that climaxed with an Academy Awards ceremony degenerating into complete chaos.

"Well," she said, "if ever that was going to happen, this would be the year."

DRESS REHEARSAL began at 7:35 with the usual red carpet montage. It was followed by a sequence reminiscent of the recent Michael Jackson video

"Black or White," in which the faces of different movie stars morphed into each other. Backstage, Goldberg tried to watch on a monitor as she waited for her cue—but she had trouble seeing because Claudia Schiffer and Naomi Campbell had planted themselves in front of her monitor and were chatting away, oblivious. "Excuse me," the host said. "*Excuuuuse* me." Finally, they turned, and Goldberg pointed at the TV screen. "My monitor," she pointed out. "Could you move?"

As usual, the rehearsal had its rough spots. Singer Gloria Estefan's voice faltered as she navigated a small stairway, always the bane of female singers in long gowns. Randy Newman's piano was never in sync with the orchestra. An hour into the rehearsal, during what was supposed to be a short commercial break following "You've Got a Friend in Me," the show simply stopped dead. Newman and singer Lyle Lovett remained onstage, crew members made small adjustments, and musical director Tom Scott was hastily summoned over the P.A. system.

Some ninety minutes into the rehearsal, the percussive dance troupe Stomp, which specialized in pounding on any and all available surfaces, delivered a rousing performance. Their moves were synced to film clips, which tenuously tied the routine to the world of movie sound effects. Then things came to a halt once more. Jones ambled onstage and talked to Stomp leader Luke Creswell; Quincy's personal photographer followed and took pictures as they conversed.

By 10:30, three hours in, the show was only about half over and the crowd was thinning out. The "satellite link" between Goldberg, Miss Piggy, and Babe was rough and awkward, and Babe's participation was so minimal that it was hard to figure out the point of the whole thing. Afterward, Goldberg frowned. "I love that pig," she said, "but my whole career's riding on this."

After the latest in a long line of "five-minute" breaks that ended up lasting ten or fifteen, Bryan Adams was introduced. He wasn't ready. Either unaware of or unconcerned with the niceties of dress rehearsal, he continued tuning his guitar when he should have been singing. Then he stepped to the microphone and said, "Could I have a little less vibrato on my voice, Mikey? Are you with me, Mikey?"

Margolis stopped the run-through and waited for Adams to get ready. Then he started again. "Here we go," he said. "Five, four . . ."

"What?" Behind the curtain, Adams was confused. "Aren't they open-ing the curtain before we start singing?"

A stagehand quickly filled Adams in on what he'd missed during the pre-vious day's rehearsal: he would begin the song behind the curtain, while dancers cavorted in front of it; then the curtain would part to reveal the band and the Spanish courtyard tableau.

Adams finally got it straight and performed the song—but when it was over, he remained in place. "Where's that stage manager?" he said. "Can we do that again?"

After a minute's hesitation, Jeff Margolis stopped the rehearsal and gave Adams more time. "Well," said a disgusted Vilanch at the production table, "Mr. Adams decided to rehearse." Nearby, Salzman got a neck massage.

At 11:35, Adams was finally done. The show lurched onward with its most mysterious segment, a tribute to the way Hollywood covers social and political issues. It was introduced by someone referred to in the script and in all production materials simply as "special presenter." A stand-in walked onstage to the theme music from *Superman*, and delivered lines that sounded preachy, simplistic, and like a defensive reaction to Jesse Jackson: "Holly-wood needs to do more . . . Let's work together . . . There is no challenge that we can't meet."

By 11:55, the rehearsal had been going on for nearly four and a half hours, but two of the show's twelve segments remained unrehearsed. Best actor, best actress, and best picture all had yet to be presented. Rather than incur union penalties, Jones and Salzman called it a night. "That is a wrap," announced Margolis. "We'll see you here tomorrow at 8 a.m."

Staffers started to gather up their belongings. "That was a very good first run-though," added Margolis. Not a person in the building be-lieved him.

AT 10 A.M., Margolis stood onstage, waiting to begin a rehearsal with Robin Williams. A stagehand greeted the director. "You probably got about three hours sleep, huh?"

Margolis looked at him incredulously. "*Three hours?*" he said. "I *wish* I got three hours."

In a backstage hallway, Michael Seligman said he had been at the Chandler until 2:30 a.m. "We had a very rough run-through last night," he admitted. "Very rough. It was the first time in nine years we didn't finish the show. Bryan Adams screwed us up, and we had some real rough spots. But I think we'll be okay."

Nearby, David Salzman tried to remain optimistic as well. "It ran long, so we just tried to shorten a couple of segments," he said. "It wasn't that bad."

Outside the executive suite, though, it was impossible to miss the chorus of grumbles. A stage manager: "This was not a good way to do things this year. This was a terrible way to do it."

One stand-in: "This is ridiculous."

Another: "The whole thing's out of control."

A manager: "The sense I get is that the whole thing is sort of rudderless. They're trying too hard to be different, and doing it on the most superficial level. And every time you talk to Quincy, it's just 'me me me.' All he wants to do is tell you how he's changed everything about the show."

At noon, there was one last rehearsal. This one was smoother than the previous night, though few staffers remained in the audience to watch, and the energy level was low; people were exhausted, or maybe defeated.

Salzman watched from the production table, while Jones stood backstage for most of the rehearsal, chatting with friends outside his office. Some segments had been shortened and streamlined; many of the film packages were trimmed as well. And Doug Stewart, it turned out, had been right to be worried about all the work he'd put into researching and assembling the mini-filmographies earmarked for the acting nominees: overnight, those montages were scrapped in favor of the old standby, single clips from the nominated performances.

In the green room, Springsteen's keyboardist, Roy Bittan, watched the show on a monitor. "It looks like every other Academy Awards show," he said. "What's so different about it?" He grinned. "Okay, they got Tom Scott instead of Bill Conti. What a difference."

Just inside the green room door, four baskets were filled with different-colored ribbons. Near the baskets, a sign read "Ribbon du jour" and decoded the palette: pink for breast cancer awareness, red for AIDS, green for the environment, rainbow for Jesse Jackson's Rainbow Coalition. In the lobby of the theater, ushers carried trays of Jackson's ribbons.

Outside the Chandler, helicopters began to circle the block, and streets around the Music Center were shut down. Though they weren't allowed near the red carpet, demonstrators for a variety of causes—but not Jesse Jackson's crew—began to appear on nearby street corners. One veteran security guard took in the increasingly feverish activity and explained what was about to happen to a pair of new recruits. "It'll get closer to six," he said. "The traffic will get worse, and Edy Williams will show up."

6:00 P.M., PACIFIC DAYLIGHT TIME: *"From Los Angeles, it's the 68th annual Academy Awards."*

The show kicked off with the usual arrivals montage, though this year there was a difference: Oprah Winfrey had been working the red carpet, so the shots of arriving stars were punctuated by a handful of quick, stilted interviews.

Oprah: "To die for, that's what you look like tonight!"

Nicole Kidman: "So do you!"

Oprah: "You're presenting tonight?"

Nicole: "Yes."

Oprah: "Oh, my goodness!"

When the cameras moved inside the Chandler, Goldberg was introduced by the morphing sequence: Elizabeth Taylor morphed into Michelle Pfeiffer, who morphed into Natalie Wood, then Meryl Streep, then Faye Dunaway, then Jerry Lewis. Once again, Claudia Schiffer and Naomi Campbell stood squarely in front of Goldberg's monitor, blind to the host's needs. The supermodels were finally shooed away in time for Goldberg to see the sequence's biggest laugh, which came when a chimpanzee from *Planet of the Apes* morphed into Arnold Schwarzenegger. At the end, Judy Garland's Dorothy morphed into an Oscar statue, which dissolved into Goldberg. "So," she said, after she walked on. "Did you miss me?"

Immediately, the host turned political. "I want to say something to all the folks who brought me ribbons to wear," she said. "You don't tell a black woman to buy an expensive dress and then cover it with ribbons. You don't. I'm sorry. But I got them all, so here it goes. I got a red ribbon for AIDS awareness. Done. I got a purple ribbon for breast cancer. Done. I got a yellow ribbon for the troops in Bosnia. Done. I got a green ribbon to free the Chinese dissidents. Done. I got a milky white ribbon for mad cow disease. Done. I got a rainbow ribbon for gay rights disease. Done, done, done again. I got a fake-fur ribbon for animal rights. Done. I got a wet white ribbon to end Whitewater. Done. A seersucker ribbon to let Martin Landau finish his speech from last year. Done. A plaid ribbon that Mel Gibson wore instead of pants in *Braveheart*. Done. And a blue ribbon that somebody swiped off of Babe. Done. Enough with the ribbons."

In the green room, Alicia Silverstone watched a monitor and nervously adjusted her pale blue boa. Kelly Preston and John Travolta stood nearby. Sandra Bullock, one of the few stars to arrive via the loading dock rather than the red carpet, walked in accompanied by a stern security guard. Kurt Russell and Goldie Hawn hovered near the doorway. Except for Preston, who was accompanying her husband, Travolta, all were due onstage during the first half of the show; in most cases, stars were escorted backstage two commercial breaks before their appearance, and waited in the green room for the summons.

Oscar staffers grew to know the look of terror in many stars' eyes when it was time—and they also grew adept at dispensing last-minute pep talks and reassurances. One of the most frequent questions from females on their way to the stage, laughed vets of the process, was "Are my nipples even?"

Awaiting their cues, the stars gathered around a skimpy buffet table and eyed several TV monitors scattered throughout the small room. "Oscar is sixty-eight—younger than Bob Dole," Goldberg said on the screen. "And I'm glad that it looks like Bob's gonna get that nomination, honey, 'cause it means he'll be too damn busy to go to the movies."

Kurt Russell, a die-hard Republican, shook his head at this jibe at the GOP candidate known for his Hollywood-bashing. "I wish somebody had the balls to make a joke about this idiot of a president we have," he said.

But Goldberg had already changed the subject to *Showgirls*, the disastrous Paul Verhoeven potboiler about cutthroat Vegas strippers. "I haven't seen that many poles mistreated since World War II," she snapped. When the host came into the wings after her monologue, said Dency Nelson, "she was almost floating, she was in such a Zen state."

Less than fifteen minutes into the show, the supermodels strutted down their miniature runway to the beat of tepid but pounding techno music. Watching a pouting Trya Banks show off a gown and tiara from *Sense and Sensibility*, Emma Thompson laughed, then shattered the silence of the green room. "That's my crown!" she shouted at the screen. "Get it *off*, Tyra!"

The glitzy number was met with polite applause, and a few minutes later Goldberg returned to the microphone. "Why do supermodels have that look on their face all the time?" she wondered. "They're getting ten grand an hour, they still look pissed off." The joke quickly took away some of the bad taste left by the fashion show, which was all but forgotten a minute later when Kevin Spacey won the best supporting actor award for *The Usual Suspects*, and followed his extremely popular win with a graceful and emotional speech.

Forty minutes into the show, Robin Williams presented an honorary award to Chuck Jones, one of the pioneers from the glory days of Warner Bros.' Looney Tunes cartoons. "I have a jones for the work of Chuck Jones!" Williams said. "He worked on Bugs, Daffy . . . He has raised speech impediments to an art form!"

On a backstage monitor, Steven Seagal watched Williams. "He's *animated* tonight," he said, grinning from ear to ear. Then he looked over to make sure his publicist, Paul Bloch, got the joke.

Seagal was the only star hanging out with his publicist backstage, and he was only doing so because of a loophole. Personal publicists, once ubiquitous backstage, had been barred from the premises by order of the Academy's Public Relations Coordinating Committee. But Jones himself was represented by the Rogers and Cowan publicity firm; his publicist, Arnold Robinson, was always on hand, as was Robinson's boss, Bloch—who also happened to be Seagal's publicist. When Seagal showed up, Bloch stuck close by.

On the green room monitors, Robin Williams was still on a roll. "Now if Chuck could only animate Bob Dole," he said, "we could have an interesting campaign."

Seagal looked back at Bloch. "Who's Chuck Jones?" he said.

When Randy Newman and Lyle Lovett performed their *Toy Story* song, "You've Got a Friend in Me," Martin Landau unself-consciously clapped along in the green room. At the same time, Sandra Bullock and a friend headed for the door. "We're going to the girls' room," they told her security guard. For once, he didn't follow.

Close to the ninety-minute mark, the second award for a supporting performance turned out to be even more emotional than the first. In something of an upset over the likes of *Nixon*'s Joan Allen, *Sense and Sensibility*'s Kate Winslet, and *Apollo 13*'s Kathleen Quinlan, Mira Sorvino won the best supporting actress award for portraying a squeaky-voiced hooker in Woody Allen's *Mighty Aphrodite*. A stunned Sorvino, who had been the subject of such an aggressive Miramax campaign that some of her supporters had worried about a backlash, gave particular thanks to her father, actor Paul Sorvino. Margolis's cameras caught him sobbing in his front-row seat. "I *love* this show!" the director shouted as he went to commercial.

Backstage, honorary Oscar recipient Kirk Douglas, suffering from the effects of a recent stroke, arrived at the artists' entrance and was immediately ushered into Jones's and Salzman's office. A few minutes later he was joined by Steven Spielberg, who'd never worked with Douglas but had agreed to present the award after Douglas specifically asked for him. (Jones had figured that Michael Douglas should do the honors, but the elder Douglas wanted to keep it out of the family.)

In the green room, Winona Ryder fretted over her upcoming trip across the stage to introduce Springsteen. "My hands are freezing, and I'm still shaking from that walk down the red carpet," she told Goldie Hawn. "I'd never done that walk before."

"You know how to handle the red carpet?" asked Hawn. "Just turn your head and smile, but don't stop. *Never* stop."

Sitting on a cream-colored couch across the room, Angelica Huston overheard Ryder and got up. "You look *so* fabulous," Huston said, nodding at Ryder's beaded, low-cut Badgley Mischka gown and old-fashioned, marcelled hairstyle. "You have nothing to be nervous about."

Springsteen and his wife, Patti Scialfa, approached Ryder. "Hey, thanks for doing my intro," said Springsteen.

"Oh, no, it's my pleasure," said Ryder. "I love that song *so* much."

Springsteen looked around the room and spotted a friend nearby. He'd taken a couple of steps in that direction when the show went to a commercial. "Next," announced Marshak, "Jim Carrey, Winona Ryder, Richard Dreyfuss, Goldie Hawn, Kurt Russell, and Bruce Springsteen."

Springsteen stopped. "Oops," he said. "That's me. I better get ready." He made a U-turn and left the room.

Near the two-hour mark, *One Survivor Remembers*, the story of a Holocaust survivor, won the Oscar for documentary short. Director Kary Antholis came to the stage accompanied by Gerda Weissmann Klein, the subject of his film. Antholis gave a fifty-five-second speech, ten seconds over the limit. When he stepped back from the microphone, Margolis gave Tom Scott the music cue, and the orchestra began to play. But Klein had stepped to the microphone, and she refused to be played offstage or escorted into the wings by trophy lady Traci McGlover. "After what this woman had been through in her life," Margolis said, "I couldn't do it to her." The director told Scott to stop the music.

"I [was] in a place for six incredible years, where winning meant a crust of bread and to live another day," said Klein. She spoke to the hushed crowd for a minute and a half. "Thank you for honoring this memory," she said before walking off.

In the producer's office, Steven Spielberg and Kirk Douglas watched the show with Jones. Jones and Salzman were beginning to feel relief: on the technical side things were running smoothly, and several of the speeches had been genuinely emotional and moving. After the young dancer Savion Glover performed an affecting tribute to the recently deceased Gene Kelly, Douglas clapped. "That was great," he said.

A few minutes later, Douglas was escorted into the wings of the stage to await his cue. "Whether . . . on-screen, or dealing with the all-too-real effects of a recent stroke, courage remains Kirk Douglas's personal and professional hallmark," Spielberg said by way of introduction.

As highlights of Douglas's career played on the large screen, Douglas turned to Debbie Williams. "I hope the words come out of my mouth," he said to her. Then he walked onstage and gave a short speech, struggling to enunciate clearly. "I see my four boys," he said, looking into the audience.

"They are proud of the old man. And I am proud, too." The crowd was tremendously moved, not so much by his simple words, but by his dignity in appearing onstage in his frail condition.

Afterward, Douglas was spared the usual press gauntlet. Where most winners were taken upstairs to the four different press rooms, Douglas was led to a makeshift backdrop erected outside Jones's office. There, an Academy photographer took pictures of Douglas and Spielberg. Then Douglas was escorted to a waiting elevator that went down to the exit, not up to the press rooms. Backstage, Michael Douglas approached Jones and Salzman. "Thank you," he said. "My dad has never been treated with this much respect and honor." He also sought out Mike Shapiro, who'd put together the film clips honoring Douglas.

After accepting Douglas's thanks, Jones had another job to do as Sharon Stone's copresenter in the two film-score categories. When he walked onstage, Jones carried with him the envelope for the musical or comedy score category; while a short film showed the nominees, Price Waterhouse managing partner Frank Johnson came out of the wings and handed a second envelope, for the best dramatic score category, to Stone. Normally, the second envelope would have been carried to the stage by the trophy lady when she brought out statuettes for the first set of winners, but this time the accounting firm had argued for a different method.

Predictably, the award for musical or comedy score went to Alan Mencken and Stephen Schwartz, who wrote the music for the animated Disney film *Pocahontas*. The custom was to give the envelope to the winner along with the Oscar statuette—but as Mencken and Schwartz walked to the stage, Jones put it on the podium in front of him. The trophy lady then gave Jones and Stone Oscar statuettes to present to Mencken and Schwartz. Stone handed her Oscar to Schwartz, but she also mistakenly gave him the unopened envelope for the next category.

Mencken thanked a laundry list of colleagues and supporters, and then picked up the opened envelope bearing his and Schwartz's names as he left the podium. Schwartz nodded his thanks, and walked off not only with his Oscar, but also with the envelope for the next category.

Stone and Jones looked at the TelePrompTer and read the nominees for best dramatic score. Then Stone looked around. "Now, I don't have the thing," she said. Jones made a beeline for the wings, looking for one of the Price Waterhouse reps who had all the winners' names memorized; a stage manager realized what had happened and tried to chase down Schwartz, but he was already in the elevator on his way to the press rooms. "I don't have the envelope," repeated Stone, "so I'd like us all to have a psychic moment. Let's just concentrate." She paused. "It's coming to me." A longer pause. "Oh, you can do better than that."

In the wings, Johnson told Jones that *Il Postino* had won. (To make the task manageable, he memorized the names of the winning films, rather than the names of the winners themselves, in all but the acting categories.) Jones walked back onstage, and whispered the name to Stone. "Oh, my God," she said. "It's *Il Postino*."

In the green room a few minutes later, Stone was still baffled. "When I went to present the award, there was nothing there," she said. "No envelope, nothing." She looked at the skimpy buffet, then turned to an aide. "Is there anything here that'll help me get through tonight?" she asked. The aide started to leave to look for different food. "I'm okay," insisted Stone. "You don't have to go." The aide left anyway, returning a few minutes later with a plate of melon.

At 8:48 p.m., the "special presenter" made his appearance. "Ladies and gentlemen," said Marshak, "Christopher Reeve." The curtain rose to reveal Reeve sitting in his wheelchair center stage. The orchestra remained silent, the *Superman* overture having been vetoed since rehearsal. After a prolonged ovation, the crowd grew still. "What you probably don't know," said Reeve, "is that I left New York last September, and I just arrived here this morning." Margolis cut to several teary-eyed stars; the green room, whose occupants usually only paid partial attention to the monitors, grew very attentive.

In the wings, a nurse was standing by; if Reeve began to have spasms, a real possibility, the plan was for Margolis to immediately cut to the audience while the nurse attended to Reeve. (A few minutes earlier, just before she escorted the actor onstage, Debbie Williams had been told by one of Reeve's companions that if she wanted to touch him, she could do so on the left shoulder. When she told Reeve that his cue would come in thirty seconds, she did just that—only to be stopped cold when he hissed, "Don't do that, I might spasm.")

Reeve was collected and controlled as he introduced a montage of clips from such socially conscious films as *Boyz N the Hood*, *Philadelphia*, *In Cold Blood*, *In the Heat of the Night*, *The Grapes of Wrath*, *Silkwood*, and *Schindler's List*. While the film played, Williams stood onstage directly in front of Reeve, purposefully blocking the audience's view so they'd watch the film rather than stare at him.

When the film ended, Reeve spoke again. "Let's continue to take risks," he said. "Let's tackle the issues. In many ways, our film community can do it better than anyone else." Lines that sounded clichéd when read by an able-bodied stand-in were no longer so trite. "There is no challenge, artistic or otherwise, that we can't meet." In the green room, the speech received a rare round of applause, and prompted quite a few tears. Sharon Stone left the room to compose herself. In Jones's office, Spielberg cried.

At the show's three-hour mark, Mencken and Schwartz won the best-song award for "Colors of the Wind" from *Pocahontas*. In the audience, an audible groan, followed by tepid applause, greeted the news that yet another Disney cartoon song had bested the likes of Springsteen and Newman.

But the rest of the show ran smoothly: Mel Gibson was charming and amusing while accepting the best-director award for *Braveheart*, which had begun to steamroll everything else in its path. Susan Sarandon and Nicolas Cage were both popular if predictable winners in the actor and actress categories.

In a hallway backstage, Jones rounded a corner, saw Salzman, and wrapped him in a bear hug. "I'm glad it worked, man," said a friend with audible relief.

Braveheart capped the evening by winning best picture. "Well, we've stomped our way through another Oscar show," said Goldberg. "And if you said three hours and thirty-five minutes, you won the pool."

In his office, Jones dispensed hugs and high fives. "God was with us tonight," he said. The consensus was that it worked, thanks to the genuine emotion of moments like Sorvino's, Douglas's, and Reeve's. Even those who'd been critical of Jones a few hours earlier conceded that things somehow came together. The supermodel fashion show didn't have many fans, but it came early in the evening and was quickly forgotten. "It was just what we wanted," Jones said. "Different, fast, emotional."

Near the musicians' trailers outside the Shrine, Jon Landau and Bruce Allen commiserated over the fact that the artists they managed, Springsteen and Adams, respectively, had lost to a Disney song. The two men posed for a photo together, and Landau commented, "It'll be in *Billboard* next week— a new partnership."

"Yeah," laughed Allen. "And the caption will be, 'Two Losers.' "

Jones and Salzman walked by, heading for the Governors Ball with an entourage that included Oprah Winfrey. "You were great," Jones said to Oprah. "You were like . . . What's that big rock over in Europe?"

"The Rock of Gibraltar?" she said.

"Yeah," he said. "The Rock of Gibraltar."

In the Governors Ball, the biggest crowd gathered around Christopher Reeve's table. Danette Herman stood by proudly. "We've been working on getting Chris here since December," she said. "He wanted to do it, but they had to figure out if he could travel, the doctor had to check out our facilities . . . It was very complicated." The few production staffers who knew about the booking used code names for Reeve, she added; most of the staff didn't know about it.

At the ball, Jones and Salzman basked in congratulations. But the two men also knew that the experience had been a rough one, and not one they were inclined to repeat. "It was nice working with you," Jones told Mike Shapiro. "I'd say let's work together again, but I'm never doing this show again as long as I live."

AFTER THE SHOW, Jesse Jackson announced that his protests and his ongoing dialogue with Hollywood executives were having positive results. He also insisted that the fact that Goldberg joked about his campaign on the show was good, because it meant she was addressing the serious issue, albeit with humor.

The ratings did not keep pace with the upward trend of the past few years: it was the lowest-rated Oscar telecast in four years, with the biggest one-year drop-off since 1985. For the first time since 1987, ABC did not finish atop the Nielsen ratings for the week in the eighteen-to-forty-nine demographic, though it did win the week overall. Still, the show was the highest-rated entertainment program since the previous Oscar show, and the 30.3 rating was higher than that of seven out of the past ten shows.

In addition, the show picked up some of the best reviews of any Academy Awards show in years. Though some of the praise was due to the fresh approach of Jones and Salzman—the appearance of Stomp foremost— much of it was due not to their attempted overhaul of the show, but to the emotional moments that no Oscar producer can truly plan. Appearing before the Academy's review committee, Jones deflected some of the credit and suggested that the Oscar vets, primarily Margolis, deserved the kudos.

4
≡

Secrets and Lies

The 69th Academy Awards

HE AMBLED THROUGH THE DOOR just before noon on February 24, 1997, one month to the day before the 69th Academy Awards. Casually dressed in blue jeans, a gray sweater, and sneakers, Billy Crystal stuck his hands in his pockets as he wandered through the nondescript office suite that was serving as a temporary home to the Oscar production staff. Crystal and his manager, a rumpled, curly haired man named David Steinberg, had come to meet with Gil Cates, but for a few seconds they stopped, looked around, and seemed lost. The hallway was nearly deserted, and no nameplates adorned the office doors in the plain high-rise building on Wilshire Boulevard in the Westwood section of Los Angeles.

But when Crystal and Steinberg turned a corner, they spotted a group of faces familiar from Crystal's four previous gigs as the Oscar host. Danette Herman immediately broke into a broad grin. "Nice to see you," she said softly. "*Really* nice to see you." She stepped back, and her smile got bigger and her voice louder. "*Really* nice to see you! *We missed you!*"

Oscar himself had missed Billy Crystal. His stint as host of the show, from 1990 to 1993, had garnered impressive ratings and almost unanimous acclaim. In that stretch, Crystal had staked his claim as the heir to Johnny Carson and Bob Hope, the ideal man for a demanding, tricky, and in some ways thankless job. Able to work a room and a television camera, both undercutting and celebrating the pomp of the occasion, he had delivered several of the time-capsule moments for which the Oscars are most often remembered. There was the entrance he made strapped to a gurney, a leather mask across his face, in homage to Anthony Hopkins's role as the homicidal Hannibal Lecter in *The Silence of the Lambs*; his running string of jokes after seventy-three-year-old Jack Palance celebrated his best supporting actor win by dropping to the stage for some one-handed push-ups; and his ad-lib when one-hundred-year-old Hal Roach decided to make a speech from his seat, without the benefit of a microphone to make his words audible. "I think that's fitting," said Crystal, "because Mr. Roach started in silent films."

But those highlights all came in 1992—and Crystal, not wanting to run his familiar bits into the ground, had walked away from the Oscar assignment following an anticlimactic show the following year. After two years off, he thought about returning to the Oscars—but that was the year Quincy Jones took the reins, and Jones went straight to Whoopi Goldberg without asking Crystal.

But Gil Cates was back the following year; after dealing with Jones, the Academy appreciated the steadier hand of the six-time producer. When Cates agreed to return, he immediately put a call in to Crystal. With a new movie, *Father's Day*, due out a few weeks after the show, Crystal was up for another turn as host.

Crystal had been in touch with Cates since he took the gig, tossing out ideas, particularly about a top-secret film he wanted to show before taking the stage. But he hadn't been by the office, and much of the Oscar production staff hadn't spoken to him in four years.

So when Crystal and Steinberg stopped outside Cates's office and waited for the producer to get off the phone, the group of staffers that had gathered nearby quickly surrounded the comic and welcomed him back. While Bill Conti and Robert Z. Shapiro shook Crystal's hand, a broad grin never left Herman's face.

"How have you been, Billy?" asked Herman. "You know," she repeated one final time, "we really missed you."

IF EVER the Academy Awards needed a host who could energize the show and draw viewers, 1997 was the year. The biggest movies of the previous season were popcorn blockbusters without a chance of winning Oscars in any but the technical categories: *Independence Day*, *Twister*, and *Mission: Impossible* were effective thrill rides for viewers who didn't mind checking their brains at the door, but they were hardly what the Academy was looking for. The films that dominated the year-end critics' polls, instead, were smaller independent films: Joel and Ethan Coen's wry *Fargo*, British director Mike Leigh's largely improvised *Secrets & Lies*, Dane Lars Von Trier's stark *Breaking the Waves*, Arkansas-born actor-director-writer Billy Bob Thornton's southern gothic *Sling Blade*. Scattered support also went to *The English Patient*, a languid romantic epic set during World War II and directed by Anthony Minghella, an Englishman whose two previous films had not been successes. *The English Patient* was supposed to have been made by 20th Century-Fox, but the studio got cold feet over money issues, and pulled out just before production was due to start. Miramax stepped in and bought the film at a cut-rate price.

When nominations were announced on February 11, indie films dominated. In the best-picture race, there was precisely one major studio movie that Middle America had been paying to see: *Jerry Maguire*, director Cameron Crowe's look at a sports agent in crisis, starring Tom Cruise and newcomers Renée Zellweger and Cuba Gooding, Jr. But the rest of the slate was filled with independent films and art movies: *Secrets & Lies*, *Fargo*, *The English Patient*, and *Shine*. The last film, released by Fine Line, was directed by a young Australian named Scott Hicks, and told the story of piano prodigy David Helfgott's lifelong battle with mental illness. The degree to which the movie followed the actual events of Helfgott's life was a matter of considerable debate, but most agreed that British actor Noah Taylor and Australian Geoffrey Rush did fine jobs portraying the tortured pianist as an adolescent and an adult, respectively.

In the acting categories, it was again a heyday for independents and unknowns. In the best-actress category, there was young Welsh actress Emily Watson versus middle-aged British actress Brenda Blethyn, neither of them familiar in the United States. For best actor, the obscure Australian Geoffrey Rush versus the obscure Arkansan Billy Bob Thornton. For best supporting actor, Armin Mueller-Stahl versus William H. Macy. For best supporting actress, Marianne-Jean Baptiste versus Juliette Binoche. In that last category, some old Hollywood glamour was provided by Lauren Bacall, who appeared in Barbra Streisand's otherwise overlooked *The Mirror Has Two Faces*, though Bacall didn't mean much to viewers under thirty.

For those concerned about television ratings—which is to say, everyone at ABC, at the Academy, and on the production team—the nominations were not good news. Viewers tuned in to the Oscars for lots of reasons—for the stars, the fashions, the host, the performers, or simply because everybody else watches—but if they didn't have a rooting interest in the races, the ratings invariably suffered.

As he looked over the nominations in his office a couple of hours after the announcement, Cates knew the show would be a tough sell. "We've got our work cut out for us, getting folks in Middle America to watch this," he said, looking over the bulletin board where he'd posted the nominations. "Thank God Tom Cruise got nominated."

Herman laughed, and went lowbrow to counter all the art-movie names on the board in front of her. "Calling Chris Farley," she said.

"IT'S BEEN A VERY BIZARRE YEAR," said Cates to three dozen staffers sitting in the production office at ten tables arranged into an enormous square. "Things have been a little bit off-kilter for these kinds of shows this year."

With the previous year's Oscar show suffering a drop in the ratings, the lackluster business done by other recent awards shows was a bigger concern than it might otherwise have been. As the staff took notes and examined the schedules and rundowns in front of them, Cates ran through his plans to keep people watching.

"To begin the show, Chuck Workman's doing a thing with clips from the big films of 1996," he said. "Because so many of the [nominated] films this year were ones that many people haven't seen, the idea is to put in scenes from *Independence Day* and *Twister* and *The Rock*, and movies that people did see. We want to get those things at the top of the show."

There was, he added, another option. "Billy might be doing something where he's in film clips from some of the nominated films. If we do that, Act two will begin with Chuck's thing."

On the musical front, Cates told the staff that Madonna would be performing the nominated song "You Must Love Me," from *Evita*. There'd been some question about this, because the singer had been considered a serious best-actress candidate for her performance in that movie's title role. Passed over by Oscar voters, she thought about it for a couple of weeks before agreeing to perform the number, her movie's one new song and a tune written by Andrew Lloyd Webber and Tim Rice specifically to secure a nomination for their otherwise ineligible music.

Another pop diva, Barbra Streisand, was in a similar situation. Streisand had received a best-song nomination for cowriting "I Finally Found Someone," from *The Mirror Has Two Faces*, but otherwise she'd been bypassed for her work directing and starring in the movie. "Barbra may or may not do it," Cates said. "If she does it, she'll obviously do it with Bryan Adams, the way she does in the movie. If not, we've discussed some alternatives."

What went unspoken was Streisand's troubled history with the Oscars. Once, the relationship had been a good one: the singer-turned-actress was allowed to join the Academy in 1967, before her first film, *Funny Girl*, was even released. Though the organization's rules dictated that membership should be granted only after an impressive body of work, Academy president Gregory Peck explained the waiver: "When an actress has played a great role on the stage, and is coming into films for what will obviously be an important career, it is ridiculous to make her wait two or three years for membership." That year's best-actress vote ended in a tie between Streisand and Katharine Hepburn. If Streisand voted for herself, she owed her Oscar to the Academy's early admittance policy.

In subsequent years, though, the Academy was not so generous with Streisand, and the singer was not so enamored with the Academy. Nominated for best actress for the 1973 romance *The Way We Were*, she agreed to attend the ceremony—but, she told Academy president Walter Mirisch, she didn't want people to know she was there unless she won, so she spent the entire ceremony in seclusion backstage. (She didn't win.) In 1984, Academy members voted five nominations for *Yentl*, but none of them went to Streisand, who'd directed and starred in the movie. Seven years later, her film *The Prince of Tides* won seven nominations, including best picture—but once again, she herself was overlooked in the best-director and best-actress categories. *The Mirror Has Two Faces* was also largely overlooked: it had picked up a pair of nominations, a supporting-actress nod for screen legend Lauren Bacall, who'd never won an Oscar, and a song nomination for "I Finally Found Someone."

"She says she'll let us know today," Cates told the staff. "It's a fifty-fifty chance."

ON MARCH 3, the publicity department of the Academy issued a press release: "Chris Farley and David Spade will be presenters at this year's Oscar telecast, producer Gilbert Cates announced today. This is the first appearance on an Academy Awards show for either of them."

WITH TWO WEEKS TO GO until show time, the second-floor lobby of the Shrine Auditorium was filled with dozens of folding chairs. At the end of the lobby, facing the chairs, was a long table. Cates, Seligman, Herman, and choreographer Otis Sallid took seats at the table. So did production designer Roy Christopher and the new director of the Oscar show, Louis J. Horvitz.

Christopher showed off a scale model of his set, which bedecked the wide stage in dozens of off-white, forty-foot-tall louvers, and topped it with a movable ceiling piece that could descend all the way to the floor. "We're trying to go for a very simple, elegant, classic look this year," he said.

"It looks inexpensive," shouted a staffer from the back of the room.

"It is inexpensive," said Christopher with a grin. "And very easy to build."

Horvitz leaned toward his microphone. "He means the model," he said. "The model was inexpensive and easy to build."

Horvitz was one of the few new faces among the show's senior staffers. The forty-nine-year-old director had been working in television, first as a cameraman and then as a director, for more than a decade. He'd spent eight years directing the music variety show *Solid Gold*, and had moved into live events with the *Live Aid* benefit concert in 1985. In recent years, Horvitz had directed music shows that included Paul Simon in Central Park, the Rolling Stones' Steel Wheels tour, and the Judds' farewell concert; he'd done Super Bowl halftime shows and the Emmy Awards. The world of televised awards shows was a fairly small, insular one, in which everyone knew everyone else, and Cates had been watching Horvitz.

Jeff Margolis had directed eight consecutive Oscar shows, but tension between him and Cates had been slowly building. Perhaps Margolis was a threat because he'd been given too much credit; perhaps he was a distraction because he'd tried to take too much control. Whatever the reasons, when Margolis showed up at the Emmy Awards in the fall of 1996, a nominee for directing the Quincy Jones Oscar show, he learned that Cates was also there—not in the audience but in the control truck, watching Horvitz direct. "I knew that Gil was there, but I didn't know why," said Margolis, who was devastated to lose the Oscar job. "I didn't know, but I did. I just didn't *want* to know." To add insult to injury, Margolis lost that night to Horvitz's direction of the 1995 Kennedy Center Honors. Cates suggested that Margolis take a year off from directing the Oscars—but when the director made it clear just how deeply the change hurt him, the rift widened further.

The new director was demanding, a perfectionist who treated his agenda as if it were a battle plan straight out of *Patton*. He had a meticulous approach and sharp visual sense—but when things didn't go right, Louis J., as he was known, could blister underlings with torrents of abuse and profanity. "I don't know why," he conceded, "but I've got a sailor's mouth."

At his first major Oscar production meeting, though, Horvitz was on his best behavior. "When Gil and I first sat down for lunch in January," said Horvitz, "he said, 'You have never in your life been through something like this.' I said, 'Well, I don't know . . .' And he said, 'Trust me. *Never*.' "

The director then led a more detailed discussion of the show. "We want to make everybody feel that one of the last places you can be part of a community is sitting in a movie house," Horvitz said, making explicit the vague and largely unpublicized theme that Cates had chosen for the show.

"We'll have sixteen cameras inside the Shrine," he added. "I think that's a couple more than last year. The idea is to add a little more variety during the three hours and ten minutes, which is the length the show is going to run this year. Right, Gil?"

Cates smiled. "Ho-ho," he said.

"EVERYBODY ELSE IS TENSE," said Otis Sallid. "*This* is where the fun happens."

On Stage 57 at ABC Prospect, the new Oscar choreographer was leading his crew through a rehearsal of a lighthearted pop-rock ditty called "That Thing You Do!" With Cates's much-maligned favorite, Debbie Allen, unavailable, the producer had turned to Sallid, who'd staged dance sequences in such films as *Do the Right Thing* and *Sister Act*. Sallid, though, didn't have much to work with in the crop of nominated songs, and although Herman had also booked Irish American dancer Michael Flatley's "Lord of the Dance" troupe, Sallid would have no hand in the choreography. "That Thing You Do!" had become the young choreographer's sole number.

A slight, peppy, and irresistible sixties-rock pastiche, "That Thing You Do!" was the only up-tempo tune among the five nominated songs. But it was not a case where the Oscars could simply book the original performers. The title song from the movie that marked Tom Hanks's directorial debut, "That Thing You Do!" was supposed to be the one hit enjoyed by a 1960s garage band, the Wonders, before success and excess drove the members apart. In the movie, actors mimed and lip-synched the song, which had been written by Adam Schlesinger (from the pop-rock band the Fountains of Wayne) and recorded by anonymous musicians who'd since become disgruntled at the lack of recognition.

Initially, Hanks and his music supervisor, Gary Goetzman, had offered Cates the services of original actors Jonathan Schaech, Steve Zahn, Ethan Embry, and Tom Everett Scott. The actors were all experts at lip-syncing, said Goetzman, who added that Cates and Sallid could surround the band with whatever kind of choreography and staging they desired.

Sallid mapped out a frenzied, sixties-style dance routine that would follow the rise of the Wonders from a garage to clubs to stardom. But to tell that story required more time and space than the two-and-a-half-minute song provided, so Bill Conti wrote an expanded arrangement that included a midsong instrumental break designed for dancing, and replete with classic rock 'n' roll riffs that had little to do with "That Thing You Do!" Hanks and Goetzman balked at asking the actors to go along with a completely new version of the song. "Bill Conti decided he would be Mr. Rock 'n' Roll, and now it's going to turn into one of those anachronistic Academy Awards production numbers," grumbled one executive with the film.

Sallid knew that he'd be dealing with anonymous lip-syncers in place of the film's actors, but that just gave him more freedom to control the number. On the rehearsal stage, silliness reigned: befitting the catchy song and the sock-hop choreography, the dancers were exuberant, playful, and giddy between takes. Their motto, they announced repeatedly to anyone who would listen, was "Happy to be here! Easy to work with!"

Sallid was dressed mostly in black—slacks, a turtleneck sweater, a baseball cap, along with a long gray trench coat and a silver watch on a chain around his neck. On a nearby stand sat a lyric sheet for "That Thing You Do!" along with the sheet music for the tune. The paper bearing the lyrics was folded so that only the first, second, and final verses were visible; the sheet music was punctuated with boxes describing the onstage action at various points in the song: PAPARAZZI, AUDITORIUM, RADIOS . . . During a break, the dancers stood around a microphone and recorded screams, hand claps, and applause that would later be mixed into the track.

A few minutes later, the dancers began going through their number, an athletic workout that required the predominantly female cast to do a lot of running from one side of the stage to the other. The women wore a variety of sweatpants, shorts, Danskins, and tank tops, and all but one wore sports bras beneath their tops. The one who didn't, Melissa Hurley, a thin brunette who had been briefly engaged to David Bowie a couple of years earlier, grabbed her black halter top as she bopped in place. "Ooh," she said with a sheepish grin. "I gotta hold my little titties."

Watching the rehearsal, Sallid grinned. "For me, working with these people is like driving a Rolls-Royce," he said. "These are the best bodies in the world."

OF THE FIVE NOMINEES, only one had the feel of a best-picture winner. *The English Patient* was far from the most critically acclaimed of the batch, but it was grandiose, epic, and romantic, reeking of seriousness and flaunting the literary pedigree it took from its source novel by Michael Ondaatje. If it was also slow, at times ponderous, and melodramatic—well, that hadn't hurt *Out of Africa*, or *Dances with Wolves*, or *The Last Emperor*, or plenty of other winners over the years. The film had been released by Miramax after 20th Century-Fox had backed out, but it wasn't nearly as quirky or offbeat as indie nominees like *Fargo* and *Secrets & Lies*.

In the past, the power of the major studios to wield blocks of votes would certainly have thrown the race to *Jerry Maguire*, the one nonindie entry. But Academy voters had become a more independent lot, and they knew that giving the prize to the sole studio production in a year that belonged to the independents would make the Academy look positively medieval. Miramax, meanwhile, worked aggressively on behalf of *Sling Blade*'s writer and star, Billy Bob Thornton, but the company's real muscle went behind *The English Patient*, the independent film that didn't look, sound, or feel like an independent film.

IN A TRAILER behind the Shrine, Julie Faust shook her head. On the desk in front of her was a hefty Oscar script; next to it was a phone that kept ringing with phone calls from publicists and agents. "There's a typo on almost every page," said Faust, one of Cates's assistants. "Don't they look at this before it goes out? I have to send this to lots of pissy movie stars!"

It was Friday, March 21, three days before the broadcast and the time when Oscar rehearsals got very serious. Billy Crystal, Madonna, and Michael Flatley were all due in. Potential trouble spots were numerous. All morning, staffers were on edge.

Crystal was the first up, arriving at the Shrine shortly after lunch. The hall was quietly cleared of stand-ins and other observers, while the staffers that were allowed to remain watched intently as the lights dimmed. On the huge center screen, a film began to play. This, everybody knew, would be the top-secret movie Crystal had shot to precede his entrance, the one only a tiny handful had yet seen. But fascination turned to befuddlement when the eagerly awaited movie turned out to be incomprehensible, an odd mélange of people wandering through the desert in an apparent takeoff on the opening scene of *Jesus Christ Superstar*.

"What is *that*?" asked Carrie Fisher, who slipped into a seat near the production table just before Crystal's entrance. "I thought it was going to be Billy going down in a plane piloted by David Letterman."

An actress, writer, and enormously well-compensated Hollywood script doctor, Fisher had been caught by surprise when Cates asked her to join the Oscar team of writers. The money was significantly less than she was accustomed to making, but Fisher was intrigued enough by the offer to accept, joining show vets Buz Kohan and Hal Kanter in writing patter for presenters, performers, and participants—in general, everybody except for Crystal, who relied on a separate team of six writers. Taking the job, she admitted, had brought her some flack from cynical friends who professed to hate the Academy Awards. "Fran Lebowitz yelled at me yesterday for doing this show," Fisher said. "She's not the only friend of mine who's done that."

As they watched the confounding movie play inside the Shrine, Fisher and everybody else in the theater slowly realized that they weren't watching Crystal's real movie. Instead, this was a dummy clip designed to do nothing more than take up the same amount of time. This came as a relief to Chuck Workman, whose montage saluting the popular films of 1996 had been dropped from the show because, he was told, it covered much of the same ground as Crystal's movie. "Well, I'm glad that wasn't his real movie," said Workman. "I'd hate to think that my film was pulled for *that*."

While Crystal went through a low-key rehearsal, Fisher approached Cates. "How are you?" she asked.

"Good," Cates assured her.

"Good," she said, "because Courtney Love isn't."

Love, the former punk singer and widow of Nirvana singer/songwriter

Kurt Cobain, was scheduled to present the Oscar for makeup—a curious category for someone whose look was not exactly Estée Lauder, though a better match than her original slot introducing Kenny Loggins. Her appearance was designed to help the show attract a younger audience, but it also solidified the acceptance the controversial Love had received in Hollywood after her creditable turn as *Hustler* publisher Larry Flynt's tortured wife, Althea, in Milos Forman's film *The People vs. Larry Flynt*.

Love, though, objected to the lines Fisher had written for her. The script began with Love talking about how actresses have to arrive for makeup early in the morning, and how if one is lucky, "she can get an extra hour's sleep while the makeup artists perform their magic, allowing her to nod out plain and wake up pretty." Not only did the lines contain what could be construed as a self-deprecating joke ("Not all of us are lucky enough to wake up pretty"), but they also included a thinly veiled reference to Love's widely publicized substance-abuse problems. One line described seeing what the makeup artists could do as "a fully sobering experience, let me tell you."

" 'Sobering experience' was the first thing to go," Fisher told Cates. But that change wasn't enough to satisfy the rock diva. "She doesn't like the jokes. She wants to be dignified. She sees this as her chance to do a makeover on her reputation."

To Fisher, this was a dubious strategy at best. "It doesn't matter what you do, how long you wait—those things will always be with you," said Fisher, whose own drug-fueled escapades formed the basis for her book *Postcards from the Edge*, which was subsequently made into a movie starring Meryl Streep. "They never left me." She paused and grinned. "Granted, I wrote a book and a movie about it."

DANETTE HERMAN stood by the artists' entrance looking anxious. At 3:45 in the afternoon, Herman's walkie-talkie crackled. "They have arrived," said a voice. "They're heading toward parking." *They*, in this case, meant Madonna and her entourage of about half a dozen, including a nanny for Madonna's five-month-old daughter, Lourdes.

There was reason for the concern that swept through the crew, because

Madonna's history at the Oscars was brief but stormy. She'd appeared on the show in 1991, singing a nominated song from *Dick Tracy*. Before rehearsals began that year, Madonna worked out on her own for weeks, practicing for hours every day with her own choreographer. She had her own costume people work on clothes, and insisted that the production install a sound system identical to the Shrine's in the rehearsal hall she was using on Vine Street in Hollywood. (That building was later purchased by the Academy, and now houses their film archives.)

During rehearsals with the Oscar orchestra, she had been as painstaking and demanding with the musicians as she had been with herself. "She was determined," said Seligman, "that it was going to be perfect."

She also took to showing up at the Shrine at odd hours. "She rehearsed her number, when we got to the Shrine, more than anybody had ever rehearsed a musical number in the history of the Oscars," said Margolis.

"We'd get a call saying, 'Madonna's here,' " remembered stage manager Debbie Williams. "We'd look at the schedule and she wouldn't be listed, but we'd have to find the time to fit her in." Once, the singer arrived late at night wearing slippers and a nightgown, determined to squeeze in a final rehearsal before bedtime. Another time, she was due to rehearse just after a female camera operator had fallen backward off the stage and into the orchestra pit, seriously injuring herself. While the crew waited for paramedics to arrive, Madonna walked onstage. Told of the delay, she looked puzzled. "But she's just lying there," Madonna said of the injured camerawoman. "Can't we do this?"

In her number, Madonna's every move had been carefully choreographed, and her entrance was to be particularly dramatic. She'd rise from beneath the stage through a trapdoor, all blond and glittering, then slink a few steps across the bare stage before turning her back on the audience and the camera. At exactly the right moment, she'd move to the side to reveal a pop-up microphone that had risen into place while she was blocking the audience's view.

"The elevator guy had to push a button at exactly the right bar of music," said Margolis, "and when she hit the floor I went to a head-to-toe shot of her looking sexy, from down low because that makes everybody look taller and it showed off the slit in her dress. After so many bars she'd start walking forward and I'd cut to a high shot. The speed of the microphone had been timed exactly with her walk. The timing was critical."

The night of the show, Madonna was nervous as she waited to perform. Stage manager Rac Clark, who was waiting with her below the stage, gave her a glass of champagne to calm her. But as the song neared, staffers found they couldn't communicate with the technician who was positioned in a small box halfway up the wall in the wings of the theater. His sole job was to activate Madonna's pop-up mike at just the right moment—but sitting in his lonely perch above the Shrine stage, the man had fallen asleep. He didn't hear the frantic attempts to rouse him over his headset, nor respond when stage manager Garry Hood shouted and threw things at him from below.

With no time to spare, Margolis made a quick decision. "Put a stand mike out there!" he ordered. It fell to Clark to tell the singer that her beloved pop-up mike wouldn't be making its dramatically choreographed appearance; instead, she'd be rising onto a stage where a mike stand already waited for her, in full view of the audience and directly between her fabulous gown and Margolis's camera. Clark, the son of TV personality and producer Dick Clark, broke the bad news only seconds before the song was due to begin.

Madonna did not take it well. *"Fucking asshole!"* she screamed at the messenger, launching into an astonishingly profane tirade, despite the fact that the area below the stage was also occupied by a group of children who'd be performing later in the show. Furious, she grabbed Clark around the neck and lifted him bodily off the ground, not relinquishing her grip until the trapdoor opened and she began to rise. The agitation was written on her face as she stumbled through the song she'd been sweating over for weeks. (The napping crew member was subsequently drummed out of the union.)

When Madonna returned to the Oscars six years later, she made it clear that she hadn't forgotten. "I don't have good feelings about this show," she said. Meanwhile, the staff went to great lengths to make her as comfortable as possible. Inside the Shrine, publicists Chuck Warn and Nicole Von Ruden did a sweep of the hall, throwing out most of the bystanders. One of those Von Ruden attempted to eject was Bryan Lourd, Madonna's agent and also Carrie Fisher's ex-boyfriend. When Von Ruden told Fisher about this later,

Fisher was delighted. "You don't wish your ex ill," she said, "but you don't necessarily wish them well, either." Seligman, meanwhile, caught a wire reporter sneaking into the rehearsal, and had the man escorted out of the building.

Using a regular handheld microphone rather than a pop-up, Madonna ran through her song once, then frowned. "I just want to make sure I'm not singing too loud," she said. The orchestra, still warming up, played a snippet of "Mission: Impossible." Madonna looked into the orchestra pit. "Is that a comment on this rehearsal?" she said.

As the rehearsal continued, a security guard spotted a French reporter sitting near the rear of the Shrine with a tape recorder. The woman insisted that she was not taping the rehearsal—but Warn discovered otherwise when he went to the security office and listened to her tape. Though the reporter had traveled from France to cover the show, her credentials were taken away.

For the next couple of takes, Madonna couldn't figure out if the sound was right. "Does it sound better in the house?" she asked, looking out at the sparse crowd. "Everybody who liked it, raise their hands." Then she looked over to where her daughter sat in the fifth row. "Did Baby Pumpkin like it?" she asked, then laughed. "She's sleeping. Oh, that's a good indication."

During a pause between takes, Horvitz's voice came over the P.A. system. "We're going to bring the dress onstage," he said.

"It's not a dress," Madonna snapped. "It's a pantsuit, *okay*?"

"Okay," Horvitz said.

An aide brought out the pantsuit Madonna planned to wear on the show, and the singer held it up for the director to see. "Notice how it picks up the art deco motif?" she said, pointing from the dress to Roy Christopher's set.

"I do," said Horvitz. "Thank you for being thematic."

"Would you like to see the shoes?"

"If you want to show me," said Horvitz. "They're thematic, too, aren't they?"

After take five, Madonna went into Horvitz's trailer to watch a playback. A few minutes later, she returned to the stage in her deco pantsuit. "Is there any way you guys can make me look taller?" she said.

"Sure," said Horvitz.

"I want to look taller and prettier," she added. Then she got serious. "As far as lighting goes, think drama. Drama, and reveal."

"Got it, babe."

Lourdes started crying. Madonna did the song again. Then the crew broke for dinner and Madonna went home. The schedule called for her to rehearse for another hour and a half after the break, but she didn't need it. At dinner, the sense of relief was palpable.

AT 7:15, as the dinner break neared its end, walkie-talkies sprang to life. "The Lord," a voice announced, "needs a towel."

Michael Flatley had arrived. The thirty-eight-year-old Irish American dancer had made his name in the original production of *Riverdance*, a high-tech, high-stepping exhibition of Irish dance set to an amped-up version of traditional Celtic music. After starring in the original production in Dublin and London in 1995, Flatley left the show in a dispute over credit. As the main male dancer in the show—and, he claimed, the originator of much of his own choreography—Flatley felt that he should be credited, and paid, as a cocreator of the show; when that credit and remuneration was denied, he created his own *Riverdance*-style extravaganza, which he modestly dubbed *The Lord of the Dance*.

The show had been a hit on its North American tour of sports arenas, and Herman—a big fan of *Riverdance*—booked him to give the Oscars a jolt of adrenaline. Flatley's reputation for being temperamental preceded him, and heads turned when he entered the Shrine with his troupe of three dozen young dancers. Wearing a black leather jacket with a high collar, black jeans, black boots, and a studded belt, Flatley didn't stand, he posed; he didn't walk, he strutted. "He's like Siegfried and Roy's cousin," whispered Von Ruden.

Flatley and company ran through their routine, while staffers watched and wondered what all this supercharged high-stepping and synchronized clog dancing had to do with film editing. To answer that entirely reasonable question, Fisher was drafted to write an intro saying that film editing, like dance, is all about rhythm. And Workman took Flatley's music and put together a film package that was ostensibly a tribute to the art of film editing—although of the hundreds of edits in the piece, all but four or five were made by Workman, not the original editors that were theoretically being saluted.

"They say it's a tribute to the editors, but it's really a tribute to *me* as an editor," said Workman as he stood in the aisle and watched Flatley rehearse. His film played on a screen behind Flatley, while Horvitz cut between the film and the live performance. While the theater audience saw it all, achieving the right balance for viewers proved to be more difficult. Some of Workman's more ingenious cuts were lost when the camera focused on Flatley and crew, while too much emphasis on the film distracted from the live performance. After one rehearsal, Flatley's agent complained to Cates that his client was being overshadowed by the film. Later, Workman watched on a monitor and was dissatisfied as well. "They're not showing enough of the screens," he said.

After the final run-through, Cates spoke on the phone to Horvitz, then approached Workman in the aisle. "It's great," he said. "And we'll put more screen in."

"Good," said Workman. "Because I was just complaining about that."

"It's a tricky balance," said Cates, "but Lou says he'll get it. And I was worried that our friend would complain about being upstaged, but he was fine."

STANDING IN the center orchestra section of the Shrine, Seligman frowned as he looked at a group of guests sitting behind the ABC table. "Folks, you have to clear the hall for the next half hour," he yelled to them, then turned to one of the two security guards who were helping him make a sweep of the room. "If they're not working a camera," he said, "they can't be here. We've got to get this room cleared."

Working his twentieth Academy Awards, Seligman usually had weightier matters to contend with than throwing people out of the auditorium. But Cates wanted this show to include several big surprises, from Crystal's opening film to the Lord of the Dance. For weeks, the staff had refused to confirm any information about many of the show's bookings, occasionally just lying outright—or, more often, having the press reps lie. The previous day, flamboyant basketball star Dennis Rodman had spoiled one surprise when he told a Chicago sports columnist that he was appearing in a *Brady Bunch*–themed segment of Crystal's film; afterward, everyone was on edge, worried about further leaks. "It's a difficult year," said Seligman as he watched guards attempt to clear the Shrine. "We've got a lot of secrets this year. That makes it hard."

At 10:30 a.m. on Saturday, two days before the Oscar show, the biggest secret was standing behind the theater. Most of the show's production schedules and rundowns made no mention of him; the few that did called him "Scott Murray." Some of the crew, who weren't supposed to speak his name (or even know it, really), dubbed him "Piano Boy"—or, less charitably, "Wacko." A thin, gray-haired man with a nervous manner and a penchant for hugging anyone with whom he was familiar, he was David Helfgott, the Australian pianist whose struggle with mental illness was the subject of *Shine*. Since he was in town for a recital at the nearby Dorothy Chandler Pavilion the night after the Oscars, his presence at the Shrine had been widely rumored—and just as widely denied by Cates.

The producer knew this booking was a gamble: as *Shine* made clear, Helfgott had frozen or fallen apart in public situations before. In recent years, though, he had clearly become more reliable and better able to cope with the pressures of performance. Still, his brief concert tour, designed to capitalize on his new visibility via the movie, drew scathing reviews from many music critics who felt he was at best an uncertain, amateurish pianist, and at worst the victim of exploitation.

The staff knew that Helfgott had to be handled with kid gloves. No stand-ins were allowed to remain in the theater, while the tables usually populated with network executives and members of the set design team were likewise cleared. Cates and Herman remained out back, chatting with Helfgott and his wife and not asking the pianist to come to the stage until they were certain everything was ready. When it was, they led Helfgott into the wings, and then Herman brought the pianist's wife and some friends into the hall. The few people who remained were told to sit toward the back of the floor, and to keep their heads low.

At 10:50 a.m., a stage manager walked to the microphone. "Ladies and gentlemen," she said, "please welcome Scott Murray." Without looking at the tiny audience, Helfgott walked onstage, ran up the few steps to his piano, bounced up and down on his heels a couple of times, then sat down. Immediately, he launched into a nervous, kinetic version of Rimsky-Korsakov's "The Flight of the Bumblebee." When it ended he stood up, bowed, then immediately sat down and played the piece again. Horvitz, who normally spoke to performers over the P.A. system, kept quiet.

When Helfgott finished, Cates left his seat and walked onto the stage shouting, "Bravo!" He showed Helfgott where to stand for his bows. Helfgott hugged Seligman once, then twice. Then he hugged Cates. By 10:55, he was gone.

At noon the next day, Cates, Horvitz, and Arthur Hiller appeared at a press conference outside the Shrine. At the end of the short Q&A session, they asked for questions from the fans who'd already begun to gather in the bleachers. "Is David Helfgott going to perform?" one woman yelled.

"No," said Cates. "Not unless you know something I don't know."

AFTER THE PRESS CONFERENCE, stars began arriving in earnest: Mel Gibson, then Nicolas Cage, then Jim Carrey. Publicist Pat Kingsley lurked by the back door, keeping an eye out for clients. "So," Tommy Lee Jones asked her, "have you seen your entire client list come through here today?"

"Not quite," she said. "But we have eighteen presenters."

In the audience, George Plimpton watched. Interviewing staff members for a piece in *The New Yorker*, he asked a lot of questions about security and seating arrangements; the writer was especially interested in the seat-fillers. "Have there been any interlopers who've gotten onto the stage since the streaker?" he asked intently. Sitting in a sixth-row seat and watching stand-ins take the stage, accept phony Oscar statues, and make mock acceptance speeches, the writer confided that his intentions were not entirely honorable.

"My goal is to get onstage during the show," said Plimpton, who made his name with such participatory stunts as playing quarterback for the Detroit Lions and getting in the ring with boxer Archie Moore. "They're getting me a seat for the show, and I think my best chance will come if *When We Were Kings* wins. I'm in the movie, so they probably won't stop me if I run up to the stage quickly."

Courtney Love arrived in midafternoon. After having *Larry Flynt* director Milos Forman make several calls to Cates and Fisher on her behalf, she brought along an Emily Dickinson poem that she wanted to read in lieu of her speech. "Then sunrise kissed my chrysalis / And I stood up and lived," read the final couplet.

"I told her that you can't say 'kissed my chrysalis,' " Fisher said to the other writers at the production table. "People will think it's sexual. They'll think it's *clitoris*."

Bruce Vilanch nodded. "It's a little vaginal," he said, "coming from a woman who named her band Hole."

In the Shrine lobby, the Pinkerton guards who were providing Oscar security grabbed a man in a tuxedo and held him in an alcove near the Governors Ball until Academy officials could arrive. The man, Scott Kerman, had been spotted and recognized outside the Shrine; he was the author of a book called *No Ticket? No Problem! How to Sneak into Sporting Events and Concerts*. The Pinkertons tailed Kerman until he trespassed, then arrested him. As he was handcuffed and led away, Kerman spotted Plimpton, who'd heard about the gate-crasher and had come to investigate. "Hey, George, you're my hero!" yelled Kerman.

A police officer immediately went to Cates's trailer to tell him of the arrest. Sigourney Weaver was sitting in the outer lobby with Julie Faust. Weaver had her hair piled haphazardly atop her head, and was dressed casually in a brown, long-sleeved T-shirt and tan pants; Faust, on the other hand, was wearing a more tailored blouse and slacks. The cop looked at the two women, took Weaver for the receptionist, and asked, "Is he busy?"

Without waiting for a reply, he headed down the hall toward Cates's desk. "Gil," yelled Weaver, "there's a guy coming to see you. And he's got a gun."

Back inside the Shrine, Plimpton was a little shaken. "The guy said I was his hero," he said, shaking his head. "Maybe this isn't such a good idea."

A few minutes later, Plimpton asked stage manager Garry Hood if he could take the place of a stand-in and accept a dummy Oscar during rehearsal. Hood agreed. When *Hamlet* won the rehearsal Oscar for best score, the writer loped to the stage and cradled the phony statue in his hands. "I'd like to thank Mr. Shakespeare and Mrs. Shakespeare," he said. "All of us down at the Old Globe Theatre are very happy."

"SO," SAID BILLY CRYSTAL, "I'm off to the Governors Ball. It's my eighth one. I've seen more of the Governors Balls than Paula Jones." To the laughter of the few staffers in the hall, he shrugged. "Should I do it?"

The off-color joke wasn't on the TelePrompTer—but as the Saturday evening dress rehearsal began, Crystal was mostly ignoring the actual jokes he'd planned for his monologue. He also withheld his opening film, lest anyone leak its contents to a media outlet with a late deadline. The host did perform his typical opening number "It's a Wonderful Night for Oscar," a medley of song parodies keyed to the best-picture nominees.

Crystal ran through the medley twice, stopping to ask Conti to increase the tempo. "All right," he said after the second take. "Close enough." Then staffers and stand-ins were let back into the hall for the full rehearsal— where, over the next four hours, it was revealed that Madonna had acquired a new outfit since the previous day (a gown rather than a pantsuit), that Piano Boy would sit out this run-through, and that Natalie Cole, who was booked to perform "I Finally Found Someone" when Streisand declined, was sick and couldn't make it. Céline Dion sat in the audience and watched the entire rehearsal, even after performing her song "Because You Loved Me."

The rehearsal ended around 11 p.m. "Thank you very much, everybody," said Horvitz. Most of the staff went home. Dion stayed, as did trumpeter Arturo Sandoval. A music stand was brought to the stage.

Cates went to Horvitz's trailer to go over a few notes on the rehearsal. Then he made a quick stop in his own trailer, where he sighed and explained that the evening was not over yet.

"Natalie Cole is not going to be on the show," he said, shaking his head. "She's been sick all week, and she canceled last night." Initially, he added, he thought about not even looking for a replacement. "I considered dropping the song entirely, but that has ramifications. I looked to see how the song is used in the movie, because I thought I might be able to just play the recording and show a clip. I thought about calling Bonnie Raitt. But I went home without really deciding what I was going to do."

Sunday morning, he added, he got a call from Céline Dion's manager, Rene Angelil. "He said, 'We heard about your problem. And if you need us, we'll help you.' So Céline's going to do Barbra's song."

The last-minute substitution, though, was not without complications. Not only did Angelil hear that Cole had canceled, but so did Marty Erlichman, Streisand's manager. Erlichman phoned Cates as well, claiming that he was calling without Streisand's knowledge. Some who heard about the call were convinced that Streisand was listening in on another line when Erlichman put a question to Cates: If Barbra was willing to do the song after all, would the show be able to clear enough rehearsal time for her? Every minute of rehearsal had long since been allotted, so Cates told an incredulous Erlichman that he'd have to pass. He was going to stick with Dion, the lesser star but by far the lower-maintenance performer.

"This is costing us a fortune," said Cates as he slid into his seat at the production table in the Shrine just after midnight. Less than eighteen hours before the Oscar show would begin, Dion sat on a stool, looked down at the sheet music, and sang "I Finally Found Someone" for the first time. After Dion belted out the song, there were whoops from the staffers, as well as a shout of "*Barbra who?*" Dion's rehearsal was quick and painless; Cates gave her a hug, and she left.

Then Cates huddled with Susan Futterman, who had a couple of problems with the show, beginning with Jim Carrey's use of the word *pissed*. "It has real implications," Futterman said. "It means I have to go to them and say I'm changing the rating. *Bugged* is fine. *Teed off* is fine. *Pissed*, I have to go to a TV-PG14."

"We'll look at it, Susan," Cates said. "I don't see where it's that bad, but we'll look at it."

"The other problem," she continued, "is Jim talking out of his butt. That puts it on a different level. It changes what we'll have to say in the future to Whoopi, to David . . . They'll think, if this guy can cross the line, why can't we?"

Futterman and Cates hashed it out for a few minutes longer. "Gil," she said, "I don't want to put the show on a delay, but . . ."

"Susan, that's bullshit and you know it."

When Cates left the Shrine after 1 a.m., nothing was resolved with Futterman.

"OKAY, SUSAN," said Cates the next morning. "*Pissed* is out. But Jim Carrey's ass is none of your business."

It had been a busy morning. After her offer to sing "I Finally Found Someone" was declined, Barbra Streisand suddenly decided that she ought to attend the Academy Awards after all. The Academy gave her Natalie Cole's tickets.

Michael Flatley, meanwhile, asked for more credentials so that he could station a few extra staffers in the wings to attend to his needs during his number. He was granted one wardrobe person to hand him his jacket.

The producer's office had also received a flurry of phone calls from Al Pacino's publicist, Pat Kingsley, and his girlfriend, actress Beverly D'Angelo. Pacino, who hadn't come to rehearsal, wanted to make sure that it was okay to cut his lines to the bare minimum and simply announce, "The nominees for best picture are . . ." Cates okayed the change.

In the morning, David Helfgott's record company, BMG, put out a press release announcing that he was on the show. "Shit," said Cates when he found out.

At noon, the final rehearsal began. For the first time, Crystal showed his opening film, which placed him in scenes from many of the nominated movies. Its climax came when the pilot of a crashing airplane from *The English Patient* turned out to be a kamikaze David Letterman, shouting out hosting advice to Crystal as he went down in flames: "Introduce Uma to Oprah, and Oprah to Uma, and then Uma to Oprah, and then do it again! Uma, Oprah, Oprah, Uma . . . !"

In the audience, Vilanch laughed. "Letterman really wanted to do this," he said. "He kept saying, 'I want to be the dumb guy.' "

At the end of the movie, Crystal made his entrance by jumping through a slit in the big movie screen that sat center stage. But as he jumped through the screen, Crystal tripped and fell, hard, on his elbow. He lay on the ground for a few minutes, then climbed to his feet. "It's too high," he said, wincing. "Damn, it's so high."

Garry Hood approached the host. "Do you need a doctor?"

"No," said Crystal, in obvious pain. "Let's get through this." He turned to the sparse audience. "Make me feel better," he said. They responded with big cheers. "A funny thing happened to me on the way to the theater," Crystal said to open his monologue. "I broke my elbow." He got through his song, holding his elbow at an awkward angle; during the first break, his arm was examined by a doctor, wrapped, and put on ice. A stand-in read Crystal's lines for the rest of the rehearsal.

In the command truck two hours later, Horvitz watched as the stage crew failed to reset the stage in time for Céline Dion's second song. The director put his head in his hands. "We're going down in flames here," he said. "Are we gonna make it tonight?"

"Yes," said an assistant director.

Horvitz sighed, then feigned collapsing on his desk. "They never told me it would be this many hours," he said.

Seligman, sitting in a row of chairs behind the director, leaned forward. "*I* told you," he said.

At 3:00, the rehearsal ended. Half an hour later, as the crew ate lunch, Crystal walked onstage in sweats and sneakers. He stood with his hands in his pockets, looking out at the seats for a long time. Then he ran through some of his lines and some of his opening song. Unmiked, he was almost inaudible. A handful of workers remained in the Shrine, but nobody paid him any attention.

6:00 P.M. PACIFIC DAYLIGHT TIME: *"Live, from Los Angeles, California, the 69th annual Academy Awards."*

Barbra Streisand, who had arrived just before show time and stopped along the red carpet to tell a couple of interviewers how the show had turned down her offer to perform, entered the Shrine at 6:04. The usher stationed at a door that led from the lobby into the theater said she couldn't go in until the first commercial break. She and James Brolin waited in the lobby surrounded by an entourage of seventeen, most of them men in dark suits.

After a welcoming speech from Arthur Hiller, Crystal's movie played on a large screen that covered the center of the stage. The audience cheered to find the host speaking to Yoda in *The Empire Strikes Back* (then in rerelease in theaters), then discussing his return to the Oscars with Tom Cruise's Jerry Maguire, as well as with characters from *Secrets & Lies*, *Shine*, *Fargo*, and *The English Patient*. When Letterman appeared piloting the doomed airplane from that last film, the crowd inside the Shrine erupted. Onstage, Crystal stood in the darkness behind the screen, listening to the screams of laughter. How, he thought, will I ever be able to follow *this*?

In his ensuing monologue, he quickly summed up the year in Hollywood. "New faces among the nominees," he said. "*Really* new faces. Who *are* you people?"

During Crystal's monologue and opening song, six cameramen roamed the audience, aware of what jokes were coming next and ready to focus on the stars mentioned in those jokes. When Crystal mentioned Billy Bob Thornton, the picture cut to him. When the next line mentioned Edward Norton, Horvitz cut to Norton. When Lauren Bacall was mentioned, though, the camera stayed on Crystal, because a seat-filler was occupying Bacall's seat. The actress had also arrived late and was standing in the lobby having a lively conversation with Streisand.

The first award, best supporting actor, went to Cuba Gooding, Jr., for *Jerry Maguire*. Gooding leapt to his feet, rushed to the stage, talked for about twenty-five seconds, then stopped to take a breath. In the truck, Cates and Horvitz thought Gooding was finished. "Go to music," said Cates. "Music!" shouted Horvitz. Conti's orchestra started playing.

But Gooding wasn't finished and wasn't about to relinquish his moment in the spotlight. As the music got louder, so did his speech; he thanked everybody, he danced, and the crowd roared. In the wings just off the stage, Sandra Bullock laughed, then clapped her hands, then threw her head back and whooped. In the trailer, Horvitz and Cates laughed and applauded as well; the moment may have made them look trigger-happy, but they knew it made for entertaining TV.

Thirty-five minutes into the show, Crystal introduced Madonna. "I think it's really classy," he said, "that Madonna showed up to sing her song." In the control trailer, Horvitz cut to camera nine. It showed an unsmiling Streisand.

This time, Madonna's mike worked, though her voice still sounded tentative. As the singer made her way back to her dressing room after her performance, Courtney Love presented the award for makeup. "The makeup artists have the power to transform us," she said, "from the cocoon of the dressing room to the butterfly of the film." There was nothing in her speech about substance abuse, and nothing about the sunrise kissing anybody's chrysalis. The winners were Rick Baker and David Leroy Anderson for *The Nutty Professor*, but Love forgot to read Baker's name. Leaving the stage with the winners, she apologized. "I fucked up," she said as they came into the wings. "I'm so fucking sorry, you guys." Then she brightened. "Well, it was just human error," she said. "It wasn't like adultery or something."

A few minutes later, Carrie Fisher grabbed Love, who was standing outside the green room. "C'mon," Fisher said. "We gotta go." As they walked toward the artists' entrance, Fisher turned to Love. "You were great," she said. "You were great." New comrades-in-arms at the end of a tough couple of days, the two women spent the next twenty minutes outside the Shrine, smoking cigarettes and chatting animatedly.

At the one-hour mark, Kevin Spacey presented the Oscar for best supporting actress. Though the seventy-two-year-old Lauren Bacall was considered a near shoo-in, she lost to an actress thirty-nine years her junior: Juliette Binoche, from *The English Patient*. It was not clear whether the win was part of an *English Patient* groundswell (the film having already won in the art direction and costume design categories) or another symptom of the Academy's apparent distaste for all things Streisand-related; Binoche, though, was as surprised as everyone else in the room. "I thought Lauren was going to get it," she said, seemingly dazed. "And I think she deserves it."

Shortly after "That Thing You Do!"—which despite Sallid's best efforts came across as downright dumb—Chris Farley and David Spade took the stage. "Maybe there was some kind of a mix-up," said Spade, "and right now Jeremy Irons is performing at the Improv and Daniel Day-Lewis is at a fat camp in Hilton Head."

Behind the Shrine, Fisher and Love continued to smoke, chat, and ignore the rest of the event. Their tête-à-tête broke up just about the time that Céline Dion sang "I Finally Found Someone," some ninety minutes into the show. Streisand was not in her seat, so Horvitz's camera could not capture her reaction. The next day, her publicist explained that Streisand had left her seat to go to the bathroom, not knowing that her song was up next. But six minutes later, when *Breathing Lessons* won the award for best documentary short and director Jessica Wu commented, "You know you've entered new territory when you realize your outfit cost more than your film," Streisand was standing in a darkened hallway at the back of the Shrine, watching from a vantage point well out of camera range. If the ushers in the lobby were following orders (the way they were when Streisand arrived late at the Shrine), Streisand could not be in the hallway watching Wu unless she had also been there watching Dion.

Two minutes later, *When We Were Kings* won the award for best documentary feature. Muhammad Ali and George Foreman both took the stage. George Plimpton did not.

During the ensuing commercial, Steve Martin left his front-row seat and went back a few rows to where Juliette Binoche sat. "I just wanted to say congratulations," he told her.

A couple of rows farther up, a teenage boy approached Kurt Russell. "I don't know if you remember me," he said. "I was in *Captain Ron*."

"Sure," said Russell. "How are you doing?"

As the show neared its third hour, Nicole Kidman took the stage and donned a pair of glasses. "Editing provides the rhythm and pace of the movie," she read. "In many ways, it's like the dance, moving back and forth at a particular pace, always pushing deftly and percussively toward its climax." Her words served to introduce Michael Flatley, who ripped across the stage sporting red and black leather, and for the second half of the number showing off a bare, oiled chest. At one point, Flatley whacked into a cameraman who didn't get out of the way quickly enough.

A short time later, David Helfgott was introduced, for the first time, by his real name. Sitting behind Horvitz in the control trailer, Cates suddenly got to his feet and pointed at the screen, where flashes of light were briefly washing out Horvitz's carefully composed shots. Immediately, Cates's security guard got on a walkie-talkie to a guard stationed inside the Shrine. "There's still more flash cameras," he said. "It's affecting what's going out, and Gil's getting upset. They're on the main floor. See if you can find them. And try to get the names."

When Helfgott finished, Horvitz let out a sigh and sank back in his chair. "Good stuff," he said quietly. "Good stuff."

In the last half hour of the show, the big awards piled up. First, Frances McDormand won the best-actress Oscar for *Fargo*. On her way to the press tent, McDormand stopped and used a cell phone to call her son. "Did you see it?" she said excitedly. "Here's Daddy!" She handed the phone to Joel Coen.

A few minutes later, Susan Sarandon presented the best-actor award to Geoffrey Rush for *Shine*. Then Pacino walked to the stage. "Bye," shouted Sarandon.

"We've come to the part of the show, now, that you've all been waiting for," Pacino said onstage. "It's the halfway mark." The audience laughed. "Thought I'd try that," he said with a slight grin.

Not having rehearsed (and apparently not having paid much attention to the show, during which *The English Patient* had already won eight awards and producer Saul Zaentz had been thanked several times, in addition to winning the Irving Thalberg award), Pacino mispronounced Zaentz's name. The insult was eased somewhat when he gave the producer the Academy Award for best picture.

When Zaentz finished his speech, Crystal said good night. In the nearby Governors Ball, the band was already playing. Pacino walked off the stage, out the back door, down the red carpet, and into a waiting limo. Sarandon and Robbins followed, as did Streisand and Brolin.

On the stage, the crew gathered and poured champagne into plastic glasses. At the front of the stage, an agitated woman approached a security guard. "My friend had his camera taken away," she complained. "Where can we go to get it back?"

"They'll have it tomorrow at the Academy," the guard explained. "He can pick it up then, after they've destroyed the film."

IN THE YEAR of the independent film, the big winners were the indie movie that looked most like a regular studio production, and the indie company owned by Disney. Miramax wound up with a dozen Oscars, including the nine for *The English Patient* and a best adapted screenplay win for Billy Bob Thornton for *Sling Blade*. The company celebrated with such fervor that its post-Oscar party, held at the trendy Sky Bar inside the Mondrian Hotel in West Hollywood, was temporarily shut down by the Los Angeles County Fire Department.

For the most part, reaction to the return of Billy Crystal was positive, with his opening film (and particularly David Letterman's cameo) singled out for particular praise. In fact, the kudos for Crystal's performance were for the most part enough to obscure the more questionable elements of the broadcast, from the lamentable attempts to play younger and more mainstream (Farley and Spade, Beavis and Butthead) to the mind-boggling production numbers from the Lord of the Dance and the "That Thing You Do!" crew.

When the ratings came in, though, the lesson was clear: *Saturday Night Live* comics, animated MTV characters, and even a best-actor nomination for Tom Cruise were not enough to get people to watch an Oscar show if they didn't care about or know about the movies in contention. As the network, the Academy, and the production team had feared all along, viewership took another hit, falling 10 percent from the previous year. The average rating, 27.4, was the second lowest in Oscar history, besting only the 1986 show at which another pretty, languid epic, *Out of Africa*, steamrollered *The Color Purple*.

Barbara Walters's Oscar special also took a hit, drawing the worst ratings ever for her annual round of interviews with select nominees. On the other hand, E! Entertainment Television garnered the best ratings in its seven-year history for its two-hour preshow broadcast, which starred Joan Rivers and her daughter, Melissa.

Scott Kerman, the gate-crasher who'd been arrested trying to sneak into rehearsals, sued Pinkerton and the Academy, claiming that the organizations had subjected him to ridicule. Over the next two and a half years, all of Kerman's claims were thrown out of court.

After the show, the Academy heard complaints about the Shrine Auditorium from many members. The main problem wasn't the traffic jam on surrounding streets—the city had waived $100,000 in traffic-control costs to keep things moving—but rather traffic inside the building, specifically the logjam that developed as some guests tried to make their way from the theater into the Shrine Exhibition Hall for the Governors Ball, and others tried to exit the theater.

Publicly, the Academy remained committed to keeping the show at the Shrine and the Dorothy Chandler Pavilion. But Academy officials knew that the Shrine was less elegant than they'd like, while the Chandler, which served as home to the Los Angeles Philharmonic and the L.A. Opera, was too busy to give them an ideal amount of rehearsal time. They quietly considered alternate venues, though all seemed to have insurmountable problems, being too old (the Pantages Theatre in Hollywood), too big (a new hockey and basketball arena being built in downtown Los Angeles), or too far away from the home of the movie business (several new theaters and arenas in Orange County, an hour south of L.A.).

Soon after the show, though, Bruce Davis was approached by David Malmuth, senior vice president of the TrizecHahn development firm. The company, which had helped with the revitalization (and, some said, Disney-fication) of New York City's Forty-second Street, was working on an upscale shopping and entertainment center in the heart of Hollywood. Located at the intersection of Hollywood Boulevard and Highland Avenue, it was next to the old Grauman's Chinese Theatre and a block away from the Hollywood Roosevelt Hotel, where the first Oscar ceremony had taken place in 1929.

Malmuth had heard that the Academy was interested in opening a film museum, an idea that had indeed been discussed by the board. But Davis had other ideas. "I suggested that if he really wanted an Academy presence, what he needed to do was build a theater large enough to hold the Oscars," said Davis. "He went away for about two weeks and came back with plans that were suspiciously far along." By August, Academy president Robert Rehme had appointed a committee of governors to study TrizecHahn's proposal.

5
≡

Size Matters

The 70th Academy Awards

THE FIRST FEW TIMES he designed sets for the Shrine Auditorium, the theater scared Roy Christopher. It was simply too big, with a stage nearly a
hundred feet wide and a proscenium arch that rose a good eighty feet above
it. So when he designed Academy Awards shows at the Shrine in 1995 and
1997, Christopher used tricks to reduce the size of the stage and make things
more manageable. Once he'd used vertical panels to focus attention inward,
and once he'd created a smaller inner proscenium modeled after the iris of
a camera.

But in March 1998, Christopher stood about five rows deep in the orchestra section of the Shrine and looked at the first stage he'd ever designed
that used all of the theater. In fact, his set *embraced* its size, with enormous
open spaces broken only by huge Oscar statues enclosed in shimmering
wraparound cones. Gold mosaic and silver leaf adorned most surfaces,
while drapes of crushed velvet hung from rods high above the stage. Across
the entire back expanse of the stage, a white, vaguely nautical riser had
room for the fifty-piece Academy Awards orchestra, a group usually tucked

out of sight in the orchestra pit. The overall effect was bold, flashy, over-sized. Titanic, you might say.

"I wanted something big and glamorous," said Christopher as he watched stagehands struggle with the enormous pieces of the set. "It just didn't seem like the year for modesty and understatement."

In 1998, Christopher's attitude made sense. Even more so than in previous years, this one had to be big. For starters, it was an anniversary show, Oscar's seventieth, always a reason to go bigger and bolder than usual.

Then there were the nominations. The previous year, ratings had suffered when the Academy membership nominated a lineup of independent movies Middle America didn't know much about. But the seventieth Oscars were a completely different story. Among the actors nominated were big movie stars like Jack Nicholson, Robin Williams, and Anthony Hopkins, young heartthrobs like Matt Damon and Ben Affleck, crossover TV stars like Helen Hunt. The best-picture nominees included the $100 million–plus hits *As Good as It Gets* and *Good Will Hunting*. The token "little movie" nominated for best picture, *The Full Monty*, also happened to be the biggest-grossing British movie in history. And nearly overshadowing them all, with fourteen nominations, was The Biggest Movie Ever Made, director James Cameron's *Titanic*, well on its way to a staggering gross on the high side of $600 million.

As Christopher said, it was not a year for understatement. Producer Gil Cates once again signed up Billy Crystal, the consensus choice for the show's ideal host. Then, to commemorate the anniversary, he and Danette Herman put in calls to movie stars and icons, legends and up-and-comers. In addition to assembling the usual lineup of presenters and musical performers (the latter group including a couple of masters of stentorian musical overstatement, Céline Dion and Michael Bolton), they sent letters to every living person who'd ever received an Oscar for acting, inviting them to appear onstage.

With Christopher watching from the audience, stagehands set the scenery so that director Lou Horvitz could try out a dramatic tracking shot. Three huge panels, a good twenty feet on each side, were pushed to the center of the stage; in the center of each panel was a cutout in the shape of an Oscar statuette. Interior edges of the cutouts glistened in gold leaf. A stand-in emerged from the darkness at the rear of the stage, walking through the panels and toward the audience, while a handheld camera followed her as she moved. Lighting designer Robert Dickinson's stark backlighting cast dramatic shadows around her.

It made for one hell of an entrance, but it wasn't even for one of the half dozen biggest awards of the night. The setup was for Sharon Stone, who'd be presenting the Oscar for best foreign film. Presenters for the awards that would follow Stone—best actor and actress, best director, best picture— were getting bigger, grander entrances.

At the production table a few rows behind Christopher, writer Bruce Vilanch took a seat, looked at the stage, and quickly punctured a little of the afternoon's pomposity. "Look!" he cried, pointing at the twenty-foot statues wrapped in glittering mesh. "It's Oscar in a pita! Oscar wrap!"

TITANIC HAD THE INSIDE TRACK; that much was a given. Sure, some people hated it, thought it was too big, too corny, too dumb. But those opinions were all but drowned out as the *Titanic* juggernaut rolled on. The movie monopolized the number-one spot at the box office through January, through February, into March. It set a new Golden Globes record with eight nominations, and won four.

Other films, meanwhile, jockeyed to see who could do the best job of being the thinking voter's alternative. *The Full Monty* certainly qualified: it was low budget, small scale, thoroughly British, the charming tale of a group of working-class blokes who tried to improve their dismal financial situation by putting on a strip show. *L.A. Confidential*, director Curtis Hanson's dense, smart remake of the grim James Ellroy novel about corruption and moral decay in the Los Angeles of the 1940s, was a strong alternative as well: it was tough where *Titanic* was soft, cynical where Cameron's epic was sentimental. It was possibly too tough and too cynical to win over enough Academy voters, but it nonetheless wound up as the most favorably reviewed movie of the year. And *Good Will Hunting* was Miramax's big entry, which meant it'd be foolish to count out the story of Boston friends, one a troubled math genius mentored by a kindly shrink played by Robin Williams. With *Good Will Hunting*, Miramax also had a good behind-the-cameras story to run with: the movie's writers were a pair of struggling actors, Matt Damon and Ben Affleck, who'd written the script to create the kind of good parts nobody else would give them, and who stubbornly refused to sell the screenplay unless they could play the lead roles.

"If Jim Cameron is saying size matters, then we at Miramax are saying less is more," Harvey Weinstein insisted in an interview with CNN. A couple of weeks after he made the comment, *Titanic* broke a record by holding the number-one spot for the fourteenth consecutive weekend.

"LOU?" said Billy Crystal nervously. "As soon as the curtain opens, bring the ship down. *As soon as it opens.*"

Crystal was standing near the back of the Shrine stage, gripping the railing of a small platform attached to a hydraulic lift. With *Titanic* so dominant, the host's all-important entrance clearly had to be themed to Cameron's film—so with the help of the lift and a drape painted to look like the prow of an ocean liner, Crystal planned to make his initial appearance atop a mock ship some twenty feet above the stage. The lift would descend and the ship would appear to sink, whereupon Crystal would hop off the boat and onto the stage.

That, at least, was the plan. At the moment, though, three days before the Oscar show, the plan was complicated by the fact that the host was terrified of starting his entrance from such a lofty perch.

"It's *really* high," he said, stepping away from the lift and eyeing it nervously. "Oy."

On the more familiar terra firma of the stage, though, Crystal relaxed and began to run through his traditional medley, "It's a Wonderful Night for Oscar," in which five familiar songs were given new lyrics that poked fun at the five best-picture nominees. Crystal had done this number every year he'd hosted the Oscars; it was his replacement, he said when he introduced it for the first time in 1990, for "that big, terrible number that usually opens the Oscars."

According to Marc Shaiman, who had provided musical accompaniment for Crystal since the comic's days on *Saturday Night Live*, the routine began with a simple question. "We just thought, how can we make fun of those

Oscar production numbers?" said Shaiman. "We decided to stick lyrics about the movies into songs that were never meant to be like that. And since then, it's just become a chance to do an entertaining musical number that has that cushion of irony so needed for the modern world to accept anything musical."

Over the years, Shaiman and Crystal had encountered a few problems getting permission to parody certain songs, though that often had more to do with the movies involved than the songs themselves. The 1991 Oliver Stone film *JFK*, for instance, set off alarms with the publishers who held the rights to music from *Fiddler on the Roof*; they didn't want that musical turned into *Gunman on the Knoll*, with "Tradition" recast as "Suspicion." Crystal's second choice, also vetoed, was to adapt "Trouble" from *The Music Man*: "You've got trouble my friends, right here in Dallas / With a capital D and that rhymes with G and that stands for Gun . . ." Crystal finally got an okay from the publishers of "Three Coins in the Fountain," which became "Three Shots in the Plaza."

Eventually, Crystal and Shaiman learned that they got better results if they cut the lawyers out of the equation and made the appeals themselves. "If Billy Crystal's on the phone," said Shaiman, "people are a little star-struck." In 1998, their medley kicked off with a *Titanic* spoof delivered to the tune of the theme from *Gilligan's Island*. It also included a riff on the relationships in *As Good as It Gets* set to "Let's Call the Whole Thing Off," a parody of "Night and Day" retitled "Matt and Ben," "Fascinating Rhythm" recast as "L.A. Confidential," and a salute to *The Full Monty* à la "Hello Dolly."

Wearing blue jeans with a black shirt and black blazer, Crystal first ran through the medley a capella and unmiked, and then to the accompaniment of Conti's orchestra. As he sang, he eyed the seat cards that showed where the stars would be sitting Oscar night. He didn't like what he saw. Jack Nicholson and Helen Hunt were situated in the first row toward the left side of the orchestra section, and Crystal wanted to come into the audience to sing part of his song directly to Nicholson. But in the medley, "As Good as It Gets" was followed by "Matt and Ben," and Damon and Affleck were on the far side of the Shrine. Crystal wanted to be standing in front of them when he sang, "Your script was tight / And damnit, so are your buns"—but given the size of the theater, that required a long dash that might leave him winded.

"Is there any way to move them closer together?" he asked. "I don't think I can get across there fast enough."

"No," explained Horvitz over the P.A. "We're locked into a nomination situation. It would have serious ramifications."

ONE OF THE INDISPENSABLE ELEMENTS of each Oscar show was the montage alternately called In Memoriam, the Late Show, or the Necrology. A roundup of about two dozen notables who'd died since the previous year's show, the montage always drew the attention of staffers the first few times it was shown during rehearsals; as it ran, crew members would invariably murmur, "I didn't know *he* died" as faces appeared on-screen.

Jimmy Stewart, Lloyd Bridges, Red Skelton, Toshiro Mifune, Chris Farley, J. T. Walsh, and Robert Mitchum were among those featured in the In Memoriam package when it screened inside the Shrine on the Friday before the show. "They had to deal with some *big* controversies this year," said Mike Shapiro, who put the montage together. "If people's family members or friends aren't included, they get very upset."

The segment hadn't always been so popular. "When I first told Gil I wanted to do the clip about people who'd died," said Shapiro, "his eyes rolled back in his head and he said, 'Oh, Christ, we tried that and it was deadly.' I told him I wanted to do it not like an obituary, but more as a celebration, and a sentimental opportunity to say good-bye to these people we've spent our whole lives with." Cates remembers the conversation differently, and says he fought for the In Memoriam piece from the beginning; both men agree that the producer had a tough job selling the concept to a reluctant Bruce Davis at the Academy, and then to a reluctant John Hamlin at ABC.

Shapiro worked at assembling clips of stars and other film notables looking their best, and setting them to a piece of music with, he said, "the right balance of celebration and sentiment." Over the years, he'd used film scores from composers like Alan Silvestri and James Horner; movies about dogs, it turned out, were often appropriate. "Some of the best stuff," he said with a laugh, "comes from scenes where the dog is finally reunited with his family and all the puppies."

The sequence had become a popular part of the Oscar show, but also a contentious one. "It is a beloved segment, but I would much prefer we didn't do it," said Bruce Davis, who often dealt with the calls from friends and relatives demanding to know why their dear departed wasn't included. "It's awful, just awful," he said. "We can only do about two dozen people, and when you sit down to do the list, the last fifteen or twenty cuts you make are people with substantial careers. You just feel like *shit* for days afterwards. And there is *nothing* you can say to somebody's wife or daughter about why they didn't make it into the sequence."

Davis shook his head as he thought about the misery the sequence caused him. "I have had a person, in midsummer, call me from the hospital to say, 'My father just died, what do I do to get him in the sequence?' " he said. "This was not a person I'd ever heard of, and I think I'm fairly knowledgeable about the industry."

Davis still had to write conciliatory letters to some whose loved ones hadn't made the cut, but as rehearsal moved on that duty wasn't exactly pressing. Instead, the biggest fuss of the afternoon was for someone known, in virtually all the production materials, as Special Guest. A list of guidelines had been issued detailing the precautions that needed to be taken when the guest appeared: "No eating or drinking around Special Guest, because he will want to share . . . Women should not wear perfume around Special Guest . . . Women on their menses should take care around Special Guest . . ."

As a joke, Vilanch rewrote the guidelines using "Miss Gabor" in place of every mention of "Special Guest." But Cates's big surprise turned out to be Bart the Bear, the fourteen-hundred-pound ursine star of the recent film *The Edge*, as well as ten other movies. Although Bart's favorite movie stars were reportedly Brad Pitt and Anthony Hopkins, Mike Myers had drawn the task of receiving the envelope from Bart in the sound effects editing category.

A forklift operator carefully lifted Bart's small, steel-lined enclosure, which had been concealed in the Shrine's parking lot for several days while the bear became acclimated to Los Angeles weather. The cage was towed into the theater and backed into the wings of the stage. There, a small railing, only a foot high, was erected to create a pen of sorts. Before the door to Bart's cage was opened, the railing was electrified. "Oh, that's *cheating*," said one stagehand. "Step over it, Bart!"

"Folks, you've got to keep this a secret," Cates said before the bear made his appearance. "No one knows about it. Talk about it, and we'll feed you to the bear." (This was not a pleasant thought: Bart stood ten feet tall when fully upright, and his daily meal generally consisted of twenty four-pound chickens, a five-pound bucket of carrots, and another bucket of apples.)

Carefully, Bart was led out of the cage by his trainer, Doug Seus, who was himself a big, bearish man. Seus slowly walked Bart around the stage on a leash, then took the bear through his paces. He got Bart to sit up, to hold a dummy Oscar envelope, to clap, and to bow to the crowd. When he complied, Bart was rewarded by having cans of Hawaiian Punch poured down his throat.

In the wings stood a man with a gun. Close by, a stagehand waited with a broom and dustpan. "Is this big enough?" he said, pointing to his dustpan.

Seus laughed. "Just wait," he said. "Just wait."

Chuck Warn watched the whole thing from a safe distance, and chuckled. "A lot of special preparations," he said. "But nowhere near Streisand."

THE NEXT MORNING, Chuck Workman approached Cates at the production table. Workman had been hired to do a fast-paced montage celebrating seventy years of Academy Awards shows—"sort of an Oscars greatest hits," he said. Though Workman's montage was finished—without, he was proud to say, using Sally Field's "You really like me!" line—he came to Cates with the offer of a last-minute addition. "I can put together a new version," he said, "that would include a shot of the bear."

"How can you do that?" said Cates, intrigued.

"I can take a video-only shot of the bear holding the envelope from dress rehearsal," said Workman, "and cut into the piece. You can have both versions in the system, and then it'll be your call which one to use."

"Well, we'd use the one with the bear, of course," said Cates. "Why wouldn't we use that?"

"Maybe the bear will run amok or something."

"Oh, great," moaned Cates. "What a thing to bring up."

"I'm not saying it'll happen," insisted Workman. "I'm just trying to be prepared."

Michael Seligman laughed. "Why don't you prepare us for a plague of locusts while you're at it?" he said.

For twenty-one consecutive years, Seligman had been the moneyman for the Academy Awards. He was the guy who negotiated everybody's contracts, came up with a budget for the show, and ran interference on all matters financial.

The job could be complicated, because for years the Academy had divided the cost of producing the Oscar show with ABC. Anything that was deemed necessary to physically stage the show for a live audience was considered to be an Academy expense, while costs related to the broadcast of that show fell under ABC's purview. For instance, explained Seligman, the total cost of lighting the Oscar stage might run around $300,000. But the vast majority of those lights were needed for the TV cameras, not the audience inside the theater; if the show weren't televised, it could be lit for about $5,000. In that case, the Academy would pay $5,000 for lighting, and ABC would chip in the remaining $295,000.

The split made for some tricky financial arrangements: even some executives' salaries were paid partly by the network, partly by the Academy. (Most of the Academy money, of course, came from the fee that ABC paid to broadcast the show.) But the union crews that worked on the broadcast, from the National Association of Broadcast Employees & Technicians, were hired and paid by ABC.

In January 1998, though, that changed. Shortly after the previous year's Oscar show, the contract NABET had with the network expired, and a new pact had yet to be signed. In November 1997, New York NABET workers walked off the job for twenty-four hours, forcing the network to cancel coverage of one round of a golf tournament. The union also made threats to disrupt the coverage of football games and other sporting events.

Knowing that Oscar night could be an irresistible target for the union, the Academy decided to make its own deal with the union and produce the show itself. "ABC now gives us a package price, and we do everything ourselves," said Seligman. "We use the same union people we always used, but we've made our own deals with them. And even though it's all the Academy's money, we still separate what would be Academy expenses and what would be ABC, in case anything ever changes."

AS A GROUP OF DANCERS stretched on the stage of the Shrine, Danette Herman came up to Cates in the aisle, a grim frown on her face. She leaned toward Cates and spoke to him softly and quickly. "Shit," said Cates. "Fuck," he added.

Cates sat down at the production table next to his wife, Judith Reichman. "We just lost Juliette Binoche," he said of the previous year's best supporting actress winner, who was slated to present the award for supporting actor. "She broke her foot doing a play in London."

While Herman tried to wrangle a replacement, Cates turned his attention back to the stage. There, the forty-one-year-old, Los Angeles–born dancer and choreographer Daniel Ezralow was readying his troupe for a segment that appeared every few years on the Academy Awards: a dance number performed to the music of the nominated film scores.

With Debbie Allen otherwise engaged, Cates had turned to the younger choreographer, who had performed with the modern dance companies Momix, Pilobolus, and one he cofounded, ISO Dance. He'd also choreographed music videos and worked on a handful of movies and TV shows.

With a mop of curly hair and a taut dancer's body, Ezralow found a few admirers in the Oscar audience. One was Judith Reichman, who smiled as she watched Ezralow take his dancers through their paces. "He's a dancer, he's talented, and he's Jewish," said Reichman, laughing. "If I were younger and not married, he'd be my ideal man!"

Reichman was best known as a physician, a gynecologist to the stars, an author, and an expert on women's health issues for the *Today* show. But she had a dance background, and often stopped by Oscar rehearsals to see the dance numbers take shape. She watched eagerly as Ezralow worked with his dancers on a mostly lighthearted routine set to music from the nominated comedy or musical scores: *The Full Monty*, *As Good as It Gets*, *My Best Friend's Wedding*, *Anastasia*, and *Men in Black*. In most cases, he tried to play off the movie itself: there was a mock love triangle to go with the *Wedding* music, a line of gyrating men for *Monty*, and a row of black suits and shades for *Men in Black*.

This last segment featured a series of synchronized, high-stepping moves done by five men joined to each other by thick black bands linking their ankles. As she watched, Reichman shook her head. "That doesn't look right," she said. "They should lose the straps around their ankles."

During a break, she walked over to assistant choreographer Susan Lonergan and told her as much. "I agree," said Lonergan. "Why don't you see if Gil will talk to Daniel about it?"

Reichman did so, and Cates went onstage to speak with Ezralow. A minute later, he returned to the production table. "They're going to try it without the bands," he said. During the next rehearsal, the men in black danced unfettered. Everyone agreed it looked better.

Dr. Reichman beamed. "The power of the bed," she said.

DIANNE WIEST had just walked in the back door of the Shrine when she found that her way was blocked by a man in chinos, a white T-shirt, and a blazer. He quickly dropped to his knees, bowed in front of her, and kissed her hand. Wiest grinned as she looked down at Warren Beatty. "Are you the welcoming committee?" she said.

In a way, he was. Beatty was at the Shrine to rehearse handing out the best-director award, but he'd stuck around for the POWs. The acronym stood for "past Oscar winners," and there were almost six dozen of them, recipients of acting Oscars who'd been summoned to help celebrate the show's seventieth birthday.

At first, the plan had been vague. "We wanted to do something to mark the seventieth, and we had this idea of inviting back past winners," said Herman. "We knew it was a little early, that we should wait for the seventy-fifth to do it. But I also thought we should do it while those people were still around, because you never know how long we'll have them." Cates lobbied to include directors, but in the end it seemed cleaner and easier to restrict it to those who'd won acting awards, and actors who'd been given honorary

Oscars. (If directors had made the cut, Beatty would have been included alongside Dianne Wiest: though he'd been nominated for four acting awards, he'd won his only Oscar for directing *Reds*.)

As RSVPs came in, the number of past winners fluctuated. It got to seventy, the number Herman "thought would be cool," then as high as seventy-eight. "It was up and down," she said. "It was seventy-two, it was sixty-eight, it was sixty-nine. And I was thinking, there's no way I'm going to have sixty-nine. It's *got* to be seventy." As the stars showed up for rehearsal two days before the show, the number stood at seventy-one.

Mindful of the insulting way that screen legends had been plopped into the production number that opened Allan Carr's Oscar show, or left to mingle aimlessly onstage at the beginning of the fiftieth-anniversary show in 1978, Cates and Herman had promised the winners individual introductions. But there was no way to move them on and off stage quickly and with dignity. The solution was to reveal them all sitting onstage together, then pan across the group while introducing the POWs one at a time.

To do that, a four-level riser was erected on the stage, with seventeen or eighteen chairs on each of the four tiers. The camera would pan down each row, introducing the past winners in alphabetical order while superimposed film clips showed their Oscar-winning performances. Not only would the stars, many of them elderly, have to get up the stairs and into their places quickly, but if they weren't in exactly the right order, the film clips wouldn't match.

Not all the POWs could make it to rehearsal, so stage manager Debbie Williams rounded up stand-ins and assigned them to play the part of those missing in action. "He's too tall to be Dustin Hoffman," she said, appraising one stand-in. "He can be Charlton Heston."

The Irish actress Brenda Fricker, wearing jeans and a sweatshirt, was one of the first to come through a metal detector at the end of a small red carpet behind the artists' entrance. She was followed, in short order, by Celeste Holm, then Susan Sarandon, Joel Grey, Ernest Borgnine, Rod Steiger, Karl Malden, Ben Kingsley, Rita Moreno, and Martin Landau. Anna Paquin, who won for her first movie, *The Piano*, at age eleven, signed in just as a car pulled up bearing Kirk Douglas, who after more than seventy movies finally won an honorary award when he was seventy-nine. Marlee Matlin (*Children of a Lesser God*) and Angelica Huston (*Prizzi's Honor*) both set off the metal detector, but nobody stopped them. Gregory Peck and his wife walked by, each carrying a black bag containing a small Pekingese dog.

After signing in, the stars were greeted by Herman, then led to what had been dubbed the POW Room, a large space enclosed by curtains and containing a few couches, lots of director's chairs, television monitors, and a huge sign that read WELCOME BACK OSCAR WINNERS. Borgnine walked into the room, took one look at the assembled star power, and exclaimed, "Oh, my God!"

In the POW Room, many of the stars gathered around eighty-nine-year-old Luise Rainer, who won in 1936 and 1937 for *The Great Ziegfeld* and *The Good Earth* and then left Hollywood, disappointed by the lack of opportunities she was given. Elsewhere, Red Buttons chatted amiably with Peck and Landau, and Jon Voight spent his time talking to a stand-in who wore a sign around his neck reading DENZEL WASHINGTON. Susan Sarandon grabbed Voight. "Have you spoken to Wayne Wang?" said Sarandon, who was about to begin shooting the film *Anywhere But Here* with the Hong Kong–born director of *The Joy Luck Club*. "Because he mentioned you to me as a possibility."

Debbie Williams, who was in charge of making sure the segment came off cleanly, led the stars to the stage, explaining that on Oscar night they'd need to form four alphabetical lines. For the first rehearsal, though, they simply milled about on the stage, then took their seats in the risers as Williams called their names.

As the stars sat in their assigned places, new conversations started up. Holly Hunter leaned across Patricia Neal and Jack Nicholson to greet her *Piano* costar Paquin, while a pair of African American juniors, Cuba Gooding, Jr., and Louis Gossett, Jr., laughed together. Marlee Matlin had an enthusiastic conversation with Karl Malden, aided by a sign-language interpreter who stood nearby, signing Malden's words to the hearing-impaired actress.

To move down any aisle of chairs was to get a jumbled, chaotic overview of film history. There was the workaholic British actor Michael Caine sitting next to George Chakiris, who was younger than Caine but had rarely been seen on screen since winning for *West Side Story* in 1961 . . . then Cher, the flamboyant singer who had to struggle to be taken seriously as an actress . . . then Julie Christie, the stunning British actress whose career, and her devotion to the movie business, seemed to fade after she made her mark in the sixties and early seventies . . . then the indefatigable Scotsman Sean Connery, equally well known as the original James Bond and as a tireless worker who was known to make his share of foolish choices . . . then the former model Geena Davis, a surprise best supporting actress winner in 1988 for *The Accidental Tourist* . . . then Robert DeNiro, about whom the only surprise was why he'd won just two Oscars after thirty years of startling performances.

You could quibble with some of Oscar's choices, and with many of those who'd been ignored. But on Saturday afternoon at the Shrine, the parade of legendary faces was too impressive a lesson in cinema history for anyone to worry about who did or didn't deserve to be included. "I'm trembling," said Roy Christopher as he and other crew members stood by and watched. Though the warm interaction between the past winners was thrilling to many of the staffers on hand, Cates had nixed the idea of having a documentary crew film the historic gathering, feeling that cameras would interfere with the winners' enjoyment of the experience.

Once everyone was seated, Cates picked up a microphone. "Ladies and gentlemen," he said, "I just want to say you're a splendid-looking group." After Cates and Herman thanked them for coming, Horvitz ran through the segment once, showing film clips as the camera panned from one star to the next. "I hope that when people see this on TV," said Christopher as he watched the dry, straightforward run-through, "they get some sense of the joy and the camaraderie we're seeing here."

Afterward, the departing POWs were given Oscar sweatshirts and hats as they left the Shrine. Jack Palance, though, didn't notice the freebie table; instead, he headed straight out the back door. Faye Dunaway noticed, and chased him down. "Did you get a gift, Jack?" she asked.

"No," he said.

"Come with me." She grabbed him by the hand and led him back to the POW Room for his loot.

As the stars departed, Michael Caine, Ben Kingsley, and Martin Landau stood outside the room, saying good-bye to everyone. Louise Fletcher walked out, shaking her head. "They must have started to do this a *long* time ago, to pull all of this together," she said.

Joel Grey complimented Williams on how well organized it was. "The night of the show," he said, "do you want my help?"

ELLIOTT SMITH could be forgiven for wondering how he got himself into this mess. A slight, dour-looking man clad in jeans and yellow T-shirt, with a wool cap pulled down low over his mop of lank brown hair, Smith was a reluctant émigré from the world of alternative rock music. He was far more comfortable on the stages of small rock clubs than swankier joints like the Shrine.

But in addition to being one of the more acclaimed of the morosely talented singer-songwriters on the ferociously hip Portland, Oregon–based independent label Kill Rock Stars, Smith was also an Academy Award nominee. Director Gus Van Sant, who came from the ranks of independent film, had seen Smith perform in Portland coffeehouses and drafted him to add several songs to the soundtrack of *Good Will Hunting*. When that movie became a hit, it gave the soundtrack enough visibility that "Miss Misery," which Smith had written specifically for the film, won a nomination.

A mournful little ditty that captured some of the self-destructive bent of the character played in the film by Matt Damon—its opening line was "I'll fake it through the day / With some help from Johnny Walker Red"—"Miss Misery" was the most unexpected of the five nominated songs, and Smith was clearly the odd man out among a lineup of musical performers that included Céline Dion, Michael Bolton, Trisha Yearwood, and Aaliyah.

Dion was a French Canadian pop diva known for thumping her chest and engaging in elaborate emotional histrionics, Bolton a gut-busting former (and failed) rock 'n' roller who took his extravagant ballads to gravel-voiced extremes. Yearwood, generally more tasteful than those two, was a country singer with a powerful voice, while Aaliyah was a young soul diva about to launch an acting career.

For the most part, their songs were big, dramatic, and more than a little overblown: Aaliyah's pop-soul manifesto "Journey to the Past," Bolton's bombastic "Go the Distance," Yearwood's power ballad "How Do I Live," and, of course, Dion's "My Heart Will Go On," a monster hit from the *Titanic* soundtrack. Against those other songs, Smith's spare, melancholy "Miss Misery" sounded downright malnourished—not a bad thing for fans of intelligent, understated pop music, but not exactly the way to hold your own sandwiched between Yearwood and Dion. And sandwiched between those two women was exactly where Smith was: to save a little time, Cates had decided to put the five songs into two medleys. (Initially, a plan had been floated to cut all the nominated songs except for "My Heart Will Go On" down to ninety seconds, but the idea didn't get far; even though the Dion song was by far the biggest hit and an almost certain winner, that kind of favoritism wouldn't fly on the Oscars.)

When Smith shuffled into the Shrine for rehearsal, stagehands directed him to a spot near the rear of the stage, just in front of the orchestra riser. Smith strummed his acoustic guitar, sang a few tentative lines, and frowned his way through a take, plainly irritated. When the song ended, he walked to the front of the stage, sat down on the steps that led to the audience, and played the song again. Then he stood up and walked to the microphone.

"I can't do it back there," he said, an edge of quiet anger in his voice. "Because the monitors are, like, forty feet away from where I'm sitting, and I can't sing like that." He pointed to the front of the stage. "What I want to do is sit in a chair right here. 'Cause that's what I do. But for some reason, I can't."

Rehearsal ground to a halt, as Cates, Horvitz, and Christopher discussed a move. The singer stood a few feet away from them, alone, his head down, a hand in his pocket. Within a few minutes, a stagehand brought out a stool, and set it near the front of the stage. Smith sang a few lines from his new location, then stopped. "It's woofy and weird," he said of the sound mix. "I can't sing on key up here if I can't hear the note I'm singing. I just need to hear myself better."

The sound mix was adjusted, and Smith tried again. "Is that better?" asked a stage manager.

"Yeah, I guess," he said, still frowning. "There's no way we could just get one monitor right here, is there?" He pointed to the floor directly in front of him.

Christopher shook his head, knowing that a clunky black monitor sitting center stage would look terrible with the clean lines of the set. Less than five minutes later, though, a soundman came out with a monitor, and stuck it at Smith's feet. The singer ran through his song one more time. He still sounded miserable—but this time it had to do with the song, not the setting.

In the audience, Michael Davies, ABC's new executive vice president of alternative series and specials, watched the rehearsal from a seat near Cates. At one point, the producer leafed through the show rundowns in front of him. Knowing that there was no way to prevent it from being a very long telecast, Cates turned to Davies. "Are you comfortable with a three-and-a-half-hour show?" he asked.

Davies laughed. One of the open secrets about the Academy Awards was that the network didn't really mind if the show ran overtime. Certainly, it wasn't ideal to go well past midnight and risk losing a chunk of the East Coast audience; the final rating established for the show was an average of the ratings for each half hour, so a drop in viewership could drag it down overall. Still, even if the Oscars lost viewers when it passed three hours, the broadcast drew significantly higher ratings than whatever else ABC might be airing. And the show delivered such a large audience, in such a desirable demographic, that ratings points had relatively little effect on ad rates.

"Gil," said Davies, "I'd be happy if the show lasted for a month."

TITANIC may have turned Leonardo DiCaprio into Hollywood's reigning heartthrob, at least among teenage girls whose repeated viewings of the movie were helping fuel the record grosses. But the Academy didn't entirely cooperate with DiCaprio's coronation as the man of the hour. Although he'd been nominated for best supporting actor for *What's Eating Gilbert Grape* in 1994, before his twentieth birthday, DiCaprio was passed over for *Titanic*, though his leading lady, Kate Winslet, and costar Gloria Stuart were nominated. He'd also turned down an invitation to appear on the show, but word of that apparently hadn't reached the throngs of young women who filled the bleachers in front of the Shrine, many of them toting homemade signs that sang his praises.

With DiCaprio out, the show's staff had to turn elsewhere for participants who might appeal to the marginally postpubescent set. That they succeeded was clear on Sunday afternoon, when the crush of youngsters around the artists' entrance reached epic proportions just as Ben Affleck and Matt Damon were arriving.

Affleck and Damon, twenty-six and twenty-eight, respectively, were childhood friends from Boston. Struggling actors until *Good Will Hunting* put them on the map and won them Oscar nominations for their original screenplay, the two arrived at the Shrine together, an hour earlier than their call time. They were accompanied by Affleck's mother, Chris, who asked if she could take a few photos inside the Shrine. Publicist Eva Demirjian ran the request by the longtime Oscar security chief, Jerry Moon, who agreed to rescind the ban on cameras just for Mrs. Affleck.

After they'd rehearsed, the two actors walked out the rear artists' entrance. A handful of teenagers, most of them the children of show staffers, worked the sign-in table there, handing out hats and sweatshirts along with the elaborate Oscar gift baskets. For the most part, the kids politely took turns dispensing the swag, but every year there were a few exceptions. When everybody wanted to do the honors, when the usually retiring volunteers fought over who got to hand over the sweatshirt and hat, you knew that the Oscars had booked somebody hot.

In 1998, the clear favorites were Damon and Affleck. Rather than pushing through the crowd and heading for their car, though, the two happily worked the room. They stood by the sign-in table for a good twenty minutes, chatting with the kids and posing for photos. At one point, Danny Shapiro, the eleven-year-old son of Robert Z. Shapiro, whispered to Affleck, "Kick *Titanic*'s ass."

Affleck broke into a huge grin and gave Shapiro a hug. "You're gonna go far in this life, kid," he said. "You speak your mind."

When they finally headed for their car, Affleck and Damon ran into Bruce Vilanch. "It's just gonna be all *Titanic* jokes, isn't it?" Affleck asked.

"No," Vilanch insisted. "We're egalitarian."

Watching Affleck and Damon charm the crowd, one veteran staffer smiled. "Everybody's so on their best behavior when they first come here," she said. "I call it the three-year plan. The first time they're nominated and they come here, they're totally nice, just taking it all in. But it only takes them three years to come back and be an entirely different human being. That's when you look at them and think, Oh, my God."

As Affleck and Damon chatted with Vilanch, a pair of pages stood by with two gargantuan gift baskets. An Oscar tradition for several years, the baskets had been steadily growing in both size and value. "Originally, we did it because we'd been having trouble getting the younger stars to show up," said Seligman. "So I said, 'Let's give them something. Let's create a little gift basket.' I called some people around town, and suddenly *everybody* wanted to be in the basket."

Perfumes, jewelry, and electronic devices were mainstays in the basket in early years; over time, the value increased dramatically as the baskets grew to include spa memberships, restaurant vouchers, hotel stays (airfare usually not included), United Airlines upgrades, and the free use of luxury automobiles. By 1998, the value was nearing $20,000, and the Academy was beginning to get a little nervous about the attention the baskets garnered. "What they don't tell you is that all the gift certificates have deadlines," laughed one Oscar participant who had received several of them. "To use everything in that basket, you'd have to make it your full-time job."

"LADIES AND GENTLEMEN," announced stage manager Garry Hood from the stage of the Shrine, "we need to clear the house for the next twenty minutes. There are no exceptions. We need to clear it for twenty minutes, and then we'll let you all back in."

With dress rehearsal about to begin, Hood's entreaties meant one thing: as usual, Billy Crystal wanted to keep secret his entrance, his opening film, his monologue, and his medley. So even though Crystal wasn't even going to show his real film, even though he wasn't going to be using many of the real jokes in his monologue, and even though he'd rehearsed his entrance and his medley two days earlier without clearing the house, Hood stood firm. "Guests, stand-ins, anybody who is not *working* personnel, we need to clear you," he said. "Security, please help me with this. Make sure everybody is out, and close the front entrances, side entrances, balcony entrances, outhouse entrances . . ."

At the artists' entrance to the Shrine, one guard took his new responsibilities a little too seriously. "Wait a minute, he doesn't have a pass," he barked, stopping stage manager Rita Cossette as she walked through the door with a companion. Cossette looked at the guard incredulously. "He's okay," she said, pointing to Billy Crystal, whom she was escorting to the stage.

The dress rehearsal began in front of a near-empty house that included Academy president Robert Rehme and director/choreographer Stanley Donen, who was to receive an honorary Oscar. Crystal ran through his song twice, then walked to the podium. "I will do the rest of the rehearsal as Jerry Weintraub," he said, switching into the croaky, gravelly voice of the long-time producer and manager. "Okay, to throw out the first fuckin' Oscar is a guy . . ."

The only star presenter required for this run-through was Mike Myers, who had the tricky task of working with Bart the bear. Myers and his wife arrived in a white stretch limo, inexplicably sent by the company hired to provide less ostentatious town cars for the presenters. "We went to the prom first," Myers jokingly said to Herman after he got out of the car. "We opened up the top and stuck our heads out all the way down Sunset."

When Myers walked to the stage, Herman immediately got on her walkie-talkie. "Get in touch with the limo company," she said, "and tell them that white stretch limos are *not* acceptable."

Myers got through his routine with the bear without incident. As planned, the curtains opened to reveal the bear sitting up and holding the envelope, with his trainer just out of sight in the wings. Myers went over to the edge of the electrified fence, gingerly took the envelope from Bart, and then returned to his podium to read it. Chuck Workman got a shot to quickly edit into his montage.

During the next commercial break, Myers came into the audience. "Mike!" yelled Cates. "Great job!"

"Thanks," said Myers. "I was good, if I can admit it myself."

"It was great," agreed Cates. "The only thing is that the trainer will not be there tomorrow."

"Are you serious?" said Myers slowly, looking as if he might believe the

ABOVE: *Ben Affleck and Jennifer Lopez hugged, kissed, and canoodled their way through an afternoon run-through in 2003. Behind them, far right, talent executive Danette Herman watched protectively over the celebrated lovebirds.*

BELOW: *Three generations of the Douglas family showed up at the Kodak Theatre for rehearsals in 2003. From left to right: Michael's son Dylan, 2; Michael, 58; and Kirk, 86.*

LEFT: *Cameron Diaz with a plaster rehearsal Oscar stowed between her legs during the run-throughs in 2002*

Jennifer Lopez stood at the side of the Shrine Auditorium stage, awaiting her cue, during 2001 rehearsals.

ABOVE: *The most low-maintenance host imaginable, Steve Martin sat in the audience and watched many of the 2003 rehearsals.*
BELOW: *Before taking the stage to rehearse in 2001, Winona Ryder snuck a peek into the audience.*

Minutes after declining to use the dramatic staircase entrance he'd planned for her in 2004, Julia Roberts made nice with Oscar producer Joe Roth.

The man who transformed Oscar campaigning, Miramax's Harvey Weinstein was a common presence in and around the green room. In 2004, he held court with Jim Carrey outside the Kodak Theatre's backstage restrooms.

Producer Laura Ziskin's big coup in 2002 was persuading the notorious Oscar-phobe Woody Allen to show up. Allen introduced a clip saluting New York City, then left the stage, pulled off his bow tie, and headed for the exit. In the background, Ziskin (blond hair, black suit) celebrated by high-fiving a pal.

ART STREIBER

ART STREIBER

TOP: *Before winning the best-actress award in 2004, Charlize Theron waited in the wings to present the award for foreign language film. To her left was a fellow presenter, Jude Law; to her right was PricewaterhouseCoopers partner Greg Garrison, one of the two keepers of the Oscar envelopes.*

BOTTOM: The Lord of the Rings: The Return of the King *director Peter Jackson and his partner, writer-producer Fran Walsh, took a breather between sweeping the Oscars and hitting the parties in 2004.*

TOP: *As best-actress winner Julia Roberts walked by the green room in 2001, a worker prepared to pull down some draperies. With the show running surprisingly ahead of schedule, backstage finery had to be dismantled to make room for the Governors Ball.*

BOTTOM: *In 2002, the stunned best-actress winner, Halle Berry, brought then husband Eric Benet along as she negotiated the hallways that led from the Kodak Theatre to the press area in the adjoining Hollywood Renaissance Hotel.*

ABOVE: *Tom Hanks used a prerogative open only to star participants: rather than wait in the long line out front, Hanks and his son Chester entered the 2001 Governors Ball directly from the backstage area.*
BELOW: *Fresh from being booed by some in the audience in 2003, filmmaker Michael Moore walked into the wings to the derision of a few union stagehands but the approval of his presenter, actress Diane Lane. "That was very inspirational," she told him of his incendiary speech.*

ABOVE: *In one of the meetings that are an integral part of rehearsals the day before every Oscar show, producer Gil Cates went over the 1997 script with presenter Sigourney Weaver.*
BELOW: *At the time Hollywood's most glamorous young couple, Brad Pitt and Gwyneth Paltrow waded through the red-carpet crowd as they entered the Dorothy Chandler Pavilion in 1996. Four years later, she'd be ducking her head to avoid him at rehearsal.*

After the show in 2002, Nicole Kidman hung out in the front row, posed for pictures with the Oscar stage crew, and was among the last to leave the Kodak.

LARA JO REGAN

LARA JO REGAN

TOP: *All that glitters is not gold: dummy Oscar statuettes, made of plaster and painted to look like the real thing, sat on a backstage table for use by stars and stand-ins during rehearsals in 1994.*
BOTTOM: *Producer Gil Cates looked over the top-secret board bearing the names of possible presenters and performers in 1994. Color-coded dots indicated who was in, who was out, and who was still under consideration.*

ABOVE: *Host David Letterman—unshaven, casual, and out-of-place—tried out a Stupid Pet Trick during rehearsals in 1995. To Letterman's immediate right was Sadie, the Dog That Spins When You Applaud.*

BELOW: *Arnold Schwarzenegger rehearsed his presentation of the Irving Thalberg Award to Clint Eastwood in 1995. On the screen behind Arnold was a scene from* Bronco Billy, *not necessarily one of the honoree's finer moments.*

ABOVE: *Antonio Banderas picked up his lavish gift basket as he left rehearsal in 1994. Within a couple of years, the baskets would be too big and unwieldy for a single person to carry.*

BELOW: *In 1996, the big Oscar recipient was Mel Gibson, who directed and produced the best-picture winner,* Braveheart. *When the show ended, Gibson used an equipment case as a seat and rested with his twin Oscars in a hallway outside the press rooms.*

TOP: *In 1997, a year after winning the supporting-actress Oscar, Mira Sorvino returned to hand the supporting-actor award to Cuba Gooding, Jr. She then accompanied the exuberant winner as he cooled down in a hallway between the Shrine Auditorium and the press tent.*

BOTTOM: *The aftermath of the Oscar show in 1995: a messy production office and an exhausted staffer, all dressed up with, apparently, no place to go. The Governors Ball was getting under way downstairs, but few of those who worked on the show were invited.*

Host Whoopi Goldberg tried to survive an awkward 1996 skit that found her chatting with Miss Piggy and with the porcine star of Babe.

Oscar statuettes arrived at the Dorothy Chandler Pavilion the morning of the 1994 show, several hours before they'd be needed. To keep them secure and out of sight, the Oscars were stashed in a small kitchen just off the Chandler stage and watched over by the building's longtime propmaster, Carmine Marinelli.

Chris Farley was booked to help lure Middle American viewers to the Oscars in 1997, a year when art movies and obscure actors captured most of the nominations. The tactic didn't work—it was the lowest-rated Oscar show in eleven years—but it did give Farley a chance to clown around with a mirror ball destined for the after party.

BELOW: *Director Renny Harlin accompanied his then wife, Geena Davis, to rehearsal at the Dorothy Chandler Pavilion in 1994. While she ran through her lines, he tried out the seat he'd have on Oscar night.*

In a quiet backstage corridor in 1996, best-actor winner Nicolas Cage grabbed a moment with his then wife, Patricia Arquette.

Wearing the lavender silk chiffon evening dress that helped put Prada on Hollywood's radar screen, Uma Thurman ducked behind the Shrine Auditorium for a smoke after losing best supporting actress in 1995.

producer. Then he broke into a grin as Cates laughed. "Now I need to change my pants," Myers said. "You'll get my dry-cleaning bill."

Myers grinned. "No, he's a sweet bear," he said. "A sweet puppy."

"Actually," said Seligman, "he *eats* puppies."

Myers walked a couple of rows away and talked to friends. "I admit, I'm nervous," he told them. "Don't think I haven't figured out an escape route: down the steps, past Brenda Fricker . . ."

After the break, Crystal returned to the podium. "The answer is, a bear doesn't shit in the woods," he said. "He does it in the green room."

The rehearsal finally ended about 11:30 p.m. At midnight, ABC's Susan Futterman informed Seligman that one of Julianne Moore's nipples was visible through her sheer blouse in a film clip from the movie *Boogie Nights*. "Who the fuck cares?" he replied. "*Billy's* nipples are bigger than hers." Futterman didn't buy the logic. Edits were ordered.

FOUR PARALLEL ROWS OF TAPE ran along the floor outside the POW Room. At the end of each row was the name of the Oscar winner who'd be leading a line of stars onto the stage: Robert Duvall, Shirley Jones, Joe Pesci, and Teresa Wright. "When we get to that part of the show, I'll have six minutes to get them from here onto the stage and into their seats before the curtain opens," said Debbie Williams. "I think it took about seven minutes at rehearsal on Saturday, and then I was able to spread them out over the whole stage. It's going to be *very* tight."

Outside, on the red carpet, a huge bottleneck developed as guests tried to make their way through six metal detectors, three for stars who'd be working the press line and three for regular guests who'd be bypassing the press. Sean Connery and Neve Campbell took the latter route.

Backstage, Jon Voight sat by himself in the POW Room, studying the script to *Varsity Blues*, a high school drama he was about to start shooting. "They gave me two tickets, but I'd really rather use the time to go over this script," he said. "Do you know anybody who needs seats up front?" Just before the show began, two seat-fillers slipped into Voight's seats, and got to stay in them all night long.

With thirty seconds to show time, actor Robert Forster, a supporting-actor nominee for the Quentin Tarantino movie *Jackie Brown*, came into the auditorium. An usher told him he'd have to wait until the first commercial break, some twenty-three minutes away, before taking his seat. "I'm a nominee," he said, "and I'm in the first row." The usher let him in just as the orchestra began to play a new fanfare composed specially for the Oscars by Jerry Goldsmith.

6:00 P.M., PACIFIC DAYLIGHT TIME: *"Live from Los Angeles, California, the 70th anniversary Academy Awards."*

Backstage, Billy Crystal moved into position as a large movie screen descended from the rafters. As he stepped onto the platform of the hydraulic lift, Crystal's opening movie began to play. As it had the previous year, his entrance film used newly shot footage to integrate Crystal into scenes from many of the year's biggest movies, beginning and ending with *Titanic*. At the end of the clip, Crystal was dangling from the prow of James Cameron's ship as it began to sink. "I can't imagine a worse disaster!" he cried.

"Oh yeah?" shouted Kevin Costner, the star and director of the year's most notable flop, *The Postman*. "Well, *I* can!" As the audience roared at the sight of Costner engaging in the same kind of self-mockery that David Letterman had done the previous year, the hydraulic lift began to rise. As it went up, Crystal grabbed the railing and gripped it tightly.

A few jokes and five quick songs later, Crystal turned the stage over to the preceding year's hyperkinetic winner for best supporting actor, Cuba Gooding, Jr. Gooding read his lines, then tossed in an ad-lib. "One quick word of advice," he shouted. "The lady that graces this stage this evening, while you're giving your acceptance speech, take your time! Don't listen to the music! Do your *thing*, please!" An astonished Kim Basinger won, thanked "everybody I've ever met in my entire life," and wrapped up her speech in an un-Cuba-like fifty-six seconds, only eleven over the allotted limit.

Backstage, Basinger spotted Danette Herman. "I can't believe it, I can't believe it, I don't believe it!" she screamed. Herman screamed, too. Basinger turned the corner by the green room, saw Cates, screamed again, and hugged him. "I can't believe it, I'm still staring at it," she said, holding the Oscar. "Oh, my God. Oh, my God."

Gooding joined Basinger at Cates's side. "Thank you," Cates said, giving Gooding a hug. "But I didn't like that advice you gave."

"Sorry," said Gooding, who didn't appear to be.

Half an hour into the show, a visibly nervous Neve Campbell introduced Aaliyah and Michael Bolton to perform the first of the song medleys. As Aaliyah sang, the bear's trailer was slowly backed into the wings of the stage. The armed guard watched. When Aaliyah finished her song, she stood in the wings and watched Bolton on a monitor, unaware that Bart, still in his trailer, was about three feet away from her.

Bart's preparations were proceeding slowly—the fence erected and electrified, the door to his cage unlatched—while Mira Sorvino announced the winner for best supporting actor: Robin Williams for *Good Will Hunting*. In the audience there was an immediate scream, and a standing ovation. "Oh man," Williams said. "This might be the one time I'm speechless." Behind him, obscured by a curtain, Doug Seus led Bart out of his cage and onto the stage.

As the curtain opened to reveal the bear, Bart dropped the envelope. Seus darted into the enclosure, picked up the envelope, and handed it back to Bart in time for Mike Myers to take it from his fourteen-hundred-pound copresenter. As Myers walked back to the podium, the curtain closed and Bart was quickly led to his trailer. "Good boy, good boy, good boy," said Seus. By the time the sound effects technicians for *Titanic* finished their acceptance speech, Bart was in the parking lot of the Shrine; by the time the next commercial break ended, Seus was at the wardrobe room below the stage, turning in his tux and following Bart out the door.

"We had a little problem backstage," Crystal said as the broadcast resumed. "You know that old joke: does a bear —— in the woods?" He shook his head. "In the green room."

In the wings of the stage, Affleck and Damon awaited their cue. Dency Nelson, who was responsible for getting them into position, approached the pair singing Crystal's parody song, "Matt and Ben." They laughed. "Wonderful," said Affleck.

"Okay, guys, follow me," said Nelson. Affleck reached into his pocket, pulled out a set of car keys, and dropped them on the director's chair behind him. "You watch these?" he said to a guard, adding, "The car is not that nice, and the phone, you gotta punch a code in." As the pair took the stage, Robin Williams rushed back into the wings after his run through the press rooms. He waited for Damon and Affleck to come offstage, then gave long, fervent hugs to the men who wrote his Oscar-winning part. A few minutes later, Helen Hunt won the Oscar for best actress. The giddy Williams stayed in the wings, waited for her, and gave her a big hug, too. "Now I can go back to comedy," he said.

A few feet away, in a curtained-off hallway just outside the green room, Sharon Stone stood in front of one of a pair of makeup tables. A makeup artist retouched Stone's face, while a second staffer adjusted the wraparound Vera Wang skirt that Stone had paired with one of her husband's white dress shirts. At the table next to her, Ashley Judd touched up her own makeup. Nobody bothered to inspect Judd's off-white Richard Tyler dress, which was slit to the top of her thigh. But when Judd walked across the stage a few minutes later, she immediately ignited a debate about what she was wearing beneath that skirt. (The consensus: nothing.)

At the show's two-hour mark, Madonna came into the wings and settled into a director's chair to await her turn onstage. A makeup artist touched her up while she watched on a monitor as director Stanley Donen received an honorary Oscar and incorporated a delightful song and dance into his acceptance speech. Watching the seventy-three-year-old Donen effortlessly serenade his statuette with "Cheek to Cheek," Madonna laughed and broke into applause. Behind the Shrine, *My Cousin Vinny* stars Marisa Tomei and Joe Pesci chatted while Pesci smoked a cigar.

During the commercial break after "My Heart Will Go On" won the Oscar for best song, dozens of pages swept through the hall, pulling past Oscar winners out of their seats and leading them to the POW Room. There, a large crowd gathered around a TV monitor as Robin Williams introduced Workman's film of highlights from past Oscar shows. Robert DeNiro got up, walked over to a monitor, and turned up the volume. Tomei, Pesci, Voight, and Landau watched with him.

A few minutes later, Frances McDormand read the nominees for best actor, and clips from each of the nominated performances were shown. When a scene of Dustin Hoffman's work in *Wag the Dog* included a quick shot of DeNiro, Rita Moreno spoke up. "Didn't you just *love* DeNiro in that?" she said to the group of POWs around her. A couple of feet in front of her, DeNiro turned around and smiled. "Oh," she said, laughing, "I didn't know it was *you*!"

Jack Nicholson won the award, completing a sweep for the lead actors in *As Good as It Gets*. After rambling for about a minute, Nicholson looked into the orchestra pit at Bill Conti. "I know Gil Cates is starting to sweat back there now, isn't he, Bill?" he said. When Nicholson finished, Horvitz cut to a shot of Judith Reichman applauding.

L.A. Confidential and *Good Will Hunting* picked up the screenplay awards, with the latter win confirming a trend that had also seen Emma Thompson (*Sense and Sensibility*) and Billy Bob Thornton (*Sling Blade*) winning in recent years. When actors wrote their own screenplays, they often won Academy Awards, no doubt courtesy of support from the large actors' branch.

In the POW Room backstage, Debbie Williams got on a microphone and directed the stars out the door and into four lines. "Mr. Robert Duvall," she said. "Mr. Duvall. Miss Faye Dunaway. Miss Faye Dunaway is after Robert Duvall. Richard Dreyfuss is after Faye Dunaway . . . Mr. DeNiro, are you coming? Okay, I hear you . . ." Obedient and orderly, the celebrities formed lines. There were exactly seventy of them, Dianne Wiest having failed to make it because of a limo mix-up. Slowly, keeping the lines together, they walked around the corner and toward the stage. Instantly, stagehands started dismantling the POW Room to make more room for the Governors Ball.

Onstage, Denzel Washington handed out yet another Oscar to *Titanic*. While cinematographer Russell Carpenter spoke, the POWs began filing into their chairs. A large curtain behind Carpenter remained closed. Williams tried to direct traffic and keep things moving without her voice carrying beyond the curtain.

Three of the night's four new Oscar winners in the acting categories— Kim Basinger, Robin Williams, and Helen Hunt—were led into the wings; the fourth, Jack Nicholson, was already part of the segment as a previous winner.

With some of the past winners still finding their seats, Susan Sarandon took the stage. She spoke very slowly and deliberately. "In celebration of this year's anniversary, the Academy invited all those who have been honored with leading, supporting, honorary, or juvenile awards for acting over the three score and ten years of Academy history," she said, pausing frequently. "And I think they're still getting in their places." She took a breath. "Ladies and gentlemen"—a pause—"Oscar's"—she brought up both hands, her fingers crossed—"family album."

The curtain opened, and the POWs appeared on-screen—all in place, in the right seats. In the wings, Williams yelled "Yaaaay!" In the seats, a camera caught Alec Baldwin mouthing "My God" as he looked at the array of winners. For the next fifteen minutes, announcer Norman Rose read the names of the seventy winners, as the camera panned from one to another. At the end, the night's newest winners were introduced.

Afterward, twenty-six pages descended upon the wings, each assigned to lead two or three POWs back to their seats. Robin Williams was a priority, because the next award was for best director—and in the unlikely event that *Good Will Hunting* director Gus Van Sant won, Horvitz wanted a reaction shot of Williams.

In the wings on the side of the stage, seven Oscars remained on a double-decker cart that had carried more than four dozen statuettes three hours earlier. With only two awards left, and none of the best-picture nominees sporting more than two producers, a maximum of three statuettes would be needed. A guard collected four of the Oscars and took them away.

To the surprise of no one, James Cameron won for best director, the tenth *Titanic* win of the night. "I don't know about you," he said, "but I'm having a really good time." He thanked his fellow producers, his family, his parents. "There is no way to express to you how I feel right now," he said. "My heart is bursting. Except to say—I'm the *king of the world*!" After this quote from his own movie, he whooped, threw his arm in the air, and walked off the stage. From the wings he was taken straight back down the steps and to his seat, to await the final category.

He didn't stay there for long. Opening the envelope containing the name of the best-picture winner, Sean Connery feigned a double take, then read the name: "*Titanic*." Producer Jon Landau spoke first, reading four dozen names in a rapid-fire minute and a half. Then Cameron took over for another two minutes, including a moment of silence for those who died on the *Titanic*. "Thank you very much," he said after sixteen quiet seconds had passed. "That's about as much as I'm sure Gil Cates can stand. All right, you really made this a night to remember in every way. Now let's go party till dawn!"

Backstage, Cameron headed not for the party, but for the press tent. "It's been a great night, we're all tired," said Crystal. "Matt Damon just hit on Shirley Temple. Good night everybody, see you next year."

It ended at 9:45, the longest Oscar show in history. Among the production staff, the consensus was that despite the length, the show was exhilarating—and regardless, everybody involved knew it was going to be long.

Guests moved on to the Governors Ball or to other parties, or simply headed out front to pick up their cars. Limo drivers returned to their vehicles and awaited orders. On the first floor of a parking structure adjacent to the Shrine Exhibition Hall, the tables where the drivers had been fed during the show were deserted. The catering crew had moved on as well, but they'd left behind an enormous pile of ice, slowly melting into the gutter outside the theater. For those who didn't mind stretching for cheap metaphors, the message was clear: this time, the boat won and the ice didn't stand a chance.

THE LESSON TAUGHT by the Academy Awards show in 1997—that the show's ratings were determined to a large degree by public interest in the competing movies—was reinforced in 1998. Despite the fact that the show contained little suspense and was of record length, it drew its biggest ratings in thirteen years, and its largest American audience ever at eighty-seven million viewers.

Though it hardly needed the extra publicity it picked up by winning eleven awards—which put it in a tie with *Ben-Hur* for the most Oscar wins ever—*Titanic* kept on rolling at the box office. It passed the $500 million mark the week of the Oscars, and by the end of the summer it had topped $600 million, making it the top-grossing movie in history. Worldwide, it topped the $1 billion mark.

After the Oscars, *Titanic* added one more week to its record-setting dominance of the box-office charts. The first weekend in April, however, its fifteen-week run at the top was finally ended by the big-screen version of the 1960s television series *Lost in Space*; although the movie was almost universally panned, it had a $20 million opening weekend that knocked *Titanic* out of the number-one spot.

Later that month, the Motion Picture Association of America's anti-piracy unit said that tapes of *Titanic* sent to Academy members had been used as the source for pirated copies of the movie, which had become a hot seller on the black market.

The film's reputation began to sink soon after the Oscars, helped along by viewers who found Cameron's acceptance-speech grandstanding to be more than a touch egomaniacal. In 2003, viewers of a BBC television show in England would vote it the worst movie of all time.

On the heels of the blockbuster ratings, the Academy had significant leverage when it opened negotiations for a new television contract. Rather than simply re-signing with ABC, the organization entertained proposals from other channels, including an extraordinarily lucrative offer to move the show to a cable outlet. It would have meant more money but a smaller audience, so the board voted to stick with the alphabet network.

In an attempt to keep viewership high in subsequent years, the Academy decided to move upcoming Oscar shows to Sunday, the one day on which the show had never taken place. (Monday and Thursday were the most popular.) In the past, the Academy had stayed away from Sunday because of a deal made in the 1950s to placate movie theater owners who were worried that a televised Oscar show might hurt theater attendance. But nearly half a century later, given the unrivaled power of television to hype movies, an agreement to avoid weekend Oscar shows no longer made much sense.

The move also enabled the network to start the show half an hour earlier, at five-thirty instead of six. Not only would West Coast viewers not be racing home from work to catch the show, but also those on the East Coast stood a better chance of seeing the best-picture winner before midnight.

During the summer, the Academy's longtime accounting firm, Price Waterhouse, merged with another company, Coopers & Lybrand, and the company name was changed to PricewaterhouseCoopers.

When Emmy nominations were announced during the summer, the Oscar show picked up eight. Most years, the Oscars would receive seven, eight, or nine nominations, and then win a single award. This time, though, it won in five of the eight categories, including direction, lighting direction, music direction, sound mixing, and performance (for Billy Crystal). No Oscar show had ever before won more than three.

A few days after the seventieth show, the Academy formally agreed to use the proposed theater in the Hollywood & Highland complex for upcoming Oscar shows. The organization signed a twenty-year lease with TrizecHahn, though the contract also included escape clauses that could be invoked after ten years. In October, TrizecHahn held a groundbreaking ceremony at the site. Quincy Jones hosted the event, and announced that the complex would include Q's Jook Joint, a restaurant and nightclub. TrizecHahn said that the first Oscar show would take place in the new venue in March 2001, and that the entrance to the theater would be dramatic. "It won't be a mall," developer David Malmuth told *Daily Variety*. "The Academy said, 'We don't want to be part of a mall.' "

6

Sunday Bloody Sunday

The 71st Academy Awards

AS ONE OF THE BIGGEST MOVIE THEATERS in Los Angeles, the 1,012-seat Samuel Goldwyn Theater was normally filled only for premieres or the hottest screenings, and rarely before sunset. But in the chilly predawn hours one morning a year, all that changed—which is why, at 5 a.m. on Tuesday, February 9, 1999, the theater inside the Academy's Beverly Hills headquarters was jammed with folks who would not normally be up at such an ungodly hour. Nominations for the 71st Academy Awards were being announced at precisely 5:38 and thirty seconds, so the Goldwyn teemed with cameras, cameramen, reporters, publicists, studio executives, Academy staffers, and the assorted flotsam and jetsam of the movie industry.

Louis Horvitz was directing the brief but momentous telecast. He sat in front of three monitors as he waited for the clock to count down to the moment when Academy president Bob Rehme and Oscar-winning actor Kevin Spacey would read the nominations. In the audience, more than 550 reporters readied their cameras and their notebooks. Throughout the hall, television reporters had final touchups done to their makeup.

Near the back of the theater, producer Gil Cates took in the entire pageant. Cates had already been working on the show for a couple of months, enlisting Whoopi Goldberg to return as host, hiring the key staff members, commissioning packages of film clips. As the clock edged past 5:30, he was one of the handful of people in the room who knew what Pricewaterhouse-Coopers executives had divulged to top Academy staffers several hours earlier: that *Shakespeare in Love* and *Saving Private Ryan* would lead the pack with thirteen and eleven nominations, respectively, and that the acting field would include stars like Tom Hanks and Meryl Streep alongside the lesser-known likes of Ian McKellen, Cate Blanchett, and Fernanda Montenegro. Waiting for everyone else to hear the news, Cates stuck his hands into the pockets of his gray slacks, looked around, and shook his head.

"What a zoo," he said with a chuckle. "What a zoo."

In a nearby aisle stood Doug Stewart, whose company, DMS, was responsible for the slides that would appear on screens behind Rehme and Spacey. Stewart had been in the building all night, after spending the past few weeks collecting photos and logos of every film and every actor he thought might have a chance at a nomination. The idea was not to be caught unprepared by any long shots—although on the occasions when that did happen, Stewart had ways to play catch-up, even at midnight in Beverly Hills. The Academy library on nearby La Cienega Boulevard, for example, was kept open all night, with a small crew of staffers ready to scour magazines and promo materials if need be.

For Stewart, a more pressing problem was locating photos that met his needs without appearing to play favorites. "Getting good material is very tricky," he said, "because the Academy does not want to give the slightest impression that they have any inkling who will be nominated." Stewart had, in fact, run afoul of the organization just a few days earlier, when Dream-Works sent him *Saving Private Ryan* materials that were oriented vertically; the screens he'd be using were better suited to horizontal images.

"I called the DreamWorks publicity people and said, 'Hey, could you make these horizontal, instead of vertical?' They said, 'Sure, no problem.' Well, it wasn't too long after that that I got a call from the Academy saying, 'It's really problematic when you do that. Please don't do it again.' "

Stewart laughed. "I have to be kept on a very short leash," he said. "And rightly so."

FOR MUCH OF THE YEAR, *Saving Private Ryan* was the clear Oscar front-runner. A World War II epic from director Steven Spielberg, *Private Ryan* opened with a twenty-minute depiction of the invasion of Normandy on D-Day that was startling in its virtuosity and in the relentless nature of its carnage. And Spielberg wasn't alone in exploring the war: the legendary but reclusive Terrence Malick, who hadn't directed a movie in twenty years, made *The Thin Red Line*, a brutally rhapsodic war movie set on the Pacific island of Guadalcanal during World War II. Even Roberto Benigni, an Italian comic known mostly for his frenetic mugging, had the nerve to make *Life Is Beautiful*, in which he played an Italian Jew who during the war is sent to a concentration camp, where he convinces his young son that it's all an elaborate game.

But 1998 also had its share of movies that weren't loud, testosterone-laden, or filled with weaponry. *Shakespeare in Love*, a Miramax film that starred Harvey Weinstein's favorite leading lady, Gwyneth Paltrow, was a lark that in its charming but insistent way tried to make much of the similarities between Elizabethan England and modern Hollywood. And if Spielberg's film had been the favorite ever since its summer release, Miramax knew how to play the underdog. When *Shakespeare* came out of early screenings with a good buzz, the company quickly went to work. Miramax did what most studios did—it hired outside consultants, sent out videocassettes, courted journalists, and spent lavishly on ads in the Hollywood trade papers—but it seemed to do so more aggressively and feverishly than others. When *Saving Private Ryan* found itself losing occasional guild or critics' awards to the likes of *Shakespeare*, *The Thin Red Line*, and writer-director Bill Condon's *Gods and Monsters*, the Oscar race suddenly seemed closer and more competitive than anyone would have predicted.

"WELCOME TO CAMP OSCAR," said Bob Rehme, as he looked around the awfully luxurious campground: an elegant conference room at the swanky

Century Plaza Hotel in Century City. The walls were a soft peach color, a crystal chandelier hung from the ceiling, and tables laden with coffee, Danish pastries, and fruit juices awaited any of the several dozen Oscar staffers who might have been looking for a quick breakfast before a 10 a.m. production meeting.

Cates then looked around the room. "Let's see, who is here?" he asked, and then grinned. "Fuck." When the producer start spewing unprompted obscenities, longtime insiders knew it meant only one thing: "Oh, yes," said Cates. "Susan Futterman." From her seat, ABC's director of broadcast standards for comedy/variety grinned and waved. After years of waging battles large and small, she was used to this kind of shit from Cates. Futterman also knew that she had her work cut out for her: while Whoopi Goldberg talked as if she were an unpredictable wild card but then behaved once the cameras were on during her first go-around as host of the Oscars, she'd been far looser and less predictable on her return engagement. Now that Goldberg was back for number three, Futterman expected the host to push things even further.

When the staffers present had all introduced themselves, Cates removed the black cloth that had been draped over a bulletin board at the front of the room. On the board was a breakdown of the entire show, though the names of most of the presenters had been omitted. "Please, please, please, let's keep this in the room," Cates implored. "The press loves to give away our secrets. That's why most of the stars' names aren't up here. When you look at the board in my office, it has such stars and glitter. This is just the bare bones."

In fact, as Cates took staffers through the show itself, his rundown was infuriatingly vague. "Then a star comes out," he said. Later: "A very funny star." Later: "A big, beautiful, wonderful star comes out and introduces the *Life Is Beautiful* clip."

With seven nominations, *Life Is Beautiful* had set a record for a foreign film. Three days earlier, the movie's director and star had been named best actor at the Screen Actors Guild ceremony, and had responded with a delirious, lengthy speech in broken English. Remembering that, Cates laughed. "And if Roberto Benigni wins," he said, "be prepared for a *very* long show."

Finally, Cates arrived at what could become a defining moment of the seventy-first Oscars: the honorary Academy Award presentation to director Elia Kazan. "There will probably be a standing ovation," Cates predicted. "Some people probably won't stand, and some people probably won't clap. Whatever happens, happens. And we'll show whatever happens."

HONORARY ACADEMY AWARDS had been stirring up controversy for decades. From the first Academy Awards in 1929, when *The Jazz Singer* was declared ineligible for the real awards but then given a special Oscar for revolutionizing the industry, the honorary Oscars were often used to correct oversights and balance the inequities of the voting. If Alfred Hitchcock, one of the premier filmmakers of the century, somehow made it into his sixties without winning an Oscar despite half a dozen nominations, the solution, in 1967, was to give him the Irving Thalberg Award, the Oscar presented to a producer for his body of work. If Paul Newman's wins-to-nominations ratio was 0-for-6 after a splendid thirty-year career, the answer was to give the reluctant actor an honorary Oscar in 1983. (He won best actor the following year.) Harold Lloyd, Buster Keaton, Groucho Marx, Cary Gant, Greta Garbo, Edward G. Robinson, Kirk Douglas, Fred Astaire, Steven Spielberg— the list of those who'd been given an honorary Oscar or a Thalberg after years of being snubbed by the voters cut across the history of film.

But the special awards—which, besides the regular honorary Oscar and the Thalberg, grew to include the Jean Hersholt Humanitarian Award and, for a brief time, special juvenile awards—were not always doled out to right wrongs. They'd also rewarded friends of Oscar like Bob Hope. They'd gone to people of power within the organization: Darryl F. Zanuck, for instance, won three. And they'd been used to honor foreign filmmakers like Akira Kurosawa, Federico Fellini, and Michelangelo Antonioni, who otherwise would have little chance outside the foreign film category. The awards were usually proposed by members, partly because the board tended to ignore lobbying from outside the Academy. "If we made decisions based on public proposals," said Bruce Davis, "all of the Three Stooges would have honorary awards."

That Elia Kazan's relatively brief film career had been influential was not in question. When he made the move into films after an acclaimed career in theater, his performers—fresh, rough faces like Marlon Brando and Karl Malden, many of them trained in what would become known as Method Acting—brought a startling level of intensity and realism to the screen. Kazan was known as an actor's director, and his actors helped revolutionize the craft. Between *A Tree Grows in Brooklyn* in 1945 and *America, America* eighteen years later, actors in his movies won two dozen Oscar nominations, and took home nine statuettes.

In those years, Kazan himself was nominated for best director five times, winning for *Gentleman's Agreement* in 1947 and *On the Waterfront* seven years later. But from the early sixties on, he rarely worked in Hollywood, making only *The Arrangement* in 1969, *The Visitors* in 1972, and *The Last Tycoon* in 1976. None was particularly successful.

Still, those who objected to giving Kazan an honorary Oscar didn't do so simply because his career had tailed off after an early period for which the Academy had already rewarded him. Instead, they attacked the director, and the Academy, because in 1952, Kazan had gone before the House Un-American Activities Committee and named names.

During the 1930s, some in the creative community, Kazan among them, had embraced communism as a utopian economic philosophy and a system they felt was more equitable than unchecked capitalism. Some remained Communists, while many others walked away when Soviet dictator Josef Stalin's abuses and ambitions came to light, and when it became obvious that the philosophy laid out by Karl Marx and Friedrich Engels was being used for destructive ends. But the House Un-American Activities Committee, chaired by Senator Joseph McCarthy, reduced the complex situation to a single question: "Are you now, or have you ever been, a member of the Communist Party?"

In 1952, Kazan was not, but twenty years earlier he had been. When the committee asked him to name others who were once Communists, he complied. Kazan had not initially intended to name names; he did so, he claimed in his autobiography, only after a crisis of conscience in which he decided that the secretive nature of Communist Party membership was proof that the party really was trying to infiltrate and subvert the movie industry, just as McCarthy had charged.

Of the many industry figures called to testify, those who refused were blacklisted from further employment in Hollywood, as were those identified as Communists. And although McCarthy was publicly humiliated during a hearing in 1954, the blacklist affected a group of screenwriters—the so-called "Hollywood ten"—for years afterward. It wasn't until the 1960s, after people like Kirk Douglas and Otto Preminger began to hire and give screen credit to banned writers like Dalton Trumbo, that the blacklist lost its force.

While the blacklist was in effect, several Academy Awards for screen-writing went to people who had little or nothing to do with the scripts for which they won; the winners were fronts for the otherwise unemployable true writers. Worse, the Academy dishonored itself by adopting a rule that stripped Oscar eligibility from anyone who'd been a member of the Communist Party, or had refused to testify before a congressional committee. But that rule was quickly rescinded, and in the 1970s the Academy began to set the record straight and give Oscars—often as not posthumously—to the blacklisted writers who had earned them.

For decades, the chances of the Academy giving any further awards to Kazan seemed remote. But Karl Malden, a past president of the Academy and a man with clout on the board, was an avid supporter of the director who'd guided him to the only two Oscar nominations of his career. (Malden won for *A Streetcar Named Desire* and was also nominated for *On the Waterfront.*) In January 1999, at a board meeting devoted to the awarding of honorary Oscars, Malden stood and made his case.

Ordinarily, a nominating speech would have been followed by other governors speaking out on behalf of their candidates. Several rounds of voting then would narrow the field to a single candidate, whereupon the governors would vote one more time; if two-thirds of the board approved the selection, an award would be bestowed. The process could be repeated up to two more times with additional candidates.

In Kazan's case, though, Malden's speech was so persuasive that the governors voted immediately, with a show of hands rather than by secret ballot. One participant at the meeting recalled that two members of the board abstained, but otherwise the vote was unanimous. "It was a really good speech, and it came at a time when a lot of the old wounds had healed," said Bruce Davis, who attended the meeting. "I think it's a legitimate question: are we about morality or are we about art? Because if we start factoring in morality, there's a lot of people who might not be eligible."

When Kazan's award was announced, the criticism started. Abraham Polonsky, who'd been blacklisted and couldn't write anything under his own name for more than a decade, called Kazan "a creep" and bluntly declared, "I'll be watching, hoping somebody shoots him." Kazan's detractors asked those attending the awards to remain seated and not applaud when he came onstage.

The man at the middle of the controversy remained quiet. Kazan's third wife, Frances Kazan, did grant a rare interview to *Los Angeles Times* columnist Patrick Goldstein, who reminded her that some might be watching to see if Kazan would apologize for his actions.

"Too fucking bad," Mrs. Kazan said. "It's not going to happen."

BY THURSDAY of Oscar week, crews were crawling over the stage and backstage areas at the Dorothy Chandler Pavilion. In the middle of the stage sat an enormous white rotunda, the central element in an old-fashioned, classically ornate set that most staffers thought was Roy Christopher's best Oscar set ever.

"It's the last Oscars of the twentieth century, so I was looking for something classic yet forward-looking to end the millennium," explained Christopher. "And I was sort of at a loss until I saw a sixteenth-century drawing of an Italian rotunda in forced perspective." In front of the designer was a bag full of supplies that might prove vital as he did eleventh-hour touch-ups: fifteen rolls of Venetian Gold Plastifoil, a glittery cover-up for surfaces that might require some flash.

Outside the Chandler, the Academy held a noon press conference with Rehme, Cates, and Horvitz. One reporter asked about the size of the Oscar viewership. "We don't know the exact number," said Rehme, "but it's in the hundreds of millions."

This marked a significant change from what had for years been the Academy's and the network's standard line, that the Oscars were watched by a billion people. "We decided to drop the one billion figure," confessed ABC publicist Dan Doran as he watched the press conference. "It got ridiculous when the Grammys started claiming a billion six, even though they're on in fewer countries than we are. When we heard that, we thought, We can't get into this game with them. So now the official figure is hundreds of millions."

Bruce Davis was even blunter. "There has never been a television event in the history of the world that had a billion viewers," he said. "It's a handy number to throw around, but it's not true. I don't mind a little showmanship, but when you look at the domestic audience of around seventy-five million, that's a *long* way from a billion."

In much of the world, the Oscars were not broadcast live—or if they were, they were shown in the middle of the night, a dismal time for big TV ratings. Even in England, most of the viewers shunned the 2 a.m. live broadcast in favor of an edited version prepared by the BBC for airing the following night, by which time the results were known. "If you already know who's going to win," Davis said, "then you're left wondering if somebody will say something funny, or if somebody will cry. Which is not uninteresting, but the essence of the experience has evaporated at that point."

At the press conference, Cates also handled what had become an annual question: how long is the show going to be? "It's like the Super Bowl," he said, trotting out the analogy he would come to use at every opportunity. "It'll take as long as it takes."

Backstage, the consensus was that it would take a long time. For one thing, the show featured a dance number, an appearance by the grandson of Roy Rogers's famous horse, Trigger, and a large number of film packages, beginning with Mike Shapiro's usual In Memoriam package. But Frank Sinatra and Stanley Kubrick, both of whom had died since the last show, were being given separate tributes of their own. Cates had also ordered film salutes to cowboy stars, and to real-life heroes depicted on-screen. The producer knew that he had overloaded the show, but he had done so for a reason: afraid that the Kazan award would cast a pall over the entire night, he'd gone out of his way to lighten the show with additional entertainment.

The last of these elements was a five-minute Chuck Workman piece to open the evening. By the standards of Oscar film montages, five minutes was an eternity—but Cates wanted Workman's piece to cover a century of film, so he made room. "Since this is the last Oscar show of the twentieth century, they wanted to show what Academy members think are the best film moments of the century," said Workman. "So they had little postcards that they sent out, along with a very official-looking letter asking everybody to vote for their three favorite moments."

About 1,700 of the Academy's 5,500 voters had returned ballots. Workman took the top 350 vote-getters, added another 150 scenes of his own choosing, and then narrowed his choice down to the 250 clips that made up the final package. "What surprised me," he said, "was how many people voted for themselves. Val Kilmer nominated three of his own movies, including *Batman Forever*, and apologized for it in the postcard. He said, 'I can't help it, these are my three favorite movies.' And then a lot of people called me afterwards and said, 'You are going to include my scenes, aren't you?'" The top four vote-getters were the final scenes of *Citizen Kane*, *Casablanca*, and *Sunset Boulevard*, and the sequence from *When Harry Met Sally* in which Meg Ryan loudly faked an orgasm while dining with Billy Crystal at the Carnegie Deli.

Late in the afternoon, Debbie Allen made her return to the Academy Awards after a three-year absence. Rather than recruit a large cast, the way she usually did, Allen had opted for a more serious, intimate presentation of dances to accompany the five nominated film scores. She chose five dancers: the Spanish flamenco sensation Joaquin Cortez; eighteen-year-old Rasta Thomas, a San Francisco–born dancer who was studying at the Kirov Academy; New York–bred ballerina Tai Jimenez, the only woman of the group; Desmond Richardson, a member of the American Ballet Theater who had worked extensively on Broadway; and the twenty-five-year-old tap dancer Savion Glover, who'd performed on the Oscars three years earlier and had also made an appearance in 1989 as the youngest and most talented of Allan Carr's "stars of tomorrow."

Allen had choreographed a series of solos, duets, and group scenes set to snippets of music from *Life Is Beautiful*, *Saving Private Ryan*, *Elizabeth*, *Pleasantville*, and *The Thin Red Line*. As usual for Allen's Oscar routines, the sheer athleticism and grace of the dancers proved far more persuasive up close and live than it did on the television screen, where questions tended to arise about such issues as whether it was appropriate to salute the bloody World War II epic *Saving Private Ryan* with a tap dance from Glover.

At the Chandler, of course, it was far too late to ask those kinds of questions. Allen arranged her dancers across the stage, and then lectured them like she was a schoolmarm and they were unruly fifth graders. "Child, be a gentleman, don't paw her," she said to Thomas, who had idly placed his hand on Jimenez's back. Then she turned to the whole group. "Once you're in place, you must not fidget," she said sternly. "Lights are all around you, and you never know when he's going to focus on you. You must be *still*."

The dancers ran through the number a couple of times in low gear, taking it easy on the most physical aspects, the lifts and leaps. "Okay, guys," Allen said finally. "I need you to do it full out this time. Please? Otherwise we don't know what we've got." The next time through, some of the crew members who were watching cheered at the sheer virtuosity of the dancers—particularly Thomas, as word swept through the Chandler that he was still a teenager.

NORMALLY, recipients of honorary Oscars gave their speeches to the Academy ahead of time, so that their lines could be placed on the TelePromp Ter. But Elia Kazan did not do that. When he made his first appearance at the Chandler on Friday morning, tensions were running high and nobody knew what he was going to say.

Walking slowly, flanked by his wife, Frances, and by several security guards, Kazan looked frail, tentative, and a little confused. At first, Cates walked him through the rehearsal, with stand-ins taking the place of Robert DeNiro and Martin Scorsese, who would give Kazan his award. But when one of the stand-ins said, "Ladies and gentlemen, Mr. Elia Kazan," and then handed over the plaster Oscar statuette used for rehearsals, Kazan studied it, a quizzical look on his face.

"Say something, Elia," said Frances.

"Here's where you say thank you," added Cates.

"That's it?" said Kazan. "And go home?" He frowned. "Where does Bobby stand?"

Cates pointed to the stand-ins. "Bobby will be right there, and so will Martin."

For the second rehearsal, Kazan was led to the back of the stage, where he waited while the tribute film played on a large screen center stage. As he waited, Frances coached him. "After they give you the Oscar, just say thank you," she said. "That's *all* you have to say."

The second time through, Kazan took the dummy Oscar, looked into the audience, and delivered a two-word speech: "Thank you." Then he walked off. The brevity of his remarks stunned staffers who'd wondered if he would use the occasion to answer his critics or acknowledge the controversy.

But Kazan was unconcerned with whatever furor he may have caused; he simply walked into the wings, sat in a chair, and watched the rehearsal on a nearby monitor. The film critic and historian Richard Schickel, who put together the tribute saluting Kazan, came up to say hello. "This must be fun for you, being on a set again," he said.

"Yeah," said Kazan. "I've never seen a show like this."

As the two men chatted, stagehands wrestled with a huge Oscar statue that had been positioned under the rotunda. On the monitor, Anne Heche ran through her lines; backstage, Renée Zellweger waited for her cue to do the same.

"Where are you going from here, Richard?" asked Kazan. "Are you going to write another book?"

"I might write a book about *you*, Elia," said Schickel. "What do you think of that?"

"I think there's too much talk about me," said Kazan wearily. "I'm just another Joe."

"STAND BY, boys and girls, or dysfunctional children," Lou Horvitz announced over the P.A. system as lunchtime ended. "Daddy's home."

Daddy, in the person of Horvitz, could be a stern taskmaster—as well as a world-class screamer whose tirades were already legendary by his third year with the Oscars. "I don't have a big patience level," he conceded. "The team I put around me are all A players, so I have incredibly high expectations of them not to drop the ball. I'm not in it to be a nice guy, and I'm not going to win a popularity contest. But I feel that I'm fair, and I feel that I'm damn humorous."

Horvitz had also won kudos for his ability to react quickly, and for the meticulous way he planned the show—from seeing the shots in his head before he ever got to the theater to laying out "relationship charts" identifying where each nominee's loved ones and costars would be sitting, in order to get quick reaction shots. "If a winner's third-grade teacher is sitting in the balcony, Lou knows about it," said Garry Hood.

Still, other staffers found the level of Horvitz's preparation—the scripts he sent out two weeks before the show, laying out every single camera move and cutaway—to be stifling. Confided one veteran staffer, "The show's not as much *fun* as it used to be."

Fun was on the afternoon agenda, though, because Aerosmith was in the house. Formed in Boston in 1970, Aerosmith was a hard-rock band that modeled itself after the Rolling Stones, both in the raucous, blues-based music, and in the offstage excesses. By the beginning of the 1980s, the band had fought, broken up, and reunited; just because they could get the band back together, though, didn't mean they could get themselves together. "There's nothing to do on the road but take drugs and fuck," lead singer Steven Tyler declared during an attempted comeback in 1984, shortly before showing for a concert in such an altered state that he fell off the stage.

The old Aerosmith would never have been booked to perform on the Academy Awards—but then, that Aerosmith wouldn't have recorded "I Don't Want to Miss a Thing," a big, generic hard-rock ballad written by Dianne Warren for director Michael Bay's big, generic hard-rock movie *Armageddon*. But Aerosmith had cleaned up and had a string of hits that included "Love in an Elevator" and "Dude (Looks Like a Lady)." The latter-day Aerosmith was calmer, its music slicker. Tyler even had a movie star daughter, Liv Tyler, who played Ben Affleck's love interest in *Armageddon*.

Still, even the new Aerosmith was an uneasy fit for the Oscars. Before the band rehearsed, Cates and Conti met with them backstage. The recorded version of "I Don't Want to Miss a Thing" featured an orchestra, but the difficulties in balancing the rock band and the orchestra were formidable. Cates, who appreciated Bruce Springsteen and loved Céline Dion but was assuredly not a rock fan, gave the boys a pep talk. "You don't need the orchestra!" he told them. "You're a *band*!"

A few minutes later, Aerosmith took the stage and ran through the song for the first time. Though it was only a casual rehearsal, Tyler gave the kind of full-out, theatrical, scarf-flinging performance for which he had become known. The second rehearsal included two columns of flame at the rear of the stage, plus an explosion and a shower of sparks. Undeniably entertaining, it was massively louder than anything else on this or maybe any other Academy Awards show.

As the band got ready to leave, show publicist Eva Dimergian returned from its dressing room. "They're really worried about their drummer, Joey Kramer," she said. "I guess he *never* gets dressed up." She laughed, and thought of the dress code that applied to stagehands. "And I don't know how they're going to get some of those roadies into tuxes."

THE FIRST TIME that Whoopi Goldberg hosted the Oscars, it was the year of *Schindler's List*; the second time, Jesse Jackson led a protest against the paltry extent of African American representation in Hollywood. And when she took the job in 1999, Goldberg was once again dismayed at what she saw as the limited opportunities for jokes provided by nominated films like *Saving Private Ryan*. But when she and Bruce Vilanch noticed that two different women had been nominated for playing Queen Elizabeth—Cate Blanchett in *Elizabeth* and Judi Dench in *Shakespeare in Love*—they decided that it might be fun for Goldberg herself to enter dressed as the queen.

"The idea sort of grew from there, because we're always looking for things that Whoopi can do during the show," said Vilanch. "And eventually we thought, Why doesn't she wear clothes from the five films nominated for costume design, and then give out that award?"

The decision to turn Goldberg into a fashion model had a twofold effect: it forced the host to spend much of her time backstage doing eleven frantic costume changes, and it made her rehearsals top secret. The theater was cleared of all guests before Goldberg's Friday afternoon rehearsal, which began when she took the stage dressed in a hugely elaborate Queen Elizabeth costume, including full whiteface. "Good evening," she said. "I am the African Queen."

Goldberg ran through her lines quietly, almost unintelligibly; the main reason for this rehearsal wasn't to test the jokes, but to see if she could make her costume changes quickly enough. When she changed into the fifties-style suburban frock from *Pleasantville*, she mispronounced the name of costume designer Judianna Makovsky. "I think you'd better spell it phonetically for the colored girl, 'cause we don't have names like that," she told the TelePrompTer operator. "We have names like Jackson, Jones . . . Anyway, the bitch made some cool costumes." Sitting in the second row in front of Goldberg, Susan Futterman laughed and shook her head.

Goldberg's ensuing costume changes put her into slave rags from *Beloved*, a glam-rock outfit from *Velvet Goldmine*, an Old Globe actor's getup from *Shakespeare in Love*, and a return to full Elizabethan garb, this time a man's outfit that included a beard, from *Elizabeth*. This last costume prompted a number of off-color gags, beginning when Goldberg stroked the beard and commented, "I feel like Ellen DeGeneres." When the audience groaned again, she snapped, "You think this is easy? I haven't taken my dress off so many times since my first audition."

A minute later, she read her intro to John Travolta, whose recent movies had included *Primary Colors* and *A Civil Action*. "Our next presenter played a politician and a personal injury lawyer, and we still like him," she said, and then paused. "Bruce?" she said, looking for Vilanch. "Did I miss the joke? It's just that I'm standing up here with my panties down, and I want to know why. So I don't fuck up the joke."

With the small audience in stitches at her gleeful, good-natured profanity, Goldberg stoked the fires even further. When it was time for her to open the envelope and present the award for costume design, the TelePrompTer flashed the word ENVELOPE. Goldberg looked at it, annoyed. "Quit flashing ENVELOPE at me," she said, holding up the dummy Oscar. "I've been here before. I *got* one of these motherfuckers."

She looked toward Futterman. "Is Susan still breathing?"

AEROSMITH'S SONG may have been the biggest change of pace from the usual Oscar fare, but it was far from the trickiest of the nominated tunes. That distinction had to go to "When You Believe" from the animated DreamWorks film *The Prince of Egypt*. In the film, the song existed in two different versions. The first was sung by Michelle Pfeiffer, who supplied the voice for one of the lead characters, and also by Sally Dworsky, who provided the singing voice for a character played by Sandra Bullock. But to run over the final credits—and, crucially, to score a pop hit that would help sell the movie—a second version of the song was recorded by the prolific pop/soul singer and producer Kenneth "Babyface" Edmonds.

Edmonds refashioned some of the music to make the song more commercial, wrote a new bridge, took a cowriting credit, and brought in Whitney Houston, Mariah Carey, and a gospel choir, the last in place of the children's chorus that sang in Hebrew in the original song. While Schwartz's song was called "When You Believe," the Babyface revision bore the title "The Prince of Egypt (When You Believe)."

Schwartz's version was the one nominated for an Oscar—the songwriter had seen to that when he declined to give Edmonds a writing credit in forms submitted to the Academy. After Houston and Carey were booked to perform on the Oscar show, the Academy insisted that they'd be performing the original song, rather than the pop version with which the singers were more familiar.

Conti wrote an arrangement that added a few pop touches to Schwartz's original song. It seemed crucial that Houston and Carey have enough rehearsal time to work on this hybrid—but at the last minute, Houston called to say she wouldn't be able to join Carey at the Friday night rehearsal.

Among the crew, there was some uncertainty about her excuse. "She missed her plane, or she has an ear condition, or some other bullshit story," snapped one top executive. And when Carey arrived and learned that her fellow diva wouldn't be showing up, her immediate reaction was to leave as well, though she eventually reconsidered.

Another drama, meanwhile, was playing out among the stand-ins. Early in the day, stand-in Janis Uhley had done a creditable job singing Céline Dion's part at a rehearsal of the Dion–Andrea Bocelli duet "The Prayer." (Bocelli's part had been handled by a young singer named Josh Groban, a protégé of songwriter and producer David Foster.) Uhley, who'd once worked as Horvitz's assistant, wanted to sing Houston's part as well, but some stage managers thought she wasn't the right choice for the job; in this situation, they needed somebody who'd blend in and stay out of Carey's way. ("Janis likes to sing too much," explained one.) Uhley went over their heads to plead her case, and word came down from Horvitz to let her sing.

At about 8:30, the members of a gospel choir took their places on a large pyramid that sat at the rear of the stage. After the choir rehearsed the song a couple of times, with Debbie Allen directing the singers in where to stand and how to wave their arms, Carey walked onstage in tight black capri pants and a snug white spaghetti-strap shirt. Allen showed her the flight of stairs she'd be walking down at the beginning of the song, and Carey laughed. "Maybe someday," she sighed, "awards shows will have escalators."

On the first run-through, Carey looked nervous and unsteady, and she couldn't remember all of the lyrics. Stand-in Uhley didn't have any such problem; in fact, she sang with a theatricality and gusto that seemed more than a little inappropriate, and even unnerving. In the audience, a few staffers exchanged glances as Carey laid back and let Uhley belt out the song. Afterward, Carey's reps spoke quickly and urgently to the production crew. "Their basic message," said one crew member, "was 'Get her off the stage.'" The next time through, a different, more subdued stand-in took over.

Sitting at the production table during the late-night rehearsal, Michael Seligman looked over his shoulder and saw Susan Futterman still sitting a few rows back. "Hey, Futterman," he yelled, "isn't it past your bedtime?"

"Have you fixed the piano yet?" she yelled back.

Seligman flinched. A few hours earlier, Futterman had informed him that the Steinway and Sons logo visible on Randy Newman's piano would have to be covered, because Steinway wasn't paying for product placement. Seligman hadn't taken care of the offending logo yet, so he cupped his hands over his ears and played deaf.

"What?" he said.

"Have you fixed the piano yet?"

"*What???*"

After Futterman gave up, Seligman shook his head. "I was in the middle of dealing with a big problem this afternoon," he said, "when Susan called me to tell me that something in the script didn't read right, because a comma was in the wrong place." He sighed. "I said, Susan, take your fuckin' comma . . ."

SATURDAY AFTERNOON, Elia Kazan returned to the Chandler for another rehearsal. Again, he was accompanied by his wife and by several security guards. This time, Kazan's speech was marginally longer. "Thanks to the Academy," he said, "for its good heart and its generosity. Thank you all." He walked off, went straight into the wings, grabbed a chair, and sat down where he could watch rehearsals on a monitor.

For the next hour, Liv Tyler struggled to read the TelePrompTer, Gwyneth Paltrow laughed out loud when she realized how extensive the ritual was with the stand-ins, and Catherine Zeta-Jones rehearsed while stagehands tried to secure a loose pipe high on a side wall in the wings. Nearby, another crew member used black paint to cover the Steinway and Sons logo on Randy Newman's piano.

Kazan, meanwhile, sat calmly in his director's chair, occasionally talking to staffers about his days in live television.

Eventually, Frances Kazan approached her husband. "I'm tired," she said. "I want to go lie down."

"Lie down in the green room," he said.

"But I want to go home."

Kazan wasn't moving. "Go ahead and go," he said.

"But you have the limo."

"Then take a taxi."

Giving up, she left Kazan in the company of his bodyguards. He remained in the wings, a slight smile on his face as he took in the activity around him. "Elia's our new mascot," Debbie Williams told Cates when the producer walked by.

Cates looked at Kazan and nodded. "It's his last hurrah," he suggested gently. "And he knows it."

DRESS REHEARSAL ran smoothly, though Goldberg continued to take particular delight in tweaking the ABC censor. Reading her introduction of the Irish actor Liam Neeson, the host began slowly and suggestively stroking the microphone stand in front of her. The audience howled with laughter at the completely inappropriate bit—particularly, it seemed, Judith Reichman, Cates's wife and, coincidentally, Futterman's gynecologist. During a break,

Reichman approached Futterman to plead that she not cut the sight gag. When Futterman said she was more concerned with Goldberg's suggestive beard jokes, Reichman quickly brokered a deal: let Whoopi stroke the mike stand and she'll keep quiet about the beard. "Every woman in America will love it," Reichman promised.

The rehearsal made it clear that it was going to be a very long show. Cates knew that the show had gotten away from him, but he tried to shrug it off. "The ironic thing," he told Rehme, "is that if you make the show shorter, it'll be more boring. If you take away what makes it long, then there'll be no entertainment."

Vilanch dropped by the production table to say that lots of jokes about the show's length had been prepared. "There's, 'While you've been watching the show, another century has passed. Get ready for Y3K.' And, 'For those of you who were upset that the show was moved from Monday night, guess what? It's Monday night!' "

As soon as the dress rehearsal ended, stagehands pulled an enormous Oscar statue off the stage and rolled in staircases for Mariah Carey and Whitney Houston. Houston had finally arrived a few hours earlier for the dress run-through, but her unfamiliarity with the song's new arrangement had left her begging for more rehearsal time. Though it meant paying overtime, Cates had quickly agreed to give the divas an additional run-through once the main rehearsal ended.

The pair returned to the stage around eleven p.m., Houston's arm around Carey's shoulders. Houston wore a tailored black suit that hung on her stylishly; Carey was squeezed into impossibly tight blue jeans and a low-cut T-shirt.

"I love divas," said Vilanch. "I live for divas."

As Bill Conti played his arrangement of the song, Houston shook her head, tried briefly to adapt, and then stopped singing altogether. "I'm sorry, Bill," she said. "We're just used to the recorded version, and it's freaking us out, man."

Over and over, Houston returned to the same complaint. "Is it okay to do it how they originally had it?" she asked, referring not to the original, nominated version of the song, but to the Babyface revision to which Schwartz had denied the nomination. "This is a totally different count. I want what was on the record, and this ain't it." She shook her head in frustration. "I'm incapable of expressing it. You know what I'm talking about?"

Finally, after about forty minutes of tinkering, Conti crafted an arrangement close enough to the Babyface version to satisfy Houston (and Carey, who'd been letting her partner take the lead). "Whoo!" shouted Houston when Conti delayed a crucial chord change just long enough. "Hallelujah, darling!"

Carey nodded. "We got it now," she said.

"Thank you, everybody," added Houston, "and God bless you."

At 11:40, the cameramen were sent home. Houston and Carey headed into the wings together, decided they didn't want to wait for the elevator, and walked up a flight of stairs to their dressing rooms. Trailed by two large entourages, they walked arm in arm, harmonizing on "When You Believe" all the way up the stairs.

AT 2:15 on the day of the show, walkie-talkies crackled backstage. "We have a request," said a voice, "for some pizzas for Aerosmith."

A minute later came the reply. "That's an okay on those pizzas."

A few minutes later, the best-picture award at the final rehearsal went to *Shakespeare in Love*. The choice was random but intriguing, because many Oscar handicappers felt that Miramax's romantic comedy had been picking up momentum in recent weeks. The company's strategy was clear. To many people, *Saving Private Ryan* did not resonate the way Spielberg's *Schindler's List* had done five years earlier. Some Academy members admired the film but couldn't embrace it; *Ryan* was too long, too violent, a return to an area the director had covered with more feeling and sensitivity. Surely some voters were ready for a lighter, wittier alternative; the trick was to make sure that they thought of *Shakespeare in Love* as that alternative.

A handful of critics' awards and a win over *Private Ryan* at the Writers Guild awards helped *Shakespeare*'s cause, and Miramax kept up the pressure with so many trade ads that DreamWorks publicly complained about having to step up its own ad campaign to keep pace. "There is no question that the aggressiveness of the extraordinary campaign Miramax has run in support of 'Shakespeare' has caused us to do more on behalf of 'Ryan' than we had initially planned," DreamWorks cochairman Jeffrey Katzenberg told the *Los Angeles Times*. *New York* magazine suggested that Harvey Weinstein was privately bashing Spielberg's movie, while others insisted that Weinstein wasn't, but that DreamWorks was trying to spread the word that he was. Campaign spending by one or both companies was estimated to be as high as $15 million.

All those charges were hotly denied, but bad blood and ill will hung in the air. By the week of the Oscars, asking who would win best picture had, in Hollywood at least, become tantamount to asking if Miramax's *Shakespeare* campaign had worked, or if the studio had gone too far and created a fatal backlash.

The Academy, for its part, was not pleased with the emphasis on campaigning. "Miramax has gone at the whole idea of campaigning in a way that just hadn't been seen before," said Bruce Davis. "They see it as a competitive sport, and look for every edge, every angle. And they're not the only ones responsible, because the others have felt the need to step up and match them."

OSCAR CAMPAIGNS weren't the only area that had been heating up. For years, ABC and the Academy had been watching as the hoopla surrounding all aspects of the Oscars grew. The growth was accelerated by outlets like *Entertainment Tonight*, the syndicated entertainment news show that began in 1981; the similarly focused *Access Hollywood*, which started thirteen years later; and E! Entertainment Television, a cable network devoted entirely to the entertainment industry.

For these outlets, the Oscars were the Super Bowl and Election Day combined; simply covering the results wasn't enough. There had to be daily Oscar updates, "backstage at the Oscars" features, and of course "countdown to the Oscars" preshows. E! enjoyed its highest ratings of the year by parking comedian Joan Rivers and her daughter, Melissa, on the red carpet, where they sucked up to celebrities' faces but lambasted their fashion choices once the stars had moved on. The ABC affiliate in Los Angeles, KABC, syndicated its preshow coverage, making it the station's most profitable show.

With the move to Sunday at 5:30, the Academy decided to produce its own half-hour preshow. During that final thirty minutes, other crews would not be allowed to broadcast live from the red carpet. "It was such an odd thing that we were doing this show and allowing six or seven other entities to do a show right ahead of our show, on our turf," said Bruce Davis. "We wanted to claim that turf, at least for the half hour."

Cates was nominally in charge of the preshow as well. But since he had his hands full with what quickly came to be called "the big show," he hired Dennis Doty to oversee the preshow. Doty, a longtime producer of made-for-television movies, was not only a good friend of Cates's, but also his partner in Cates-Doty Productions.

Promising looks into areas of the show that viewers had never seen, Doty and his crew prepared a variety of features, including the history of Oscar fashions and the making of Oscar statuettes. He also hired a pair of hosts, CNN reporter Jim Moret and actress Geena Davis, and set up bases along the red carpet and in the Founders Room, an elaborate private room on the mezzanine level of the Dorothy Chandler Pavilion.

Since it would have been folly to rely on the right people to be on the red carpet at the right time, Doty planned to pretape several of Moret's and Davis's interviews. (Home viewers wouldn't be apprised of this.) At 4 p.m. in the Founders Room, Davis prepared for one of those interviews. Standing on a small circular stage in front of an elaborate backdrop, the actress looked over cue cards bearing questions for the nominated Australian actor Geoffrey Rush. Besides the camera crew, about a dozen other staffers and bystanders stood around, watching.

"I'll ask him about Australia first, and then *Shine*," Davis said. "And then I should just pick one of those other questions. I think the one about costume design is more interesting."

A few minutes later, Rush showed up. At first, he spoke so softly that the interview had to be halted in order that a staffer could reposition Rush's microphone closer to his mouth. Then Davis tried again. "Seven of your fellow Australians," she began. "And yourself, of course." She stopped. "Can I start that again?" She tried again, and flubbed the opening question again.

When she finally finished the interview, an aide informed her that it was thirty seconds too long for the slot where they'd be using it. "When you ask me that last question about the costumes," suggested Rush, "I'll just say, 'Yes, I liked the costumes,' and end it at that."

After a few more false starts, Davis completed the interview to everyone's satisfaction. Then she looked around the room. "Could there be more people watching?" she said, mildly annoyed. "Actually, I wouldn't mind if we cleared the room."

What Davis didn't know was that the entire episode—the false starts, the flubbed lines, the muttered conversations between takes—continued to be shown, unedited, on monitors throughout the backstage area. It also played on a pair of monitors at opposite ends of the Dorothy Chandler Pavilion lobby, where the crowd had already begun to arrive.

"I'm such a novice," Davis sighed, as Academy guests and staffers listened in.

An hour later, home viewers saw the completed version of the interview, along with a breathless but tepid collection of other interviews and clips. At the end of the preshow broadcast, cameras inside the command truck showed Cates standing behind Horvitz. "Two minutes to air, ladies and gentlemen, to over a billion people watching," Horvitz said. "Have fun."

5:30 P.M., PACIFIC DAYLIGHT TIME: *"Live from the Dorothy Chandler Pavilion in Los Angeles, California, the 71st annual Academy Awards."*

As the traditional montage of arriving stars played, best supporting actress nominee Judi Dench rushed through the lobby and arrived at a door into the hall moments after it had been shut. "I'm sorry," said an usher. "You'll have to wait until the first commercial break."

"No, we have to get her inside!" yelled a stage manager who was scanning the latecomers. "Lou wants her in the audience for Whoopi's entrance!" Dench was quickly and quietly whisked to her third-row aisle seat.

At the same time, several guards brought Whitney Houston into the backstage area through a small hallway. Grasping the folds of her dress in one hand and her young daughter in the other, Houston looked at the pages and guards who had been stationed in that area. "Who *are* these people?" she snapped impatiently.

An usher watched the diva and her entourage sweep past. "Some people," the usher muttered under her breath.

As Houston fled to her dressing room, Goldberg walked onstage as Queen Elizabeth, wearing whiteface and an enormous gown and wig. Horvitz cut to Judi Dench, who was laughing. "Good evening, loyal subjects," Goldberg said. "I am the African Queen. Some of you may know me as the virgin queen, but I can't imagine who."

Then she tried to head a few critics off at the pass. "This will be a long show," she said, "so we don't want to read about how damn long it was. We know it's long. Tough." She brought out Bob Rehme, and as soon as the Academy president took the stage Goldberg rushed offstage and hurried through a black curtain in the wings. She headed to her left down a short, heavily guarded corridor, made a quick right, ducked into her dressing room, and ripped off the heavy gown.

As Chuck Workman's film of memorable movie moments played, stage manager Dency Nelson led Kim Basinger out of the wings and into position behind an enormous Oscar statue that sat center stage. Behind the statue was a stool for Basinger to sit on, but she didn't use it.

Goldberg returned to the stage in a less ostentatious gown, wiping the last of the white makeup off her face. With Basinger and Nelson hidden behind the huge Oscar statue, all eyes were on Goldberg as she ran through a seven-minute monologue. "I thought the blacklist was me and Hattie McDaniel, shit," she said, muttering the last word softly but clearly. About twenty feet behind Goldberg, Basinger swayed back and forth. Hidden from the audience, she bounced on her heels and took occasional sips from a bottle of water she then placed on the base of the giant Oscar statue. Nelson sat on the floor behind her, consulting his notes.

"Armageddon ready to hand out some little bald boys," cracked Goldberg. "Our first presenter went home last year with two of the best-looking men in Hollywood: Oscar and Alec Baldwin," said Goldberg. "Lucky girl." From her hiding place behind the statue, Basinger grinned. Nelson got up off the floor and cued Basinger, who presented James Coburn with the best supporting actor award for *Affliction*.

"I finally got one right, I guess," said Coburn, a veteran of more than seventy films. As he talked, five handheld cameras remained focused on the other nominees, in case he decided to say something about them. Coburn went well over the suggested forty-five-second limit, ignoring the TelePrompTer, which was flashing PLEASE WRAP UP! against a red background. A minute and a half into Coburn's speech, Horvitz cued Conti to begin playing music. "Wait a minute, *wait a minute*!" Coburn shouted. "I've gotta say something else here!" The orchestra continued playing, but softly, as Coburn finished his remarks.

At 5:55, the show cut to its first commercial break. Upon its return, members of the gospel choir took their places on the stage. At the same time, Mariah Carey and Whitney Houston stood in the wings stage right and left, respectively. Houston dabbed at her nose and mouth with a tissue.

As the two divas sang "When You Believe," Matt Damon, Ben Affleck, Edward Norton, and Billy Bob Thornton stepped outside the theater for some fresh air.

An hour into the show, Goldberg came onstage in her *Pleasantville* frock. "Good evening, I'm Marilyn Quayle," she said. She described the movie's clothes as being "inspired by those memorable black-and-white television series of long ago. More white than black, as I recall. But let's just leave that to beaver." A pause. "I didn't say whose." She grinned wider. "You know, I may not be doing this show ever again. So let's just go right to the edge and go over, what do you say?"

When Robin Williams took the stage to present the best supporting actress Oscar, Damon, Affleck, Norton, and Thornton headed back into the lobby to watch a monitor. As they went through the door, a catering employee dashed toward them, shouting "Mr. Norton!" Norton stopped. "I just wanted to say hi," she told him—violating the first rule of working at the Oscars, which was "Don't bother the stars."

"Thank you," Norton said politely. The catering employee headed back to her coworkers, who greeted her with whoops. Damon, Affleck, Norton, and Thornton watched as Williams made a suggestion. "In terms of the Kazan controversy," he said, "let Lainie sing!" Then he gave the supporting-actress award to Judi Dench for *Shakespeare in Love*. In the lobby, Damon clapped.

During a commercial break after the award, the aisles were clogged with stars coming and going. Coburn returned to his seat, where he was congratulated by his *Affliction* costar Nick Nolte. A few seats away, Emily Watson hugged Rachel Griffiths, her costar in (and fellow nominee for) *Hillary and Jackie*. Robin Williams headed in a side door, walked over to Norton, and shook his hand. "Powerful stuff," he said to the star of *American History X*. Jack Nicholson left his seat and made his way toward the exit, pausing to shake Damon's hand. As Nicholson went out the door, Harvey Weinstein stopped him to say hello. Aerosmith's roadies, wearing everything from tuxes to black T-shirts, set up the band's equipment as Conti's orchestra played "Over the Rainbow."

Back from the commercial break, Goldberg spotted Goldie Hawn and Kurt Russell standing in the aisle, pointing at the seat-fillers who'd taken their seats. "Hi, Goldie," she said. "Siddown. Shiiiii . . ." She trailed off before supplying the final consonant. The seat-fillers quickly vacated Kurt's and Goldie's seats.

As Chris Rock presented the award for sound effects editing, the members of Aerosmith took their places behind a screen that hid them from the audience. Drummer Joey Kramer was wearing a gold lamé suit. "It's a big, controversial night," said Rock as the band members picked up instruments. "I saw DeNiro backstage. You better get Kazan away from DeNiro, 'cause you know he hates rats." There were audible groans from the crowd. "Now, somebody has a death wish if they wanted me to come up here," said Rock.

After Rock's introduction, a short film spotlighting the nominees played on the screen in front of Aerosmith. During the few seconds when the home audience could only hear that film's soundtrack, the band members quickly tested their instruments. Hearing the rock 'n' roll riffs blasting from behind the curtain, a few audience members hooted. As the film ended, a stage manager cued the band to stop playing and wait for their introduction from Liv Tyler. The group's performance was typically spirited; leaving the stage, Steven Tyler high-fived his huge bodyguard, who was waiting for him in the wings.

In the green room, Nicolas Cage talked to a page. Andie MacDowell watched the show on a monitor. Outside the room, Bruce Vilanch smiled. "Two *shits* and one *beaver* so far," he said. "I'm counting. And Chris Rock took care of Kazan for us." He looked pleased. "Susan Futterman keeps putting little notes on the mirror in Whoopi's dressing room: DON'T GO THERE; NO MORE SHIT; THIS IS SUSAN: WATCH YOUR MOUTH, GIRL."

Cheers sounded in the green room as *Life Is Beautiful* won the award for best foreign-language film. As expected, Roberto Benigni went crazy, walking on seat backs and rambling through an exuberant two-and-a-half-minute speech in amusingly broken English. "I feel like now to dive into this ocean of generosity," he said.

Immediately afterward, John Travolta introduced a tribute to Frank Sinatra. In the west lobby, a huge group of seat-fillers stood around the monitor, watching. Just outside the lobby, in a secluded area by some of the control trailers, Nick Nolte stood by himself, hands in his pockets. Behind a black drape not far from Nolte, Val Kilmer was led through a stage door and into the wings. He was followed quickly by Triggerson, the grandson of Roy Rogers's famous steed. As the trainer held Triggerson, Kilmer walked around the horse, petting and talking to him.

On the stage, Goldberg introduced Liam Neeson, stroking the microphone stand as she spoke. The audience tittered. Backstage, Triggerson started stomping his foot, a trick for which he was usually rewarded with a treat. (To ensure he didn't leave an unsightly souvenir onstage, the horse's feeding schedule had been changed.) Though the trainer tried to calm Triggerson, Kilmer didn't feel comfortable trying to ride the skittish horse—so when he took the stage to introduce a tribute to cowboy actors, he was beside Triggerson rather than astride him. The horse walked in circles and resisted Kilmer's attempts to control him. "Debbie Allen didn't choreograph this part," Kilmer said.

A few minutes later, Helen Hunt read the nominees for best actor. Peter Gabriel and Randy Newman stood in the wings, waiting for their turn to perform. Roberto Benigni won, in a huge upset over Ian McKellen's remarkable performance in *Gods and Monsters*. "This is a terrible mistake because I used up all my English!" Benigni shouted. "My body is in tumult! I would like to be Jupiter and kidnap everybody and lie down in the firmament making love to everybody . . ."

Newman and Gabriel, due up next, watched the spectacle from the side of the stage. "It'll be like following an animal act," said Newman as Benigni went on and on.

After a minute and a half, the music came up to play off Benigni, and the show cut to a commercial. During the break, three of the best-actor nominees—Nolte, Norton, and McKellen—ran into each other in the bar and teased one another about losing to the hyperactive Italian.

Paltrow, meanwhile, stepped outside for a smoke. Danette Herman stuck her head into Cates's office, where Elia and Frances Kazan sat with Scorsese and DeNiro. "One more segment," she said, "and then it'll be time." It was already eight o'clock, two and a half hours into the show. "It's Sunday *and* Monday at the Oscars," Herman said apologetically.

When the word spread backstage that the upcoming segment would include the award to Kazan, there was a sudden flurry of activity. Damon and Affleck, who were presenting the award immediately before Kazan's, asked Debbie Williams if there was any way they could get back to their seats to see the honorary award. "I'm sorry," she told them, "but there's no time to reseat you."

With thirty seconds left before the commercial ended, a page approached stage manager Rita Cossette. "Val Kilmer would like to return to his seat to see the Kazan award," she said. "Is that possible?"

"I can do it," said Cossette. "Where is he?" She rushed to the green room, but returned a minute later shaking her head. "He's got his girlfriend with him, and they're three seats in from the aisle," she said. "It'd be impossible."

The act began with Goldberg wearing a glittery silver glam-rock ensemble from *Velvet Goldmine*; bedecked with feathered plumes, she tottered on massive platform boots. After introducing Lisa Kudrow, Goldberg dashed into the wings and headed for her dressing room to change into a costume from *Shakespeare in Love*. Garry Hood saw the look on her face as she passed, and thought the host was probably regretting her decision to wear so many outfits.

While she was changing, Scorsese and DeNiro began to speak about Kazan. The green room got very quiet. A huge crowd also gathered around another backstage monitor, this one hanging just above the stage door. Nicolas Cage stood about two feet from the monitor, watching intently. Kudrow and Renée Zellweger hurried to the monitor in Horvitz's office.

In the theater lobby, Geoffrey Rush and David Geffen were among those gathered around a different monitor. "What about all the movies that didn't get made because of what he did?" Geffen was overheard asking, rhetorically.

In the hall, reaction to Kazan was sharply divided. Applause was steady but subdued; the standing ovation was spotty, and some of it was made up of seat-fillers, who were always told to stand for the honorary Oscar winners. Horvitz cut to shots of Karl Malden standing and applauding, then to Warren Beatty doing the same, then to Spielberg clapping from his seat, then to Ed Harris and Amy Madigan sitting silently, arms in front of them and frowns on their faces.

"Thank you very much," said Kazan. "I really like to hear that. And I want to thank the Academy for its courage, generosity, and I want to tell you that I've been a member of the Academy, on and off, for I don't know how many years. So I'm pleased to say what's best about them, they're damn good to work with. I also want to thank . . ." He stopped, and looked around. "Marty, where are you?" he said. "Hiding behind me? C'mon here." Scorsese walked up to Kazan, who hugged him. "Thank you all very much," he concluded. "I think I can just slip away."

After leaving the stage, Kazan headed into Cates's office. "I need to use the bathroom," he said.

Affleck and Damon walked through the backstage area. "Whew," said Affleck, shaking his head.

The show had already passed the three-hour mark by the time Annette Bening introduced the In Memoriam package, which included footage of such notables as E. G. Marshall, director Alan J. Pakula, Maureen O'Sullivan, Phil Hartman, Akira Kurosawa, and Roddy McDowall. Goldberg watched it from the wings. When Bowery Boy Huntz Hall appeared on the screen, she sighed. "Oh, Huntz," she said.

In the green room, a very slinky tête-à-tête was taking place: Geena Davis, Uma Thurman, and Goldie Hawn, all in long gowns, stood around a silver tray laden with strawberries.

A few minutes later, Thurman was led into the wings. A stagehand going the other direction stepped on the full skirt of her Chanel couture gown, bringing her to an abrupt, jarring halt. "You okay?" asked Debbie Williams.

"Yeah," said Thurman uneasily. "He nearly pulled my dress off. That would have been unfortunate." She paused. "For me."

Three and a half hours in, Gwyneth Paltrow won the best-actress award, the fifth win of the night for *Shakespeare in Love*. She immediately broke down, delivering a teary two-and-a-half-minute acceptance speech. In the green room, Harrison Ford and Kevin Costner watched stoically, sitting side by side. Eyeing the same monitor from a nearby seat, Renée Zellweger got a little misty-eyed. Geena Davis applauded. On the fourth floor, in the general photo room, half a dozen weary photographers started heckling the monitor. An Academy publicist warned them to keep it down.

Ten minutes later, with four awards yet to be handed out, Robert Shapiro stepped outside the Chandler. "What do you think?" he asked. "Longest show ever?"

A security guard looked at his watch. "Oh, yeah," he said. "You're in the record book."

"All *right*," said Shapiro.

Ten minutes later, Kevin Costner walked out to give the best-director award. "They say the show's running a little long," said the star of the epic films *Dances with Wolves*, *The Postman*, and *Waterworld*. "I like things that run long."

The winner was Spielberg, who received a standing ovation. "Am I allowed to say I really wanted this?" he asked. After the award, Spielberg was rushed straight back to his seat to await the best-picture category. As Spielberg sat back down, Harrison Ford paced backstage. In his right hand, Ford carried a piece of paper that contained his lines. In his left, he held the night's final envelope.

When Ford opened that envelope onstage, a brief flicker of dismay seemed to cross his face. "The Oscar goes to *Shakespeare in Love*," he said. To huge cheers from the Miramax contingent and gasps from other sections of the audience, the film's five producers came to the stage—including Harvey Weinstein, who pulled a sheet of paper from his jacket pocket as he walked up the steps to the stage. After Donna Gigliotti and David Parfitt spoke, the pale, hefty Miramax chief leaned toward the microphone. "This was an ensemble film, and it took an ensemble team to make it," said Weinstein, who thanked Michael Eisner and Joe Roth at Disney, then moved to the Miramax staff, then to his "loving wife," his "two rotten kids," his two nieces, and his mother. At this point, Cates had heard enough. For the first time in memory, the orchestra played off a best-picture winner.

When the credits finally ended, Seligman checked his watch. "4:02," he said. The show was, officially and irrevocably, the longest Academy Awards telecast in history.

Backstage, Roberto Benigni headed for the elevator, only to be chased down by Goldie Hawn. "Thank you," she said, "for your great heart."

A few minutes later, Elia and Frances Kazan left Cates's office. In the hallway, they ran into Warren Beatty and Annette Bening. Beatty wrapped Kazan, who had directed him in *Splendor in the Grass* in 1961, in a big hug. "Warren," said Kazan. "I'm so glad to see you! I haven't seen you in so long! And now you're a producer and a director. I haven't seen your movie yet, but I'm going to."

"*Bulworth*?" said Beatty. "It's funny." The couples chatted awhile longer. Then Beatty asked Kazan, "Are you going to the ball?"

"I don't know," said Kazan. He pointed to his wife. "She's telling me what to do tonight."

Beatty laughed. "So is mine," he said.

Upstairs in the press rooms, Paltrow began to do interviews. One reporter told her that many people in the room cried during her acceptance speech.

"Come on, you are all a bunch of hardened, cynical journalists," said Paltrow. "Don't try to pull that on me."

While guests began to filter into the Governors Ball, crew members gathered onstage, tried to shoot the corks from a few bottles of Moët & Chandon champagne off the head of a giant Oscar statue, and cut a cake decorated with a picture of the set.

Amid the hugs and thank-yous and snapshots, Whoopi Goldberg was presented with a souvenir that had been fashioned backstage since the dress rehearsal: an ample, hand-carved, polished wooden dildo. She laughed at the gift, and then—at the urging of just about everyone who'd worked on the show—marched across the stage and bestowed the item on Susan Futterman.

And as the Oscar seventy-one crew hooted and hollered and the host beamed, ABC's Madame Censor Lady broke into a big grin, grabbed hold of her new dildo, and began stroking.

BACKSTAGE after his big win, Harvey Weinstein claimed that he'd talked to Warren Beatty, who'd spoken to Jeffrey Katzenberg, who'd admitted that DreamWorks spent more on the *Saving Private Ryan* campaign than Miramax spent on *Shakespeare in Love*.

The move to Sunday couldn't stop a nearly inevitable ratings skid after the previous year's record-setting mark. The show was down 18 percent over those titanic numbers—while, to use a fairer comparison, it improved on the dismal figures from two years earlier by a paltry 4 percent.

The preshow was widely panned. The show itself received the usual range of reviews, with Benigni receiving a mixture of approval and ridicule, and reaction to Debbie Allen's dance number leaning toward the latter.

A few days after the show, Roy Christopher got a call from a friend who worked at the Metropolitan Opera. "When I started doing the Oscars, I didn't put much value on it," said Christopher. "I wanted to do opera, I wanted to do something meaningful, something beautiful, something amazing. But this friend called me after seeing the show, and he said, 'Let me tell you something. You may think that you're not doing art, but you would never get the opportunity at the Met to do anything that beautiful. So you might as well shut up and appreciate it.' "

After four years of separate awards for dramatic and comedy scores—years in which, crucially, animated Disney films were beaten by the music for *Emma* and for *Shakespeare in Love*—the music branch went back to a single award for best score. Unwilling to completely relinquish a category, the branch reinstated the award for best song score, though it wouldn't be given out unless enough films qualified during the year.

In June, the board of governors also voted to change the rule governing the best-picture award. In the future, it announced, no more than three producers could be awarded Oscars in the best-picture category. The Academy did not say that the rule change was due to the five people who trooped to the stage on behalf of *Shakespeare in Love*, and then spoke until the orchestra stopped them—but considering that it had been twenty years since a best-picture winner had more than three producers, it was impossible not to lay this one at the feet of Harvey Weinstein and crew.

The young singer who'd served as Andrea Bocelli's stand-in, Josh Groban, signed a recording contract with Warner Bros. before the year was over and began recording with producer David Foster. When his debut album came out in November 2001, it contained a version of "The Prayer," the song he'd sung at Oscar rehearsals.

By the end of the year, on the corner of Hollywood Boulevard and Highland Avenue in the heart of Hollywood, construction was under way on the entertainment complex that would house the new, permanent home of the Academy Awards. The initial plan was to have the theater ready in time for the Oscar show in 2001—but that was beginning to seem unlikely, considering that the property was little more than a hole in the ground, surrounded by fences bedecked with murals advertising *Toy Story 2* and *The Tigger Movie*. Quincy Jones, meanwhile, had changed his mind about opening a nightclub in the new complex.

Two blocks away, in a sleepy shopping center that sat between a multiplex theater and the Hollywood Museum (an attempted tourist attraction usually devoid of tourists), the Tower Records chain had opened a video clearance outlet. As the next Oscar season began to heat up, a big table near the entrance to the Tower outlet was piled high with *Oscar's Greatest Moments* videocassettes, which were selling for ninety-nine cents each.

7

Everybody's Talkin'

The 72nd Academy Awards

SITTING ACROSS THE TABLE from Richard and Lili Fini Zanuck, Lou Horvitz couldn't figure it out. The couple, he knew, was Hollywood royalty—particularly Richard, a small, trim, white-haired man of sixty-five whose father, the legendary Darryl F. Zanuck, had cofounded 20th Century-Fox studios and helped create the Hollywood studio system. Richard Zanuck himself ran Fox for a spell, then formed his own company and produced such films as *Jaws*, *The Verdict*, *Cocoon*, and *Driving Miss Daisy*. For that last film, he and Lili Zanuck, his third wife and a producer and director in her own right, received best-picture Oscars.

But now the couple had agreed to produce the 72nd Academy Awards show, which is why they were meeting with Horvitz. To the three-time Oscar director, though, their decision didn't make sense. Of course it was a prestige gig, but what's left to prove when you've already won the Thalberg and a best-picture award?

"I was sitting in front of people whose careers I'd really studied, and they were asking me questions about how the show worked," remembered

Horvitz. "I just stopped and said, 'Can I ask something? You have Oscars, Thalbergs . . . Why would you possibly want to produce the Oscars?' "

Richard Zanuck's reply came quickly. "I don't," he told Horvitz. Then he nodded toward his wife. "She does."

Months later, Lili Zanuck laughed about how she'd essentially forced her husband to produce the Academy Awards. "From the time we said yes, which I think was in September or October," she said, "I always knew there was going to be this moment when my husband was going to say, 'I never wanted to do this, you're the one that wanted to do it.' I thought that moment was going to come around February. But actually, he said it the very next day."

RICHARD ZANUCK may not have wanted the job, but when he and his wife took it they were ready to change the face of Oscar. "The minute we said yes, we had ideas for every single thing," said Lili Zanuck. "We wanted to revamp it as much as we could, because we thought for years it had had a similar look."

In certain ways, Gil Cates had created the template for the modern Oscars. His shows differed from year to year, but they all relied on a familiar blend of film clips, musical numbers, and dance routines that sometimes struggled to find a connection with the movies. They'd also been growing steadily longer, from three and a half hours or less in the early 1990s to more than four hours in 1999. Bob Rehme thought it was time to bring in new producers—and when he called on the Zanucks, the couple had some immediate priorities: "We wanted to freshen it up a bit, make the pace faster, make the show shorter," said Richard.

As the Zanucks got to work from production offices in the heart of Beverly Hills, they made plans and they made promises. They immediately announced that the show would not include any dance numbers, and that it would be far shorter than other recent Oscar shows. In some of the interviews they gave, the Zanucks promised to bring in the show at three hours and fifteen minutes; in other conversations, Lili hinted at hitting the seemingly unattainable mark of three hours.

Their new vision involved elaborate changes. They hired art director

Bob Keene to design a set that featured towers of high-tech video screens, along with a stage floor that was lit from beneath. They booked actor and commercial voiceover artist Peter Coyote to be the voice of Oscar, and to appear on-screen when Horvitz's cameras ventured into the wings. And Lili Zanuck had ideas for a dramatically different use of music, incorporating a pit band led by pop-rock producer Don Was and another combo under the direction of legendary songwriter Burt Bacharach.

When Michael Seligman heard the new producers' plans, he knew the Academy was going to have to write some big checks. The usual Oscar show was budgeted at about $10 million, but the longtime associate producer quickly realized that the Zanucks' plans were far more extravagant. Seligman listened, took notes, ran the numbers, and reported to the Academy that the show would cost significantly more than the usual Oscar telecast. Not wanting to rein in the new producers, the Academy agreed to the largest budget in Oscar history.

ON VALENTINE'S DAY, 2000, on the eve of Oscar nominations, the Internet struck in the familiar form of Harry Knowles. An overweight twenty-eight-year-old with flaming red hair, Knowles ran a Web site called Ain't It Cool News out of his father's house in Austin, Texas. AICN was respected in some quarters and tolerated in others, but it occasionally infuriated Hollywood studios with inside news, gossip, and particularly reports from what were supposed to be confidential test screenings of upcoming movies. The Web site spread positive word-of-mouth about films like *Titanic*, but it also broke the bad news after its spies infiltrated screenings of *Batman and Robin*.

Knowles relied on a network of informants and insiders, and tried his best to determine which of them could be trusted. The day before the Oscar nominations were announced, he trumpeted a major scoop. "From Deep Within the Halls of The Academy of Motion Pictures Arts & Sciences [*sic*] comes the list," he wrote, claiming to have obtained "the list that they narrow down from." It consisted of eight potential nominees in seventeen different Oscar categories.

The fact that the Academy never had such a list didn't deter Knowles, who reported that for best picture, the top eight vote-getters were British theater director Sam Mendes's twisted drama *American Beauty*; *The Green Mile*, another Stephen King adaptation from Frank Darabont, director of *The Shawshank Redemption*; *The Insider*, director Michael Mann's look at a tobacco industry whistle-blower; Indian-born writer-director M. Night Shyamalan's blockbuster thriller *The Sixth Sense*; Anthony Minghella's stylish and morally ambiguous *The Talented Mr. Ripley*; Neil Jordan's World War II romance *The End of the Affair*; Mike Leigh's Gilbert and Sullivan story *Topsy-Turvy*; and Norman Jewison's biography of imprisoned boxer Ruben Carter, *The Hurricane*.

As soon as the list hit the Internet, other media outlets jumped on it, spreading the information that Ain't It Cool News had somehow hacked into the Academy's computers.

EARLY THE NEXT MORNING, the Samuel Goldwyn Theater once again filled with reporters, publicists, and studio reps anxious to see just how accurate Ain't It Cool News had been. In an aisle seat near the back of the theater was Tony Angelotti, a publicist and awards consultant who had helped run campaigns for such films as *The English Patient*, *Shakespeare in Love*, and *Pulp Fiction*, and was considered one of the savviest Oscar predictors in town. "*Toy Story 2* has no chance for a best-picture nomination," said Angelotti to those around him. "It won't happen. First of all, it had three directors, so the directors' branch isn't going to vote for it. You don't see the actors in it, so it won't get support from the actors' branch . . ."

"What about Hilary Swank?" asked someone sitting near Angelotti. Swank, best known for a stint on the TV show *Beverly Hills, 90210*, had won raves and critics' awards for *Boys Don't Cry*, in which she played a true-life teenage girl who passed herself off as a boy and was raped and murdered when her ruse was discovered.

"She might get a nomination," Angelotti announced, "but she can't win. She came out of nowhere, and the movie wasn't successful. The Academy likes to give the supporting-actress award to unknowns, but never best actress. If she wins, she'll be the first unknown actress since World War II to win for a movie that wasn't a big hit. Marlee Matlin was an unknown when she won, but she was in a big movie from Paramount, *Children of a Lesser God. Boys Don't Cry* is a small movie from Fox Searchlight. She can't win."

A few minutes later, Angelotti and the rest of the room learned that Swank had indeed been nominated—and that the Miramax movie on whose behalf he was working, Swedish director Lasse Hallström's *The Cider House Rules*, had won seven nominations, the same as *The Insider* and one less than the year's leader, *American Beauty*.

Ain't It Cool News, it turned out, had missed the best-picture and best-director nods for *Cider House*, even though its list contained eight contenders instead of five. It also erred on a few other crucial nominations, such as the best-director citation for Spike Jonze, a former video director who'd made the delightfully twisted *Being John Malkovich*.

But proving Ain't It Cool wrong wasn't the biggest treat for the Academy's staff, which had known all along that the Internet list couldn't possibly be accurate. Instead, Bruce Davis was more delighted to find relatively little overlap with the Golden Globe Awards, which reveled in its widely disseminated reputation as the harbinger of the Oscars. It had long grated on Davis that an organization made up of around eighty reporters for foreign newspapers and magazines, a group widely considered susceptible to being wined, dined, and flattered, was thought to have any impact on the votes of the Academy.

"The thing that bothers me, and it's not just with the Golden Globes but with all the other shows and the guilds, is this fallacy that because one thing follows another, the first thing was the cause of the second," Davis said. "Our members do not need the Hollywood Foreign Press to show them what a good movie is."

It was true that the nominees and winners for the Oscars and the Globes often did coincide—but to a large degree, the overlap was based on a statistical quirk. The Globes split their main awards into separate categories for drama and musical or comedy, which meant that it named ten best-picture nominees each year. With twice the number as the Academy, that usually made it a safe bet that the films nominated for the best-picture Oscar had already been up for Golden Globes.

But that wasn't the case in 2000. "Even with ten slots," a delighted Davis said to executive administrator Ric Robertson, "they only got two of our best-picture nominations." (The two were *American Beauty* and *The Insider*, which were nominated along with *Cider House*, *The Sixth Sense*, and *The Green Mile*.)

Standing in the rear of the theater with Davis, Danette Herman was particularly interested in the five nominees for best song. She'd expected four of the nominations: the title song to *Music of My Heart*, written by Diane Warren and sung in the film by Gloria Estefan and the up-and-coming boy band 'N Sync; "Save Me" from *Magnolia*, written by alternative-rock singer-songwriter Aimee Mann; "When She Loved Me" from *Toy Story 2*, written by thirteen-time nominee Randy Newman but sung by the Canadian singer Sarah McLachlan; and "You'll Be in My Heart" from the Disney film *Tarzan*, written and sung by Phil Collins.

Herman had figured that the fifth nominee would probably be "Beautiful Stranger," a new Madonna song written for *Austin Powers: The Spy Who Shagged Me*. Though few staffers relished the idea of telling the pop diva that she'd have to cut her song down to a minute and a half to fit into the medley the Zanucks had envisioned, Madonna was the kind of big name that ABC loved.

Her name, though, was nowhere on the list of nominees. Instead, the fifth slot went to "Blame Canada," from the gleefully but astonishingly profane animated film *South Park: Bigger, Longer and Uncut*. The movie, based on the series that had brought the Comedy Central cable network its highest ratings ever, took vicious swipes at society's tendency to look for pop-culture scapegoats; along the way, according to one count, it contained more foul language per minute than any movie ever made. The two masterminds behind *South Park*, Trey Parker and Matt Stone, fought Paramount Pictures over the editing and marketing of their movie, and waged a lengthy and bitter battle with the MPAA to keep it from being rated NC-17.

South Park: Bigger, Longer and Uncut was a very funny movie, and a full-fledged musical that not only mocked the conventions of Disney-style animated musicals, but worked extraordinarily well on its own terms. In addition to being a foul-mouthed malcontent who hated the movie business, Parker was also a fanatic devotee of Broadway musical theater. Together with Marc Shaiman he came up with the richest song score in years, one that would have been a shoo-in in the recently restored category of best song score had 1999 seen the release of enough musicals for the category to be implemented.

Of course, the *South Park* songs included lyrics like "Shut your fucking face, Uncle Fucka / You're a boner-biting bastard, Uncle Fucka," lines completely unsuitable for the Oscars. So Paramount put a small push behind "Blame Canada," a song in which a group of mothers, concerned over the foul language their kids pick up at a movie starring a pair of Canadian comedians, decide that the fault lies with the country to our north. Parker, who six years earlier had won a student Academy Award and, he claimed, stiffed the Academy for his bar tab, was astonished when the song was nominated.

So was Herman. "Who sings 'Blame Canada'?" she said with a frown.

Told that some of the voices were done by Parker and Stone themselves, along with voiceover artist Mary Kay Bergman, who had committed suicide two months earlier, Herman shook her head. "Trey Parker?" she said, envisioning how that name would go over with the network and its advertisers. "Oh, great."

"I know," said Ric Robertson, who was standing nearby. "Let's get Ann Reinking to sing it."

Herman laughed at the idea of inviting the Broadway star Reinking, who had famously butchered Phil Collins's song "Against All Odds" in 1985, while an appalled Collins sat in the audience and watched. "Well," she said, "I'm sure we'll work something out."

THE NEXT DAY, a chastened Harry Knowles admitted that the Oscar nominations made him look "like a complete moron." After complaining about reporters who'd written that he'd hacked the Academy's computers—"I wouldn't even begin to know how to do any hacking," he said—Knowles explained that the trouble began two days earlier, when he received an e-mail from a source who claimed to have found the preliminary list of nominees in an unprotected FileMaker database on an Academy computer.

Knowles said he immediately began double-checking the names on the list to make sure they were all eligible for nominations, and he looked up past articles about the nomination process. Knowles then had a more tech-savvy friend check the Internet address from which the material had supposedly come. The friend suggested, wrongly, that it had indeed come from an Academy computer.

After more correspondence with the original source, who said that the files were a database earmarked for the Oscar.com webmaster, Knowles decided that the material was legitimate. It wasn't until the real nominations were released that he was able to figure out the truth, which was that his list was simply the best guesses of a staffer for ABC.com, who didn't realize that his cable modem allowed outside computers access to his files.

On AICN, Knowles apologized to the Academy, blamed "faulty research" for the confusion, and added, "[T]here never was an attempt on an Academy computer. The nominations were never in any danger. And both Price Waterhouse [*sic*] and the Academy can sleep well at night knowing that at no point was there any failure in their security."

AS FAR as the Zanucks were concerned, the big musical number of the 72nd Academy Awards was going to be Burt Bacharach's medley of past Oscar-nominated songs. But they still had to deal with the five new songs. Calls went out to Randy Newman, Aimee Mann, Phil Collins, Gloria Estefan, and 'N Sync, all of whom agreed to perform and, reluctantly, to cut their songs to ninety seconds.

But dealing with the disgruntled likes of Newman and Mann—and they were indeed disgruntled at the prospect of cutting their songs in half—was nowhere near as tricky as figuring out what to do with "Blame Canada." Not only were the song's original performers either dead (Mary Kay Bergman) or unknown and unpredictable (Trey Parker and Matt Stone), but the song itself made little sense to people who hadn't seen the movie. In addition, the lyrics called Canadian singer Anne Murray "that bitch," took a swipe at perennial Oscar favorite Céline Dion, used the word *fart*, and included the immortal couplet "My boy Eric used to have my picture on his shelf / But now when he sees me he tells me to fuck myself."

The Zanucks approached "Blame Canada" songwriters Parker and Shaiman for ideas. "The first big kick in the balls we got," said Parker, "was that they were going to do all the songs together as a medley. And another part of their master plan was to get rid of the orchestra and let it be Don Was and a couple of synthesizers. And we were like, 'You've got to be kidding. These are Broadway-type songs, and they should be done in Broadway fashion.' They were like, 'No, this is young and hip and cool, let's get Jewel to come out and do it with a guitar.' "

Parker and Shaiman fought for an orchestra and a chorus. Shaiman, who for years had cowritten Billy Crystal's "It's a Wonderful Night for Oscar" medley, used the clout he'd accumulated to plead his case. "Billy's medley is totally in the Rat Pack style of big band and strings," he said, "and 'Blame Canada' is a big musical comedy number. As the composer, I didn't want my songs to be on the grandest of presentations with, like, a synthesizer playing trumpet and trombone parts, not to mention oboe parts and bassoon parts and piccolo parts."

Initially, Shaiman took his case to the laid-back Was—whose response, he said, was, "Hey, man, whatever. Call Burt Bacharach." The call to Bacharach was not a pleasant one: "It's like going to Olympus and speaking to the gods, and yet having to have this sort of antagonistic conversation with him. And he didn't want to be bothered. I felt terrible having to piss off Burt Bacharach, but it was the Academy Awards, and I was going to really fight for an orchestra."

At the same time, ABC's standards and practices department had more bad news for Parker and Shaiman. The word *fuck* was out, of course, but so was *fart*. So was calling Anne Murray a bitch—because, they reasoned, she might sue.

ON WEDNESDAY, March 1, the Academy staged its annual ballot-mailing photo op for the Oscar-hungry press. Afterward, staffers from Pricewater-houseCoopers took the ten bags, which contained forty-two hundred ballots going to Academy members in California, and left them on the loading dock at the Beverly Hills post office. (Out-of-state ballots had already been mailed.) The bags, though, were mislabeled third class and sent to a routing center in the industrial town of Bell, twenty miles southeast of Beverly Hills.

On Saturday night, March 4, at the annual Scientific and Technical Awards ceremony, Academy officials began to hear from anxious members who had yet to receive their ballots. The problem was tracked down, new ballots were mailed, and the deadline for returning them was extended for two days, from March 21 to March 23, just three days before the ceremony.

Two days after the Sci-Tech dinner, a shipment of Oscar statuettes from Chicago arrived at a loading dock that was coincidentally also in Bell. Six boxes, weighing 470 pounds and containing fifty-five Oscars, disappeared. Still reeling from the embarrassment of the mislabeled ballots, the Academy decided to keep quiet about this new loss.

WHILE THE ZANUCKS struggled with "Blame Canada" and the Academy tried to track down ballots and statuettes, the battle over best picture began to resemble nothing so much as the previous year's fracas between *Saving Private Ryan* and *Shakespeare in Love*. Again, on one side was DreamWorks, with a film generally acknowledged to be the front-runner; on the other side was Miramax, trying its best to turn a one-time dark horse into an upset victor.

This time, DreamWorks had *American Beauty*, stage director Sam Mendes's caustic look at anomie, voyeurism, pedophilia, homosexuality, and other undercurrents running through American suburbia. One of the best-reviewed movies of the year, it was tough stuff, narrated from beyond the grave by Kevin Spacey's malcontent suburban dad, who began the movie masturbating in the shower and ended it dead on the garage floor. The movie wasn't for everybody, but it won most of the major critics' awards, and led the Oscar nominations with eight.

The Miramax entry was *The Cider House Rules*, Lasse Hallström's adaptation of the John Irving novel about a beloved small-town physician. Dr. Wilbur Larch, played by Michael Caine, watched over generations of orphans and, on the side, had a thriving business performing illegal abortions. Somewhere along the way, he'd also become addicted to sniffing ether. Gorgeously shot, languid, and unabashedly sentimental at times, the film picked up mixed reviews and didn't win any major awards—but Miramax saw a chance to position it as the perfect choice with voters for whom *American Beauty* was too dark. On their side was the fact that brilliant but risky movies usually won the screenplay award but lost in the best-picture race to safer fare: *Forrest Gump* over *Pulp Fiction*, *The English Patient* over *Fargo*.

If *American Beauty* was the liberal choice, *Cider House* could be the conservative alternative. Of course, to position it as such required emphasizing the romantic, feel-good side of *Cider House*, and ignoring the fact that it dealt with drug addiction and incest, and at heart was a fairly passionate defense of the right to abortion. Miramax's ad campaign, almost as lavish as the one the company had mounted the year before on behalf of *Shakespeare in Love*, emphasized the love affair between characters played by Tobey Maguire and Charlize Theron, the kindhearted benevolence of Doc Larch, and the lush visuals. To look at the ads, on television and in newspapers and in the trades, you'd never guess that the philosophical heart of the movie might offend hard-right conservatives as much as the perversion on display in *American Beauty*.

At first, Miramax's strategy appeared to be paying dividends. Prognosticators routinely referred to the best-picture competition as a two-horse race, and the consensus was that *Cider House* was picking up momentum. Even Trent Lott, the conservative Senate majority leader from Mississippi, weighed in with the news that *The Cider House Rules* was his favorite movie—though when *Entertainment Weekly* pressed a Lott staffer as to why the senator liked such a prochoice movie, the spokesperson grew evasive.

At the same time, though, distaste for the misleading ad campaign began to surface—actively encouraged, suggested many, by DreamWorks, which was determined not to see its Oscar favorite lose to Miramax two years in a row. Meanwhile, *American Beauty* continued to win awards: best dramatic film at the Golden Globes, best actor and actress at the Screen Actors Guild Awards, plus top honors from the Directors Guild and Producers Guild. As the Oscar show neared, most insiders felt that *The Cider House Rules* was losing momentum, and that for a change Miramax might have been out-campaigned.

The battleground even moved to the Oscar show itself. Chuck Workman was supervising all the film clips that would run during the show, including clips of the best-picture nominees. But the piece he'd put together saluting *The Cider House Rules* was, he said, too true to the movie—and as such, it flew in the face of a studio marketing campaign that was misrepresenting the film as a feel-good love story.

"Miramax hated what I did, and they screamed at me that it wasn't the way they wanted us to present the film," said Workman. "They said, 'The movie's about the relationship between the young man and the doctor, and about the love story between Tobey Maguire and Charlize Theron. You can't use any shots of Delroy Lindo,' " who played the boss on the farm where Maguire worked picking apples.

Workman's argument was simple: "It's my job to show people why the movie was nominated," he said. "The movie is called *The Cider House Rules*, and we need to show the Cider House. But they didn't care about that— they just wanted us to help their marketing."

It was not, he added, the first time Miramax had caused problems with Oscar clips. "They push the rules as far as possible to sell their movies," he said, "and no one ever tells them that the way they do business is reprehensible."

TREY PARKER had spent the weekend in Las Vegas, one of the favorite haunts of a thirty-year-old with lots of new money and a zest for partying. But on the morning of March 12, Parker returned from his two-day binge in time for a more sedate soiree, the Oscar nominees' luncheon.

Standing by the bar before the lunch got under way, Parker looked around; nearby were Tom Cruise, Annette Bening, and Warren Beatty. He laughed at the incongruity of the setting. "I was in a strip club in Vegas at four o'clock this morning," he said. "I was pretty fucked up, but I do remember looking up at a stripper and yelling, 'Hey, you wanna go with me to the Academy Awards nominees' lunch tomorrow?' And she looked down and yelled, 'Sure!' "

In the end, Parker left his stripper friend back in Vegas and came to the luncheon with his more presentable assistant, Jennifer Howell. He was still amazed at the furor "Blame Canada" had caused. "They say you can't say the word *fart* on TV," he said, baffled. "I don't believe it. That really shows where America is at."

The producers, he added, still hadn't booked a singer. "I don't know what we're going to do," he said. "They want Bette Midler or somebody, they want one vocalist. We said, 'No, we need a chorus,' and they said, 'No, we're not doing that this year.' It's like, goddamnit, we're pulling our hair out trying to get them to see that this has to be a *big* number."

When the hundred-or-so Oscar nominees were seated, Bob Rehme welcomed them. "I had a speech prepared," he said, "but the Beverly Hills post office lost it." He didn't mention the missing statuettes, still a secret outside the L.A.P.D. and the Academy. But later in the week, the Academy decided that publicity was its ally and announced that the statuettes had been stolen.

At a press conference, Bruce Davis noted the coincidence that both the missing ballots and the statuettes had passed through the town of Bell. "We have told Billy Crystal not to go anywhere near Bell," he said. Privately, Crystal and his writers were asked not to prepare too many jokes about the theft.

FOR WEEKS, concerns about the extraordinarily complex stage had been growing. Particularly troublesome were the tower units, thirty-five-foot columns designed to spin and slide. Together, the towers made up a wall of video screens that could show individual images, or come together to display one large image. "It was a kluge of every piece of equipment that existed in the world," said Lou Horvitz. "There were twenty-two video sources, all these graphic playbacks. Lili would say, 'Oh, this is great,' but every day we just kept getting in deeper and deeper."

In addition, the stage floor had to be raised so that it could be lit from beneath, but the heat from those lights threatened to buckle it. A cooling system was implemented to pump in cold air as a countermeasure, but that caused sound problems. The only way to make sure it would all work, that the towers wouldn't topple and the images could be synced, was to build and set everything up and try it out.

The entire stage was erected on a soundstage at ABC Prospect, and rehearsals were held using stand-ins. The towers remained upright and the digital projections were sharp. "There was a tremendous amount of choreography that had to go into it, but it worked," said a relieved Richard Zanuck. After an initial bit of panic while Keene tried to find a route that didn't pass under any low bridges, the stage was moved to downtown Los Angeles and the entire operation shifted to the Shrine Auditorium.

Horvitz, meanwhile, struggled to mark his script with everything that was needed. Normally, he'd use the script to indicate cuts, camera moves, and cues for video packages—but this time, he realized as he started working on it, the video towers alone complicated his task enormously. "It took me almost an hour and a half to write the first cue, out of twenty-six," he said. "It was 'Tower one shows this, tower two, tower three, tower four . . .' After I wrote that first page, I looked in the mirror and went, 'Louis J., what the fuck did you do?' "

As the production relocated, a sixty-one-year-old junk scavenger named Willie Fulgear found all but three of the missing Oscar statuettes behind a drugstore in the Koreatown neighborhood of Los Angeles. A Roadway employee admitted involvement and implicated a fellow driver. The two men were arrested. Although Roadway wanted to wait until he'd been officially cleared of any involvement by the police, the Academy quickly gave Fulgear tickets to the Oscar show, and encouraged the shipping company to give him the $50,000 reward it had offered.

INSIDE THE SHRINE, the Zanucks were a study in contrasts. Richard was low key, dressed Beverly Hills casual: sports coats, slacks, and dress shirts. Lili was more energetic—as one staffer put it, she was "an unassuming-looking fireball" in tattered jeans and untucked men's shirts.

"She is a pistol," said stage manager Garry Hood. "She speaks her mind and she *goes*. Richard's more the old Hollywood-style producer and mogul type. He just sits back and puts in his two cents. But she just goes all over the place, and there is such great energy that it's great fun."

Still, even crew members who admired and liked the couple were confused as the week wore on. Instead of spending Tuesday and Wednesday doing lighting and camera tests, and then bringing in the stand-ins to begin proper rehearsals, the schedule bogged down with an unusual number of camera tests, film tests, music tests . . .

By now the Zanucks knew that three hours and fifteen minutes was a lost cause. Instead, they cautiously mentioned three and a half hours as a goal. But besides Bacharach's lengthy medley and several packages of film clips (including a baffling six-minute montage presenting the history of the world as seen through Hollywood movies), the show contained many small elements that could slow it down. Categories that had often been handled by a single presenter, like the two documentary or short-subject categories, were being presented separately, while an unusually large number of awards were being handed out by multiple presenters, necessitating the kind of chitchat the producers once seemed eager to cut.

"It's going to be a very long show, and we all know it," said one crew member. "But I don't see Lili and Dick worrying about that. They just keep doing all these tests. That's what you do when you're making a movie, but you don't have time for that stuff on live TV. They're just not on terra firma anymore."

IN DOWNTOWN LOS ANGELES, the crew at the Shrine Auditorium was getting ready for a day devoted largely to rehearsing the Oscar show's musical numbers. Across town, in Pacific Palisades, Randy Newman sat in his backyard and looked out toward the Pacific Ocean. He was due at Oscar rehearsals in a couple of hours, but first he spent a few minutes mulling over his experiences with the Academy Awards.

"You know, I've been seeing these shows for fifty years," said Newman, whose uncles Alfred and Lionel had each conducted the Oscar orchestra. "As a little boy I remember looking at them. And they said the same thing every year: 'This year it's going to be better than a really bad vaudeville show.'" He shrugged. "Billy Crystal's funny, but I don't know if there's any such thing as a good Oscar show."

Newman thought back to the previous year, and Savion Glover's tap dance set to music from *Saving Private Ryan*. "I will miss the dances," he said with a grin. "I mean, that evocation of World War II was one of the most unbelievable things I've ever seen. I had my mouth open when I saw that at rehearsal."

Newman, one of the smartest but toughest songwriters in pop music and a man who freely described himself as "an old crock," also took issue with the musical choices the Zanucks had made. "They wanted the show to be entertaining," he said, "so they cut Sarah McLachlan, Phil Collins, Robin Williams, and Gloria Estefan. And it really is ludicrous how they cut the orchestra. I like to hear the band hacking away at *American Beauty* or whatever."

One could, of course, accuse Newman of a modicum of sour grapes—after all, his nomination for the song "When She Loved Me" was his thirteenth without a single win. The previous year he'd scored a rare trifecta with nominations for best song ("That'll Do" from *Babe: Pig in the City*), best dramatic score (*Pleasantville*), and best musical or comedy score (*A Bug's Life*), only to lose to music from *The Prince of Egypt*, *Life Is Beautiful*, and *Shakespeare in Love*, respectively.

"Always, the nomination really is what matters," he insisted. "Because it's musicians voting. But in the final voting . . ." He paused, looked down at his ensemble of Hawaiian shirt and rumpled chinos, and laughed. "I mean, why should I be able to vote for costume design? *Look* at me. Or makeup. What the hell do I know about it? I sort of liked *The Talented Mr. Ripley*, so I voted for the makeup of Jude Law, but who the hell knows if the makeup of Jude Law was really any good. And the same is true of music. People think they know—they say, 'I like that little tune in *Il Postino*,' or whatever beat me that year—but they don't really know. There have been scores lately that actually hurt the movie, that slowed it down, but they won."

Newman stopped and chuckled. "I hear myself complain, and I think, it's a wonder I ever get a job," he said.

"THIS," said Don Was, "is a ritual at the foot of a modern Mount Olympus."

Was, born Donald Fagenson in Detroit, cut an unusual figure on a show that usually turned to the old-school likes of Bill Conti for its musical director. The forty-eight-year-old musician wore his hair in dreadlocks and favored sweatpants and sandals regardless of the occasion. The onetime leader of an adventurous rock/dance group called Was (Not Was), whose biggest hit was the novelty tune "Walk the Dinosaur," Was had become well known as a producer, engineering the remarkable comeback of singer Bonnie Raitt and producing hits for everyone from the Rolling Stones to the B-52's.

Was had also assembled and led versatile bands for the Grammys, among other shows, which is why Lili Zanuck hired him to be one of the two Oscar bandleaders and threw him into what had become a complicated and unprecedented musical setup. By this point, there were four separate bands performing on the show—including the Oscar orchestra, which the Zanucks had reluctantly agreed to reinstate. Don Was's eight-piece band, which occupied the orchestra pit stage left, included three synthesizer players and one deejay; they played music for entrances and exits. Bacharach's ten-piece combo, which included three singers, sat in the pit stage right to handle entertainment during commercial breaks. The orchestra, forty-eight players strong, was ensconced in a room on the third floor of the Shrine. And a nine-piece onstage band combined members of all three groups to perform Bacharach's medley.

It was, as one staffer put it, "an audio nightmare"—not to mention the fact that orchestral musicians accustomed to sitting in the pit were not happy about being exiled upstairs and out of sight. Still, the orchestra *was* in the building, a tribute to the persistence of Marc Shaiman and Trey Parker, who insisted that "Blame Canada" just wasn't the type of song you could toss off unobtrusively.

"We decided to highlight the whole piece, instead of hiding it," explained Richard Zanuck. "It wasn't the most exciting song, but we made a big, colorful number out of it." To do so, the Zanucks brought in a large group of background singers and dancers. This was a curious move on a show that up to then had so avidly proclaimed "no dance numbers," but it wasn't technically a violation of the producers' promise; "Blame Canada" was simply a nominated song that would include dancers, not a dance number per se.

Partly, the more extravagant staging came about because Shaiman had persuaded Robin Williams, a fan of *South Park*, to perform the song. "Once Robin was in, it changed everything," said Parker. "That's what you learn about the Academy Awards: all they're trying to do is get ratings. They're selling fucking dish soap, and once Robin Williams was on, it was like, 'Great, we're gonna sell more dish soap.'"

Richard Zanuck had also talked the network into relenting and allowing Williams to say *fart*. Anne Murray sent word that it was fine to call her a bitch, and Williams promised to neither say nor mouth the word *fuck*.

The presence of an orchestra, meanwhile, had repercussions that Don

Was hadn't anticipated. Even though the orchestra was only being used for Billy Crystal's medley, "Blame Canada," and an overture that Bacharach had written, union regulations for the American Federation of Musicians required that they be paid for all the music played on the show.

"You can't just say, 'Okay, you're hired for this hour,'" said Was. "I'm using some drum loops and samples from a record I made in 1992 that was never released—and even though it was recorded in '92, it was deemed to be done for the Oscars, because that'll be the first public performance. It's costing $30,000, because every member of the orchestra has to be paid for something I did seven years ago."

Was had already run afoul of many Oscar music vets. One of his first ideas had been to do away with the traditional way of bringing winners and presenters onstage, which was for the orchestra to perform a snippet of the score from the film with which they had won, or the film with which they were most closely identified. In an attempt to modernize the tradition without completely junking it, Was decided that his band would bring people onstage to some sort of steady groove or drum pattern—but at the same time, the deejay in the orchestra pit would layer in recorded samples from the appropriate film score. The music director was particularly proud of the intro he'd worked up for Steven Spielberg: the theme from *Jaws* sawing away while a thudding groove kept the beat.

To Was, using recorded samples of the original scores was a matter of respecting the original composers. Since, say, John Williams had recorded the score to *Angela's Ashes* with a large orchestra, Was felt the composer would be better served by his original orchestration than the scaled-down version that would have been necessitated by the smaller Oscar forces. But orchestral musicians and the support staff that surrounded them didn't agree. "There's an infrastructure that doesn't have anything to do with the people producing the show," said Was. "It's a permanent bureaucracy of copyists and contractors and rehearsal studios, and I think everyone's just freaked out that they're not going to be part of the proceedings. I don't get a whole lot of help from them. I get a lot of hostility."

At rehearsal on Friday, Was also got lots of advice about how to deal with the hot boy band 'N Sync, which would be performing with Gloria Estefan on "Music of My Heart." Warned that the group was used to lip-syncing onstage and probably couldn't cut it vocally in live performance, Was recorded their harmony parts and sampled them so that they could be triggered by his keyboard player. But when Estefan first rehearsed, the tempo required by the samples seemed sluggish.

So Was approached Justin Timberlake, Lance Bass, and the other band members. "You guys can sing live, right?" he said. "Forget about the samples, let's try it." On the next take, the group nailed the harmonies. Afterward, Was felt vindicated. " 'N Sync can absolutely sing," he said. "People talk about how these boy bands can't perform live, but maybe it's because nobody gives them a chance."

BURT BACHARACH had spent months painstakingly crafting his big number. When the composer and performer signed on late in 1999, Lili Zanuck sent him a list of every song that had been nominated for an Oscar, highlighting about thirty of her favorites.

Bacharach chose the tunes he wanted to use in an extended medley; through January and February, the medley was his passion, and his obsession. He carefully dovetailed more than a dozen songs, plotting the dynamics and keying everything to the singers who'd agreed to perform: Ray Charles, Garth Brooks, Queen Latifah, Isaac Hayes, Dionne Warwick, Whitney Houston, and Bacharach himself. Early versions of the medley were more than twelve minutes long, far too lengthy for the show. Bacharach slowly and deliberately trimmed it, until he had it down to about eight minutes: "We fought for every bar," said Was.

Bacharach had been involved with the Oscars on and off over the years, presenting the best-song award a few times and winning three Oscars himself, most recently in 1982 for the song "Arthur's Theme (Best That You Can Do)," from the film *Arthur*. The writer of dozens of stylish pop hits in the 1960s and 1970s, including the movie themes "The Man Who Shot Liberty Valance," "What's New Pussycat?" and "Alfie," he hadn't been a steady presence on the pop charts for more than a decade. But he'd always had admirers in the world of rock 'n' roll, including the acclaimed singer-songwriter Elvis Costello. Bacharach's hip cachet was unassailable, as was his reputation as a brilliant, painstaking, and demanding bandleader and arranger. Bacharach was not a strong singer—he had a thin, breathy voice without much range—but he knew exactly what he wanted, and his musicians knew that he would instantly hear every flat note or missed cue.

Early the week of the show, Bacharach rehearsed his medley in studios at Paramount Pictures, running through the number with all of the singers except Whitney Houston, who failed to show up. A remarkable singer and sometime actress who'd had a string of number-one hits in the 1980s and one of the biggest singles of all time with "I Will Always Love You" (from the movie *The Bodyguard*) in 1993, Houston had once been considered demanding but professional. In recent years, though, she'd become increasingly erratic, unreliable, and disruptive. Rumors had long been rampant of drug use by Houston and her husband, R&B singer Bobby Brown, though Houston always denied them. She faced a charge of drug possession in January 2000 when a guard at an airport in Hawaii allegedly found marijuana in her purse, though the charges were later dropped.

Still, the rail-thin thirty-six-year-old was capable of turning in stunning performances, and Bacharach knew her well. In the sixties he'd often worked with her mother, gospel singer and background vocalist Cissy Houston, and he'd written and produced a dozen top-twenty hits for her aunt, Dionne Warwick.

At the Shrine, rehearsals for the medley took place on Friday night, in front of a small, tense group of staffers. Most of the medley's singers were in good spirits and good voice—Garth Brooks being a particular favorite among the stagehands—but from the start it was clear that Houston wasn't at her best. She looked puffy and a little disoriented; watching her stumble as she tried to navigate the stairs onstage, staffers described her in terms that ranged from "out of it" to "completely fucked up."

Houston was assigned two songs, the *Wizard of Oz* standard "Over the Rainbow" and the Barbra Streisand chestnut "The Way We Were." She wasn't happy with the keys in which Bacharach was asking her to sing, but he'd arranged the medley to build in a specific way, and he wasn't about to change that for Houston. During an early run-through, Bacharach played the introductory music to "Over the Rainbow" as Houston gingerly walked down the stairs. When she got to the bottom, she began singing "The Way We Were."

Bacharach immediately stopped the music and tried to tactfully point out her mistake. "Gosh," he said gently, "I love that song, but . . ."

Houston looked at him, realizing what was wrong. "Oh, yeah," she said, vaguely. "I don't know why I sang that."

For the next few minutes, Bacharach tried again. But Houston's voice was shaky, she seemed distracted and jittery, and her attitude was casual, almost defiant. Finally, Bacharach slumped over the piano, his head down on the keys. "I thought he was having a coronary," said Was.

During a break, Bacharach huddled with the Zanucks. He told them he didn't think Houston could cut it, that they were taking a big risk if they kept her on the show. Lili Zanuck wasn't necessarily convinced—"Dick and I thought she might have just been walking through rehearsal to save her voice, though nobody else was doing that," she said—but she agreed to back her musical director. "We cued off of Burt," she said. "We told him we'd do whatever he wanted because, quite frankly, it would be so easy for this show to be about something else. We all remember those years. We didn't want to work for six months for this to be a show about how fucked up Whitney Houston was."

Dionne Warwick took Houston's side and argued with the Zanucks. But before they went home for the night, the producers made a decision: Houston was off the show. Richard Zanuck called Houston's agent and manager to break the news, while Lili Zanuck placed a 1 a.m. call to the manager for country singer Faith Hill, for whom Zanuck had directed a music video.

"They absolutely made the right decision," said stage manager Garry Hood, who watched the rehearsal closely. "Sometimes somebody needs to say no instead of continuing to enable a situation, which we all do in this business. You want that name, so you're willing to put up with unfortunate situations. But they said no and they stood by their decision, and that doesn't happen very often."

Don Was, for his part, was not convinced that Houston would have been a liability once show time arrived. "Whitney's personal problems are well documented, but there was a certain amount of protest in her cavalier approach that I thought was not pharmaceutically driven," he said. "Burt deserved to have the medley done properly, and there was reason to question whether she would have done it properly. But if you ask me, I say she'd have come through in the end. I think she was maybe fucking with everybody a little bit. It's not un-diva-like behavior to leave everybody worrying about whether you're going to show up, or you're going to deliver, until the last minute, and then to deliver. But there's no black or white in this, everything's gray. It's hard to say . . ." He trailed off, then shrugged.

"Certainly she was loaded," he said with a smile, "but I wouldn't want to do urinalysis on a number of people involved in the show. Let's leave it at that."

AS USUAL, star day was tightly controlled and chaotic at the same time. Roberto Benigni flirted with the trophy ladies, Gwyneth Paltrow wore shades and nursed a hangover, and Mike Myers discussed the difference between the words *asshole* and *butthead* with an ABC standards and practices rep. When Russell Crowe took the stage to rehearse his lines, he looked into the audience and saw that the seat card marking his chair was one of the few not to include a photo. "What, nobody has a fucking picture of me to put up there?" he asked. As soon as he finished rehearsing, Crowe borrowed a pen and drew a stick figure on his card. Then he did the same with the blank card that marked the seat of *American Beauty* star Wes Bentley. "Okay," Crowe said when he finished. "Now I can go."

But when he walked out the back door of the Shrine to light up a cigarette, Crowe ran straight into Brad Pitt, who was standing near the artists' entrance wearing a powder-blue shirt unbuttoned to the navel. "No way!" shouted Pitt. The two men hugged, then launched into an animated conversation. As they talked, Paltrow rounded the corner and was headed for the back door when she spied Pitt, her old boyfriend, standing in her path. She turned away from him, ducked her head so he couldn't see her, and blew past him quickly.

Later, Keanu Reeves stood by the artists' entrance and watched Myers make a beeline for the green room buffet. "Damn actors, man," he said. "Them and their free lunches." Tommy Lee Jones walked by in a jacket and tie. "Oh, my God," Reeves said. "That's Tommy Lee fucking Jones. He is the *man*." Then Peter Coyote shook Reeves's hand. "My God," said Reeves. "Peter Coyote and Tommy Lee Jones in one day."

In midafternoon, Lili Zanuck huddled with Antonio Banderas and Pené-lope Cruz, who were giving out the award for foreign film. The odds-on favorite in the category was *All About My Mother*, a film from the flamboyant Spanish director Pedro Almodóvar, with whom both Cruz and Banderas had worked. Almodóvar had given an extremely long, meandering, and often incomprehensible acceptance speech a month earlier at the Golden Globes. At rehearsal, Lili Zanuck pleaded with the presenters to speak to Almodóvar. "Please tell Pedro that if he wins, we do not want to play him off," she said. "But we *cannot* afford for him to take five minutes, like he did at the Golden Globes." Banderas and Cruz assured her that they'd pass along the message.

Arnold Schwarzenegger arrived late in the afternoon, hours past his scheduled 9:30 a.m. rehearsal time. He was smoking a cigar, and had two little girls in tow. Onstage, Schwarzenegger had trouble with his introduction to the visual effects award. After stumbling over his lines, he snapped at the TelePrompTer operator. "You're running it too fast, too fast," he said.

In the audience, a staffer looked at the testy scene—typical, she thought, for Schwarzenegger—and rolled her eyes. "And you can't read, okay?" she muttered under her breath. Richard Zanuck went to the podium and asked that Schwarzenegger's microphone be turned off. The actor and the producer went over the lines seven or eight times, until Arnold got it right.

"IT'S CHAOS DOWN THERE," yelled stage manager Alissa Levisohn as she ran up the stairs to the stage level of the Shrine. Dress rehearsal was under way, and Levisohn had just been to the dressing rooms beneath the stage, checking on the progress of the singers and dancers who would be needed shortly for "Blame Canada." What she found, rather than the usual costume crew moving with dispatch, was the slower, more deliberate pace of a six-foot-three-inch former model named L'Wren Scott, whom Lili Zanuck had hired to be the Oscars' "Style Designer."

"The stylist has no idea what it is to get people in and out of makeup," complained Levisohn to other stage managers. "She's playing around with costumes now, and she doesn't understand we have rehearsal." Other staffers were sent downstairs to speed things up.

But costume problems with "Blame Canada" were nothing compared to the trouble that awaited when it was time for Bacharach's medley. Except for Faith Hill, who'd been at the Shrine all afternoon, the singers arrived around 9 p.m., at which point they were quietly informed that Whitney Houston had been replaced.

Garth Brooks heard the news when Lili Zanuck and Danette Herman visited his trailer, but Garth was not in an understanding mood. The singer, by far Nashville's biggest-selling artist for much of the 1980s and '90s, worked hard to sustain his image as a down-to-earth guy—but once his first two albums had sold twenty million copies and he'd been all but anointed the savior of the country music industry, he hadn't been shy about using his clout to get what he wanted.

Brooks was supposed to be the first artist to perform during the medley, kicking things off with the hit song "Everybody's Talkin' " from *Midnight Cowboy*. (Curiously, the song had never been nominated for an Oscar, and shouldn't have even been included.) But when Debbie Williams went to Brooks's trailer to tell him it was time to rehearse, the thirty-eight-year-old Oklahoman wouldn't leave. "You're gonna have to buy some time for me here," he told her. "I need to make some calls."

Garry Hood, who lived in Nashville and knew Brooks from other shows, was sent to talk to the singer; he got nowhere. Brooks punched numbers into his cell phone and paced outside his trailer, furious that Houston had been replaced, that he hadn't been told about the move right away—and, some suggested, that Houston's replacement, Faith Hill, also happened to be a country singer with crossover success.

Lili Zanuck tried to reason with Brooks, as rehearsal ground to a halt. Firing Houston wasn't right, Brooks told Zanuck. It wasn't fair. Whitney had to be reinstated.

Zanuck did not budge. Quietly, a stand-in was told to be ready to take Brooks's place if need be. The other artists stood by and waited.

But after what seemed to be an interminable delay, Brooks suddenly walked back into the Shrine, took his place onstage, and said he was ready. Bacharach's band launched into "Everybody's Talkin'," Brooks crooned the song as he walked down a flight of stairs, and the dress rehearsal resumed.

"Ultimately, he got through to Whitney on the phone, that's why he came back," said Don Was. "Garth was trying to be humanitarian, and he told her, 'If you want to come back, I'm holding out for you.' And Whitney said, 'I'm not going back to that fucking show.' And that was pretty much the end of it."

THE NEXT AFTERNOON, as show time neared, most of the crew changed into tuxedos and formal dresses. An exception was made for stagehands who'd be moving scenery on and off the stage. Because the floor was illuminated from beneath with bright white light, those stagehands were issued white jumpsuits that would allow them to blend in more easily. "They look like a bunch of sperm running around the stage," said one staffer upon first spotting the crew.

By 4:00, when the doors to the Shrine were opened, almost everybody was formally dressed. There were exceptions, though. Lili Zanuck walked around backstage in her usual baggy men's shirt, not changing until almost show time.

Trey Parker and Matt Stone arrived wearing knockoffs of notable awards-show dresses worn by Jennifer Lopez and Gwyneth Paltrow, respectively. They were accompanied by Marc Shaiman, who hadn't been told of their plans far enough in advance to work out his own drag act; if he had, he said he would have gone as Cher the year she wore a towering feathered headdress to the Oscars. Instead of donning a dress, Shaiman huddled quickly with stylist Scott, who helped him work up a garish baby blue outfit complete with fedora and puffy faux fur jacket. On their way down the red carpet Paltrow shot the trio a dirty look. Michael Caine walked over to tell them he loved their outfits. "Awesome," he said.

Inside the theater, Jack Nicholson had no sooner arrived at his front-row seat than he got up and strolled down the aisle that ran across the front of the theater. It surprised nobody that Nicholson was on the move: of all the stars who regularly attended the Academy Awards, he was almost definitely the most fidgety. That's why directors tended to show reaction shots of Nicholson with disturbing frequency. You needed to take advantage of the times you had him in his seat, because you never knew when it would happen again.

At the previous year's Oscar show, Nicholson had been seated in the third row, six seats in from the aisle, which proved to be predictably problematic. When Roberto Benigni started climbing over seat backs or Elia Kazan divided the audience into opposing camps, Jack's sunglassed countenance was backstage, out of camera range. So the following year, Nicholson was back up front, where he'd be more likely to stick around for a few good reaction shots—particularly reactions to Billy Crystal, who *loved* to talk about Jack.

Still, Nicholson had barely arrived before he took a stroll. As he did, he glanced into the orchestra pit, knowing that he'd see the usual complement of forty or fifty tuxedo-clad musicians awaiting a cue from their elegantly attired conductor.

Instead, Nicholson found himself looking down on eight casually clad musicians, three of them standing behind synthesizers and one with a pair of *turntables* in front of him. Nicholson took it all in—the musicians, the electronics, the fact that the guy in charge had dreadlocks and was wearing sandals. He frowned. "What the fuck is *this*?" he said.

5:30 P.M., PACIFIC DAYLIGHT TIME: *"This is the 72nd annual Academy Awards."*

Minutes after preshow cohost Tyra Banks gave a backstage high five to Academy president Bob Rehme, Peter Coyote kicked off the Oscar show from his desk just off the stage. Richard Zanuck sat in the wings near Coyote, ready to greet winners and producers. Lili Zanuck settled into a seat behind Horvitz in the command truck.

Rehme delivered a brief opening speech, and then walked off during Crystal's opening film. In it, the host found himself in a variety of famous movies, from *The Gold Rush* to *Taxi Driver* to *Psycho* to *The Godfather*. In this last clip, he asked for advice from Marlon Brando's Don Corleone: "Godfather, I don't know what to do . . . These producers, they're movie people. They've never done the Oscars. They don't want to have a dance number!" Crystal kept up the no-dancing theme when he segued into a scene from *West Side Story*, where he was serenaded by an angry musical gang: "The Jets ain't gonna get their chance tonight / They're telling us that we can't dance tonight . . ." Crystal broke into a rendition of one of that musical's signature songs, "Tonight": "Tonight, tonight / Please Billy, make it tight / Cut the clips, cut the jokes, cut the songs . . ."

Backstage, it seemed to some crew members as if babies were everywhere, courtesy of an unusually large number of new mothers. A trailer just outside the artists' entrance was turned into a center for nannies and breastfeeding moms. Another facility, nearer to the stage, was earmarked for the nine-months-pregnant Annette Bening. The crew called it "the Sinatra Bathroom," in honor of the facility that had to be kept in the wings during Frank Sinatra's final shows.

From the stage, Crystal introduced Willie Fulgear, who'd found the missing statuettes. "Willie got $50,000 for finding the fifty-two Oscars," said Crystal. "Not a lot of money, when you realize that Miramax and Dream-Works are spending millions of dollars just to get one."

After Crystal's opening, the three stars of *Charlie's Angels*—Cameron Diaz, Drew Barrymore, and Lucy Liu—walked onstage together. To accompany their entrance, Don Was took a sample from the movie's soundtrack, laid a thudding drum loop beneath it, and had his band play over the top of the sample. But while the drum track boomed, the soundtrack sample, which was supposed to be providing the melody on which the band was riffing, was completely inaudible. "It sounded like people were walking on to tribal drums," said Was, who stopped short of saying he was sabotaged but found it astonishing that nobody noticed the missing samples or tried to fix them.

Backstage in the green room during the first commercial break, Erykah Badu's two-year-old son, Seven, banged his head on the corner of a glass coffee table and began screaming. Winona Ryder, James Coburn, and the other stars in the small, tastefully appointed room studiously tried to act as if nothing untoward was happening. But the timing was particularly unfortunate: Badu was due to present an award during the show's next segment, which meant it was time for her to head to the wings. A talent staffer quietly suggested to Badu's nanny that she move the child to the trailer outside, lest he really erupt when his mom was taken away.

At the end of the show's second segment, forty minutes into the broadcast, James Coburn awarded the first major Oscar of the night, best supporting actress, to Angelina Jolie for *Girl, Interrupted*. Afterward, in an Oscar rarity, the cameras followed Jolie offstage, where she hugged Jude Law and Cate Blanchett. During the commercial break after Jolie's win, fellow nominee Chloë Sevigny headed for the lobby. This was typical: the lobby was often crowded with those who didn't win in the last couple of categories.

By the one-hour mark, it was clear that the high-tech video presentation and funkier music had indeed given the show a more modern, accelerated feel—but at the same time, the band had trouble stopping quickly when winners and presenters got to the microphone, and the new trophy ladies, models without awards show experience, didn't always get the winners offstage quickly. The show felt faster, but in some ways things were moving even more slowly than usual. In the truck, Lili Zanuck checked the time and figured the show was running ahead of schedule.

In the orchestra pit, meanwhile, Don Was didn't know what to think. During rehearsals, Was and his former Was (Not Was) partner David Weiss, who was working the turntables, had looked into the audience and found themselves staring at a field of seat cards bearing famous names: Warren Beatty, Annette Bening, Kevin Spacey, Tom Cruise, Nicole Kidman . . . They'd imagined the electricity that must come from that kind of star power—but when the show started, the musicians quickly realized that the stars inside the Shrine were too distracted, preoccupied, or nervous to give back much energy to the performers onstage or in the pit. "This room," muttered a disappointed Weiss to his partner, "is *smaller* than life."

At about 6:40, LL Cool J and Vanessa Williams introduced Randy Newman and Sarah McLachlan, the first performers in the medley of nominated songs. The five songs made up a twelve-minute medley that was capped by Robin Williams's showstopping romp through "Blame Canada," accompanied for much of the song by two dozen singer-dancers and another two dozen Rockette-style hoofers in Mountie garb.

"Blame Canada" got the biggest reaction, but the best-song Oscar went, as expected, to Phil Collins's Tarzan song, "You'll Be in My Heart." During the ensuing commercial break, nominees Diane Warren and Aimee Mann headed for the lobby. So did Trey Parker and Matt Stone, who stood against a wall accepting congratulations and ignoring stares. "This is cold and uncomfortable," said Stone of his pink spaghetti-strap gown.

"I'm getting sick to my stomach," added Parker. "Everybody up there's just patting themselves on the fucking back. And the last thing these people need is to be patted on the back, because they get it every fucking day." They sent an assistant to fetch the suits they'd brought with them, then changed clothes and left the Shrine. "I never even knew you could do that," laughed Shaiman, who'd also lost during his four previous stints as a nominee.

An hour after Jolie's supporting-actress win, the second major award of the night, best supporting actor, was given to Michael Caine for *The Cider House Rules*. His gracious acceptance speech included nods to his fellow nominees but lasted almost three minutes, the longest of the night so far. When he saw the TelePrompTer flashing PLEASE WRAP UP, Caine frowned. "Well, Dick, I wasn't here last time I won," he said, referring to his no-show when he won for 1986's *Hannah and Her Sisters*. "So give me a bit extra on my speech." Dick Zanuck, though, was sitting in the wings; it was Lili in the control trailer, with the power to tell Horvitz to cue the band and cut off Caine. She didn't.

By this point, Lili realized that the show was falling well behind schedule. She just hoped that people would be entertained.

The next segment, though, was the driest of the night. It started with Jane Fonda presenting a special Oscar to Polish director Andrzej Wajda, who gave a subtitled acceptance speech in Polish. Then came awards for sound effects, followed by a recap of the scientific and technical Oscars, followed by the award for visual effects. *The Matrix* was a popular winner in this last category—but when John Gaeta's acceptance speech passed the one-minute mark with no end in sight, Zanuck reconsidered her unspoken rule not to play winners offstage. Reluctantly, she gave the cue to Horvitz, who yelled "Shut that motherfucker up!" into Was's headphones. Earlier, Was had pretended not to hear a suggestion that his band interrupt the documentary winners, but this time he complied, cutting the speech off as it reached a minute and a half.

In the lobby, Jude Law waited at the bar with a group of friends that included Gwyneth Paltrow. They both ordered Heinekens and drank them straight from the bottle. (Before the show, drinks were free; after 5:30, the bars started charging but the lines stayed long.)

By the two-hour mark, many stars were finding refuge and refreshment in and around the green room. But Crystal had planned a comedy bit in which he would "read the minds" of many of the notables in the audience. For the jokes to work, those actors had to be in their seats. So during a commercial break at 7:35, staffers and pages rounded up the likes of Jack Nicholson and Judi Dench and asked them to please return to their seats. "Why am I going back out there?" asked Dench as a stage manager escorted her into the auditorium. "It's for something Billy is doing," the staffer said vaguely. Nearby, Meryl Streep returned to her own seat, while Brad Pitt and Jennifer Aniston talked to nominee Catherine Keener.

With the stars reseated, Crystal told us what they were thinking. Streep: "The designated hitter rule is ruining baseball." Dench: "This thong is killing me." Michael Clarke Duncan: "I see white people." Russell Crowe: "Boy, I could use a cigarette right around now." Crowe nodded after hearing this line; though the camera had been cutting to him all night, he had yet to crack a visible smile.

Then Bacharach led his medley of past nominated songs. Isaac Hayes was obscured by an overactive fog machine during his rendition of "The Theme from *Shaft*," but otherwise things went without a hitch. As the performers left the stage at the end of the medley, Richard Zanuck made a beeline for Garth Brooks and pumped his hand.

At about 8:00, *All About My Mother* won the Oscar for foreign film. As Lili Zanuck had feared, Pedro Almodóvar began babbling in broken English with no apparent intention of stopping. The band came in after a minute and a half, but that didn't faze the hyperactive Spaniard, who remained at the microphone until Antonio Banderas dragged him off by the arm.

A few minutes after Almodóvar cleared the stage, Edward Norton introduced the In Memoriam film. Besides the usual array of Academy members and Oscar winners, the montage featured several stars with indelible ties to the Oscar ceremony: George C. Scott, who refused to accept the best-actor trophy when he won for *Patton*; Abraham Polonsky, a blacklisted writer and outspoken foe of Elia Kazan who'd helped lead the fight against Kazan's honorary award; Charles "Buddy" Rogers, who'd starred in the first best-picture winner, *Wings*, and sixty years later sat onstage during part of the gruesome production number that kicked off Allan Carr's show; and Carr himself, who'd died the previous June of liver cancer.

As the show hit the three-hour mark—with a full eight awards yet to be handed out—Jack Nicholson came into the wings, ready to give the Irving Thalberg Award to Warren Beatty. He looked at a particularly large stagehand, clad in the regulation white jumpsuit. "Who are you?" he asked. "The baker?"

Beatty turned out to be a gracious recipient, but also a troublesome honoree late in a show that was already running long. His speech, which he had refused to show to the Zanucks ahead of time, was amusing, but also meandering and very long—almost six minutes, putting it neck-and-neck with Greer Garson's legendary speech in 1943, which was later reputed to have lasted as long as an hour. In fact, Garson had spoken for five and a half minutes—but she did so at the end of a long, slow show, after 1 a.m., when everybody was ready to go home.

By the time Beatty left the stage, the show was already close to the 3:15 mark that was the Zanucks' original goal. At this point, though, the evening was just getting to the prestige awards, the ones that had a bearing on the best-picture race. And clearly, the contingents from DreamWorks and Miramax knew it. When *American Beauty* won for cinematography, a large DreamWorks crowd jumped up as one. When *Cider House Rules* writer John Irving won the adapted-screenplay award a few minutes later—and pointedly referred to the movie as "a film on the abortion subject" at the beginning of his speech—the Miramax crowd did the same. When Alan Ball won the original-screenplay Oscar for *American Beauty*, DreamWorks celebrated anew.

Before cutting to a commercial a few minutes later, the camera focused on Peter Coyote in the wings. "He's back," said Coyote. "Academy Award winner Roberto Benigni presents the best-actress Oscar when the 72nd annual Academy Awards return." Benigni stood a few feet away, out of sight of the camera. "Get in there, get in there!" crew members whispered to him, pushing the actor toward Coyote. Suddenly shy, Benigni protested; when they insisted, he jumped into the frame and mugged with Coyote for a few seconds before the commercial.

During the next segment, Benigni handed the best-actress Oscar to Hilary Swank for *Boys Don't Cry*. When she left the stage, Swank embraced Gwyneth Paltrow, who then presented the best-actor award to Kevin Spacey for *American Beauty*. It was too late for funny intros, so Crystal dropped the joke he'd planned and said simply, "Ladies and gentlemen, Mr. Steven Spielberg." Spielberg walked onstage as Was's band played along with a sample from the *Jaws* soundtrack. As had happened all night, the sample was inaudible.

Spielberg presented the best-director Oscar to *American Beauty*'s Sam Mendes, then Clint Eastwood named that film 1999's best picture. The show finally ended at 9:38 p.m. "I've been told that this is the shortest Oscar show of the century," said Billy Crystal. "So how about that?" Four hours and eight minutes after it began—roughly half an hour of clips, eighty jokes, and sixteen songs after Crystal sang "cut the clips, cut the jokes, cut the songs"—the longest Academy Awards show in history was over.

AT THE GOVERNORS BALL, Lili Zanuck was accosted by an angry Pedro Almodóvar, who said he was offended that he had been played off, and mad at Banderas for grabbing his arm. Then he threw in a few more complaints for the hell of it: he thought it was terrible that a committee voted for the foreign films rather than the entire academy membership, he was mad that foreign nominees weren't invited to the nominees' luncheon . . . "He took me aside for thirty fucking minutes," said Zanuck. "And I thought, God, what if this guy hadn't *won*?"

Across town in West Hollywood, Billy Crystal's daughter was at the *Vanity Fair* party. "I'm so glad it's over," she told a friend. "You have *no idea* what the pressure is like."

In his *Daily Variety* column on Monday morning, Army Archerd reported that during Friday's rehearsal, Bacharach "decided not to go with Whitney Houston and she was taken off the show!" Almost immediately, urgent calls went out from the producers' office to many of those who worked on the show. The story that *must* be used, everyone was told, was that Houston had to drop out because of a sore throat. It would be months before the Zanucks admitted the truth.

Ratings were up by 2 percent over the previous year. Many viewers found the show to be a fresh update over the usual Oscar show, though the use of Peter Coyote was roundly panned. More than a few observers were amused that after the early promises of a shorter show with no dance numbers, the Zanucks produced a show of historic length highlighted by a rendition of "Blame Canada" that featured about forty dancers.

"We made all these pronouncements about how we were going to make it a faster show, and we failed miserably," Lili Zanuck freely admitted a few months later. Still, she said, she wouldn't rule out producing the show again. "It was about as much work as I expected, but it was a lot more fun than I thought it was going to be."

Whitney Houston's rocky year didn't get any better after the Oscars. Just weeks after the show, she was a no-show at the Rock and Roll Hall of Fame ceremony, where she was supposed to help induct Clive Davis, the record executive who'd signed her to Arista Records and guided her career. Not long afterward, she was sued for nonpayment by a company run by her father. Her husband, Bobby Brown, spent two months in jail for parole violations after he tested positive for cocaine. At the end of the year, Houston appeared on ABC's *Primetime*, swearing to interviewer Diane Sawyer that her self-destructive days were over—and adding that contrary to rumors, she'd never smoked crack cocaine. "I make too much money for me to ever smoke crack," she said.

A little more than two months after the Oscar show, Willie Fulgear reported to police that a five-hundred-pound safe, containing what was left of the reward he'd received for finding the Oscar statuettes, had been stolen from his Los Angeles apartment.

The Roadway Express truck driver and loading dock worker arrested in the theft of those statuettes pleaded no contest. The truck driver, Lawrence Ledent, received a six-month jail term, while the dock worker, Anthony Hart, received probation. In October, charges were filed against a third man, John Harris, who was the half-brother of Fulgear. Police admitted they found the relationship suspicious, but Fulgear said he and Harris were estranged, and no charges were filed.

The final three Oscar statuettes were never found.

In the aftermath of what also turned out to be the most expensive Oscar show ever—a show that was reputed to cost half again as much as the usual show—the Academy decided to change the way in which it financed the Oscars. Instead of having Seligman talk to the producers and work up a budget that he'd submit to the Academy for approval, the organization decided that future producers would be given a dollar figure up front and would be expected to stick to it.

In July, the Eastman Kodak Company agreed to pay $75 million for the naming rights to the theater that was being built in the Hollywood & Highland complex.

8

Short Cuts

The 73rd Academy Awards

THE SPEECHES were always a problem. No matter what a producer told the nominees, once they heard their names announced they talked too long, or they pulled out a list and read a bunch of names of people the audience didn't know or care about. Most of them, sad to say, had no idea how witty and entertaining you could be in forty-five seconds. They got in the spotlight, they looked at the famous people in front of them, they froze, and they rattled off names until the orchestra cut them off.

It hadn't always been like that. "The thing that's most striking if you look back at the shows from, say, the early eighties, is that most of the accepters just said, 'Thank you,' " recalled Bruce Davis. "Now everybody makes a speech, everybody has their VCR turned on back at home. People who used to walk up almost embarrassed, grab the statuette and smile and say 'Thanks' and get off, are now giving long speeches."

In the winter of 2001, as Gil Cates prepared to produce his tenth Academy Awards show, he was determined to try to change that. He had to: the last time he'd produced the show, in 1999, he'd been responsible for what had been, for one year, the longest Academy Awards show in history. For years, Cates had been using sports analogies to shrug off questions about the show's length, comparing it to major athletic events: "It'll take as long as it takes." But with the show's overall rating an average of each half-hour segment, the metaphor was no longer working.

"We can't compare it to the Super Bowl anymore," said Davis. "That's too self-indulgent. In fact, we have to get this thing in in three and a half hours or shorter. We've been looking at the breakdowns from ABC, which can give you each city at fifteen-minute intervals. And you can just see the sets clicking off on the East Coast when you run past midnight. It hurts the rating. You're hurting yourself in the second hour if you run into a fourth."

That was one of the reasons the Academy, two years earlier, had moved the show from Monday to Sunday night, and from a 6:00 p.m. start time to 5:30. But while the earlier start time was partly designed to let East Coasters get to bed before midnight, that hadn't happened. In both of the shows since the time change, the final awards weren't handed out until after 12:30 a.m.

So when Cates agreed to take over the seventy-third Oscar show, time was a priority. The producer had certain ideas about how to streamline the show, but none of them meant much if the speeches ran long. The key, he knew, was to convince nominees that he was serious about that forty-five-second limit on acceptance speeches, and serious when he said they should not pull out written lists.

His best chance to make that point came at the nominees' luncheon on March 12, a little less than two weeks before the Oscar show. The room contained about a hundred nominees from all categories, including actors Jeff Bridges, Russell Crowe, Willem Dafoe, Tom Hanks, Ed Harris, Kate Hudson, and eighty-one-year-old producer Dino De Laurentiis, who had been voted the Thalberg Award. As they sat at tables spread out across the grand ballroom of the Beverly Hills Hotel and lunched on sea bass with red pepper coulis and chateaubriand in merlot sauce, Cates walked to a podium at the front of the room and made his plea.

"I've done this every year for ten years," he said. "I've tried to be charming and humorous. I've tried persuasion and bribery. It all comes down to my belief that brevity is next to godliness . . . I just beg you, *please*, keep your speech to forty-five seconds, and don't read off a list of names. Studies have shown that most of those people won't hire you again anyway." As usual, Cates showed a montage of bad acceptance speeches—all of them lists of names—and then a second montage of what he said were good speeches, including Joe Pesci's terse, "It's my privilege, thank you" in 1991 and Alfred Hitchcock's minimalist, "Thank you very much" upon receiving the Irving Thalberg Award in 1968.

He neglected to supply the backstory to both of those speeches. Hitchcock's, for instance, was widely taken to be the normally eloquent sixty-eight-year-old director's slap at the Academy, which had never given him an Oscar despite more than fifty movies, many of them classics. As for Pesci, the supporting-actor winner for *GoodFellas* was so overcome upon winning that he couldn't have said anything more if he'd wanted to: as soon as he got offstage, the actor collapsed in a heap on the floor, right at the feet of the startled British actress Brenda Fricker. "I can't beeeelieve this, I can't beeeelieve this," he kept muttering, crouching on the floor in the dark.

"When you come off the stage," Cates continued, "you can hand us a list of all the people you want to thank, and we'll post it on the Oscar.com Web site right away. It'll be up there that night, and if people ask why you didn't thank them, you can tell them to go to the Web site."

Before he sat down, Cates had a final offer. "As an incentive, the person with the shortest speech gets a special award: a brand-new high-definition TV." At the tables, nominees laughed. Nobody was quite sure if Cates was serious.

FOR NOMINEES, the matter of acceptance speeches had always been a tricky one. To unfold a written speech and a list of names risked incurring the wrath of the producers and earning a rude sendoff from the orchestra. To speak off the cuff, unprepared, was to run the risk of leaving out someone important in the heat of the moment and the glare of the lights. But to have an eloquent speech memorized—well, that could be seen as the height of presumption. The happy medium was to have remarks prepared, but to deliver them in such a way that you appeared to be speaking off the cuff, but that was a tough one to pull off. Still, people tried: even Greer Garson prefaced the most famously lengthy acceptance speech in Oscar history by saying, "I am practically unprepared."

Many winners found the time constraints almost impossible to deal with. "When I watch our acceptance speech now, the panic is written all over us," said Lili Zanuck, who coproduced the 1988 best-picture winner *Driving Miss Daisy* with Richard. Their own acceptance-speech anxiety fueled their desire not to rush winners offstage when they produced the Oscars in 2000. "We know what it's like to go as fast as you can because you're afraid you're going to get played off in forty-five seconds."

Then there was the matter of whom to thank and whom to leave out. While it wasn't as blatant as Oscar campaigning, acceptance-speech campaigning also took place in Hollywood. Virtually every nominee could tell stories about the congratulatory calls he'd received, first after the nominations were announced and then, again and again, in the weeks leading up to the show itself.

Richard Sylbert, the set decorator who was nominated for six Oscars and won for *Who's Afraid of Virginia Woolf?* in 1967 and *Dick Tracy* twenty-four years later, once recalled getting a surprisingly pleasant phone call from Jeffrey Katzenberg, then the chairman of Walt Disney Studios, not long before the Academy Awards in March 1991. Sylbert and Katzenberg were not exactly friends; in fact, many of those associated with *Dick Tracy* were furious at the executive for a twenty-eight-page memo he'd written two months earlier. The so-called "Katzenberg memo," which was supposed to be kept in-house at Disney but was quickly leaked to the press, laid forth Katzenberg's philosophy of low-cost, low-risk moviemaking, and held up Warren Beatty's lavish $100 million salute to the comic strip hero as an example of the kind of movie Disney should no longer make. "As profitable as it was," Katzenberg wrote, "*Dick Tracy* made demands on our time, talent, and treasury that, upon reflection, may not have been worth it."

So when Sylbert got a call from Katzenberg just before the Oscar show, he didn't know what to think. "He said he was calling just to say hello, to see how I was doing," said Sylbert several years before his death in March 2002. "When I hung up I was very confused, so I called Warren and told him about it. And Warren said, 'Don't you know what that call was about?' I said, 'No, I don't.' And he said, 'The little prick wants you to thank him if you win.' " Sylbert did win. He thanked Beatty, but not Katzenberg.

IT WAS A RARITY: a year in which there was no true front-runner in the best-picture competition. *Gladiator* and *Crouching Tiger, Hidden Dragon* received the most nominations, but neither of them was typical Oscar fare: the first, from *Blade Runner* director Ridley Scott, was the kind of violent, big-budget, crowd-pleasing action movie that usually won in the technical categories but nowhere else, while the latter, shot in Mandarin Chinese with subtitles for English-speaking viewers, was director Ang Lee's tribute to the martial arts movies from Hong Kong he'd loved as a child. They may have been expertly crafted films with more depth and resonance than most genre movies—but genre movies, whatever depth and resonance they may have, seldom won many Academy Awards.

Director Steven Soderbergh's *Traffic* was more typical Oscar bait, but the high-minded three-hour film about the drug trade along the U.S./ Mexican border was also inconsistent, and Soderbergh's fondness for mixing in grainy film stock and jerky handheld cameras didn't figure to endear him to older Academy voters. In addition, Soderbergh might well split the vote, because he'd also directed another best-picture nominee, *Erin Brockovich*, a more conventional film that had won raves for Julia Roberts's performance as a hell-raising legal assistant.

The fifth nominee was *Chocolat*. The morning that nominations were announced in the Samuel Goldwyn Theater, a slight groan had run through the crowd of reporters, publicists, and studio reps when its name was announced. A trifle from Lasse Hallström, the director of *The Cider House Rules*, *Chocolat* was to most viewers a lesser achievement than, say, Christopher Nolan's intriguing *Memento*, Darren Aronofsky's unrelentingly bleak *Requiem for a Dream*, the Coen Brothers' romp *O Brother, Where Art Thou?* or a number of other movies. *Chocolat*, though, fulfilled the apparent requirement that Miramax must produce one best-picture nominee each year.

Since *Gladiator* received the most nominations, twelve to *Crouching Tiger*'s ten, it began to assume the mantle of a front-runner almost by default. DreamWorks, which had coproduced the film with Universal, used its campaign to play up the movie's heroic, epic qualities rather than its blood and gore. But *Crouching Tiger* remained a sentimental favorite, and USA Films quietly worked to position *Traffic* as not only the best, but also the most important movie of the batch. The best-actor race narrowed to a two-man competition between the always-popular Tom Hanks, who spent most of *Cast Away* acting alongside a volleyball, and *Gladiator* star Russell Crowe, who in the past year had become a world-class movie star, hell-raiser, and tabloid staple via rumored romances with everyone from Meg Ryan (confirmed) to Nicole Kidman (denied). The only sure bet, most observers felt, was in the best-actress category, where it seemed a foregone conclusion that *Erin Brockovich* would bring home the gold for Julia Roberts.

With so many races presumably up for grabs, Oscar campaigns kicked into overdrive, and each move by one studio was countered by another. No sooner had Universal sent a "Making of *Erin Brockovich*" DVD to every *Daily Variety* subscriber than a rival publicist called writers to suggest that the move was a sneaky way to reach Oscar voters by skirting the Academy's rules against such items. DreamWorks rereleased *Gladiator* at a deluxe theater in Century City, and for the first week trotted out Russell Crowe, composer Hans Zimmer, and five other nominees to speak after the screenings—again, a violation of Academy rules if the screenings hadn't been open to the public. Sony Classics, determined to fill the art-movie-with-a-real-chance slot that Miramax usually occupied, sent *Crouching Tiger, Hidden Dragon* to twenty different film locations for special cast-and-crew screenings.

ON THURSDAY, March 22, three days before the seventy-third Oscars show, Steve Martin pulled into the parking lot behind the Shrine Auditorium. Like all presenters, performers, and previous hosts, Martin had been offered the use of a town car and driver at Academy expense—but to the astonishment of Cates and many staffers, Martin turned it down in favor of driving his own Lexus to and from the downtown theater. What's more, he brought his own laptop computer to meetings, and took his own notes.

Martin had appeared on several Oscar shows in the past, and he'd declined one offer from Cates to host the show. But when first-year Academy president Frank Pierson approached Cates in the fall and asked him to over-see the show, the producer knew he wouldn't be able to turn to Billy Crys-tal. At the September wedding of Crystal's daughter, the comic's manager had already told Cates that his client would be too busy directing the HBO movie *61** to even consider the gig.

"Steve was an easy choice," said Cates, sitting in the lunch area of the Shrine Exhibition Hall and waiting for Martin's first rehearsal. "And this is the Oscars, so you don't have to worry about contracts and negotiations and all that bullshit. I called Steve's agent, Ed Limato, and asked if he thought Steve would be interested. Ed said, 'He might be, why don't you call him?' So I called Steve, asked him if he wanted to host, and he said yes."

By the time he showed up at the Shrine, Martin had already been to the production office several times, testing his monologue before small groups of staffers. The host had also declined suggestions that he incorporate props into his duties: he wanted to keep his initial Oscar stint classy.

Just before 2:30, Martin showed up on the stage and stepped to a micro-phone. "Testing," he said. "Testing, one, two, three." He paused, and looked into the audience. "That's my opening line," he said.

Looking calm and composed, with a pair of glasses hanging around his neck, he peered toward the TelePrompTer. "I'm not going to do the mono-logue, because you'll tell everyone," he said. "So, blah blah blah . . ." Then he stopped. Tired of throwing out nonsense, he looked toward a group of his writers, including Bruce Vilanch, comedian Rita Rudner, and Martin's manager, David Steinberg. "What are some of the jokes we have that we're not going to use?" he asked. "You know, the ones that are too mean."

He thought for a minute, then launched into the first of the rejected jokes. "Michael Douglas this year became a father to Catherine Zeta-Jones," he said. "Wait, did I say *to*? I meant *with*." The audience let out a low groan. "See why we're not going to use it?" Martin said. Then he ran through more of the rejected jokes. "One of the nominees is *Chocolat*, starring Juli-ette Binoche and . . . some guy who gets to touch Juliette Binoche."

He looked back at his writers. "What else?"

"Madonna and Guy Ritchie!" yelled Vilanch.

"Oh, right," said Martin. "Madonna married Guy Ritchie—who before the wedding was known as Guy Poory . . . Any others?"

"Travolta!"

"Our next presenter is John Travolta, who can still wear the suit he wore in *Saturday Night Fever* . . . as a bib."

After this line, ABC's Susan Futterman yelled to the stage, "You should put that back in!"

"Should I?" said Martin. "Isn't it a little mean?"

"No," yelled Futterman. "Use it!"

Martin shrugged, then forged ahead. "Here's another one we're not using. This just in: Erin Brockovich has found toxic mold on Dino De Laurentiis. Or this one: I'm so envious of Russell Crowe, because he's been in some *fabulous* things this year."

After rehearsing for about half an hour, Martin left the stage and chatted with Cates. As they spoke, Martin's publicist, Catherine Olim, approached Vilanch.

"I know you're not using that joke about Russell," she said uneasily. "But as his publicist I have to tell you, they're *just good friends*."

Vilanch looked confused. "What?" he said. "Russell and who?"

"Nicole Kidman. She's my client, too."

"You have nothing to worry about," Vilanch assured her.

AT THE OSCARS, as in much of the rest of Hollywood, one of the true signs of power was the proximity of one's parking space. At the Shrine Auditorium, the parking lot at the rear of the building was prime but rarefied territory, reserved for the likes of Cates, Horvitz, Herman, Seligman, and a handful of other bigwigs, along with top executives from ABC and the Academy. Those who didn't rate quite so highly parked farther away, with a hundred or so allocated spaces in a parking structure adjacent to the Shrine Exposition Hall.

But out of the fifteen hundred or so workers who came to the Shrine during Oscar week, most were exiled to outlying lots. The bulk of these lots were to the south of the Shrine, past the USC campus, on the outskirts of a large complex of city buildings known as Exposition Park. The area included the Los Angeles Memorial Coliseum, the Sports Arena, and the Museums of Natural History and Science and Industry; it also had abundant parking, and during Oscar week a fleet of shuttle buses made constant trips to and from the Shrine.

On Friday morning, two days before the Oscar show, one of those shuttles had a typical cross-section of riders: a couple of technicians, some office staffers, and one security guard. Most of the bus, though, was occupied by stand-ins, who spent the ride to the Shrine mulling over their version of a typical Oscar question: what should I wear?

For rehearsals, the stand-ins had been separated into two teams, with twenty in each team. The first team was due in the theater at 8:15 in the morning, in order that they could spend the day playing the part of presenters and nominees whenever Horvitz got the chance to run through the show. The second team wasn't due until 8 p.m.; they'd handle the same chores for the night shift. Nobody talked about it out loud, but everyone knew that stand-ins Horvitz liked got the day shift, ones he wasn't so sure about the night.

On the bus, though, they weren't talking about the stand-in hierarchy; after all, this was the day shift, which meant they were all on Horvitz's good side. Instead, they were trying to figure out what to do about a new edict. For dress rehearsal the next night, the stand-ins had been told, Horvitz wanted them to dress as if they were really attending the show.

"How can I dress like that?" complained one woman. "I'm staying at my friend's apartment this week—I didn't bring my best clothes with me."

"Do they expect us to wear our best clothes if we're here all day," griped a man, "or are we supposed to bring them and then change before the dress rehearsal? It's just not practical."

"It's ridiculous," summed up a third stand-in. "We're supposed to dress like the stars, but we don't have their budget."

FRIDAY WAS DEVOTED largely to rehearsing the nominees for best song. The importance of the songs was more pronounced than usual, because the telecast didn't include any medleys of past songs or dance numbers to illustrate sound effects or film editing. (A tentative plan to feature a ballet number themed to the British film *Billy Elliott*, in which a small-town working-class boy yearned to become a dancer, was scotched when that movie received only a single nomination.)

The slate of songs was wildly mixed. It included Randy Newman, now up to fourteen nominations without a win, for a bouncy tune from *Meet the Parents*; the chirpy Icelandic alternative-rock princess Björk, with an atmospheric track from *Dancer in the Dark*; former rock god turned mainstream balladeer Sting with a languid song from the animated Disney film *The Emperor's New Groove*; and writers Jorge Calandrelli, Tan Dun, and James Schamus for a lush ballad sung by Asian star Coco Lee in *Crouching Tiger, Hidden Dragon*.

The last slot was filled by the biggest name of the group, rock legend Bob Dylan, with "Things Have Changed" from *The Wonder Boys*. Once it would have been inconceivable to find the iconoclastic and often perverse Dylan performing on the Academy Awards—and from the moment he received the nomination, serious doubt existed about whether he could be persuaded to appear. Even before the nominations, Dylan had scheduled an Australian tour for the month of March; some suggested that he was well aware of what he was doing when he booked himself on the opposite side of the globe.

Over the ensuing weeks, negotiations took place to secure Dylan's participation on the show. Columbia Records, Dylan's label, offered to buy out the conflicting Australian shows, to pay off promoters and give the singer time to get back to the United States. Dylan refused, meaning the Oscars would need to either find somebody else to sing the song, or set up a remote broadcast.

Remotes were rarely used on the Academy Awards. The last time a nominated song had been performed anywhere but at the show was twenty-five years earlier, when Diana Ross had sung "Theme from *Mahogany* (Do You Know Where You're Going To)" from Amsterdam, lip-syncing the song while riding the streets in a horse-drawn carriage. Nobody wanted a return to that kind of foolishness—but at the same time, nobody wanted to book an inappropriate substitute for a nominated singer, especially one as legendary as Dylan. Besides Ann Reinking's famously awful rendition of "Against All Odds" in 1985, other regrettable choices included a 1984 rendition of "Maniac," Michael Sembello's driving rock song from *Flash-dance*, by Herb Alpert and the Tijuana Brass, who at the time hadn't had a hit in twenty years; a stab at the pile driver "The Eye of the Tiger" (from *Rocky III*) by the odd coupling of the action-film actress Sandahl Bergman and the vocal group the Temptations; and Paul McCartney's James Bond theme, "Live and Let Die," entrusted to the actress and one-time teen-pop singer Connie Stevens.

Both options—a satellite link or a different performer—were distasteful. With some inside the production and the Academy adamantly opposed to doing a live remote, a few replacement names were bandied about, among them the gravel-voiced bard Tom Waits. Still, it was hard to take what seemed to be a meaningful, personal song from the greatest songwriter of his generation, and hand it over to somebody else. In the end, Cates decided that it was better to have Dylan from afar than somebody else in person. "If it were anybody but Dylan," said Robert Z. Shapiro, "the decision would have been a lot harder."

On Friday, Björk was the first of the nominees to rehearse, arriving at 8:30 in the morning with her fourteen-year-old son, Sindri, in tow. The singer wore a long, gauzy white dress, and kicked off her shoes as soon as she got to the stage. Her son watched, wearing a black Oscar cap.

In the film, Björk's nominated song, "I've Seen It All," was performed as a duet with Thom Yorke, the leader of Radiohead, the most influential and acclaimed British rock band of the past ten years. Though he tended to be somewhat reclusive and didn't enjoy performing, Yorke had initially agreed to appear on the Oscars with Björk, until the Academy's time constraints quite literally got in the way. "Thom was definitely up for it," said Björk's publicist, Joel Amsterdam, as he stood in the aisle and watched her pace the stage. "But the song's five and a half minutes long, and they told us we had to cut it down to three minutes. There's no time for his part."

Over the course of several rehearsals, Björk slowly became acclimated to the stage. At first she stared at her sheet music as she sang the droning song, which was set to a lurching, mechanical train rhythm. With each take, though, she loosened up a little more, meandering around, then bouncing on her heels, swaying, and turning into an oddly, endearingly magnetic performer.

Over a walkie-talkie, an assistant director radioed one of the stage managers. "This may sound like a weird question," he said, "but you may want to ask Björk if she's going to be wearing the glass dress."

The stage manager looked over at Amsterdam. "Um, is Björk going to be wearing a glass dress?" she asked.

"No," he said, as if the question were a completely normal one. He pointed to a small gym bag sitting on a nearby seat, and grinned. "Her dress is in that bag."

By the end of the day, Randy Newman had also come through, as had Sting and the striking Asian singer Coco Lee. But Cates was most excited about a midafternoon appearance by the classical virtuosos Itzhak Perlman and Yo-Yo Ma, who'd been booked to perform a suite of music from the nominated scores.

"Did you hear the joke that Itzhak told?" Cates asked Seligman a couple of hours after Perlman and Ma had rehearsed. "Jean-Claude Van Damme, Sylvester Stallone, and Arnold Schwarzenegger got together, and they decided to make an action movie about famous composers. Van Damme said, 'I'll be Tchaikovsky.' Stallone said, 'I'll be Mozart.' And then Schwarzenegger said, 'I'll be Bach.' "

Seligman and a handful of staffers laughed politely, and Cates shrugged. "It's not so funny when I tell it," he insisted, "but it's *very* funny when Itzhak Perlman tells it."

AS REHEARSAL WOUND DOWN, a couple of ABC pages got on the shuttle bus that would take them back to the lot where their cars were parked. The pages, most of them men and women in their twenties, were used to escort stars to and from their cars, to stay with them when they were in the Shrine, and to make sure they got their gift baskets and other freebies. Because the stage managers and talent staff had so many stars to deal with, they relied on pages to offer the kind of constant attention the show staff couldn't, both during rehearsals and during the show itself.

On the shuttle bus, the two young men looked over the schedules they'd been given for the next day.

"I have Hilary Swank tomorrow morning at ten," said one.

"How is she?" asked the other.

"She's really nice."

The second page looked at his sheet. "Tomorrow at four I've got Penélope!"

"I've got Kate Hudson at five. I'll trade ya."

"No thanks."

"I thought you liked blondes."

"Yeah, but Penélope's *hot*."

DURING A NORMAL YEAR, getting stars to the Oscars involved an intricate game of scheduling. Actors with movies in production needed at least a day off if they were nominees, a minimum of two if they were presenters; for those whose films weren't shooting in Southern California, travel time had to be factored in as well. In 2001, though, things were even trickier than usual, because the Screen Actors Guild and the Writers Guild had both threatened to strike in early summer if new contract negotiations weren't concluded. To make sure they'd have enough product to see themselves through the possible strikes, the major studios and production companies rushed films into production, anxious to finish as much as possible by Memorial Day.

"With the strikes coming up, everybody is just fried," said Danette Herman as she stood at the top of the steps overlooking the artists' entrance to the Shrine. It was 9 a.m., and in fifteen minutes a procession of movie stars were due to arrive. "Some people are doing two movies at once," added Herman. "But everybody's going to show up."

As usual, that wasn't quite true: Tom Cruise was skipping rehearsal, per his custom, and so was Julia Roberts. But more than two dozen others, including Michael Douglas, John Travolta, Russell Crowe, Kate Hudson, and Renée Zellweger, were due at the Shrine. On the way to his trailer, Cates stopped for a minute to talk with Herman. "This is a rough morning for me," he said. "I have to sit in my trailer and talk to lots of beautiful women."

First up was the previous year's best-actress winner, Hilary Swank, who arrived early. When she got to the podium for the first time, Swank looked into the audience at the seat cards.

"Oh," she said, "Jeff Bridges has my seat from last year. Anthony Hopkins has Meryl Streep's seat."

Debbie Williams was incredulous. "How do you remember that?" she asked.

"I remember *everything* about last year," said Swank.

The day's rehearsal proceeded uneventfully, with a few exceptions. Russell Crowe, reportedly the object of a recent kidnapping plot, was accompanied by two handlers and a pair of large, stern men in suits. Afterward, a stage manager asked the gum-chewing Crowe to go to the sound truck, where he could record the nominees' names in a voiceover that would run while film clips were being shown. Crowe declined to do so. Cates was summoned to the green room to convince the recalcitrant actor—but once again, Crowe refused. "It's a *live* show," Crowe said. "Why would I do that?"

The other presenter who needed careful handling was Ben Stiller, who was handing out the award for short subjects. Stiller wasn't thrilled with his category—but, as he told the show's writers, "It was either that or some technical award." The actor also didn't care for the copy that had been written for him, so he tried to substitute a bit of his own that drew on the fact that Stiller, Woody Allen, and Martin Scorsese were all short—"but not our private parts." When that line failed to pass muster, Stiller sat at the writers' table and hashed out a new version that was less juvenile, but still phallic: "It's not the length of your film, it's what you do with it." By the time Stiller was finished rewriting his lines, he didn't have time to record his own voiceover.

Outside the hall, Cates left his office and escorted Penélope Cruz to the green room. He waved good-bye to Winona Ryder and Jennifer Lopez as they were leaving, then stopped to say hello to Sigourney Weaver. As they were talking, Kate Hudson dashed in the artists' entrance, ten minutes past her call time. "I'm so sorry I'm late," she said to Cates.

"It's no problem," he told her, giving her his arm. "C'mon, let's go to my office." On the way, he stopped, turned around, and grinned. "Hard job," he said.

BOB DYLAN hadn't been the easiest performer to deal with—and neither had his crew in Australia, key members of which were dubbed "flakes" by Seligman. Staffers at the Shrine were clearly tense as the time approached for an early evening test of the satellite link to Dylan. It was, perhaps, appropriate that to get his song down to the three-minute mark required by the Oscars, Dylan had eliminated the second of the four verses in "Things Have Changed"—the verse that began, "This place ain't doin' me any good / I'm in the wrong place, I should be in Hollywood."

Guitarist Charlie Sexton, eighteen hours ahead and seven thousand five hundred miles from Hollywood, subbed for his boss during the brief rehearsal. Sexton had been playing with Dylan for close to two years, and he even obliged by singing one verse in a creditable Dylanesque drawl that drew hoots of laughter back in Los Angeles. "I've been walkin' forty miles of bad road," snarled the Texas-born guitarist. "If the Bible is right, the world will explooooode." Meanwhile, a beefy, middle-aged, white-haired roadie stood in Sexton's usual spot, absently strumming a nonexistent guitar.

Once they'd rehearsed the song, the next order of business was to practice what would happen if Dylan won—a distinct possibility, since the song was the odds-on favorite. To keep things as simple as possible, presenter Jennifer Lopez was due to open the envelope immediately after Dylan's performance. While the band waited, a stand-in did the honors. "The Oscar goes to Bob Dylan," she announced, whereupon Horvitz cut back to Sexton, who once again was playing the part of his employer.

"Uh, thank you," Sexton mumbled in his best Dylan voice. At the Shrine, many observers figured that Sexton's three-word speech was probably the exact same one they'd hear from Dylan if he received the award.

Cates, though, breathed a sigh of relief when the satellite rehearsal went off without a hitch. "I think if Dylan wins it will actually be an exciting moment," he said to Seligman. "I'm not nearly as worried about it as I was."

STEVE MARTIN didn't seem worried, either. In fact, as the first dress rehearsal neared, the host was to all appearances completely relaxed. While Horvitz counted down the minutes from his truck and Cates settled behind the production table inside the Shrine, Martin wasn't in his dressing room fretting about last-minute changes; instead, the tuxedo-clad host stood in the center aisle, chatting with friends and posing for photos. It wasn't until Bill Conti's orchestra started playing the overture—the Richard Strauss theme from *2001: A Space Odyssey*, which made sense given the year, but had also been used to kick off David Letterman's ill-fated gig at the Oscars six years earlier—that the host left the aisle and ambled onstage.

There, he delivered what was essentially a dummy monologue: a few jokes, some mumbling, and lots of lines like "blah blah blah, I'm so funny now, standing ovation, blah blah blah . . ." After one joke, he listened to the applause—more than ought to be coming from the small group of stand-ins and staffers watching the rehearsal—and shook his head. "Is that sweetening I hear?" he scolded, accurately identifying the canned laughter coming from the P.A. system. "Oh, thanks. That's a real confidence builder."

Martin remained loose and relaxed throughout the rehearsal. Unless he was needed onstage, he watched the show from a seat near his writers, putting his fingers in his ears during every musical performance. The rehearsal ended at the unnervingly early time of 10:46, just a few minutes past the three-hour mark. Stage manager Garry Hood, who was in charge of cuing Martin during the show, was impressed. "There's low-maintenance, there's high-maintenance, and there's Steve Martin: no maintenance," he said. "Normally a host comes off, I hand them their script for the next bit and tell them how long they've got. Steve comes off, and before I can say anything he says, 'I know. Item forty-two, I'm introducing Julia. I'll see you in five minutes.'"

After Martin left, Cates shook his head. "He is a man," he said admiringly, "totally without angst."

ON THE MONITORS in front of Horvitz, Itzhak Perlman and Yo-Yo Ma alternately caressed and ripped into music from the five nominated scores. They sounded great, but Horvitz didn't like what he was seeing during the final rehearsal. The two men sat in chairs that had been placed atop a center-stage platform, while behind them large screens showed footage from the films whose scores they were performing. Horvitz needed to capture both the musicians and the screens—but as the pair ran through their number, he scanned the dozens of monitors in front of him with increasing impatience, nowhere seeing the kind of shots he wanted.

"That's fucked," said Horvitz into his headset. "We need a wider shot somewhere in here. This *has* to be dealt with."

"We can't stop to fix it, right?" an assistant director asked.

"No," the director replied. "We'll have to fix it on the show." He turned and focused on the monitors in front of him. "Ready camera two. Dissolve to three. Dissolve to four." He stopped. "Damnit, Hector, how many fucking times did we do that shot?" He put his head in his hands. "Guys, I gotta have some help here, goddamnit."

Outside the truck, the atmosphere may have been unexpectedly relaxed for an Oscar show; inside, where decisions were made on the fly and there was no such thing as a second take, the usual tensions gripped the crew.

Sitting in a chair behind Horvitz, Cates leaned forward after the Perlman and Ma performance. "By the way," he said, "if they get a standing ovation, you can really milk it. I love those guys."

A COUPLE OF HOURS LATER, Björk returned to the Shrine, turning heads in the dress she'd had stuffed into her gym bag during rehearsal. A swan's head curled around her neck; the swan's body formed a fluffy tutu of sorts. When she arrived backstage in the outfit most people stared, though Anthony Hopkins walked by without noticing.

From the outside, the green room was draped in dramatic red velvet curtains, shielded by an entry corridor that contained two makeup tables. Inside, things were a soothing shade of pale blue, the translucent curtains dotted with small stars. The furniture—a couple of couches and a few chairs arranged around a handful of tables and a small spread of hors d'oeuvres and drinks—was a subdued, quietly tasteful beige. Early arrival Ben Stiller sat in there with his wife, Christine Taylor, while PricewaterhouseCoopers partner Lisa Perozzi held one of the two briefcases that contained complete sets of envelopes announcing the winners. (Her colleague Greg Garrison, stationed on the far side of the stage, had the other set.)

An hour before the show began, Itzhak Perlman entered the auditorium on his motorized cart. He rolled into the backstage area, accompanied by an aide carrying his priceless Stradivarius violin.

"How are you doing?" said a bystander as Perlman passed.

"Just schlepping," replied the virtuoso.

The Oscars themselves were wheeled out of a small, locked room about half an hour before show time, accompanied by a phalanx of guards. Academy historian Patrick Stockstill, wearing white gloves, walked alongside the surprisingly nondescript, even dingy cart on which the gleaming statuettes rested. Stockstill would be the only one to touch the Oscars until he handed them to one of the show's trophy ladies.

5:30 P.M., PACIFIC DAYLIGHT TIME: *"Live from the Shrine Auditorium in Los Angeles, California, the 73rd annual Academy Awards."*

Just outside the artists' entrance at the rear of the Shrine, Michael Douglas and Catherine Zeta-Jones stood in what passed for a smoking section. Between drags on her cigarette, Zeta-Jones studied the lines she'd be reading as the night's first presenter. (Her husband would be the last.) Shortly before a stage manager took her into the wings, Zeta-Jones began fanning herself with her script pages.

On the stage, Steve Martin launched into a monologue that dealt largely with show business—in fact, the subtext of most of it was the venality of the entertainment industry. "Please hold your applause," he said at one point, "until it's for me."

Eighteen minutes into the show, the first major award of the night, best supporting actress, went to Marcia Gay Harden for *Pollock*. When Harden and presenter Nicolas Cage were almost off the stage, a crew member yelled "*Go!*" and stagehands immediately began sliding a large center screen and two huge side panels off the stage. One of the panels almost hit the two actors.

Onstage, Martin mentioned how the phrase "and the winner is . . ." had been changed to "and the Oscar goes to . . ." "Because God forbid anyone should think of this as a competition," he said. "It might make the trade ads seem crass." He introduced Russell Crowe, who gave the editing award to *Traffic* and then immediately headed for the smoking area, trailed by a page, a publicist, and two guards.

A few minutes later, Martin reminded the nominees about Cates's offer of a free TV for the shortest speech, then introduced Ben Stiller. "You loved him in *There's Something About Mary*," he said. "You loved him in *Meet the Parents*. And you were just fine with him in *Mystery Men*." Stiller presented the award for best animated short to Dutch filmmaker Michael Dudok de Wit for *Father and Daughter*. De Wit thanked three people and the Academy, and wrapped up his speech in eighteen seconds.

As the show neared the one-hour mark, Benicio Del Toro won the award for best supporting actor, for *Traffic*. In the wings, Danette Herman let out a whoop. As Del Toro exited, stagehands began to move the huge scenic elements into place for the nominated song from *Crouching Tiger, Hidden Dragon*. "There's gonna be a lot of scenery coming through here, folks," yelled stage manager Peter Margolis. "We need everybody up against the walls."

While the scenery was being set, Mike Myers came onstage to present the awards for sound. "Now, ladies and gentlemen, the award we've all been waiting for," he said in a portentous tone. "Sound and sound editing. Now, I know what you're asking yourself: will the winner this year be Chet Flippy, or Tommy Bloobloo?" As he mocked the anonymity of the nominees, some members of the sound branch began to stew.

When Myers walked offstage and returned to the green room, he passed dozens of waiters and workers in the Governors Ball area. Nearby, Yo-Yo Ma and Itzhak Perlman warmed up in a quiet corner, then headed for the stage. On the way there, Ma spotted a woman walking off the stage with an Oscar in her hand. It was Tracy Seretean, the winner of the award for documentary short. Although he didn't know her, the cellist stopped and congratulated Seretean.

At this point the show was flowing easily; on backstage monitors, a countdown clock had it coming in at almost exactly three and a half hours. During a break, Cates left his usual post in the command truck. Trailed by a security guard, the producer walked past the green room and into the wings of the stage, where he greeted writer Buz Kohan.

"How's it playing out here?" said Cates.

"Good," Kohan assured him. "It's playing really well."

Cates nodded. "It's light, airy, pizzicato," he said. "And we'll be at three and a half hours, unless somebody does something stupid." Then he smiled, and his smile was informed by the experience of producing ten Academy Awards shows. "Which they may."

On the stage, Randy Newman and Bangles singer Susanna Hoffs performed "A Fool in Love." In the wings, Perlman slowly climbed up a set of steps to the platform on which he and Ma would perform. Ma followed. Casually, unheard by anyone except those nearby, Perlman and Ma began to play along with Newman's song.

While they played, a visibly nervous Renée Zellweger came into the wings, where she chatted with Goldie Hawn. "I'm going to trip over my dress, I know it," Zellweger fretted.

Cates walked over to greet the women, but he refrained from offering hugs. "He's done this for so long," said Zellweger, "he knows better than to wrap his arms around us."

After Newman's performance, Steve Martin returned to the stage. "The FBI has just announced a suspect in the plot to kidnap Russell Crowe," he said. "And all I can say is, Tom Hanks, you should be ashamed of yourself." The camera caught a priceless reaction from Hanks, who looked chastened and guilty. Behind Martin, the wings of the stage were plunged into chaos: Newman's bandstand and grand piano had to come off the stage and out of the way so that Perlman and Ma's platform could be pushed into place, but other scenery initially blocked the way. Stagehands rushed around trying to maneuver the huge set pieces. Hawn and Zellweger stood nearby and chatted, while Winona Ryder tried to stay out of the way.

When Perlman and Ma began their own performance a few minutes later, Julia Roberts took up residence in a corner of the Governors Ball, away from the hubbub of the green room. Accompanied by her boyfriend, Benjamin Bratt, and a group of about eight friends, she ate from a plate of sushi that Bratt had brought to her.

Behind the theater, the crowd steadily grew as some people stepped outside to smoke, others to escape the congestion in the green room. One woman approached Kevin Spacey and Ben Affleck. The two men were hanging out together, Spacey with a drink in his hand, Affleck with a cigarette.

Even amid the debris of setup, Oscar exerted a powerful lure. Days before the show in 1998, a local television reporter found herself irresistibly drawn to the big guy outside the Shrine.

The biggest and potentially the deadliest Oscar presenter in 1998, Bart the Bear wandered inside an electrified rail on the Shrine Auditorium stage, watched closely by an armed guard and some curious stagehands.

ANTONIN KRATOCHVIL

ABOVE: *Before rehearsing in 1998, presenter Sean Connery waited in the wings with a stage manager. Behind him, another crew member moved a panel to reveal the orchestra riser at the rear of the nautical-themed stage, an appropriate look in the year of* Titanic.

BELOW: *The same year, Matt Damon would win an Oscar for co-writing* Good Will Hunting. *The day before the show, Damon was escorted through the artists' entrance behind the Shrine by stage manager Rita Cossette. Damon arrived at rehearsal with pal Ben Affleck and Affleck's mother; the next day, Damon brought his own mom to the Oscar show.*

ANTONIN KRATOCHVIL

TOP: *Elia Kazan, whose presence dominated the show in 1999, practiced his succinct, unapologetic acceptance speech on the stage of the Chandler. Behind him, between a stage manager and a stand-in, stood director Martin Scorsese and Kazan's wife, Frances.*

BOTTOM: *The Kazan year also marked the first time the Academy produced its own pre-show. To prepare for that broadcast, stand-ins gathered outside the Shrine and donned name tags.*

ABOVE: *In 1999, stage manager Jason Seligman signaled host Whoopi Goldberg and the presenters when to read from the TelePrompTer. He wore white gloves to make his gestures easily visible from the stage.*
BELOW: *Dame Judi Dench took home the supporting-actress Oscar that same year for her six-minute role in* Shakespeare in Love. *After winning, she waited with an escort on the fourth floor of the Dorothy Chandler Pavilion.*

Adjusting Oscar outside the Shrine Auditorium, 2000

ART STREIBER

In 2000, Cameron Diaz couldn't keep her hands off the hair of her Charlie's Angels *costar, Lucy Liu.*

Sitting at the podium where, in 2000, he would serve as the first on-camera voice of Oscar, actor Peter Coyote was flanked by stage manager Dency Nelson, left, and soon-to-be best-actor winner Kevin Spacey, right.

Prepping for a 2000 show whose producers had proudly boasted of no dance numbers, Robin Williams led a line of hoofers through the profane and problematic song "Blame Canada."

"Do you mind if my boyfriend takes a picture of me with the two of you?" she asked.

"No problem," said Affleck. Then he pointed to Spacey. "You know, he *won* last year." When Penélope Cruz walked by, Affleck quickly left Spacey for a whispered conversation with the Spanish actress.

Closer to the back door, Winona Ryder nursed a cigarette. Goldie Hawn, who'd introduced Perlman and Ma, stepped outside for a smoke as well. Zellweger and John Travolta immediately rushed over to Hawn. "How did it go?" asked Zellweger. "We can't see anything out here."

"That's not true," joked Travolta. "We saw it, and you were *shit*." Then he laughed. "No, no. You look fabulous tonight, Goldie." He paused, and leaned forward intently. "And it's not just the dress," he added. "It's you."

Zellweger sighed. "He knows just the right words," she said.

As Winona Ryder was escorted to the stage to introduce Björk, Hilary Swank rushed out the back door, holding up her dress. "Hurry hurry hurry," she said, making a beeline for the women's room. A minute later, Julie Andrews headed in the same direction.

Two and a half hours into the show, the satellite link to Sydney went off smoothly. As Bob Dylan performed "Things Have Changed," Horvitz kept the singer in extreme close-up on a big screen that sat center stage. The idea was for Dylan's image to be big enough that shots from the back of the theater could show both the live audience and Dylan's facial expressions—though it meant that guests at the show found themselves staring at the enormous, grizzled visage of the fifty-nine-year-old Dylan, who sported a pencil-thin mustache and piercing blue eyes.

His head cocked to the side, Dylan drawled and snarled his way through a strange, riveting performance. Ang Lee watched from the wings, holding the best foreign film Oscar he'd just won for *Crouching Tiger*. Jennifer Lopez stood nearby, accompanied by the night's largest security guard. In midsong, an audience shot caught Danny DeVito munching on a carrot stick. From the booth where they were watching the show, Martin and Vilanch noticed this, and sent a staffer into a nearby hospitality room to fetch some dip.

Dylan won the Oscar and gave a surprisingly long speech that ended, "I want to thank the members of the Academy, who were bold enough to give me this award for . . . a song that doesn't pussyfoot around nor turn a blind eye to human nature. God bless you all with peace, tranquillity, and good will."

Outside the green room, a minor brouhaha developed when stagehands, trying to make room for the Governors Ball, began taking down the drapes covering one side of the room. Seligman chewed out a supervisor—but the Governors Ball organizers were scrambling, because the show was actually running ahead of schedule.

The next time he took the stage, Steve Martin walked into the audience and gave a bowl of dip to DeVito.

A few minutes later, Russell Crowe won the best-actor award for *Gladiator*. But when Crowe took his Oscar and headed out the back door, he didn't follow the usual winners' path toward the press tent; instead, he turned the other way and hung out in the smoking area with a few buddies.

While Crowe stood there, security guards suddenly asked guests and bystanders around the artists' entrance to clear the area. Despite three days of star comings-and-goings, this was a first, and it puzzled credentialed guests who wondered why the guards were suddenly so paranoid. The answer came a minute later, when a limo pulled up to the end of the red carpet and Tom Cruise got out, accompanied by a friend and by publicist Pat Kingsley.

Wearing a suit instead of a tux, with no tie and an unbuttoned blue shirt, Cruise had arrived less than half an hour before he was due onstage. While security guards tried to keep people away from him, Cruise hustled down the red carpet. He was almost in the back door when he spotted the newly crowned best actor lingering by the entrance. "Russell!" he shouted. "You won!"

The two men spent a few minutes embracing, laughing, and doing some mild but manly head- and fist-butting. Then Cruise ducked into the green room and Crowe went back to his seat—though he was temporarily blocked by a carpet sweeper cleaning the corner of the Governors Ball.

As the show neared the three-hour mark, Julia Roberts was named best actress. Deliriously giddy, she gave a three-and-a-half-minute speech that began, "I have a television, so I'm going to spend some time here to tell you some things." Besides being studded with cries like "I love it up here!" and whoops of delight, her speech was also full of warnings to Conti—"stickman," she called him—not to start the music. In truth, she was in no danger; one reason for the forty-five-second rule was so that at the end of the night, big stars like Roberts could have all the time they needed.

As the orchestra played the music from *2001* for the sixth time (but not for the last), Roberts came into the wings, hanging on to presenter and past winner Kevin Spacey. "Oh, my *God*," she said, hugging him. "My knees are weak."

"I know," Spacey said. "You need to sit down, you need to have a drink." He looked at the staffers around them and took charge. "Julia needs a drink," he announced. Then he turned to Roberts. "What would you like to drink?"

"Champagne?"

"Okay," Spacey said. "Julia needs champagne."

A staffer pointed to the nearby watercooler. "We have water right there."

"No," said Spacey quickly. "Only champagne will do. You have to understand."

Debbie Williams ran through the wings and into the Governors Ball, which was in the final stages of preparation. "I need a bottle of champagne!" she shouted to the bartender.

He shook his head. "I can't give it to you," he said.

"Julia Roberts just won," insisted Williams, "and she wants champagne!" The bartender promptly passed her a bottle. Williams grabbed two glasses, and back in the wings Roberts and Spacey shared a toast and quietly talked for a few more minutes. "I really see why they have the tradition of previous winners giving out the awards," he said. "You need somebody who understands what you're going through."

Roberts hugged Spacey a few more times, took some sips from her champagne glass, looked at her Oscar, and shook her head. "I know that everybody was writing about how I was going to win," she said, "but I didn't believe the stuff I read in the papers." She looked down again at the statuette in her hand. "My God," she said with a huge grin, "I just won an Oscar!"

Spacey turned to Roberts's publicist. "You'll be hearing that a lot for the next couple of weeks," he said.

Onstage, Martin introduced Tom Hanks, who himself introduced Arthur C. Clarke, the writer of *2001: A Space Odyssey*, to hand out the adapted screenplay award from Clarke's home in Sri Lanka. The segment was pretaped; Clarke had done five different takes, one for each of the nominees. Greg Garrison left his spot in the wings and went to the truck, where he told Horvitz which clip to run.

As Julia Roberts finally headed back to her seat, the two screenwriting winners—Stephen Gaghan for *Traffic* and Cameron Crowe for *Almost Famous*—stood in the wings talking to Hanks. "This," said Crowe, "is a psychedelic experience."

Up to this point, awards had been split fairly evenly between *Gladiator*, *Traffic*, and *Crouching Tiger, Hidden Dragon*, which had four, three, and three wins, respectively. In something of an upset, the best-director Oscar then went to Soderbergh for *Traffic*, confounding handicappers who figured that his dual nominations for that film and *Erin Brockovich* would split the vote. "Suddenly, going to work tomorrow doesn't seem like such a good idea," said Soderbergh, who was shooting *Ocean's Eleven* in Las Vegas.

When he came offstage, Soderbergh waited in the wings to see the best-picture winner. Though at this point the race suddenly seemed to be wide open, the winner was the preshow favorite, *Gladiator*. All the night's big winners were quickly herded backstage for commemorative photos. Russell Crowe finally headed for the press rooms, where he greeted the assembled scribes by saying, "Ask me questions that I can answer yes or no to, and we'll all get along really well."

At about 8:55 Pacific time, the show ended—less than three and a half hours after it began, forty minutes shorter than the previous year. Afterward, the show's staff gathered on the stage to share cake and champagne as usual, and the stage managers posed for a photo with Julia Roberts. "I see you guys more often than my family," said Roberts, who'd been hitting the awards show circuit hard.

The Governors Ball had taken over much of the backstage area, and the party was just beginning. But the green room still sat in its corner; no longer protected by thick drapes or a shielded entryway, it was still a place of refuge. Before gearing up for the press and the parties, Roberts went in and flopped down on the couch. Kate Hudson and Goldie Hawn followed her in—and Hudson, relieved that the big night was coming to an end, whipped out a cigarette. "Okay," she yelled, "let's light up!"

From her couch, the new best actress looked up and broke into a huge grin. "Honey," she said, "*it's that time!*"

FOR THE MOST PART, reviewers found the slimmed-down Oscar show to be a welcome change. "Neat and clean, tasty and cheery," *Daily Variety* said the next day. But the numbers were not as favorable: the show drew the second-lowest number of viewers in ten years, and its lowest rating and share ever.

Dutch filmmaker Michael Dudok de Wit, who took home the Oscar for animated short, won the television set Cates had promised for the shortest speech. But de Wit said he was giving the set to a children's charity. "I did not write the shortest speech to win the television set," he said. "I have many television sets."

The day after the show, the Academy heard from members of the sound branch, who were not amused to hear Mike Myers making fun of the nominees in their category. Bob Rehme wrote the branch a formal letter of apology.

In June, the Academy announced that the Kodak Theatre would be ready in time for the seventy-fourth Oscar show.

The same month, the board of governors voted to tighten the rules regarding eligible producers of the best-picture nominees. The number of producers eligible had been reduced to three the previous year, but the board went further, pointing out that the Academy "shall not be bound by any contract or agreement relating to the sharing or giving of credit." Aimed principally at studio executives and personal managers who had increasingly negotiated for producer credit regardless of their actual day-to-day input during production of the movie, the new guidelines made it harder for managers or studio bosses—say, for instance, Harvey Weinstein—to go home with an Oscar.

The governors also approved the rules for the new category of animated feature film, specifying that it would be given out anytime at least eight eligible films were released. The award, the board said, would go to "the key creative talent most clearly responsible" for the film, usually a single person and never more than two people.

In July, the fourteenth branch of the Academy, the documentary branch, elected its first governor.

In August, with Bob Rehme's tenure ended, the board of governors chose screenwriter and director Frank Pierson as the new president of the Academy. Pierson, best known for writing *Cat Ballou*, *Cool Hand Luke*, *Dog Day Afternoon*, and the 1976 Barbra Streisand remake of *A Star Is Born*, had served as president of the Writers Guild twice, once in the early 1980s and again a decade later. His first WGA tenure coincided with Gil Cates's election to the presidency of the Directors Guild. As leaders of the two famously combative guilds—among other things, the writers were still upset that directors had seized the "a film by" possessory credit—Pierson and Cates had not gotten along especially well.

Work proceeded on what was now called the Kodak Theatre, and on the Hollywood & Highland complex. Academy officials and key members of the Oscar production crew were consulted about what they needed to make the theater an ideal home for their show. In addition, the Academy was given veto power over the other tenants in the center. That stretch of Hollywood Boulevard may have been home to lots of discount electronics shops, T-shirt emporiums, and cheesy souvenir shops, but Oscar's immediate neighborhood had to be classier.

"From the beginning," said Bruce Davis, "we made it clear that there was not going to be an Oscar Drugstore or an Academy Awards Haberdashery, or whatever. We had a whole list: there could be no T-shirt shops within the mall, that kind of thing. There would be a dignity about the place. And we also told them, 'Look, whether you guys admit this or not, this is a mall. You're asking us to do our show in the middle of a shopping center, so you're going to have to shut down your mall and clear those businesses out for the day of the show and a portion of the night previous.' "

Quickly, TrizecHahn agreed to the stipulations. "Even though we would only be there one month out of the year, we were a very large gorilla," said Davis. "So they gave us a lot of control."

9

Movin' on Up

The 74th Academy Awards

"AS A LITTLE GIRL, I dreamed that I produced the Academy Awards," Laura Ziskin told Bruce Vilanch in one of their first meetings. "Now I think I've gone insane."

From the early September day when Frank Pierson had asked Ziskin to produce the seventy-fourth Oscars, her life had been tumultuous. Ziskin was a movie producer whose films included *To Die For* and *What About Bob?*, a Hollywood vet of more than twenty years who'd gotten her start as an assistant to the fiery producer Jon Peters. Pierson had met Ziskin in 1975, when he was directing the remake of *A Star Is Born* and she was working with Peters and Barbra Streisand. She also lived with screenwriter Alvin Sargent, an old friend of Pierson's—and though Ziskin's only experience with live television had come on the George Clooney project *Fail Safe*, which ran on CBS in April 2000, the Academy president knew that she was interested in the Oscar job.

Before accepting his offer, though, Ziskin told Pierson some of her ideas. She wanted an orchestra conducted by film composer John Williams.

She wanted to hire a production designer who usually worked in film. She wanted to commission notable filmmakers to put together the show's film packages. And she didn't want to open with the traditional arrivals montage from the red carpet, since that was a reprise of what viewers had just seen on the preshow. Pierson signed off on all the ideas and Ziskin took the job, even though she was already producing *Spider-Man*, which she'd be delivering to Sony Pictures right around Oscar time.

A few days after she accepted Pierson's offer, terrorists flew passenger planes into the World Trade Center and the Pentagon. "I don't know exactly how it's going to affect us, but those events are going to resonate forever," she said a few weeks later. "I think everybody in the movie business has started to think, God, what we do is all so insignificant. And then another part of me takes over and says, No, it's significant. Movies are really powerful, they're a big part of people's lives, they give us solace and stimulation and they provoke us. Those things are important."

Still, Ziskin knew her concerns would have to be openly addressed on Oscar night. "I feel an obligation at the top of the show to say what is really in my head," she said. "The world is a tricky and dangerous and serious place, and we're gonna sit there and congratulate ourselves. Is that a lot of bullshit?"

IN NOVEMBER, the Kodak Theatre opened with a gala concert featuring tenor Russell Watson. Designed like a European opera house, the inside of the Kodak was lush and dramatic. Opera boxes lined the walls, rich cherry-wood surfaces ran throughout the theater, and three balconies rose toward the "corona," a large oval ring that hung eight stories above the orchestra seats.

But the theater was not without problems—and the Academy, admitted Bruce Davis, was "sweating bullets." In the fall, TrizecHahn had sent the organization a letter that appeared to renege on previous agreements to close all of Hollywood & Highland's shops on Oscar day, and to secure nearby space for production and satellite trucks. Both items were deal-breakers to the Academy, but after a few tense meetings and some posturing in the press, TrizecHahn agreed to abide by the original agreement.

Still to be settled, though, were issues of traffic control and security. The

Kodak was situated at one of the busiest intersections in Hollywood, an area jammed with cars on a good day. In addition, a subway stop sat directly beneath Hollywood & Highland. Not only had the problem of securing the entire area added more than a million dollars to the security costs of the show, but Los Angeles's Metropolitan Transit Authority had yet to agree to close the subway stop during the Awards.

"Particularly in light of recent events, we are determined that the MTA skip that stop for a few hours that evening," said Davis. "Basically, the entrance is within our security perimeter, so it's not a good idea to have crowds come up those stairs and be inside our security line."

As the show approached, the board of governors took an additional, unprecedented step. Mindful of the unstable world situation, they paid a million dollars for a catastrophe insurance policy that would pay off in case of a terrorist attack that delayed, disrupted, or canceled the Oscar show.

TO ENTER the Samuel Goldwyn Theater required walking a security gauntlet unprecedented at previous nominations announcements. Invited guests with laminated passes had to pass security guards, submit to scanners, and walk through metal detectors. "What's with all the security?" asked one studio rep as he settled into a seat in the Goldwyn Theater. "Like they're gonna blow up a room full of publicists?"

In fact, things didn't really get ugly until after the nominations were announced. To go by the numbers, the race was dominated by *The Lord of the Rings: The Fellowship of the Ring*, the first of director Peter Jackson's trilogy based on the classic fantasy epic by J.R.R. Tolkien. But while it received thirteen nominations, five more than any other film, Jackson's movie was the kind of special effects–laden extravaganza that rarely won major Oscars; many of its nominations were in the technical categories. In the best-picture race, front-runner status gravitated instead toward Ron Howard's *A Beautiful Mind*, the kind of high-minded, serious film the Academy usually loved. Baz Luhrmann's delirious musical *Moulin Rouge!* also picked up eight, while veteran director Robert Altman's witty drawing room comedy *Gosford Park* was surprisingly strong with seven; the French romance *Amélie* and the intense low-budget drama *In the Bedroom* received five each.

In the best-actor category, the strongest contenders appeared to be Denzel Washington for his explosive role in *Training Day*, along with two actors playing real people: Will Smith as the flamboyant boxer Muhammad Ali in *Ali*, and Russell Crowe as troubled mathematician John Nash in *A Beautiful Mind*. In the labyrinthine logic of Oscar calculations, though, Crowe's chances were thought to be hurt by his win the year before for glowering and fighting his way through *Gladiator*—an award that was in itself partly attributed to Academy remorse over not giving him the Oscar the year before that for *The Insider*. In best actress, the front-runners were actresses from three smaller movies: Sissy Spacek from *In the Bedroom*, Judi Dench from *Iris*, and Halle Berry from *Monster's Ball*.

To become an Oscar front-runner, though, was to become an immediate target. Working on information from unidentified sources, Internet reporter Matt Drudge had already lit into *A Beautiful Mind* for omitting any mention of Nash's alleged homosexual encounters, and after the nominations he stepped up his attacks. The film, he charged, whitewashed Nash's life, leaving out anti-Semitic statements made in the grip of his schizophrenia and idealizing Nash's marriage when in fact he and his wife, Alicia (played as a long-suffering supporter and muse by Jennifer Connelly), were divorced, and Nash had fathered a child with another woman.

The whispering campaign against *A Beautiful Mind* continued, though nobody could pin down who was behind it. The usual reaction to underhanded campaigning was to blame it on Miramax, but that studio's best-picture nominee, *In the Bedroom*, was such a long shot that many figured that Harvey Weinstein didn't have enough motivation to slander *A Beautiful Mind*. At one point, Universal even took the unusual step of publicly absolving Miramax of responsibility for the attacks. New Line, meanwhile, tried to stay out of that fray and draw voters' attention to the fact that *The Fellowship of the Ring* dealt with the battle between good and evil, a pertinent theme after September 11.

By the time of the nominees' luncheon on March 11, even the normally mild-mannered Ron Howard had heard enough. The campaign to undermine his movie's credibility, he told reporters in the press room, was "an attack strategy" reminiscent of the one the late Republican strategist Lee Atwater had developed during the 1988 presidential campaign, in which

George Bush had defeated Michael Dukakis. Meanwhile, Stacey Snider, the chairman of Universal Pictures, made her own statement. "Lines that should be clear to all of us," she said, "have recklessly been crossed."

THE EIGHT-FOOT OSCAR statue that stood in the lobby of Laura Ziskin's office on the Sony Pictures lot was a loaner from the Academy, a courtesy extended to Oscar producers who wanted a tangible sign of the job. But Ziskin wasn't content to simply stick the giant Oscar in the corner and leave it at that: instead, her statue sported a curly black wig, a pink boa, and a pair of lightly tinted aviator-style sunglasses. A cigarette dangled from the corner of its mouth.

One of Ziskin's requirements when she took the producing job was that she had to keep her office on the Sony lot; otherwise, there was no way she'd be able to work on the show and finish *Spider-Man* at the same time. Her first-floor office suite, tucked into a corner of the lot not far from the main gate, was decorated with posters from the films she'd worked on—*No Way Out*, *Murphy's Romance*, *Hero*—as well as a signed photo of actress Drew Barrymore and a ticket stub from the 1998 World Series at San Diego's Qualcomm Stadium, signed by record-breaking St. Louis Cardinals slugger Mark McGwire (whose team didn't play in that series).

The Monday before the Oscar show, Ziskin welcomed preshow host Leeza Gibbons to the office. Gibbons, the former host of *Entertainment Tonight* who had moved to the competing show *Extra*, arrived bearing a lavish basket of beauty products for Ziskin. The producer responded with a gift of her own: a small, sterling silver egg timer with exactly forty-five seconds' worth of sand inside it. "I gave these to all the nominees at the luncheon," she told Gibbons, "just to encourage them to keep their speeches short."

"Oh, my gosh, that's adorable," said Gibbons. "I feel very inside."

Gibbons took a seat on Ziskin's brown leather couch, while other members of the preshow production team arranged themselves around a low, rectangular coffee table covered in dark fabric. The meeting included Ziskin, preshow director Bruce Gowers, producer Pamela Oas Williams, and researcher Simbiat Hall, as well as producer Marty Pasetta, Jr., the man whose father had directed seventeen Oscar shows before his unceremonious departure in 1988. (It was hardly unusual for the children of awards-show vets to follow their fathers into the business: the sons of Michael Seligman and Jeff Margolis worked the awards circuit as well.) As the staff took seats, Ziskin set Gibbons's gift basket behind her desk, near two Spider-Man action figures and a copy of the book *Inside Oscar*.

"Tentatively, we've planned that your first interview will be live with Julia Roberts, and all the rest of your interviews will be pretapes," Williams told Gibbons. "But we're throwing in a few live segments, to give the illusion that the whole thing is live."

Gibbons looked at the script, which included introductions to and possible questions for the people she'd be interviewing. "Can I be more casual with this intro?" she asked.

"Of course," said Ziskin. "In terms of dialogue, feel free to rewrite it and make it comfortable for you."

"Of these questions for Julia, I feel like the question about George Clooney and the rat pack has been asked so many times before," Gibbons said. "I'd rather talk about the year since she won, what the differences have been."

"Fine," said Ziskin with a quick laugh. "More than that, George Clooney isn't coming to the show. So screw him."

For the next twenty minutes, they mulled over the best questions to ask several of the stars on the preshow. The freshest approach for Ian McKellen, they decided, would be to ask him about hosting *Saturday Night Live*, though Gibbons was also inclined to ask the openly gay McKellen about his thoughts on John Nash's sexuality, or on the ugliness of the Oscar campaigns. For Cameron Diaz, they decided to focus on future projects, though Ziskin was also fascinated by the fact that Diaz didn't use a stylist. "Even the seat-fillers have stylists," she said.

Finally, they discussed the end of the preshow, and Gibbons's interaction with her two cohosts, talk show host Ananda Lewis and veteran movie reporter Chris Connelly. "We'll start with a shot of Ananda on the red carpet," said Williams, "and then she'll throw it to you at the bottom of the stairs. You have your last words, and then you throw it to Chris at the top of the stairs."

Gibbons frowned. "Why can't I be where Chris is?" she said.

"It's easier to light at the bottom of the stairs," explained Gowers. "Chris will be walking to the door of the theater, and that's an awkward walk for a lady to do, because we can't light it. At the bottom of the stairs, you'll be completely gorgeous all the time."

"I understand," she said, pouting a little. "But that's the big ending, there at the top."

"Also," said Ziskin quickly, "the opening of the show is going to be seeing the stars in the theater, not on the red carpet. So when we go to you at the bottom of the stairs, it'll be an exciting shot—there will be a lot of activity behind you as we get the stars into the theater."

"Okay," Gibbons said, clearly trying to show—or at least feign—some enthusiasm. "I'm so excited about it. It's going to be a blast. And I love the people I'm going to talk to."

Gowers sighed. "If you really want to be at the top of the stairs . . ."

"Only because that's the ultimate shot," said Gibbons. "But it's okay, really." She chuckled. "Who's sleeping with Chris?"

At the end of the meeting, Ziskin walked Gibbons to the door. After Ziskin returned, Pasetta looked at her. "Leeza's going to be at the top of the stairs," he predicted.

BY THE MIDDLE OF THE WEEK, the Kodak Theatre was tightly secured. The system of passes was more extensive and complex than ever before, with seven different levels of access and seventeen different ways to classify each staffer, from ACADEMY and PRODUCTION to BLEACHER CREW, SEAT-FILLER, and BODYGUARD. Passes were scanned each time an employee came onto the property, to make sure the bearer matched the picture stored in the system's memory; metal detectors also stood at each entrance to the grounds. When staffers applied for passes, their names and stats were fed into a computer that flagged possible security risks—including one Governors Ball staffer whose pass was voided when he turned out to have the same name as someone who'd been detained by the L.A.P.D.

Outside, Hollywood Boulevard had been shut down in front of the Hollywood & Highland complex. Workers erected scaffolding, laid the red carpet, and went to great expense to disguise the mall. One by one, storefronts were obscured by hanging banners or hidden by platforms; even a huge Kodak Theatre sign, which sat atop an enormous arch through which every guest would pass, was painstakingly covered by a framework that held an ACADEMY AWARDS banner.

Inside the theater, staffers who'd been consulted by the builders were surprised at what they found. For starters, the wings of the stage were far smaller than at the Shrine Auditorium—particularly stage left, where there was almost no room at all. There was a spacious green room, but in an unusable location: a couple of hallways and one flight of stairs below the stage itself. And the backstage rest rooms were woefully inadequate.

"Plenty of thought and planning went into it, and a lot of good stuff ended up being in there," said Horvitz. "But it was not what we thought it would be. It started out to be bigger and wider, but then retail came in and retail was very important. And suddenly it's a vertical house, and it seems my stage left was now the Krispy Kreme Donuts store." (This was not technically correct: stage left was truncated to leave room for a driveway between the Kodak and the Orchid Suites Motel. Krispy Kreme was farther away, out in the mall.)

While Horvitz tried to figure out how to shoot a vertical theater in TV's horizontal aspect ratio, a small hallway near the stage was commandeered to serve as the new green room. Production designer J. Michael Riva's staff transformed the space, which was fifty feet long but less than fifteen feet wide, using lots of red velvet drapery, tiger-print carpet, and black deco furniture. Clearly influenced by the look of *Moulin Rouge!*, the new green room was variously and affectionately compared to both a train car and a bordello. The rear door of the room led onto the loading dock, to a small patch of carpet designed to serve as the stars' smoking section. A fire marshal set the capacity of the new room at twenty-five, less than a third of the capacity of the room downstairs.

Along a hallway that led from the Kodak's lower lobby to the backstage area were offices for Ziskin, Seligman, Horvitz, and host Whoopi Goldberg. At the rear of the stage were large doors to the loading dock, where Horvitz's command truck was parked. Dressing rooms, the main production office, and offices for Herman and her staff were located one floor below the stage. Other offices, including the three press rooms, were located in the Renaissance Hollywood Hotel, which was connected to the Kodak by a rather complicated and lengthy series of hallways.

Production designer Riva, a veteran art director whose films included *The Color Purple*, *Lethal Weapon*, and *Charlie's Angels* (and who was the grandson of Marlene Dietrich), had spent much of his budget on an enormous art deco proscenium arch that framed the Kodak stage; the idea was to create the look of a vintage movie palace.

As workmen positioned the arch during one of the days devoted to loading in the set, the Kodak's sensitive alarm was triggered by stray smoke somewhere in the building. The system had been designed to suck smoke (or, given the times, poison gas) out of the building in a matter of seconds, using huge fans concealed behind panels in the ceiling. But with the doors between the stage and the loading dock wide open for the load-in, the fans sucked air in the back door and blew it out the ceiling with such force that stagehands struggled to keep the unsecured proscenium from toppling onto the orchestra seats.

Determined to make sure the system wouldn't be triggered again, supervising producer Seligman met with building supervisors, who assured him that the automatic sensors would be switched off.

"WE KNOW it's going to be longer than four hours," said Bruce Vilanch. "We're blaming that on the fact that we've got a new award, animated film, plus three honorary awards."

Standing backstage three days before the show, Vilanch shrugged as he considered what had become the only real question among Oscar staffers: would it simply be one of the longest Oscar shows, or would it beat the Zanucks' show to become *the* longest?

"Laura seems convinced that Lili's show was 4:20," said Vilanch. "But I think it was more like 4:11." In fact, the 2000 show was a mere 4:08.

The dilemma, clearly, was that Ziskin had lots of ideas—and since this was her first and perhaps only time producing the Oscars, she was determined to use them all. There were five film packages, an orchestral medley, a circus performance, long introductions . . . When the board of governors voted in January to give three honorary awards, she knew she should probably jettison something, but she couldn't bring herself to do it.

"All of her concepts were really quite good, and everything had a tremendous impact," said Horvitz. "But it's like going to a baseball game that goes into extra innings. After a while you're going, 'Somebody please break this up so I can go home.' "

According to several participants, Ziskin hadn't wanted to hire Horvitz; she'd heard about his temper and preferred somebody less volatile. But Horvitz had prominent supporters within the Academy and the production, who persuaded the first-time producer that she needed an experienced hand in the director's seat. She found out just how tricky the job was at a large production meeting, when Horvitz took his turn at the mike.

"We talked about the profiles, we talked about the floor, we talked about the aspect ratio," said Horvitz. "Then we talked about getting the big screen out, the stair unit, the new theater, this and that, item after item, department after department. And finally she turns to me and she goes, 'You are *really* underpaid.' She said, 'Directors don't do this in film.' And I said, 'Well, we do here.' "

Ziskin was one of the few who liked the way Peter Coyote had served as the voice of Oscar in 2000, so she took Lili Zanuck's idea one step further. She hired two actors, Glenn Close and Donald Sutherland, both of whom had thriving careers doing voiceovers.

Close arrived for a Thursday afternoon rehearsal wearing an open-necked white blouse under a black blazer, while Sutherland was clad in a dark suit and tie, with a heavy muffler wrapped around his neck. They sat at a black, deco-style table in the wings, stage right; behind them were a video monitor and three shelves that would bear Oscar statuettes.

At first, they ran through their copy simultaneously, testing different pronunciations. "Mar-eesa Tomei," said Sutherland. "Mar-issa Tomei."

Next to him, Close read the names of the stars she'd be identifying during the show's opening segment. "Dame Judi Dench, Dame Maggie Smith, Sir Ian McKellen, Sir Ben Kingsley." She went back over the lines. "Dame Judi Dench, Dame Maggie Smith, Dame Ian McKellen, Dame Ben Kingsley . . ."

For much of the rehearsal, the voices of Oscar kept things light and playful. Close joked with everyone around her, while Sutherland affected a grave, deadpan manner that didn't obscure a dry wit.

During a short break, he suddenly turned to Close. "Glenn, do you like sushi?" he asked, apropos of nothing in their conversation.

"Yes," she said, a little confused. "Is that what we're having for dinner?"

"No, I'm not having dinner tonight," he said. "I just wanted to let you know that the best sushi restaurant in town is on Sawtelle, between Olympic and Pico."

A minute later, stage manager John Best pointed to a hardcover book sitting in front of Sutherland. "Can I move that over here?" he said, pointing to a nearby shelf.

"No, you may not," said Sutherland solemnly. "I think I'll put it here in my pocket." He paused. "Do you want to see what it is?"

"Okay," said Best.

Sutherland held up the book: *Cod*, by Mark Kurlansky. "What do you think it's about?" Sutherland asked.

"Uh . . . fish?"

"Yes," said Sutherland. "It's about the fishing industry. The author has another book called *Salt*. You know, you can't understand salt until you understand the history of refrigeration."

About an hour into the rehearsal, Sutherland suddenly closed his script and got out of his chair. "Somebody is smoking," he said. "I can't stay here if people are smoking." He turned and headed for his dressing room downstairs.

The offending smoker, it turned out, was in a designated smoking area on the loading dock, a good 125 feet away from Sutherland. "I'm sorry he's smelling smoke, but that's the way it goes," snapped one stagehand as the doors to the loading dock were closed. "I can't load the goddamn set if I have to close the door."

Ziskin and Seligman came into the wings, and new edicts came down: don't smoke on the loading dock, and keep the doors closed as much as possible. With large pieces of the set coming in and out through those doors, this last order would clearly be problematic. Making matters worse, the smoking area attached to the green room was located just outside those doors.

"What can we do?" Ziskin asked Debbie Williams and Rita Cossette.

"We really can't do anything," said Williams, who knew full well that the smoking area was often the most crowded area backstage. "All the talent is going to be out there smoking."

"Well, let's keep this door closed for now, and we'll have to figure something out," said Ziskin. Then she spotted a crew member with a cigarette on the loading dock. "You can't smoke here," she yelled. "Please go as far away from the door as possible!"

EVERY OSCAR PRODUCER knew that one of the trickiest parts of the job was keeping the branches happy. The Academy was made up of fourteen different branches, and invariably most of them were unhappy about the fact that come Oscar time, their members weren't lavished with quite as much attention and love as were the members of the actors' branch.

Over the years, changes had been made to appease various branches. Nominated writers got their pictures on-screen during the show, then had their categories added to the list of those read at the nominations announcement. Bowing to a request from Oscar show producer Howard Koch, in 1997 Gil Cates added photos of the nominated producers to the package when best-picture nominees were read.

Bruce Davis always tried to look over Oscar scripts and identify potential trouble spots: a common one, he said, was when a star presenting the award for cinematography would applaud the nominees and their fellow directors of photography for putting actors in a flattering light. "They *hate* to have their art form reduced to making the star look good," he said. "That is one thing that just drives them up the wall, but the actors all think it's a great and original joke. Every time it happens, there's an uprising in the cinematography branch."

Through no fault of her own, Ziskin had stepped into a major brouhaha started the year before by Mike Myers's cavalier introduction of the sound categories. When Ziskin was hired, she received a letter from Don Rogers, one of the governors of the sound branch, reiterating the members' concern. "Don't worry," she told Rogers. "I'm going to do something great for you."

Originally, Ziskin's plan was to bring back Myers and have him tortured by foley artists, who create sound effects in a variety of unusual—and in this case, presumably punishing—ways. But she jettisoned that idea early on, and instead went looking for a screenwriter who could honor the category.

Ziskin had already farmed out much of the script to a group of noted screenwriters. She'd asked David Mamet to write about editing, Buck Henry to explain makeup, James Cameron to rhapsodize on visual effects, Joel and Ethan Coen to explicate art direction. She also asked William Goldman, an Oscar winner for *Butch Cassidy and the Sundance Kid* and *All the President's Men*, to write about sound, but he declined, saying he didn't know anything about it.

Vilanch suggested songwriters (and Academy governors) Alan and Marilyn Bergman. His logic was twofold: songwriters might know about sound, and the Bergmans' positions on the Academy board might make it harder for touchy soundmen to criticize them. The couple came up with a lengthy introduction that scanned like a song lyric—"Sound is the sensation that is due to stimulation / It's transmitted by vibration to the centers of the brain"—and included a long list of noises: "A smack, a whack, a quack / A creak, a squeak, a shriek / A punch, a crunch, a munch / a breeze, a wheeze, a sneeze . . ." In the right hands, it might work—but on paper, it also seemed light, frivolous, and maybe even silly. As soon as the script was distributed to show participants, Ziskin got a call from Frank Pierson, who didn't like the copy and had written an alternative introduction himself. Ziskin said she'd look at it, but she encouraged Pierson to keep an open mind.

Friday morning, Pierson arrived early to watch Halle Berry rehearse the sound awards. With the Academy president sitting in the third row and a rep from the sound branch lurking nearby, the Bergmans sat with Ziskin and Vilanch at the production table. Berry walked onstage wearing a black cap, a long-sleeved pink T-shirt, and beige pants with silk piping and a dangling drawstring. She delivered the intro with flair, turning the Bergmans' lines into a surprisingly charming ode to the art of sound. When she finished, Marilyn Bergman clapped heartily. Her husband looked over at Pierson, who smiled and gave a thumbs-up sign.

"She is darling," said Marilyn Bergman. "*Darling*."

For her part, Berry was relieved to have a task that took her mind off her best-actress nomination. "This is great for me," she said after going over the lines. "It gives me something to think about. I won't be so nervous about the award if I'm concentrating on this."

BACK IN THE FALL, Ziskin had spent weeks obsessively watching past Oscar shows, taking notes and looking for inspiration. She'd been most impressed by the shows that departed most drastically from the template, by Quincy Jones's Oscars in 1996 and the Zanucks' marathon four years later. Uncomfortable with dance numbers but determined to give her show a shot of adrenaline around the halfway mark, she was particularly fascinated by Jones's booking of the percussion troupe Stomp. That, she decided, was precisely what she needed: "some wham-bam entertainment in the middle, 'cause that's usually when the show sags."

Doug Stewart, who'd known Ziskin since their days at USC film school, suggested she look into the bizarre but frequently hilarious Blue Man Group. But at the top of Ziskin's wish list was Cirque du Soleil, the arty French-Canadian circus troupe. When they surprised her by agreeing to appear on the Oscars, Ziskin gave Stewart the task of finding a connection between the circus performers and the movies. He responded by putting together a split-screen video that put Cirque acts side-by-side with movie special effects they seemed to echo. Using Stewart's as the model, Cirque choreographer Debra Brown then prepared her own film to run on screens behind the performers.

On Friday night, the result was showcased for staffers and a handful of guests inside the Kodak. Wholly different from anything seen on the Oscars before, twenty-nine performers (recruited from five different Cirque shows around North America) ran through a four-minute act that incorporated acrobats, trapeze artists hanging high above the stage, and a few of the inexplicable but artsy touches for which the troupe was known, including a headless giant toting an umbrella.

As a woman onstage spun four hula hoops around her body, a screen at the rear of the stage showed a figure enclosed in rings of electricity in Fritz Lang's 1927 classic *Metropolis*. As a powerfully built performer twirled a flaming ball and chain around him in a large circle, the screen showed the ring of power from *The Lord of the Rings*, gleaming with fiery light. The film also showcased visual effects from movies like *The Wizard of Oz*, *E.T.*, *Star Wars*, and *Royal Wedding*, in which Fred Astaire appeared to dance on the walls and ceiling of a room.

Despite the stylish juxtapositions, though, the Cirque number was a virtuoso exhibition by a company whose work never really had anything to do with motion pictures. As the performers were warming up, a Cirque vice president, Roslyn Heward, approached Seligman. "We made a few cuts," she said, holding the script page that bore Maggie Smith and Ian McKellen's introduction. "I took out that part about how much we were influenced by the movies. Because we weren't."

The most dangerous part of the act was the ring of flames. For the first few run-throughs, the troupe did the number without fire. Then, while three fire marshals watched attentively, Cirque performer Mike Brown lit a heavy round torch that was attached to a long chain. Grabbing the end of the chain, he spun the flaming ball in circles around him, just a few inches off the ground. But when he finished, the stage continued to burn for several seconds before going out, leaving a scorched ring some twenty feet in diameter.

A crowd gathered and tallied up the damage: seventeen of the shiny blue tiles that covered the stage would have to be replaced. "Just a little pyro thing, man, nothing could possibly go wrong," said one technician with a rueful grin. "Isn't that what they said?"

"Well, we were going to repaint that floor anyway," said another, well aware that the burn went deeper than one level of paint.

Stage manager Garry Hood shook his head. "Well, we're not gonna do *that*," he said.

Seligman walked around the stage and surveyed the damage. He didn't say a word. When he returned to the production table, Horvitz's voice came over the P.A. system. "Michael Seligman, your insurance broker on line one," he said. "Michael Seligman, line one."

At the production table, Heward quickly conferred with Ziskin, Seligman, and Riva. "I've never seen that happen," she insisted.

"I don't want to lose the fire, but we can't have them burning our stage," said Ziskin. "What do we do about this?"

"In our other shows, there's a lot of other martial arts stuff with fire that doesn't touch the ground," Heward suggested. "I could bring in a different fire act."

Heward walked away, punching the buttons on her cell phone. A minute later, she returned. "Okay, we're calling the Mystère guy," she said, referring to a Cirque show in Las Vegas. "Mystère uses fire, but it doesn't have to touch the floor." She turned to Riva. "We talked to your pyro guy," she said, "and apparently you use something in your paint."

"Yeah," he snapped. "It's called lacquer."

When Heward left, Riva turned to Ziskin. "You know, we sent them a sample of this floor weeks ago," he said.

Over the next hour, the plan changed constantly. Ziskin considered dropping the fire segment from the performance, but that entailed cuts in the backing film and the music as well. The technical director and one of the performers from Mystère agreed to make the five-hour drive to Los Angeles first thing Saturday morning—but the clip from *The Lord of the Rings* was designed to go not with just any fire performance, but with a ring of fire. Seligman suggested laying a false floor over the real floor and letting that burn, but the stage crew doubted it could get a phony floor on and off in time, and Riva resisted the idea of putting something on top of his floor.

They continued rehearsing the performance without the fire, making additional changes and struggling to get everything finished by eleven o'clock. Aerialist Yuri Maiorov had to scale down a stunt that had him soaring in circles above the audience, but landing far too hard in the vicinity of Nicole Kidman's seat. Across the Kodak, another performer flung hula hoops into the audience, where Nathan Henderson, an acrobat with his hair teased into devil horns, was supposed to catch them. During one of the final rehearsals, the last of the hoops landed squarely on Julia Roberts's seat card. Afterward,

Henderson was defiant. "If Julia Roberts was sitting there," he insisted, "I *definitely* would have caught it."

As they struggled to get the twelve different acts in sync, Seligman came up to Heward. "We're gonna do this three or four more times," he said. "We're gonna go past eleven, so we can get it right." He paused, and grinned. "And you can write me a check."

At the production table, Ziskin put her head in her hands and sighed. "Whose idea was this?" she asked.

"Yours, thank you very much," said Riva.

As the chaotic rehearsal wound down, Ziskin left the Kodak and went to her room at the adjoining Renaissance Hotel. She called Alvin Sargent and bemoaned how she'd tried to cram more stuff—more junk, more crap—into the Oscar show than it could possibly accommodate. "I feel suicidal," she told him.

IT HAD BEEN A LONG WEEK for the stand-ins, too. The gig looked easy—read from the TelePrompTer, walk to the stage, pretend you've just won an Oscar, collect your twenty-three dollars an hour—but it was full of unexpected land mines. Even when they were sitting around waiting to see if they'd be needed, stand-ins needed to be alert: reading the newspaper while on the clock, for example, was definitely out. (At the American Music Awards or other shows produced by Dick Clark, so was chewing gum.)

Mock acceptance speeches, too, were trickier than they looked. There were unwritten rules about what should and shouldn't be done when a stand-in took the stage and received a dummy Oscar statue. Thanking the Academy, of course, was a must. But thanking other stand-ins was a definite mistake; people had been fired for that. A good speech was unobtrusive but not completely generic, with enough detail to suggest that the stand-in took this job seriously. Sometimes, if the mood was right in the theater and in the truck, jokes and a bit of frivolity were acceptable; other times the production staff might be getting tense, and it was best to get on and off without any silliness.

When movie stars were in the house, the job was even more delicate. Stand-ins were expected to treat the stars with respect, to give them space, but not to fawn. The important thing was to help the star do his or her job, without overstepping the bounds of the job. A star might ask a stand-in what was happening with a certain entrance or bit of staging; in those cases, it was always best to defer to the director or stage manager.

Boyce Miller was one of twenty-three stand-ins who had the day shift, and by Saturday afternoon he was exhausted. Miller had his SAG and AFTRA cards, did some acting, and also worked as a freelance writer; he'd been doing stand-in jobs for more than fifteen years. On Saturday, Miller was assigned to stand in for nominees. As a succession of stars arrived to rehearse their lines, he'd check his script for each item; if he had an assignment for whatever award the star was rehearsing, he'd move into the seat that would be occupied by one of the nominees. If his nominee won, he'd go onstage and make an acceptance speech; if not, he'd check his script to see whose seat he'd be occupying next.

Before Will Smith took the stage to practice presenting the award for editing, Miller checked his script. He was assigned to be Pietro Scalia, who'd been nominated for *Black Hawk Down*. Scalia was sitting in the sixth row of section C, way off to the side of the theater; if he won, he'd have the longest walk of any of the nominees. Miller settled into his seat and hoped he didn't win.

Smith walked onstage wearing a black T-shirt emblazoned with the Batman logo. He read his lines, watched snippets from the nominees' work play behind him, then opened the dummy envelope. "For this rehearsal only," he read, "the Oscar goes to Pietro Scalia for *Black Hawk Down*."

Miller stood up and walked toward the stage, trying to figure out what to say when he got there. He'd seen *Black Hawk Down*, which helped. When he got to the stage, Smith smiled, handed over the phony Oscar, offered insincere congratulations; like many stars, he was amused by how elaborate the whole ritual was. Just as Miller was about to start speaking, Smith interrupted.

"You ain't no Pietro Scalia," he said.

Miller turned to look at Smith, and the words just came out. "And you ain't no Ali," he said.

Smith burst out laughing, while Miller thought to himself, I am *so* fired. Quickly, the stand-in tried to repair the damage: "But you *could* be," he added. Smith, still laughing, drew his arm back as if to throw a punch. When Miller finished his acceptance speech and the two men walked off, Smith kept bumping into the stand-in, nudging him closer to the lip of the stage and the fifteen-foot drop into the orchestra pit.

"We came offstage and people were howling," said Miller. "And Debbie Williams, God bless her, said very loudly, 'Best line by a stand-in this year: Boyce Miller.' And I thought, Well, thank you, dear, but maybe you shouldn't have announced exactly who I was." When he showed up at the Kodak the next morning, Miller was still wondering if he'd be fired. Instead, Garry Hood handed him a videocassette of the previous day's rehearsal. "Here's your Oscar moment," Hood said. "Congratulations."

WHOOPI GOLDBERG hadn't been the first choice to host the Oscar show— except for the Quincy Jones year, she never was, a fact that didn't seem to bother her. And as the dress rehearsal began, Goldberg made the sort of showstopping entrance that the acrophobic Billy Crystal or the studiously tasteful Steve Martin would never have considered: clad in an outlandish collection of glitter and feathers, she descended, Moulin Rouge style, from a swing that hung from the rafters eight stories high. "She's fearless," laughed Vilanch. "She won't fly in a plane, but she'll hang on a trapeze."

"I'm the original sexy beast," Goldberg said as she took the stage. That line had been deemed a more seemly beginning than the runner-up, which was, "Welcome to the vagina monologues."

Ziskin watched the rehearsal from the production table in the middle of the house, drinking from a can of caffeine-free Diet Coke and making an occasional note on her laptop computer. At times the producer looked lively and energized; other times she appeared drawn and weary, her mouth pursed into a slight frown.

Early in the show, Goldberg introduced a stand-in for director Nora Ephron, who according to the show's lineups was going to introduce her own film paying tribute to New York City. By now, everyone on the crew knew that Ephron's name was a phony, put into the lineup simply to hide the identity of a top-secret guest. Somebody else—a bigger name closely associated with New York City, the reasoning went—would in fact be introducing Ephron's film. But few staffers had any idea who that might be. Speculation centered on politicians like Hillary Clinton and Rudy Giuliani. Word spread that the guest would come in through the loading dock and spend the show in Seligman's or Ziskin's office.

Ziskin and Herman knew the guest would be Woody Allen, who was legendary for never showing up at the Oscars; Ziskin had been working to get Allen since *Premiere* magazine's Women in Film luncheon the previous October, when she'd pitched DreamWorks cochairman Jeffrey Katzenberg on the idea and he'd promised to make it happen. But she'd shared that information with almost nobody except, reluctantly, ABC consultant John Hamlin, who'd stormed into Ziskin's office in the middle of rehearsals wielding a rundown and demanding to know why she was wasting so much time on Ephron.

At the dress rehearsal, when Ephron's film finished, Ziskin and Herman shared a smile. "I think that's my favorite thing on the show," said Herman.

Almost two hours into the rehearsal, Cirque du Soleil's performance ran smoothly. Michael Riva had broken down and bought rolls of the material that Cirque used for its performances, covering the center of the stage with a round mat that could burn without damaging the tiles beneath it. Everything was synced to the film clips, and when the performance ended it drew an immediate and enthusiastic standing ovation from the staff. Ziskin jumped to her feet, thrust her right arm high in the air, and gave Seligman a resounding high five. Then she slumped back into her seat, exhausted.

A few minutes later, Goldberg introduced a stand-in for Denzel Washington, one of the presenters of Sidney Poitier's honorary Oscar. When a white stand-in walked onto the stage to read Washington's lines, she returned to the microphone. "Don't tell me we ran out of black people already!" she shouted. "Even here, when we ain't gettin' no goddamn Oscars, we don't have enough black people!" Tired and more than a little punch-drunk, the small audience went into hysterics.

Two and a half hours into the rehearsal, Goldberg walked through the wings with a friend. "It's endless," she said. "There's another fucking hour." Nearby, the show's "trophy boy," Silas Gaither, gave a neck massage to Kimberly Painter. Gaither, the first male to serve in that capacity since the Allan Carr show, had been a contestant on the popular CBS reality series *Survivor*. On that show, he seemed to be one of the more clueless contestants—but when he appeared on a special *Survivor*-themed week of the game show *Hollywood Squares*, panelist and head writer Vilanch had found him "adorable" and convinced Ziskin to hire him. "Maybe we'll get a few more fourteen-year-old girls to watch," said Vilanch.

For his part, Gaither was anxious to become something other than a Survivor who didn't survive. Among the crew he quickly became known for hitting on every woman backstage, and for the goofy grin that rarely left his face. He took the gig seriously, though: when a reporter asked to interview him, Gaither said he'd talk only if the story didn't mention *Survivor*. Deprived of the only reason people might want to read about the guy, the reporter declined.

While Gaither sat in the wings, Ziskin remained at the production table as the show ground on. Past the three-hour mark, at about 10:15, she turned to Riva. "At this time tomorrow night," she said, "we'll be drunk. *Soused*."

Rehearsal ended a few minutes after eleven, some three hours and fifty minutes after it started. After going over her notes with the staff, Ziskin finally walked back to her hotel. But when she got in bed, the producer couldn't sleep. Hour after hour, all night long, the Oscar show played in her head. Around 5 a.m., with dawn breaking over the mountains to the east of downtown Los Angeles, she finally slipped into about forty-five minutes of slumber. Then she got up, threw on blue jeans and a sleeveless T-shirt, and walked over to the Kodak Theatre to put on a show.

ZISKIN HAD only been back in the theater for a couple of hours when disaster struck once more. Early in the final rehearsal, a huge gust of wind suddenly rushed into the theater, sucking dust and debris into the Kodak and threatening to topple the large panels onstage. Near the back door to the loading dock, a heavy tool kit began sliding across the floor toward the stage. Glenn Close ducked her head and grimaced, while Donald Sutherland immediately grabbed a piece of cardboard and held it up in front of his face.

After a moment of sheer panic at the production table, Ziskin and Seligman looked up and saw that emergency panels had once again opened in the roof of the theater. The fans mounted up there were sucking air through the loading dock, into the theater, and then out the roof.

Immediately, Seligman ran backstage and confronted a building supervisor. "Do we know what happened, and how to prevent it tonight?" he asked.

"We have a technician in the elevator room working on it," she told him.

"So we don't know yet."

"No."

"Tell me when you find out."

Slowly, details emerged: smoke in one elevator shaft had triggered the automatic response. "Apparently," the building supervisor reported to Seligman, "there was a legitimate smoke reading in one shaft. So it's a real call, and we can't disconnect the system without disabling the elevators."

"Well, we need to figure this out," said Seligman. "Those are the elevators that lead to the winners' walk, and we need them."

He turned to Kirk Smith, an L.A.P.D. officer who was serving as the head of security at the Oscars. "If we can't get these elevators running again, we'll need to find a different way to get the winners to the hotel," he said. "That'll probably involve using the escalators in the mall, but we'll need more people from you to keep things clear out there."

"No, you won't," said Smith. "Once the show starts, we seal everything off in the mall. There won't be anybody else out there."

"Well, let's keep that as an option," said Seligman.

As building officials tried to figure out what triggered the alarm—speculation centering on the smoke machines at the rear of the stage, which ran continuously so that the lighting effects would look more dramatic—others studied just how much of the system could be shut down to prevent a midshow recurrence. Within a few minutes, Smith's security team presented Seligman with four alternate routes for getting winners to the press rooms without using the elevators.

Ziskin, meanwhile, walked into the lower lobby of the Kodak, and noticed that the air appeared to be full of particles of some sort. "This is hellish," she said, heading for her office.

In the hallway, Danette Herman tried to find a silver lining. "Well," she offered, "thank God the sprinklers didn't go on."

As rehearsal started up again, two violinists from John Williams's orchestra were walking down a hallway beneath the stage. Suddenly they stopped and stared at a fifty-nine-year-old man with messy brown hair standing in the doorway of a dressing room. "Oh, my God," said one of the women. "It's—"

Before she could finish the sentence, the man looked over at her and grinned. "Yes!" he said brightly. "It's Paul McCartney!"

The ex-Beatle, who'd written the title song to the Cameron Crowe movie *Vanilla Sky*, was one of the performers in a medley of best-song nominees. Sting, Faith Hill, Enya, and Randy Newman (with John Goodman) were the others, but none of them had the star power of McCartney, who arrived at the Kodak midmorning and quickly got a tour of the premises from Debbie Williams.

Along the way, Williams told him that she'd seen the Beatles' final concert at Candlestick Park in 1965, when she was fourteen.

"Could you see me?" he asked.

"No, not really," she confessed.

"Could you hear me?"

"Not very well."

McCartney grinned. "It was a double," he confided.

"What do you mean?"

"It was a double," he repeated solemnly. "The crowds were so far away and the girls were all screaming so loud that it didn't matter if it was us or not. We used doubles sometimes, and nobody ever noticed. It wasn't me at Candlestick."

Williams stared at him incredulously. "The biggest moment of my life," she moaned, "and you're telling me it wasn't you?"

McCartney laughed. "Gotcha," he said. "Just joking. It was me."

On the side of the stage, McCartney waited for his turn to perform. "I'm not going to win," he told Williams. "It's taken me twenty-eight years to get back here"—his previous nomination having come for the title song to the James Bond movie *Live and Let Die* in 1974—"and it'll probably take me that long to get back again." He shrugged. "Randy Newman's going to win." Newman had sixteen nominations without a single win, making McCartney's prediction something of a long shot.

McCartney rehearsed "Vanilla Sky" a couple of times, drawing big cheers from the small audience. He grinned, threw his left fist in the air, and affected a surprisingly persuasive Elvis drawl as he spit out the first line of "Blue Suede Shoes": "Well, it's one for the money . . ."

The crowd went wild, but McCartney stopped and shook his head. Then the cheers continued, mixed with a few shouts of "Yes!" and "Do it!" McCartney grinned, leaned back toward the microphone, and continued. "Two for the show, three to get ready, now *go cat go*!"

AS SHOW TIME APPROACHED, the biggest worry had to do with the show's opening. Normally, footage shot on the red carpet was edited into an opening montage, but Ziskin was determined to show the stars—twenty-two of them, if possible—sitting in their seats inside the theater. That meant they all had to be seated before 5:30, something that almost never happened.

But concerns about the Hollywood traffic, along with incessant urging from Ziskin's office, had its effect. By 5:00, most of the stars had in fact arrived; by 5:15, all but one were inside the theater.

Staffers were not surprised to learn who the latecomer was. The day before, a few crew members had flipped a coin to see who'd be saddled with escorting the three most demanding stars: Barbra Streisand, Jennifer Lopez, and Kevin Spacey. But coming up fast on that list was Russell Crowe. The Australian actor was the only star who'd been downright unpleasant to Ziskin when she outlined the new regulations against smoking on the loading dock; in addition, he'd refused to record a voiceover the previous day, and had purposely mixed up the names of the best-actress nominees when he rehearsed.

Crowe finally arrived at the door of the Kodak just as Donald Sutherland announced, "Five minutes to show time." A stage manager and an ABC page met him at the door and offered to whisk Crowe and girlfriend Danielle Spencer to their seats. He refused. "I can find my own way, thank you very much," he said gruffly, and headed for the men's room.

"He is *such* an asshole," muttered one staffer under her breath.

From the stage, Ziskin saw that virtually all the stars had arrived—but most of them were standing in the aisles talking, not sitting in their seats. She walked down the stairs and began to make personal appeals. "Julia, I've got to start the show, could you please sit down?" she said to Julia Roberts, who was standing in the aisle chatting with Hugh Grant.

"Oh, yeah, okay," said Roberts. When Ziskin walked away, Roberts and Grant resumed their conversation.

Ziskin went up to Ron Howard. She nodded toward Russell Crowe, who was finally near his seat but not in it. "Please make your actor take his seat," she said to Howard.

Finally, Ziskin threw up her hands, went onstage, and took the microphone from Garry Hood. "I'm here as a stage manager, not as the producer," she told the audience. "*We need you all to please take your seats.*"

Outside, the preshow was ending. Ananda Lewis, who stood at the bottom of the stairs leading into the Kodak, threw it to Chris Connelly and Leeza Gibbons, who stood together at the top of the stairs. "We better get going!" shouted Connelly as the two hosts ran toward the doors of the Kodak.

In the wings of the stage, Bruce Vilanch talked to Tom Cruise, who had just come in through the loading dock. Goldberg walked by in a glittery, spangled outfit, plumes of feathers sticking out behind her. "*Moulin Rouge?*" asked Cruise with a grin.

"Yeah," said Vilanch. "Either that, or it's show time at the Apollo."

5:30 P.M., PACIFIC DAYLIGHT TIME: "*Tonight, the highest award in film-making will be awarded to one of these motion pictures.*"

As Sutherland and Close read their opening lines, Horvitz's cameras captured nominees, presenters, and notables, all of them safely in their seats. The camera trained on supporting-actor nominee Ethan Hawke also had a bird's-eye view into the voluminous cleavage sported by Hawke's wife, Uma Thurman. A chorus of whoops erupted in the wings. "Uma's frisky tonight!" shouted one writer.

After the opening, Tom Cruise delivered a speech written for him by

Cameron Crowe, and designed to answer the question of why the Oscars remained important in the aftermath of September 11. "What of a night like tonight?" intoned the bestubbled Cruise. "Should we celebrate the joy and magic that movies bring?" He paused dramatically. "Well, dare I say it: more than ever." The remarks quoted director Billy Wilder, who was watching the show from his home, and introduced a delightful film by documentarian Errol Morris (modeled on an earlier one by Chuck Workman), in which First Lady Laura Bush, rock stars Lou Reed and Iggy Pop, composer Philip Glass, writer Fran Lebowitz, and a host of lesser knowns rhapsodized about movies from *The Wizard of Oz* to *Godzilla vs. Mothra*, *The Bicycle Thief* to *Ernest Goes to Jail*. Backstage, Dency Nelson brought Benicio Del Toro into the wings to watch on a monitor. Del Toro moved as far to the side as he could, so as not to block anybody else's view.

Ten minutes into the show, Whoopi Goldberg descended on her swing, singing a rewritten version of "Diamonds Are a Girl's Best Friend" and shouting Nicole Kidman's signature line from *Moulin Rouge!*: "Come and get me, boys!" As Goldberg walked to the stage, Horvitz cut to a shot of an amused Russell Crowe—perhaps the first reaction shot of the actor laughing in the history of the Oscars. "So much mud has been thrown this year," said Goldberg when she got to the stage, "all the nominees look black." She scanned the front row. "Oh, look, the Smith family are seated together," she said. "Will, Jada, and Maggie Smith."

Del Toro presented the first award of the night, best supporting actress, to *A Beautiful Mind*'s Jennifer Connelly. "This is Jennifer Connelly's first Academy Award nomination," Glenn Close read as Connelly walked to the stage. "She made her screen debut at the age of eleven in Sergio Leone's *Once Upon a Time in America*." Factoids about the other four nominees occupied the same page in her script, but they went unread.

During the first commercial break, Owen Wilson entered the green room, followed a minute later by Jodie Foster. Ryan O'Neal and Ali MacGraw entered the building via the loading dock.

Early in the next act, husband and wife Reese Witherspoon and Ryan Phillippe read the nominees for best makeup. "Can I open it?" Witherspoon asked when Phillippe held up the envelope.

"Go ahead," he said. "You make more money than I do." The line wasn't on the TelePrompTer, but Witherspoon and Phillippe had tried it out earlier during an interview on the red carpet.

Backstage, Will Smith posed for a photo with a security guard. Then he spotted the Academy president outside the green room. "Frank Pierson!" he yelled to the staffers standing around. "Everybody get to work!"

Smith approached a talent coordinator. "I need, like, an inside connection that can get me some *stuff*," he said conspiratorially.

"There's food in the green room, Will," said Debbie Williams, who brought him a martini glass filled with strawberries and cream. Smith beamed, but asked for a couple more glasses. "We'll eat 'em real fast in the commercial, and then hand 'em off," he promised. Finally, he went into the green room himself, where he filled two more glasses with strawberries and loaded a small plate with sushi.

Shortly after 6 p.m., the door to Ziskin's office opened. *"Woody's here!"* whispered a friend to Julia Roberts outside the green room.

Staffers stared, incredulous, as Allen made his way down the hallway and into the wings of the stage. "That is *much* cooler than any of the people we were guessing," said one.

The atmosphere changed as another special guest made her entrance. Barbra Streisand came in from the loading dock, walking through the backstage area accompanied by James Brolin and a phalanx of staffers and security guards. Streisand looked to be wearing no makeup; she walked fast, pulling a red coat up tight around her neck and barely glancing at staffers and bystanders. When a page showed her the location of the green room, Streisand didn't even look up; instead, she ducked into a waiting elevator and went to her dressing room beneath the stage.

"Ladies and gentlemen," said Goldberg as Streisand was on her way downstairs, "it is my pleasure and my honor to introduce Mr. Woody Allen."

Allen took the stage to a standing ovation. "Thank you very much," he said. "That makes up for the strip search." Watching on a monitor in the truck, Ziskin had no idea what he was going to say; all she knew was what Allen had told DreamWorks marketing chief Terry Press—that when he practiced his speech in the shower, it lasted two minutes. Onstage, stretched by two standing ovations and frequent gales of laughter, the delightful monologue took four.

When Allen left the stage, Ziskin bolted from the truck and caught up with him in the hall. "Thank you!" she said.

Danette Herman ran to Ziskin, and the two women exchanged an enthusiastic high five. "I was crying," said Herman.

Ziskin turned to head back to the trailer and stepped squarely on the dress of Catherine Martin, who was holding the Oscar she'd just won for costume design for *Moulin Rouge!* Ziskin apologized, straightened Martin's dress, and went back outside.

Backstage about an hour into the show, Susan Futterman left the control truck and ran into Vilanch. "I was just on a nipple check," she said. The nipples in question, it turned out, belonged to Cameron Diaz. "She's wearing a beautiful dress," said Futterman, "but under the lights . . ." With her fingers, she outlined a pair of areolas.

In the trailer, Futterman had suggested to Ziskin and Horvitz that they show Diaz from the shoulders up. Horvitz complied most of the time, though he did occasionally cut to a shot that was framed in such a way that the offending nipples were visible—barely, and only if you looked very closely.

While Horvitz dealt with Diaz's nipples, Julia Roberts wandered around the loading dock in search of the smoking section, which was largely obscured by plants and equipment cases. (Prohibited during rehearsal, smoking had been restored to a small area of the dock.) As Roberts gave up and turned to go back inside the Kodak, Kate Winslet spotted her and yelled, "Julia!"

"Darling!" shouted Roberts, running to Winslet for a long, lingering embrace. Then she lit up a cigarette. Jennifer Lopez and Harvey Weinstein also puffed away. The large doors from the loading dock to the stage remained closed, shielding Donald Sutherland from the smoke. A minute later, Woody Allen and his wife, Soon-Yi Previn, left the theater via the loading dock, unnoticed by any of the smokers.

A few minutes before seven, Catherine Martin won her second Oscar of the night, for the art direction of *Moulin Rouge!* During the next commercial, director Baz Luhrmann accepted congratulations on Martin's two wins as he stood in an aisle. "Can you believe it?" he said. "It's all downhill from here."

When the show returned from the commercial, twelve empty seats were noticeable in the first three rows. In the truck, Ziskin, who had considered doing away with the seat-fillers but in the end had chosen to simply cut their numbers, realized how bad the vacancies looked. She also knew that Cirque du Soleil was due up shortly, and she wanted lots of famous people applauding. Ziskin went into the wings and corralled Herman. "I want them back in their seats," she said. "Get Julia back to her seat!"

In the next act, Cirque du Soleil performed and won a rousing standing ovation—including cheers from Roberts, who had been coaxed back into the auditorium. When the performance ended, whoops and hollers resounded through the backstage area. A stagehand sighed. "Fuck, it's over," he said. "Time for a deep breath and a big cocktail."

During the ensuing break, the large doors that led from the stage to the loading dock were opened wide in order for Cirque du Soleil's props to be moved out and the four bandstands rolled in. Almost miraculously, the smoking section outside the green room was deserted.

After presenting the Oscar for best score to Howard Shore for *The Lord of the Rings*, Sandra Bullock and Hugh Grant left the stage. Costars in *Two Weeks Notice* and a rumored real-life couple, the pair stopped in the hallway outside the green room.

"How much time is left in the show?" Grant asked.

"An hour," guessed an aide.

A stagehand looked at a show rundown. "An hour and a half," she said, generously.

Grant grimaced. "An hour and a half?" He turned to Bullock. "What do you want to do now?" he asked. "We can sit, or we can go to the bar."

"I don't know," said Bullock. "Do you want to sit in the audience? We can't sit down until the next break. Do you want to go to the bar?"

Grant shrugged. "We can go to the bar, or we can go to the green room . . ."

They stood in the hallway dithering for a few more minutes. "I don't care what we do," Bullock finally said with a faintly exasperated sigh. "I just want you to make a *decision*." He did, and they headed for the bar.

As the two-and-a-half-hour mark approached, Sidney Poitier received standing ovations both before and after his eloquent five-minute speech. He left the stage to a round of applause from stagehands and bystanders, and was about to leave the wings when Nelson ran up. "Sidney!" he yelled. "Sidney, wait for a minute! Whoopi wants to see you, Whoopi's running this way." Poitier turned around and waited for the show's host, who ran up to offer her congratulations.

Outside the green room, Paul McCartney talked to Carrie Fisher, a member of the writing team Vilanch had assembled. Kevin Spacey stood near them, staring at McCartney and looking for all the world like an enraptured fan.

A few minutes later, after the medley of song nominees, Sting and Randy Newman were led away from the monitor where they'd been watching the other performers and positioned closer to the stage. On the other side of the stage, McCartney and Enya took a similar position. The move was designed to more quickly catch the winner's reaction. In a huge upset, Newman won. "I told you so," said McCartney to Williams.

Newman walked onstage to a healthy round of applause. "Randy Newman has sixteen Academy Award nominations," read Close, "and now the Oscar." Throughout the hall, people who'd been sitting and applauding got to their feet.

Newman looked out into the audience, stunned. "I don't want your pity," he said, before thanking the music branch "for giving me so many chances to be humiliated over the years." When the TelePrompTer began flashing numbers, indicating the time left before his forty-five seconds were up, Newman stared into the orchestra pit, which was filled with musicians he'd hired to play on his film scores over the years. "Are you really gonna play in four seconds?" he asked. "Don't play." They didn't.

During the next commercial break, Gwyneth Paltrow came into the wings to present the screenwriting awards with Ethan Hawke. Before going on, she took out her chewing gum and put it into a ball of tissue. Nelson took the tissue from her and threw it in a nearby trash can. Paltrow's top was more transparent than Cameron Diaz's had been, and Futterman had ordered Horvitz to frame her tightly—but since she was copresenting with Hawke, the director needed a wider shot to show both stars. As Paltrow and

Hawke presented the adapted-screenplay award to Akiva Goldsman for *A Beautiful Mind*, Robert Redford paced outside the green room. He walked slowly back and forth, hands in his pockets, opening and closing his mouth and rolling his tongue around, clearing his throat and stretching his mouth for his upcoming speech.

When Redford walked onstage to accept his honorary Oscar, a page approached Debbie Williams in the wings. Visibly shaking, the page told Williams that Will Smith's daughter had just been taken to the hospital with an ear infection and Smith and his wife had left the theater to be with her. Smith did, however, leave a cell phone number so that he could be called if he won.

The show reached the three-and-a-half-hour mark with the four major awards still to come. Waiting in the wings to present the first of them, best actress, Russell Crowe turned to Garry Hood. "I want to thank you for being so good to work with," said Crowe, who then praised the Kodak. "This is the best place I've ever been for actually watching a show." Crowe proceeded to mispronounce Sissy Spacek's name as he read the nominees.

Halle Berry won for *Monster's Ball*, marking the first best-actress win for an African American. The stunned winner delivered an impassioned four-minute speech that began, "This moment is so much bigger than me." Choking back sobs, she continued: "This moment is for Dorothy Dandridge, Lena Horne, Diahann Carroll. It's for the women that stand beside me: Jada Pinkett, Angela Bassett, Viveca Fox. And it's for every nameless, faceless woman of color that now has a chance, because this door tonight has been opened." Three minutes later, the tearful Berry got around to thanking her agent and lawyer.

Inside Whoopi Goldberg's waiting room in the wings, Vilanch and the other writers quickly came up with a variety of punch lines. Just as quickly, they decided that the moment was too big to joke about. The next time she took the stage, Goldberg simply said, "First of all, I would like to congratulate Miss Halle Berry."

Backstage, a shell-shocked Berry was still making her way behind the stage, where a small walkway led to the path to the press rooms. As she headed down that hallway, her mother and husband were hustled through the wings to catch up with her. They did so on the far side of the stage, where the best-actress winner and her family shared some long, tearful embraces.

While Berry was navigating the passageway known as "winners' walk," Julia Roberts presented the best-actor award to Denzel Washington, completing a historic and unprecedented sweep of the top acting categories by African Americans. In his speech, Washington bowed to one of the night's honorary recipients, Poitier. "I'm proud to follow in your footsteps, Sidney," he declared.

In the wings, Mel Gibson and then Tom Hanks came up to Washington to offer congratulations. An ecstatic Roberts hung on to Washington the whole time. Gibson, about to present the award for best director, approached Rita Cossette. "Is my collar flipping up?" he said. She assured him it wasn't.

Four hours and seven minutes into the show—in other words, the point when the credits were rolling during what had previously been the longest Oscar show ever—Gibson presented the directing Oscar to Ron Howard for *A Beautiful Mind*. Howard came offstage with his Oscar, but he was held in the wings close to the stage, because he'd need to go back out if his movie also won for best picture. It did, and Howard returned to the stage to accept the final Oscar of the night from Tom Hanks.

As the credits began to roll, Hanks put his arm around Howard in the wings. "You got *two*!" said Hanks, who won his two Oscars in different years. "I had to split 'em up, but you got two."

A huge crowd gathered around Howard and his producer, Brian Grazer. Hanks laughed again. "Now I'll need a string of new anecdotes about the two of you," said Hanks, who had been directed by Howard in *Splash* and *Apollo 13*. "I'll have to do more interviews about you now." Photographers gathered to snap the winners, and Hanks looked at them and quoted the title of the low-budget 1976 movie Howard had acted in for producer Roger Corman, who in return gave him a chance to direct his first film. "Ron Howard says, 'Eat My Dust!'"

Four hours and twenty minutes after the show began, Donald Sutherland read the voting rules to cap off the longest Oscar telecast ever. Glenn Close came out from behind the announcers' table and hugged Mel Gibson. Ziskin ran into the wings and kissed Howard and Grazer, then hugged

Sutherland and Close. Hanks's wife, Rita Wilson, hugged Howard. The *Beautiful Mind* winners lingered on the stage, mingling with the staff and crew. The stage crew pulled Nicole Kidman out of the audience and posed for photos with her. Michael Riva's cell phone rang. "Wasn't it wonderful?" he said.

"I DID ABOUT 75 PERCENT of what I wanted to do, and I never get that percentage on anything I do," said Ziskin a few days after the show. "I did what I wanted, it was a historic night, and I was lucky to have that happen on my watch."

The show received mostly positive reviews, as did the Kodak Theatre. The ratings, though, were another matter: continuing the downward trend, the number of viewers was the lowest in five years. The average rating, dragged down by the loss of viewers in the show's final hour, was the lowest ever.

In Laura Ziskin's office on the Sony lot, it was easy to ignore that bad news amid the congratulatory messages that poured in. Harvey Weinstein, for instance, sent over a bottle of Cristal champagne along with a note. "Dear Laura," it read, "You can print this: 'This was the best Oscar show in ten years.' You did a brilliant job." Other letters came in from Marilyn and Alan Bergman, Jenna Elfman, Hugh Jackman, and many others.

In a way, Ziskin's favorite was the one she received from Sidney Lumet, the veteran director whose films included *Dog Day Afternoon*, *Network*, and *The Verdict*. "We don't know each other," Lumet wrote, "but I must tell you it was the best Oscar show ever. It was moving, funny, dramatic—all good words. I'm sure they'll give you a hard time about the length. Don't even think twice about it. That's what the evening was for. All those people bubbling over to a point where they were uncontrollable. It was terrific."

Three days after watching a show that had begun with a speech that quoted him, Billy Wilder died.

In the aftermath of the show, the Academy's review committee was left facing one inescapable fact: the broadcast had gotten to be too long. With the three longest shows in history all occurring in the last four years (the exception being Cates's relatively breezy three-and-a-half-hour show in 2001), the committee and the board of governors grappled with ideas for making things shorter.

The In Memoriam segment, always a bone of contention, was considered a candidate for elimination, though this was not simply because of the length of the show. The segment had caused an uproar by omitting actress Dorothy McGuire, whose near-fifty-year career had included an Oscar nomination for 1947's best-picture winner, *Gentleman's Agreement*. Some insiders insisted that the Academy, Ziskin, and segment directors Gary Ross and Michael Johnson simply forgot about McGuire, though the official explanation was that she was duly considered.

"There was this wave of criticism," said Bruce Davis. "And it wasn't just family, it was fans and a lot of other people. There were a couple of people in the segment who had much less extensive careers, and the board just thought, this seems to be hurting as many feelings as it's making people happy. Why are we doing this? So they decided to drop it."

That decision later changed—in part, said Davis, because the following year would provide the opportunity to salute such notables as Wilder, Milton Berle, Lew Wasserman, Rod Steiger, Richard Harris, and James Coburn.

At its monthly meeting in July, the board of governors tightened up the rules for giving honorary awards. In the future, the first award—be it a Thalberg, a Hersholt, or an honorary Oscar statuette—would require a two-thirds vote of the governors; the second would require a three-fourths majority. After two consecutive years in which three honorary awards were bestowed, a new rule stipulated that no more than two would ever be allowed in a single year.

In addition, new guidelines were formulated to tighten the Academy's financial oversight of the Oscar show. "Because Gil had been doing the show so consistently, it had not been necessary to really look at the process," said Frank Pierson. "Everything was done by estimate and guesstimate, and there was no procedure so that you knew when you were beginning to go over and you could cut back. That was okay because we were in good hands when Gil was the one who was estimating and improvising. But Laura went spectacularly over budget and overtime because she and I were both doing it for the first time." Cates helped formulate the new procedures, which included an auditor to constantly track the production; the Academy president also took over some responsibility for eliminating elements when a show was running overtime, so that the show's producer wouldn't have to spend valuable time explaining to a star why he'd been cut from the show.

Still, Pierson avidly defended Ziskin's show. "She bit off an awful lot, but I personally loved the show," he said. "The only thing I think was a mistake was the Cirque du Soleil sequence. It was beautiful, it was wonderful in the theater, but it meant nothing on the tube. And it was lengthy, and very, very expensive."

Ziskin's Oscar show received seven Emmy nominations. It won in one category, choreography. The award went to Debra Brown, who designed the Cirque du Soleil number.

10

War Games

The 75th Academy Awards

GIL CATES liked to say that the Academy Awards always reflected the year in which they took place. As the seventy-fifth Oscar show approached in early 2003, that was not necessarily a good thing.

For months, the administration of George W. Bush had been talking about removing Iraqi dictator Saddam Hussein from power. The president spoke of ties between Hussein and the Al Qaeda terrorist organization, responsible for the September 11 attacks on America, of the dictator's record of brutality and violence within his own country, of the likelihood that he had or was preparing weapons of mass destruction. By January, military action against Iraq seemed likely, perhaps inevitable.

If not for the threat of war, Cates would have been focusing on celebrating Oscar's seventy-fifth anniversary, while at the same time keeping the show to a reasonable length. The past four years had seen three Oscar shows of record-breaking length; ratings had continued to decline, and the Academy knew it needed to hand out the final awards before TV sets up and down the East Coast were switched off. Given that priority, the obvious choice as producer was Cates, who'd brought in the 2001 show at an elegant three hours and twenty-five minutes, and who didn't feel the need to stick every one of his ideas into the show. After all, he'd already done it ten times and figured to do a few more before he was through.

Still, Pierson felt the need to put a little extra pressure on his producer. Before the nominations were announced on February 11, the Academy president went to Cates and said he'd like to publicly promise that the best-picture winner would be revealed before midnight, East Coast time.

Cates considered the request. He knew Pierson's scenario had happened only once in the past twenty-five years, and that the final winner wasn't usually revealed until after 12:30 a.m. He knew that an Oscar show stripped of everything—no film packages, no dance numbers, nothing but two dozen awards, five songs, and half an hour of commercials—would still take three hours. He thought about it all, and he agreed. Make your promise, he told Pierson, and I'll give you a three-and-a-half-hour Oscar show.

Just past 5:30 a.m., Pierson and Marisa Tomei read the names of the year's nominees. "And for those of you on the East Coast," concluded Pierson, "here's a presidential promise: you'll know the best-picture winner before the clock strikes twelve."

At the back of the hall, executive consultant Robert Z. Shapiro shrugged off the pressure. "Actually," he pointed out, "all we have to do is give out best picture first."

IF YOU JUST WENT by the numbers, the year's nominations were a triumph for director Rob Marshall's musical *Chicago*, which led all films with thirteen nominations. Also for Martin Scorsese's *Gangs of New York*, which had ten, for British director Stephen Daldry's adaptation of the Michael Cunningham novel *The Hours*, with nine, and for fugitive director Roman Polanski, whose Holocaust-themed drama *The Pianist* won seven nominations, including nods for best director, actor, and screenplay.

Inside the film industry, though, the nominations were not simply seen as a victory for *Chicago* or *Gangs of New York* or *The Pianist*, but as a triumph for Harvey Weinstein.

It had been a rough few months for the bellicose and controversial Miramax chief, the subject of a scathing profile in *The New Yorker* the previous December. The piece went into great detail about the bullying manner Weinstein was known to employ, delighting Harvey-bashers and infuriating his supporters. The nominations, though, played as vindication: the Miramax releases *Chicago*, *Gangs of New York*, and *Frida* accounted for twenty-nine nominations, plus one for *The Quiet American* and another for the Chinese film *Hero*. (Miramax also held some foreign rights to *The Hours*, while Harvey and Bob Weinstein received executive producer credit on another multiple nominee, *The Lord of the Rings: The Two Towers*, though their credit was simply a condition of the deal made when Miramax sold the property to New Line.) Miramax's total far outstripped the combined nominations for Warner Bros., Universal, Disney, 20th Century-Fox, and Sony.

Of the Miramax films, *Chicago* seemed the best bet for a serious Oscar haul. Weinstein, though, made no secret that he was playing favorites in one of the categories. Martin Scorsese, the director of *Gangs of New York*, had never won an Oscar despite having one of the most distinguished careers of the past three decades. Twice, he had lost in the best-director and best-picture competitions to films that, in retrospect, seemed markedly inferior to his: the first time in 1980 when his brutal masterpiece *Raging Bull* lost to actor Robert Redford's directorial debut, *Ordinary People*, then again ten years later when his *GoodFellas* was beaten by the first directing job of another actor, this time Kevin Costner with *Dances with Wolves*.

Weinstein wanted badly to be the man who finally brought home an Oscar for Scorsese—and he didn't care who knew it, even if that meant alienating *Chicago* director Rob Marshall. If *Gangs of New York* was far from Scorsese's best work, that was okay: Miramax would subtly play up the idea of a directing Oscar as a de facto lifetime achievement award for Scorsese by suggesting, vociferously if a bit foolishly, that *Gangs* was in some way a summation of the director's craft and style.

Another best-director nominee, Roman Polanski, was not available for campaigning. The director had fled the United States in 1978 after pleading guilty to the statutory rape of a thirteen-year-old girl, and couldn't enter the country without exposing himself to possible arrest. Actor Adrien Brody, the largely unknown star of the film, handled many of the promotional chores in Polanski's stead. But the focus kept slipping back to the director's legal troubles: the girl with whom he'd had consensual sex emerged to say that Polanski should be judged solely on his work, and then a transcript from his court case showed up on the Web site thesmokinggun.com. Suspicions grew that a rival studio had actually put the girl up to it—not to support Polanski, but to remind voters of his crime. Focus Features, the small company that had distributed *The Pianist*, kept up a low-key campaign and hoped that Miramax's relentless politicking on behalf of *Chicago* and *Gangs* would prove to be off-putting to Academy members.

ON MARCH 6, President Bush gave a press conference in which he pushed for a United Nations vote authorizing the use of force to remove Saddam Hussein from power. "Iraq is a country that has got terrorist ties," he said. "It's a country with wealth, it's a country that trains terrorists, a country that could arm terrorists. And our fellow Americans must understand, in this new war against terror, that we not only must chase down Al Qaeda terrorists, we must deal with weapons of mass destruction."

The same day, about a hundred crew members gathered in the lower lobby of the Kodak Theatre for a production meeting. At the meeting, Cates spent some time discussing the most problematic and surprising of the best-song nominees. The troubled but charismatic young rapper Eminem had been nominated for the song "Lose Yourself" from *8 Mile*, a film from director Curtis Hanson in which Eminem played a character loosely based on himself. The song was a hit, an assured, tough-minded statement of purpose, and more central to its movie than any of the other nominees—but it was also a rap song, the first the Academy had ever nominated. And for every person who saw Eminem as a conflicted but brilliant young writer and performer, others simply viewed him as a sullen, foul-mouthed thug.

When he'd performed "Lose Yourself" on the Grammys a month earlier, Eminem had refused to clean up the song's language; ABC had simply bleeped out the two *motherfuckers* and three *shits*. To do that on the Oscars meant going to a delay, something the producers had been fighting for years. But handing the song to a different, more compliant performer ran the risk of offending the nominee and making the Academy look stodgy.

"We don't know if Eminem will do it," said Cates at the production meeting. "But we're auditioning in the back of the room if any of you have a feeling for it."

At the end of his talk, Cates made one final point. "The question has been asked about security, and what happens if we go to war," he said. "The thing is, we're going to do the show on the twenty-third. If a war happens, it'll probably be a week before or a week after. We have several contingency plans in place, so I think we'll be okay."

Then the Oscars' security chief, Kirk Smith, had some final advice. "Security will be tighter than ever this year," he said. "We ask that you tell your folks, please empty out your trunks before you come to the theater. We will be searching cars, and we don't want to have to go through your vacation stuff every time you drive into the building."

For its part, the Academy's board of governors decided not to renew the $1 million catastrophe insurance policy it'd bought the previous year. "If we decide to postpone because of the war, our contract with ABC says we'll still get paid," said Bruce Davis. "And if there's some terrible terrorist thing that happens in the auditorium, a million dollars' worth of insurance isn't going to cover your losses anyway." Some board members made it clear that they thought the decision was foolhardy.

LOUIS J. HORVITZ couldn't help but get a special kick out of auditioning trophy ladies. Years earlier, when he was working for Dick Clark's company, the director had met his wife, a statuesque blonde named Steffanee Leaming, at one such audition.

"I went to Dick Clark's, I was a little late, I'd been playing tennis, I walk in and there's a whole room of models," he remembered. "Some new faces, some who'd auditioned before. I looked across the room and I saw Steffanee, and she looked at me and my heart started palpitating and I thought, Oh, God, no, I don't want to be in love." When he told producer Al Schwartz that he wanted Leaming in addition to the two women who'd already been hired, Schwartz knew something was up. "He said, 'Do you want her for the show, or do you want to date her?' And I said, 'I'll marry her if I can.' "

A month shy of Horvitz and Leaming's seventh wedding anniversary, another lobby full of beautiful women waited for him and Cates. The two men sat in Cates's small corner office on the twelfth floor of a building on the eastern edge of Century City. The producer sat in a black plastic chair behind a modest natural wood desk, while Horvitz took a spot on the small couch. The board laying out the Oscar show dominated one wall, but a white shade had been pulled down to cover the privileged information.

When each prospective trophy lady entered his office, Cates greeted her, glanced at her eight-by-ten glossies, made small talk, and got through the interview quickly. He'd ask if she'd done a show like the Oscars before; most had. He'd inquire where she was from, drawing answers as diverse as Michigan, Connecticut, Mexico, and Austria. He'd ask if an audience of a billion people intimidated her, and she'd assure him that it didn't. He'd wonder about her career goals, and she'd tell him she wanted to act.

"Well," he'd say after less than ten minutes, "you're a beautiful woman, you're great, nice to meet you, and I don't have anything else."

Horvitz occasionally took the interviews a step further. "Do you feel comfortable onstage?" he asked a tall brunette from New England wearing a low-cut, long black dress.

"Oh, yes," she said. "I've done theater."

"Could you stand up and do your runway walk for us?" he said.

She walked across the small office, through the door into an adjoining conference room, then back.

"Okay, good," said Horvitz. "You'd get onstage and stand there . . ."

She stood there, smiling.

". . . and if people give a speech you listen to them, and if they're funny, laugh . . ."

She giggled, just a little.

". . . and then escort them off."

She walked toward the office door.

"Well, listen, you're a terrific, wonderful woman," said Cates. "And we'll get back to you when we decide."

The next model, a blonde named Joanna Krupa, got an even more comprehensive audition. Horvitz asked his assistant, Deborah Read, to bring in a candy dish with the standing figure of a cat on it. Then he had Krupa take the dish as if it were an Oscar, do her walk, hand the dish to Read, and stand by smiling while Read made a mock acceptance speech.

When she left, Cates sighed. "You don't even recognize it when it's happening," he said, shaking his head. "But it's terrible to realize you've gotten older and turned into a dirty old man."

ROBERT Z. SHAPIRO walked into Cates's office. In his hand, he held a piece of paper.

"Gil," he said, "look at this."

"What is it?" said Cates, taking the paper.

"The show's running time."

Cates looked at the page and frowned. The listed time was three hours, fifty-five minutes, and forty seconds.

"Who came up with this?" he said.

"The script department."

Cates turned away and walked to his desk. "Jesus fucking Christ," he muttered under his breath.

AT THE NOMINEES' LUNCHEON on March 10, Cates made his usual welcoming speech, showed his usual film of good and bad acceptance speeches, and delivered his usual spiel about keeping the speeches under forty-five seconds. To Adrien Brody, Chris Cooper, John C. Reilly, Salma Hayek, Diane Lane, Queen Latifah, and others, this was something new; to Nicolas Cage and Julianne Moore, it was old hat.

Then the producer veered into uncharted territory. "To make sure that the show doesn't run long, we have two new rules this year," he said. "If you pull out a list, you're done. The orchestra is going to play you off. Even if you don't have a list, if you start naming names, you can thank five people. When you mention the sixth, you're done. The music is coming in."

Nominees looked at each other nervously, silently counting up the people they knew they'd *have* to thank. "These are harsh measures, but necessary," Cates insisted. "We'll have Bill Conti, our music director—or stickman, as Julia Roberts so eloquently called him—play you off."

In the pressroom outside the main ballroom, reporters asked the nominees if they thought the Oscars would be appropriate if a war was taking place. "It would seem obscene if we were seen bouncing up the red carpet grinning when people are dying," said Daniel Day-Lewis. "It's going to be very difficult to find a way to do this."

THE SAME DAY as the nominees' luncheon, a full-page ad ran in the Hollywood trade papers. The ad reprinted an article that had run a few days earlier in the *Los Angeles Times*, as well as other local papers. The piece bore the byline of Robert Wise, the eighty-eight-year-old director of *The Sound of Music* and *West Side Story*, and a past president of the Academy. Wise lavished praise on Martin Scorsese and *Gangs of New York*, calling it "a summation of his entire body of work." Miramax headlined the ad "Two-time Academy Award–winner Robert Wise declares Scorsese deserves the Oscar for 'Gangs of New York.' "

Miramax competitors and some neutral observers cried foul, particularly with regard to Wise's suggestion that Scorsese deserved the Oscar because *Gangs* summed up his entire career. In an ideal world, of course, a director's body of work was not supposed to enter into a voter's judgment of a specific film; more grievously to the Academy, Wise's article violated an unspoken Academy rule that members were not to publicly reveal their votes to anyone.

In its defense, Miramax said that it was simply answering an opinion piece that had run in *Daily Variety* the previous month. In that article, Oscar-winning screenwriter William Goldman bluntly stated that Scorsese did not deserve to win the best-director Oscar. "*Gangs of New York* is a mess," he declared. While eviscerating Scorsese's epic, Goldman also detoured to point out that he would never forgive Miramax "for hyping the Oscar to Roberto Benigni, the scummiest award in the Academy's history."

When the firestorm hit, Wise admitted that he'd signed the ad at the urging of Miramax, but denied having written it. (Privately, a source close to the director said that Wise didn't really like *Gangs* very much, but was a fan and friend of Scorsese.) Wise credited the piece to Mike Thomas, who had done some ghostwriting for Wise in the past, and who'd also worked as Cates's publicist on the Oscar show two years earlier. Thomas denied having anything to do with the ad. On Friday the fourteenth, Murray Weissman, a publicist hired by Miramax to work on the studio's Oscar campaign (and a member of the executive committee of the Academy's public relations branch), admitted having written the article. Some Academy members, furious at the underhanded way Miramax had used Wise, asked for their ballots to be returned so they could change their votes. PricewaterhouseCoopers refused. According to people close to *Chicago* director Rob Marshall, the ads sent Marshall over the edge as well; he angrily confronted Weinstein about playing favorites so blatantly.

The Academy was furious at Miramax, but it didn't feel that it could punish the studio by taking away any of its tickets. The problem, said Bruce Davis, was that the previous year the Academy had taken no action when 20th Century-Fox took out an ad in which Robert Wise voiced his support of *Moulin Rouge!* (another movie, said a source close to Wise, with which the director was not particularly enamored). If Miramax was punished for doing the same thing Fox had done the year before, Weinstein could have made a strong case that he was being unjustly persecuted.

"We didn't do anything last year, and we should have," conceded Davis. "You have to hand it to Harvey. He knows every angle, and he knows *exactly* how much he can get away with."

ON THURSDAY, March 13, Chuck Warn and Toni Thompson looked at a calendar that covered the wall of a room in ABC's Burbank headquarters. Warn, the press rep for Cates, pointed to Friday the fourteenth. "Bush is scheduled to speak here," he said. "Then we'll know more about what's going on in the war. The beginning of next week I'll go back to Larry King and see if he wants to devote a show to something lighter."

Thompson, a publicist for the Academy, pointed to the following week, the seven days leading up to the show on March 23. "We have to feed the monster every day," she said. "We already have two things for Friday, but we need something Thursday. Is just letting them into the theater enough?"

"Yeah, that's enough," said Warn. "They'll be happy to just get in the building."

As Warn and Thompson plotted strategy, Cates walked out of the room where he and Bruce Vilanch had been doing radio interviews to promote the show. "What do you think is going to happen with the war?" an ABC staffer asked the producer.

"I think we're going to war," said Cates, sighing. "I only hope—and I know this sounds awful—I hope it either starts Monday the seventeenth, or March 24. If it starts anytime between the twentieth and the twenty-third, we're fucked. *We are fucked*."

ST. PATRICK'S DAY was Monday, March 17, the last day off the union crew would enjoy before the Oscar show. In the Kodak Theatre, the stage sat empty and unattended. The doors between the stage and the loading dock remained closed. In the production office, TV monitors were turned to CNN. SHOWDOWN IRAQ, read the on-screen graphics.

Fears grew that if the war began Thursday or later, blanket news coverage would make televising the show impossible. Although the Academy's contract with ABC obligated the network to broadcast the ceremony, nobody thought it'd be a good idea to force ABC's hand during wartime. Besides, said Warn, "if a war starts two days before the show, celebrities are going to start pulling out, and we won't have a show anymore."

On a less serious front, the staff was still struggling to wrestle the show down to three and a half hours. On the previous day's run-through, the show had timed out to three hours and fifty-six minutes, with the best-picture presentation not slated to occur until 12:19 a.m., East Coast time. The latest round of cuts, one of which moved a Penelope Spheeris film of past Oscar hosts into the preshow, reduced the running time by six minutes.

That night, George W. Bush addressed the nation. He gave Saddam Hussein forty-eight hours to relinquish power and leave Iraq. Tuesday, Hussein rejected Bush's ultimatum. CNN changed its graphic to THE BRINK OF WAR: FINAL PREPARATIONS.

At the Kodak, though, it was starting to look like the Oscars. Seat cards were in place in the orchestra section of the theater. Roy Christopher watched the crew make adjustments to his set, which was dominated by a giant white latticework, shaped like a champagne flute, at the rear of the stage. Above the stage hung a huge ball, fourteen feet in diameter and encircled around its equator by four-foot letters that spelled out 75TH ANNUAL ACADEMY AWARDS as they slowly spun. The piece was a clear homage to the historic spinning-globe logo of Universal Pictures—and, said Christopher, the kind of nod to the past that he'd only do in an anniversary year.

Working in the Kodak for the first time, the designer wondered what had happened to the notes he'd given the builders while the theater was in the planning stages. "Gil and I, and Louis J., and Bob Dickinson spent hours poring over these plans they sent us," he said, exasperated. "We made our notes, we had our meetings, and not one thing we suggested was processed. It was essentially a charade. They used all of us as consultants, but they didn't do anything we asked them to do."

Still, Christopher didn't have to worry about turning a dingy hallway into the green room, the way Michael Riva had done the previous year. *Architectural Digest* had made a deal to underwrite and assist with the room; it was located in the same place it had been in 2002, but there was more space and more money to work with.

Down a long hallway from the green room, a sign had been posted on the door to Cates's office. WHEN THIS DOOR IS CLOSED, it read, IT MEANS PLEASE DO NOT COME IN.

Danette Herman posted a different sign on her door. THE BUNKER, it read. Will Smith's publicist called to say that the actor no longer felt it was appropriate for him to be on the show. Herman quickly replaced Smith with Brendan Fraser. Increasingly, Cates and Herman fielded phone calls from reps for actors who were uncertain about walking the red carpet, who said they'd rather quietly slip in the back way. Warren Beatty, whose wife, Annette Bening, was booked to be a presenter, ran into Cates's wife and told her he thought the show should be canceled.

For days, the staff had also been under pressure from executives at ABC, which was pushing not to cancel but to delay the show. Cates and Pierson repeatedly discussed the ramifications of various delays: with a one-day postponement, the show might lose a few stars, but most people would stick around; a delay of four or five days or a week would require buying out the run of a Scooby-Doo musical coming into the Kodak Theatre, an expensive proposition, and would probably wreak havoc with the lineup of presenters and performers; beyond that, they'd have to look into changing venues, which could become enormously expensive, particularly given the Academy's lack of insurance.

ABC kept arguing for a one-week delay, while Cates remained adamant that a seven-day postponement wouldn't solve anything and could be catastrophic for the show. He was supported by staffers who'd worked on the fall 2001 Emmy Awards, which were postponed after September 11, postponed a second time after military action began in Afghanistan, and finally took place almost two months later in a smaller theater with a different producer and a scaled-down presentation. For his part, Pierson was also determined that the show take place on time—particularly, he thought, since it would be shown on aircraft carriers and in other places where American troops could watch.

At lunch on Tuesday, a group of production and Academy staffers met at the Grill, a restaurant in the Hollywood & Highland complex. After reiterating his desire for the show to proceed as planned, Cates proposed doing away with the bleachers of fans along the red carpet, suggesting that it wouldn't be appropriate for celebrities to run that shrieking gauntlet. Warn pointed out that if the Academy took that step, the press that lined the other side of the carpet would just keep asking questions about the absence of fans.

"Well," said Cates, "then maybe we should get rid of the press, too."

At four o'clock, in the main Oscar press room at the Renaissance Hotel, Cates and Pierson took their places at a small table and faced several dozen reporters and camera crews.

"For some months now, Gil and his crew have been preparing for our show on Sunday while the clouds of war were gathering around us," read Pierson from a page in front of him. "We always knew there were some changes we would make if we needed to . . . We need the show to reflect a kind of soberness and seriousness we are all confronted with."

Cates then announced that the portion of the red carpet that ran along Hollywood Boulevard, between bleachers filled with fans and the press, would be eliminated. Interviews on the red carpet would not be permitted, and only a few crews would be allowed to photograph arriving stars. The preshow broadcast would be scaled back, and its tone changed to reflect events in the world.

"Is there a consideration for canceling the show?" asked a reporter.

"We're not prepared to address that question now," said Pierson.

"Have you been in touch with Washington?"

"No."

"Are the changes in the arrival area related to security?"

"No," said Cates. "Just the concerns of the celebrities."

"Do you plan to shorten the show at all?"

"That's a question we get every year," said Cates, allowing himself a slight smile.

Afterward, Cates headed back to his office. "Tough day, eh?" asked a bystander.

"Fuckin' A," said Cates. Then he smiled and shrugged. "It's exciting. It'll be great."

"YOU KNOW there's no red carpet?" David Jones said. "Photographers are going to be *pissed*."

Sitting behind a console at the Capitol Recording Studios in Hollywood on Tuesday night, Jones's sister laughed. "Oh, poor photographers," said Catherine Zeta-Jones, who was embroiled in a lawsuit against a British paper that published unauthorized wedding photographs. "I feel *so* sorry for them."

Due to have her first child in two weeks, Zeta-Jones was wearing black stretch pants and a black-and-white-print shirt. Her hair was tied back and she wasn't wearing makeup. She'd come to the studio to record vocals to the nominated *Chicago* song "I Move On," this prerecord being an Oscar tradition designed as insurance in the event of last-minute attacks of nerves or laryngitis.

In the movie, Zeta-Jones performed the song with her fellow nominee Renée Zellweger. But Zellweger didn't feel comfortable performing live, so another *Chicago* star, Queen Latifah, was booked instead. The Academy deliberately didn't announce that news until after the polls had closed, for fear that it might reflect poorly on Zellweger while voters still had their ballots.

While she waited for Latifah and for *Chicago* director Rob Marshall, Zeta-Jones grilled her brother and her publicist about the afternoon's press conference. "There's no chance it'll be canceled, right?" she asked.

"Oh, no," said David Jones. "They won't cancel."

"Actually, there is a small chance," said Zeta-Jones's publicist. "If the war starts Saturday, it might be postponed a couple of days."

Zeta-Jones looked at her bulging belly. "Oh, no," she moaned. "What am I going to do?"

ON WEDNESDAY MORNING, five laminated, blown-up pages had been affixed to the wall next to the entrance to the production office inside the Kodak. Three dealt with the protocol on handling bomb threats, two with suspicious mail. During the day, Jim Carrey and Cate Blanchett pulled out of their spots as presenters. Blanchett said she didn't want to leave her family in London. Angelina Jolie canceled as well.

On Thursday, March 20, ABC anchorman Peter Jennings made an announcement. "The war has begun in earnest," he said, "if not in full."

At 8:30, a few key staff members met for what had become the first order of business every morning: a security meeting that covered everything from terrorist threats to gate-crashers.

Small cuts, meanwhile, had been made throughout the script. Now the show was down to three hours and thirty-eight minutes—still too long, but closer to Pierson's goal. A major savings came with the decision to drop "Lose Yourself" from the show, Eminem having sent word that he didn't want to do it but didn't feel comfortable with anybody else taking the song, either. (That hadn't stopped Cates from asking actor Patrick Stewart to consider reciting the song; Stewart came to the studio and rehearsed what witnesses say was a creditable version of the song, but afterward the classically trained actor said he wasn't comfortable with the material.)

At lunch, Cates sat at a table with Warn, Seligman, John Hamlin, and a few others. The conversation turned to *Are You Hot?*, ABC's appalling reality show in which a panel of judges rated the physical characteristics of wannabe sex symbols. Cates laughed at the idea of the network that put it on the air telling him what was and wasn't acceptable on the Oscars.

"Susan Futterman was in Australia when it aired," said Hamlin. "She said she'd never have let Lorenzo Lamas point at a woman with his laser pointer and say something like, 'Your titties are too small.' "

"Well, if Susan gives me any shit," said Cates, "I'm just going to say, 'You can't talk to me about standards and practices, because ABC doesn't have any standards or practices anymore.' "

In the middle of the discussion, Cates's cell phone rang. He had a quick conversation and then hung up. "My wife says she was talking to a detective who said he heard from a friend of his that the Oscars were canceled," said Cates. "She said, 'Oh, I'll have to let my husband know.' "

He frowned. "Fucking rumors," he said.

"WERE THERE ANY JOKES you didn't like?" Steve Martin looked around the room at a group of Oscar staffers who'd just heard his opening monologue. "Anything I should take out? If there are, let me know and I'll meet with the writers."

Nobody responded. "Okay, good," said Martin. "Now, remember your vow: not a word."

Martin was standing one floor below the stage, in the Kodak Theatre's main green room. He'd taken over the space to try out his monologue in a controlled setting, asking that the audience be made up of staffers who hadn't heard the material during the few times he'd tested it in the production office. About two dozen of them had been recruited. With a TV monitor in the corner serving as a makeshift TelePrompTer, the host ran through the whole monologue with casual élan, and drew an enthusiastic reaction.

Cates, who'd come in late with Shapiro and Seligman, hugged Martin as the gathering broke up. "It was great," he said. "Thank you."

"You missed the beginning," said Martin. "I said, 'You'll notice that there was no red carpet tonight. Boy, *that'll* send a message.' " Shapiro and Seligman laughed, and Cates nodded. "Also, I had another one: 'Saddam, if you're watching, I hope your communications are knocked out just before best picture.' "

Cates frowned. "Let's see what happens before we use that one," he said. "He could be dead by then."

"If he's dead," Martin promised, "I'll cut it."

As the afternoon wore on, things were quiet. There were no big meetings, no press conferences, no emergencies. Martin's well-received appearance, both in the green room and later on the stage, seemed to have reassured the staff that it was okay to proceed as if it were business as usual—to take note of the situation in Iraq, but then move forward and put on a show.

Still, it was impossible to ignore the war for long—especially for Cates, who was asked to participate in constant conference calls with ABC about the network's options for canceling or postponing the show. Just after 7 p.m., as the orchestra settled into the pit and the stage was reset to rehearse a song from *Frida*, Cates walked to the production table and sat down with a sigh.

"It's been a very strange year," he said softly. "Very strange. I was literally on the phone with Annette Bening, I hung up, and the second I hung up the phone it rang again, and somebody was calling me to say, 'Did you hear Annette Bening canceled?' I do not know where the rumors come from, but you *cannot* control them. And eventually, it makes you wonder—is somebody spreading these things deliberately?"

He shrugged. "We've lost people, sure. We always lose people at the last minute. We'll probably lose more than usual this year, because people are afraid to travel. But we're back up to full strength now, and we'll be at full strength Sunday night."

FRIDAY MORNING, Cates had his usual conference call with ABC executives. The network, which was showing war coverage around the clock, continued to push for a one-week postponement; Cates and Pierson continued to lobby for a less glitzy, more appropriate Oscar ceremony taking place as scheduled. Alex Wallau, the president of ABC networks, wanted the

Oscar crew to plan for and have answers to all possible situations that might arise, from a dramatic escalation in the war to an abrupt end to hostilities. Cates argued that they simply couldn't plan for everything, and would have to deal with some eventualities only if and when they occurred. When Cates got off the phone, he sighed, "We're doing it," and then repeated the phrase as if to convince himself. "We're doing it. We're doing it."

At noon, on what would have been the red carpet along Hollywood Boulevard, Cates, Horvitz, and Pierson held a press conference. This Q&A session took place every year, and had been on the schedule well before any questions of cancellation or postponement arose. In front of dozens of reporters, many of them still smarting over the fact that they'd lost access to the red carpet, the three men reiterated that the show would go on. Cates admitted that "one or two" presenters had dropped out, said that some "flippant stuff" had been taken out of the script, and added that he anticipated some speeches to acknowledge the war.

When the press conference ended, a large group that included Cates, Horvitz, Warn, Bruce Davis, Ric Robertson, and others headed for the producer's office. On the way, a man approached Cates's assistant, Capucine Lyons, and began babbling about tickets, asking her if she wanted to go to the show with him.

When she got back to her desk, Lyons called the security staff. A few minutes later, they called her back. "They arrested him," Lyons said when she hung up the phone. "They found crystal meth on him." She smiled sweetly. "That's the second person I've had arrested in the last two days."

FIVE YEARS EARLIER, when seventy Academy Award recipients gathered at the Shrine Auditorium to celebrate another anniversary, the past Oscar winners had been referred to by their acronym: POWs. Cates and Herman had decided to have a similar segment on the seventy-fifth show—but this time, given the events in Iraq, the acronym went unused.

Sixty-three Oscar winners had originally agreed to participate, but by Friday afternoon the number was down to sixty-one. The winners straggled in over the course of an hour, starting with Ernest Borgnine, Teresa Wright, Kathy Bates, and Shirley Jones.

The stars filled up several rows in the parterre, the Kodak's name for a raised rear section of orchestra seats. Nicolas Cage, looking very Elvis-like in a white shirt and blue blazer, sat near Jon Voight and Martin Landau. Sean Connery showed up, hugged Michael Caine, and shook hands with Ben Kingsley, Landau, and Voight. Cage leaned over a row to greet Caine. "Hello, sir," Cage said. "Nice to see you again."

Cuba Gooding, Jr., walked up the aisle looking tentative, then brightened when he spotted Lou Gossett, Jr., who sat next to him at the reunion five years earlier. Mira Sorvino, stunning in a simple black miniskirt, sat by herself, the most glamorous wallflower in town.

When the past winners had all taken seats, Cates and Herman welcomed them. Then stage manager Peter Margolis took over. "Okay," he said, "I am going to give everybody a number. Julie Andrews, you are number one. Kathy Bates, number two . . ."

Margolis went through the entire list, assigning numbers to each of the stars. When Connery received number ten, Jon Voight turned to him. "Can you remember that?" he said.

In groups of seventeen, winners walked backstage and took their places in long lines outside the green room. Everyone navigated the stairs and hallways easily except for ninety-three-year-old Luise Rainer. The actress had already informed the Academy that she didn't like her hotel room and that as the oldest of the past winners, she expected special treatment. Moving from her seat to the aisle, she stumbled and grabbed her thigh. "My leg, my leg!" she yelled, before resuming a fast hobble.

Backstage, the winners formed two long lines, with stand-ins taking the place of those who couldn't make it to rehearsal. Enthusiastic conversations sprang up between Oscar recipients who found themselves next to each other: Louise Fletcher and Eva Marie Saint here, Sean Connery and Tatum O'Neal there. When Mickey Rooney showed up late, cheers erupted all the way down the lines. "Mickey la Rooney la Rooney la Mickey!" shouted Red Buttons.

Watching the tableau, Herman smiled. "The last couple of days have been horrible," she said. "But today is much better. There's been all this talk about people canceling, but we have five wonderful, courageous women who have flown a long way to get here. Olivia de Havilland from France,

Luise Rainer from London, Brenda Fricker from Ireland, Teresa Wright from New York, and Celeste Holm from Hong Kong. This reminds me why we love the movies, why we do this show. My heart is full."

LATE FRIDAY NIGHT, Bono paced the stage of the Kodak, gazing at the opera boxes lining the walls. Then he turned and eyed the giant, translucent, fluted panel that dominated the rear of the stage. Around him, the other three members of U2 settled into their places. "I just realized that we've never performed this song before," said Bono, who was wearing a backward cap and a loose brown jacket over a green V-neck sweater, along with black cargo pants and clunky black shoes. "So anything can happen."

U2, the Irish quartet that over the past fifteen years had become the biggest and most successful rock 'n' roll band in the world, had been nominated for the song "The Hands That Built America" from *Gangs of New York*. A brooding, conflicted look at a journey many of the Irish had made, it built from an acoustic opening to a near-psychedelic middle section featuring Bono's distorted, wordless moans. The last verse was spare and intimate as it lamented the destruction of September 11: "It's early fall / There's a cloud on the New York skyline / Innocence dragged across a yellow line . . ."

For the first couple of takes, the band, and particularly its famously intense and combative lead singer, seemed ill at ease. During the third runthrough, Bono stopped singing altogether, walked down the steps into the audience, took Catherine Zeta-Jones's seat card out of her front-row seat, and slouched down in her spot to listen to the band. Then he turned to Hal Wilner, a music producer who had accompanied the band to rehearsal.

"I'm not really enjoying it right now," Bono said.

"What do we need?" asked Wilner.

"I don't know," said Bono. "Talent?"

He looked back at the stage, where the flute glowed with white light, and grimaced. Then he picked up the wireless microphone he'd carried with him and spoke into it. "This time, whoever's doing the lighting, I'd like to try it without the crystal lit," he said. "I'd like to see what it looks like with darkness." He waited for a minute, but nothing changed. "If anybody didn't understand that last comment, feel free to ask me about it."

Slowly, the band began to get a handle on the song. As the balance between U2 and the orchestra improved, Bono pushed himself harder, though he never approached the kind of intensity he was capable of displaying on-stage. Screens behind the band showed vintage black-and-white photos of workers building New York's skyscrapers, images the band had requested. "Thanks a lot," Bono said after the final run-through. Then he turned and looked at the image frozen on the video screens: a row of workmen sitting on a beam high over New York City, their backs to the camera. "That's a great shot," he said. "That's a great ending."

Afterward, Bono went into the control truck and watched a playback with Cates and Horvitz. At midnight, he stood in a hallway outside his dressing room. "The room is shit," he said bluntly. "I fucking *hate* the room. We're singing a song about poverty underneath a huge fucking Waterford crystal. But it doesn't look like that on TV, and the director, Lou, has none of the ego that directors can have. I just have to forget the room and let it go."

From behind his lightly tinted bubble glasses, Bono looked determined. "We know what to do," he said. "I haven't found a way yet, but I will."

BEN AFFLECK and Jennifer Lopez stood on the edge of the Kodak stage, their arms around each other. Looking into the audience, Affleck pointed out Harvey Weinstein's seat card, which identified the Miramax chief as one of the producers of *Gangs of New York*. "He was listed as a producer on *Shakespeare in Love*," said Affleck, who'd made *Good Will Hunting* for Miramax. "He puts his name on movies he doesn't produce."

By Saturday, focus inside the Kodak had shifted to the day's parade of stars: to Affleck and Lopez, who barely left each other's sight and rarely kept their hands off each other; to a disconcertingly effervescent Renée Zellweger, who kept up a steady line of chatter the entire time she was in the building; to the young Mexican star Gael García Bernal, who left a trail of giddy women in his wake.

So did the Irish actor Colin Farrell, who arrived sporting a blue knit cap and a T-shirt that read YOU OUGHT TO BE IN PICTURES, BECAUSE EVERY-THING YOU DO IS A BIG PRODUCTION. Farrell's copresenter was the star of *Frida*, Salma Hayek, who was similarly dressed down in a long-sleeved T-shirt and charcoal sweatpants. As she stood in the wings waiting for her turn onstage, Hayek picked up one of the dummy Oscar statues and examined it closely. "He doesn't have a penis," she said.

"He does," insisted stage manager Dency Nelson, "but it's hidden behind his sword."

Sitting in the third row of the Kodak, Capucine Lyons had a big grin on her face. "You know who the sexiest man alive is?" said Cates's young assistant. "Colin Farrell. Every woman in the office got weak in the knees when he came in. And he stopped in midsentence to say hello to me."

Near the green room, Herman was similarly stricken. "I have a new favorite," the veteran talent booker admitted. "Colin Farrell. He's a sweetheart, in addition to being *adorable*."

In Iraq, bombs continued to drop, and most of the networks kept up their nonstop coverage of the hostilities. But in the Kodak, with star day winding down and dress rehearsal looming, some of the monitors that had been showing combat footage were switched to a golf tournament. Staffers no longer gathered to watch CNN and see if events would affect the show; instead, they glanced at it as they worked, assuming that the Oscars would take place as scheduled. The show was being played out against a backdrop of rumors, and with the constant adjustments that needed to be made as presenters and reunion talent dropped out, but it had gathered what seemed to be an inexorable momentum.

BEFORE DRESS REHEARSAL, Cates took part in a conference call with ABC executives to discuss how to handle the war coverage during the Oscars. ABC's news division asked for four minutes of time in the show, to update viewers on any developments from Iraq. This, of course, meant that Cates had to shorten the show even more if he wanted to hand out the best-picture award before midnight. In addition, Alex Wallau wanted a hotline phone installed at his seat in the twelfth row of the Kodak, so that he could be notified in the case of events so momentous that the show would have to be taken off the air. The production staff was becoming increasingly frustrated with the network's demands, but they acquiesced.

Early in the rehearsal, Cates spotted *Chicago* director Rob Marshall, who was on hand to stage the musical number from his movie. The producer pulled a seat card from one of the chairs in the Kodak, went over to Marshall, and said, "Here, Rob, this'll make you feel better." He turned the card over and set it in front of Marshall. On it was the smiling face of Harvey Weinstein. Marshall grimaced and threw up his hands in mock horror.

Half an hour later, Julie Taymor and Elliot Goldenthal arrived. Taymor was the director of *Frida*; Goldenthal, her partner, was a double nominee for writing the score to that movie, and for cowriting the song "Burn It Blue." "Did you go to the party?" Cates asked them.

"Yeah, we were at the Miramax party," Taymor said. "It was boring. We did 'Burn It Blue.' We were the life of the party."

Cates laughed. "Harvey wanted to come to rehearsal," he said. "I told him no."

This was not the first time Weinstein had made a fuss over access to the Oscars. Miramax initially made a splash at the show in 1990, when Daniel Day-Lewis won the best-actor award for *My Left Foot*, Brenda Fricker won the supporting-actress Oscar for the same film, and *Cinema Paradiso* picked up best foreign film. That year, Day-Lewis had given his extra front-row ticket to Alison Brantley, who worked in acquisitions for Miramax—but according to Peter Biskind's book *Down and Dirty Pictures*, Harvey and Bob Weinstein had tried everything possible to wrest the prime seat from Brantley so that Harvey could use it.

This time, Harvey already had a good seat—fourth row, on the center aisle, right behind Scorsese and across the aisle from Marshall. But in his year of Oscar triumph, Weinstein also wanted to drop in on rehearsals. He'd had assistants call on his behalf, then made a personal appeal to Cates, who explained that the policy was not to allow studio heads at rehearsal. Weinstein didn't back down until Cates suggested that it wouldn't look good for Weinstein to be granted special access, given the furor over Robert Wise's Miramax-ghosted endorsement of Scorsese.

Late in the rehearsal, Steve Martin took the stage to test a new joke. "We just realized something about that," he said, pointing at the giant globe that was hanging, and slowly rotating, above the seats where the biggest stars in Hollywood would be sitting. "It's not supposed to spin," said Martin in mock concern. "We think it's *unscrewing*."

During the next break, Cates approached his host with a big grin. "That's the best joke of the show," he said. "The audience is going to be aware of the globe spinning up there all night long, and then you'll say it's unscrewing . . ." He grinned. "It'll be a great moment."

After the reunion of past winners, Martin returned to the stage and told the audience how thrilling the segment had been—"though backstage smells a little like Grandma's house," he added.

In the audience, some staffers and guests groaned. Martin stopped. "Yea or nay?" he said. "Let's see a show of hands."

He proceeded to poll the crowd. "Yea?"

Big applause.

"Nay?"

Silence.

"Oh, you're just afraid," scoffed Martin.

By the end of the dress rehearsal, the mood was one of exhaustion, mixed with irritation. Still, Bruce Davis proclaimed himself happy. "I'm tremendously relieved," he said. "We just have to be aware that ABC News has the option of taking four minutes of news promo time—and you know they're going to take the whole fucking thing. That's $5 million worth of promotion, and Peter Jennings is not going to give it up."

Cates then headed to the control truck, where Seligman, Horvitz, and Hamlin were waiting. "It's coming along," said Seligman. "3:26:30 is what I timed it at, and that includes people speaking in every category."

SUNDAY MORNING, some top Oscar staffers received calls alerting them to a tug-of-war still taking place within ABC. According to the caller, Michael Eisner, head of the network's parent company, the Walt Disney Company, had been golfing that morning with his chief operating officer, Robert Iger; during the round, Eisner announced that he wanted the Oscars canceled. Iger reportedly talked his boss out of it.

Frank Pierson, meanwhile, heard from Warren Beatty. "He called me and said he'd consulted with a number of his friends, including Jack Nicholson," said Pierson. "He said, 'Do you really think we should go ahead with this?' And I said, 'Yes, I don't see any reason not to.' " But Pierson was also feeling pressure from circles far to the east of Beverly Hills, from no less than George W. Bush's chief political strategist. "I do know," he said flatly, "that Karl Rove was calling from the White House to some people, pushing for us to cancel."

Determined to ignore those urgings, the production crew pressed on with rehearsal.

During the second full run-through on Sunday afternoon, Martin sat in the audience with his writers when he wasn't onstage. At one point, he turned to Dave Barry, Rita Rudner, and Andy Breckman. "Gil has made a case for cutting 'Grandma's house,' " he said.

When Martin left, Breckman turned to Barry and complained, "There's no edge at all to this show."

In the truck, Horvitz guided the final stages of the rehearsal. "With a little bit of luck," Cates said to Seligman as the rehearsal wound down, "this show could be something like 3:25. Which would be fucking fantastic."

"It would be great," agreed Seligman.

"If nothing else," said Cates, "it would make sure we got hired another year."

As the crew reset for the past winners' segment, Cates looked at the CNN monitor. "What's going on in the war?" he asked. He put on a headset connected to the news channel, listened for a few minutes, and then took off the headphones. "It's all babble," he said. "It's fucking babble."

He turned to Horvitz. "Just one comment," he said. "If someone makes a speech that's very political, cover both sides. Like you did with Elia Kazan, so we don't get accused of favoring one side. If somebody says something political, show both sides."

UPSTAIRS IN THE LUNCH AREA half an hour later, Cates allowed himself a few minutes to relax. "The only way I'd call it off now," he said, "is if a nuke goes off."

With the war temporarily restricted to the background, the producer began to speculate about the night's winners. "I'm sensing a lot of support for Roman Polanski," he said.

"You don't think it'll be all *Chicago*?" asked Vilanch.

"I don't know," said Cates. "Lately, it seems like everybody I've talked to has told me they voted for Polanski. I think *Chicago*'s still going to win best picture, but it wouldn't surprise me if Polanski wins best director."

As show time approached, John Travolta and Robert Duvall discussed diets in the green room. Jack Nicholson and Nicolas Cage stepped out the back door onto the loading dock for a cigarette. Renée Zellweger joined them, but didn't smoke. A semicircle of crew members stood about fifteen feet away, just watching.

With five minutes to go, Zellweger left the loading dock and headed for her seat. Just before she went through the final door into the Kodak, she stopped. "Wait!" she said to the page escorting her. "Do I have time to call my mom?" Without waiting for an answer, she pulled out a cell phone and dialed. "Hi, we're just about to go in," she said into the phone. "I just wanted to call to tell you how much I love you!" She paused. "Thanks, Mom! Thanks, Dad! Okay, we have to go in now!"

5:30 P.M., PACIFIC STANDARD TIME: *"Since 1928, the Hollywood community has gathered together to honor the finest motion picture achievements of the year."*

The show began not with the usual red-carpet recap, but with a shot inside the theater. A boom camera panned past the giant globe—which, during the opening fanfare, had suddenly stopped turning. The letters that spelled out OSCAR 75 were on the opposite side from Horvitz's camera. Almost immediately, the staff realized that there'd be no way to fix the problem during the show.

"Well," said Martin, looking around the theater, "I'm glad they cut back on all the glitz." The audience laughed nervously. "By the way," he added, "the proceeds from tonight's telecast—and I think this is so great—will be divvied up between huge corporations." This time, the laughter was heartier.

"This year, some people in Hollywood were insulted by the use of the term *gay mafia*," said Martin. "And I say to them . . ." Before the host could get to his punch line, a crew member stationed in the rafters high above the stage brushed up against a railing, dislodging a small two-way radio clipped to his belt. The radio fell to the back of the stage and noisily broke into pieces, one of which ricocheted toward Martin. The host stopped and looked back. "They seem to be *extremely* upset," he said. "And I say to them, 'Hey, fellas, don't get your thongs in a knot.' " Laughter was tepid at best. "Well, there's a lesson for you," Martin said. "It's not a good idea to throw a cell phone in the middle of a joke."

In the Kodak, the audience slowly loosened up during the monologue, as Martin moved from current events to the movie business. In the wings, Cameron Diaz watched on a monitor and laughed uproariously. "He is one funny motherfucker," she said.

As the show approached the half-hour mark, Jennifer Connelly introduced the nominees for best supporting actor. Warming up in the wings, the dancers in the *Chicago* number—many of whom had appeared in the movie—clapped for that film's John C. Reilly. The winner, though, was Chris Cooper for *Adaptation*. As he thanked his wife about forty-five seconds into his speech, Cooper began to tear up. "In light of all the troubles in this world," he said, "I wish us all *peace*."

When Cooper and Connelly left the stage, she declined to follow protocol and accompany him to the press rooms. Instead, she headed back to the green room. "That wasn't too bad," Connelly told a friend. "Painless."

As the show cut to a commercial, the TV audience saw a close-up of the globe. It was spinning, because this time they were viewing bumper footage shot the previous day.

At 6:10, ABC News cut away from the Oscars for a two-minute newsbreak. Peter Jennings said that American forces were less than one hundred miles from Baghdad but were experiencing heavy resistance, and that fifteen U.S. soldiers were believed to have been killed during the day. "I'm Peter Jennings," he concluded. "Back to the Oscars."

A few minutes later, Catherine Zeta-Jones won the best supporting actress Oscar for *Chicago*, that film's third win of the night. "My hormones are just too way out of control to be dealing with this," she said.

Leaving the stage with her Oscar, Zeta-Jones ran into Zellweger in the hallway. "Way to go, baby!" shouted Zellweger. "Well done!" Zeta-Jones was hustled toward the elevator that would take her to her dressing room on the lower floor, unaware that her husband was in a rest room only a few feet away.

In the green room, Julia Roberts told staffers that she didn't want to read the introduction that had been written for the cinematography category. To be sure, her lines were lengthy and a bit florid: they began with "Cinematography is the art and science of putting the moving in moving pictures," and included the notion that the job involved "the art of lighting shadows and shadowing lights." Roberts said she preferred to simply read the list of nominees. Cates huddled with Kohan in the wings, and then sent the writer into the green room to speak with Roberts.

Onstage, Gael García Bernal introduced the performance of "Burn It Blue" with some lines that weren't on the TelePrompTer. "The necessity for peace in the world is not a dream, it is a reality, and we are not alone," he said. "If Frida was alive, she would be on our side, against war."

Outside the green room, Diane Lane retouched her makeup, then joined Zellweger in line outside the rest rooms. A minute later, Hilary Swank walked up. "Is this a line?" she asked.

"We're the line, honey!" said Lane.

The rest room door opened and Julie Andrews walked out. Zellweger, Lane, and Swank burst out laughing.

"Yes," said Andrews, "Mary Poppins really does go to the bathroom."

An hour after its first newsbreak, ABC News took a second. This one was less than one minute long, and repetitive: a hundred miles from Baghdad, heavy resistance, fifteen dead. "The war grinds on," said Jennings.

Back at the Kodak, Zellweger was still outside the rest rooms when Julianne Moore came offstage. "Is there somewhere I can get a drink?" she asked the page who was escorting her.

"You can go to the green room," said the page.

"No, I don't think they have real drinks," said Moore. "I think they just have water. I want a beer or something."

"My girlfriend brought cans of malt liquor," offered Zellweger.

"I'm right there with her," said Moore with a laugh.

"She's my most white trash girlfriend," said Zellweger. "She goes to all these events and wears a dress and carries a can of malt liquor."

The show approached the two-hour mark without much in the way of political speechmaking, but Michael Moore changed all that when he won the feature documentary award for his incendiary *Bowling for Columbine*. As Moore walked to the stage accompanied by all the other nominees in his category, the audience greeted the filmmaker with a standing ovation. Moore told the audience that the other nominees "are here in solidarity with me," and then launched into a denunciation of the U.S. policy in Iraq. "We like nonfiction," he said, "and we live in fictitious times. We live in a time when we have fictitious election results that elect a fictitious president."

Cheers for Moore continued, but one audience member shouted, "No!" and a smattering of boos began to come from the back of the theater.

"We have a man sending us to war for fictitious reasons!" Moore shouted, as the boos grew to about the same volume as the cheers. "We are against the war, Mr. Bush! Shame on you, Mr. Bush!"

In the wings of the stage, stagehands began shouting at Moore. "That's bullshit!" yelled one.

"Get him *off*!" shouted another.

Vilanch, who'd been standing in the wings stage right, looked at the angry stagehands and made an immediate beeline for the other side of the stage.

In the truck, Horvitz cut to a line of stars, most of whom were reacting with stone faces as the boos grew louder. Worried about the growing tension in the hall, Cates ordered Horvitz to cue the orchestra.

As the music began to play, Moore shouted out one more line. "Anytime you've got the pope and the Dixie Chicks against you, your time is up!" he yelled, before leaving the stage to a mixture of applause and derision.

Before Moore could go to the press rooms, Diane Lane pulled the director aside. "That was very inspirational," she said. "Thank you."

A few minutes later, Steve Martin returned to the stage with the line that had just been crafted by his team of writers in the wings. "It was so sweet backstage, you should see it," he said. "The teamsters are helping Michael Moore into the trunk of his limo."

Martin then introduced Julia Roberts. "It is my honor to present the Academy Award for cinematography," Roberts said, before heading straight for the area that most infuriated the cinematographers' branch: "I find this a personally fantastic award, because I happen to know what I look like at five o'clock in the morning when I go to work."

During a commercial break at 7:30, the members of U2 walked through the wings on their way to the stage. Bono spotted Roberts, grabbed her arm, and began nuzzling her neck. She beamed. On the other side of the stage door, many of the past Oscar winners began to gather.

When U2 performed "The Hands That Built America," Bono changed the lines that had initially dealt with September 11. Instead of "a dark cloud on the New York skyline," he introduced a timelier image. "Late in spring," he sang softly. "Yellow cloud on a desert skyline / Some father's son / Is it his or is it mine?"

After U2, Susan Sarandon took the stage to introduce the In Memoriam segment. On her way to the podium, she flashed a peace sign. Backstage, Peter O'Toole walked into the green room. Mickey Rooney jumped up and stuck out his hand. "I've wanted to meet you for years," Rooney said. A timer in the wings indicated that the goal of a three-and-a-half hour show was within reach.

In an upset that drew an immediate standing ovation from the crowd, Adrien Brody won the best-actor award for *The Pianist*. He seized presenter Halle Berry in a passionate embrace and kiss, and then faced the audience, dazed. "There comes a time in life when everything seems to make sense," he said. "This is not one of those times."

Two and a half minutes into Brody's speech, Conti's orchestra began to play. "One second, one second, one second, please," Brody implored. "Cut it out." In the truck, Cates told Horvitz to stop the music, and Brody went on to decry "the sadness and the dehumanization" of war. "Whether you believe in God or Allah, may he watch over you, and let's pray for a peaceful and swift resolution," he said.

Immediately after Brody left the stage, Dustin Hoffman introduced a film clip from *The Pianist*. Outside the green room, Julia Roberts looked at all the past winners who had gathered there. "I'm overwhelmed," she said softly to Louise Fletcher and Eva Marie Saint.

Onstage, Barbra Streisand awarded the best-song Oscar to the one nominee who had neither performed nor attended, Eminem. "This all goes to Marshall," said cowriter Luis Resto, who was wearing a long jacket over a Detroit Pistons basketball jersey. "He's a good man, good heart."

As he spoke, Peter Margolis addressed the past winners backstage. "Could everybody line up on your numbers, please?" he said. They began to form long rows.

Adrien Brody came out of the green room. The past winners saw him and began applauding. "Bravo!" shouted Karl Malden. "Welcome to the club, Brody!"

During the next commercial break, the doors to the loading dock were opened and the three large risers for the past winners were pushed to the stage. "Okay," said Margolis to Herman, "now the last people get pulled, and then we walk."

The last arrivals were Daniel Day-Lewis, Jennifer Connelly, Jack Nicholson, Kathy Bates, Sean Connery, and Nicolas Cage. Meryl Streep waited in line outside the bathroom. When the door opened, Brody emerged. Streep screamed, opened her arms wide, and embraced him. "Yeahhh!" she yelled. "It was wonderful!"

As Herman ran back and forth, checking the line and helping round up new winners, Denzel Washington gave Nicole Kidman the best-actress Oscar. "Why do you come to the Academy Awards when the world is in such turmoil?" said a teary Kidman. "Because art is important, and because you believe in what you do and you want to honor that."

In the wings, the past winners began to walk to the stage. Luise Rainer moved very slowly. Julia Roberts stopped, held her hand, and walked with her every step of the way.

Kidman came into the wings, dazed. "I don't know what I said," she said.

"Congratulations," Dency Nelson told her. "Now stay right here. As a winner tonight, you get to join this group." He pointed to the past winners. "So stay right here, collect yourself, and enjoy."

Onstage, Olivia de Havilland introduced the group of fifty-nine past Oscar winners. As the camera panned from one face to another, time seemed suspended in the truck. "Lose it," Horvitz said. "Pan. Announce roll. And lose it. Pan. Announce roll . . ." The cadences went on and on for more than eight minutes, but it seemed much longer.

In the wings, Kidman walked in small circles, fanning herself with the envelope that bore her name. She hugged Zeta-Jones, then Brody, losing an earring in the process. Brody dropped to his hands and knees, retrieved it, and handed it back to her. She put it on, then poked Zeta-Jones in the stomach. "Oscar baby," she said. A few feet away, the night's other acting winner, Chris Cooper, stood by himself quietly.

A timer now estimated that the show wouldn't end until 12:06 a.m., East Coast time.

When the roll call of past winners finally ended, Horvitz sighed. "That's a Zen moment, let me tell you," he said. "It'll lull you right out of it if you're not careful."

In the middle of the next act, Martin introduced Marcia Gay Harden. Then he walked into the wings. It was 8:39. Garry Hood approached Martin, a show rundown in hand. "You're not going to believe this," he told the host, "but your next item is good nights."

With twenty-one minutes left until midnight on the East Coast, four awards and six minutes of commercials remained. In the truck, thoughts of the war had been banished; the struggle to find an appropriate tone for the show was forgotten. One thing mattered: handing out that last award before midnight.

First, Marcia Gay Harden gave the award for adapted screenplay to Ronald Harwood for *The Pianist*. "Roman Polanski deserves this," said Harwood, to a huge round of applause.

In a small foyer stage left, Peter O'Toole waited for an elevator to take him to the press rooms. He spotted a bucket full of water bottles and frowned. "Any booze?" he asked.

"There's some in the press room, sir," his escort said.

A minute later, Pedro Almodóvar won the original-screenplay Oscar for *Talk to Her*. The Spanish director, who three years earlier had been furious at Lili Zanuck for cutting off his three-minute speech when he won for best foreign film, this time spoke for only one minute. He dedicated the award to "all the people that are raising their voices in favor of peace, respect of human rights, democracy, and international legality," then apologized for going overtime.

During the last commercial break, it was 8:51. For the show to come in at less than three and a half hours, the final act would have to be a short one. In the truck, Cates leaned forward. "Whatever you can do to hustle it would be good," he told Horvitz.

When the break ended, Harrison Ford took the stage to hand out the best-director award. Horvitz whipped through his changes, stopping the music quickly and cuing Ford to read the nominees. An assistant director leaned to a microphone and reminded the cameramen, "One no-show in this, Roman Polanski."

Ford opened the envelope. "And the Oscar goes to Roman Polanski for *The Pianist*," he said.

"Wow," said John Hamlin, who was sitting in the truck. Cates nodded and smiled. No acceptance speech meant he had his three-and-a-half-hour show.

As the audience stood and cheered for the exiled director, Horvitz shouted cues for reaction shots at breakneck speed. "Ready twelve, twelve! Ready eleven, eleven! Ready ten, ten! Read it, Harrison! Show it to him!"

"Roman Polanski cannot be here tonight," read Ford off the TelePromp-Ter, "but the Academy congratulates him and accepts this award on his behalf."

"Music!" shouted Horvitz. Cates grinned and gave two thumbs-ups.

When Kirk and Michael Douglas took the stage for the final award, the elder Douglas began talking in a slow, halting manner. "It's okay," Cates said to Horvitz. "We're fine on time."

Kirk Douglas opened the final envelope and saw that the best-picture winner was *Chicago*. He ripped the card in two and handed half to his son. They'd rehearsed this the day before, though they planned to do it only if the right movie—the one that featured Michael's wife and Kirk's daughter-in-law—won. The two men put the pieces together, and then shouted, in unison, *"Chicago!"*

"Fantastic!" Horvitz yelled.

Producer Martin Richards, a seventy-one-year-old veteran of the

Broadway stage, took the final Oscar and began to speak. Horvitz directed his cameramen to get reaction shots. "Camera twelve," he said, "get Harvey!" When Richards thanked Weinstein, Horvitz cut to the beaming Miramax chief.

After stumbling through a minute and a half of thank-yous, Richards stopped. "God, I'm forgetting someone," he said.

In the truck, Cates grew impatient. "Oh, come on, you old fart," he said. He leaned toward Horvitz. "Start a little music, quietly," he said.

"Oh, yes, one thing!" said Richards.

"Stop," said Cates quickly. "No music."

"I couldn't end it without thanks to my two angels who sat on my shoulders all the time," said Richards, who didn't name those angels. He ended his speech without music, then walked off.

At one minute to midnight on the East Coast, Steve Martin returned to the stage. "To our young men and women who are watching overseas, we are thinking of you," he said. "We hope you enjoyed the show, it was for you."

As the credits rolled, applause ran through the truck. Cheers rang out when Cates's and Horvitz's names appeared on the screen. Bob Dickinson shook Cates's hand. "Congratulations," he said. "I was proud to be here. And I think it was great live television."

Leaving the auditorium, Pierson found himself walking alongside Michael Moore. "Did I make an ass out of myself up there?" asked Moore.

"No, Michael," said Pierson to the normally rumpled filmmaker, who'd actually worn a tux for the occasion. "I want to thank you for coming—and I particularly want to thank you for wearing a tie."

AT THE GOVERNORS BALL, Pierson thanked Martin and Cates. Then he tried out a variation on his line to Moore, this time thanking the Oscar winner "for wearing a suit." A few partygoers booed.

The next day, police said they had arrested twelve people at both pro- and antiwar demonstrations on the streets surrounding Hollywood & Highland.

That same day, Barbra Streisand gave *Daily Variety* a copy of the speech she said she would have liked to deliver at the Oscar show—but didn't, said the paper, because she was "respecting the wishes of the producers of the Oscar ceremony." Her remarks offered prayers for American servicemen, faulted the Bush administration for its failed attempts at diplomacy, and celebrated the freedom to offer dissenting views.

"It was a very powerful night," said Danette Herman afterward. "There was a very interesting connection that happened. Steve gave people permission to feel comfortable about being at the show, and everybody that was there had a sense of purpose about being there."

While reviews were split on the balancing act of a wartime Oscars, the choices of Academy voters grabbed attention from the show itself. Belying the organization's image as a stodgy, conservative institution, Oscar voters had made unexpectedly daring choices in several categories. Adrien Brody for best actor, Roman Polanski for best director, Pedro Almodóvar for best original screenplay (for a script that wasn't written in English!), Eminem for best song, even the stylish piece of Japanese anime *Spirited Away* over the homegrown major studio films *Ice Age* and *Lilo & Stitch* in the animated-film category. The fact that in many cases these were probably the correct choices did not lessen the surprise.

The ratings, though, were not good. With an average viewership of just over thirty-three million—a drop-off of more than 20 percent over the previous year's lackluster totals—it was the smallest audience ever recorded for an Oscar show. Few blamed the Academy or the producer for the numbers: the war had given CNN and Fox News almost four times their usual number of viewers.

In previous years, even when its ratings fell the Oscar show had still been the most-watched entertainment program of the year. In 2003, however, it couldn't even beat the numbers from the final episode of Fox's tawdry reality show *Joe Millionaire*.

Michael Moore received much attention in the weeks following the show. The filmmaker published his own version of the night's events on his Web site, claiming that everyone down front was clapping, and that all the boos came from the Kodak's balconies. The Oscar review committee did not agree with Moore, but it also realized that the television broadcast didn't accurately capture the sound of the audience. At future Oscar shows, the committee decided, a microphone should be mounted in a position that would allow it to accurately capture crowd noise.

In April, the Academy issued its timetable for the Oscar show in 2004— and as expected, the show was moved from late March to February 29. The purpose, essentially, was to boost ratings—both by placing the show into February's Sweeps Month, in which the networks try to attract larger audiences through a variety of special programs and stunts, and by placing the Oscars closer to the year in which the competing movies were released.

"There was a growing feeling that we had been awfully polite waiting until the end of March, while every year it seemed like there was a new set of film awards in ahead of us," said Bruce Davis. "Everybody still concedes that we're the most important show, but in terms of expecting the public to get excited, if you've seen Julia Roberts win that award three other times before Oscar night, it's hard to go 'Wow!' "

The date change was frequently interpreted as an attempt to reduce the length of Oscar campaigns, but Davis insisted that was not a factor. "That literally never came up in the discussion," he said. "And I don't even understand how that was supposed to work. It seems to me to be obvious that it would just start earlier or become more intense while it was going on."

Which is not to say that campaigning wasn't an issue within the Academy as well. "For the past ten years, we've been watching Academy campaign techniques that we felt unleveled the playing field," said former Academy president Richard Kahn, chairman of the Public Relations Branch Executive Committee. "And the seventy-fifth show was the apogee of ruthless Academy campaigning. It was something that appalled us."

Kahn's committee issued new guidelines—which were retitled *regulations* as a statement of purpose—in July, and sent an eight-page booklet summarizing those rules to all Academy members in September. After decrying the very existence of the phrase "Academy campaign," the regulations insisted that ads "be free of endorsements from Academy members," while campaigns "designed to engender sympathy votes on behalf of filmmakers because of the strength of their bodies of work" were deemed inappropriate. Extreme caution was recommended in hosting the ubiquitous Oscar-season parties that had become, the guidelines suggested, "one of the most distasteful aspects of the Awards process."

Elsewhere, the regulations stated that members found to be in violation could be suspended or expelled from the Academy, and that more serious violations could result in films losing their Oscar eligibility. And in a deliberate attempt to prevent zealous campaigners from obeying the letter of the law while flaunting its spirit, a paragraph late in the booklet specifically pointed out that the new rules did not pretend to address every possible infraction.

"Members presumably have their own moral compasses that let them know with reasonable reliability when they are playing Oscar's game fairly," it read. "It is essential for the well-being of our award that we monitor those compasses closely."

Richard Kahn conceded that the Academy's position opened it up to criticism, but he made no apologies. "We do take a rather puritanical view of Academy Awards campaigns," he said. "For years we liked to pretend they didn't exist, and when we found out about them we were like Inspector Renault in *Casablanca*—we were shocked, *shocked* to find it was going on. Now we are accused of being rather haughty, stiff-necked, and arrogant. But that is the stance we choose to take."

11

Young Blood

The 76th Academy Awards

"BEAR WITH ME ON THIS ONE," began Joe Roth, looking across the table at Danette Herman and Michael Seligman. The two Oscar vets, with fifty-three Academy Awards shows between them, exchanged a quick glance, then turned back to the producer who'd just begun to work on his first.

"I know I have lots of crazy ideas, but just listen," continued Roth. The director, producer, and studio chief sketched out his version of a new, improved Oscar seating chart: movie stars in the center section, nominees in half of the craft categories in the first couple of rows of the side sections. "When they win," he said, "they can get to the stage more quickly because they're already close to it."

Seligman and Herman nodded slowly, reserving judgment. "So, during one of our four-minute commercials halfway through the show," continued Roth, "we literally take all those people, the nominees in the first categories, and we move them to the back of the house. And we bring up the nominees for the categories we haven't presented yet. I bet you could save fifteen minutes of shoe leather. And they couldn't complain about having to move back,

Young Blood

because if we didn't do that they'd have to sit in the back for the whole show."

Seligman and Herman grimaced at the prospect of reseating close to one hundred sound editors, documentarians, costume designers, and their guests in the middle of a live television show. "I know it'd be a fun break, when we move people from the front to the back," admitted Roth. "That's when I'd go out for a smoke."

"One problem," suggested Herman gently, "is that the winners do press after they win. So when they came back to the theater, they'd have to find a different seat."

"And Lou will go crazy when you mess with his seating chart," added Seligman.

"No," corrected Herman. "He'll go *more* crazy."

"Well, it's something to think about," said Roth. "Let's talk to the Academy about this. Because I don't have the nerve to ask them if we could give out the documentary awards during a commercial break."

JOE ROTH HAD IDEAS, and he had energy, and he certainly had connections. What he didn't have was any experience producing live television—or, for that matter, any desire to produce an Oscar show by all the old rules. But with the show's ratings on a precipitous decline, the Academy was ready for somebody with a new vision, particularly if that person also had the clout to lure stars who might normally avoid the Oscars.

The head of Revolution Studios, the former production head of 20th Century-Fox and Disney Studios, and a producer whose movies ranged from *Bachelor Party* and *Young Guns* in the 1980s to *Mona Lisa Smile* in 2003, Roth was fifty-five, but he looked and acted younger. Well liked by talent, he was a lean, unsentimental man who refused to stand on ceremony. He never wore ties or used e-mail, when necessary delegating the latter chore to an assistant so as to keep his reputation clean.

By early fall Roth was already planning the show, though he couldn't devote full time to it: he was still running Revolution, which had been experiencing a tough year with the monumental Ben Affleck–Jennifer Lopez flop *Gigli*, as well as with the disappointing returns for films like Ron Howard's grim Western *The Missing* and the poorly received buddy cop movie *Hollywood Homicide*.

Revolution's headquarters occupied a modern three-story building on Olympic Boulevard in Santa Monica. On the second floor, a wing that had recently been used for postproduction on the Revolution movie *Peter Pan* was being converted for use by the Oscar production crew. Directly above that space was Roth's office, which occupied a corner of the third floor. It was a comfortable, wood-paneled room well lit by a skylight above his desk and windows that covered most of two walls.

Roth's executive assistant, Angela Pierce, was on hand for a morning meeting; so were Seligman and Herman, the latter of whom had been given the title of coordinating producer after more than two dozen years working talent on the Oscars. Roth looked at the board on which the show had been laid out. "I really want young people," he said. "This may be selfish of me, but this is the only time I'm going to do the show, and I'd love for it to be a show with ten or fifteen really hot young stars."

After he took the job, Roth had asked ABC for a demographic breakdown of the last few Oscar telecasts, and the figures disturbed him. In addition to the fact that the ratings had been in a slow, steady decline for close to a decade— with the exception of a few big shows, the *Titanic* year foremost among them—the audience had been growing older and more female. Roth was de-termined to change that by making the show younger, faster, and funnier, though he'd also gone back to Billy Crystal, who hadn't hosted the show for four years. "The most important thing is to get a young enough group of pre-senters," he said, "and to get people like Jack Black for the boys."

The new producer was also determined to revamp the promotion for the show, which in the past had often consisted of ads on ABC, morning show appearances on the same network, and a trailer in movie theaters shortly be-fore the show. At the urging of Roth and some members of the board of governors—including Gil Cates—the Academy spent $1.5 million to buy ad time on a variety of cable channels that had never before run Oscar spots. They also made a deal to run the Oscar trailer in Blockbuster video stores for the first time, and gave Oprah Winfrey access to rehearsals and produc-tion meetings for a series on her show.

"I don't want to do all that work and have nobody watch," Roth told Seligman. "I want to know that they've got a whole promo package going to get the demos hipper and younger."

One of the key factors in that promotion was the Oscar trailer. "The Academy sent this over with three different songs attached to it," Roth said as Pierce cued up the tape and turned on a plasma screen monitor.

The trailer consisted of a barrage of familiar Oscar clips, ranging from Billy Crystal's entrance as Hannibal Lecter to Whoopi Goldberg in Queen Elizabeth whiteface. Dropped throughout the barrage of quick clips were phrases like "It's Oscar night," "Anything goes," and the unofficial motto of the show, "Expect the unexpected." The three versions were identical except for the music. One was set to "Hey Ya," a new single from the acclaimed rap group Outkast, one to Madonna's "Hollywood" ("Everybody comes to Hollywood / They're gonna make it in the neighborhood"), and one to Pink's anthem "Get the Party Started," which had been the National Basketball Association's theme song a year earlier.

"I told them," said Roth after the clips ended, "that I love the first song, I'm going to quit the show if they use the second song, and the third song is okay but it's been used ten thousand times. So we're trying to clear the Outkast song."

Seligman and Herman stared, trying to figure out just how serious their new boss was. "You guys haven't worked with me before, but that's the way I am," he laughed. "Like I said, I have lots of crazy ideas."

He turned to Seligman. "I even had a great idea for Billy's entrance, but you shot me down, Michael."

"What did I shoot down?" asked Seligman.

"Well," explained Roth, "remember, Mel Gibson's movie *The Passion* comes out the week of the show. Don't you think it's going to be on everybody's mind?"

Seligman groaned, and Roth forged on. "So I say, bring Billy out in a loin cloth, carried on a cross through the Academy."

THE ACCELERATED OSCAR schedule was already putting a pinch on voters who wanted to see many of the 254 eligible films. With a few exceptions, studios had long been holding their top Oscar contenders for the last few weeks of the year, particularly after past years in which early front-runners like *Saving Private Ryan* had had trouble maintaining momentum. But with nominating ballots due at PricewaterhouseCoopers by January 17, the schedule didn't leave much time for voters to catch up with all the contenders.

Films that in normal years might have been released in late December began to trickle out earlier. Clint Eastwood's grim tragedy *Mystic River*, which drew raves for a cast that included Sean Penn, Tim Robbins, Kevin Bacon, Laura Linney, and Marcia Gay Harden, was released in October, and immediately seized something of a front-runner status. *Lost in Translation*, a quietly unnerving movie from director Francis Ford Coppola's daughter, Sofia, came out in limited release the same month, drawing attention as the film that might finally win an Oscar nomination for the perennially over-looked Bill Murray.

Also in October, Jack Valenti, the president of the Motion Picture Association of America, announced that the MPAA's member studios would no longer send out DVDs or cassettes, dubbed "screeners." The move was designed to combat the proliferation of pirated movies on the black market and on the Internet, where many were routinely available for download before they even hit theaters. But independent studios immediately cried foul, charging that the move was designed less to prevent piracy than to freeze out the smaller films that had been doing surprisingly well at Oscar time. Since at least 1978, when airings of Woody Allen's *Annie Hall* on Los Angeles's Z channel were considered instrumental in that movie's best-picture win, lower-budget films had been relying on alternative avenues to draw the attention of the electorate; in recent years, *The Pianist* and *Monster's Ball* were among the films that had depended heavily on screeners. A slate of prominent directors, including Robert Altman, Robert Redford, Francis Ford Coppola, and Joel Coen, wrote an open letter to Valenti protesting a ban they felt would kill the Oscar chances of independent, risky films.

The Academy originally took no position on the MPAA ban, but Frank Pierson contacted Valenti when he saw that the credibility of the Oscars might be at stake. The men worked out a compromise in which Academy members who signed an agreement to not let the screeners out of their control would receive videocassettes. The deal infuriated members of the various critics' groups and smaller awards shows, all of whom were excluded from receiving screeners. A coalition of independent producers, meanwhile, went to court to end the ban. On Friday, December 5, they succeeded when a federal judge in New York City ruled that the MPAA's ban violated federal antitrust laws.

Still, most observers figured that the odds-on favorite was a film that didn't need any help from screeners, because it stood to be on thousands of screens by Christmas. While the first two movies in New Zealand director Peter Jackson's massive *Lord of the Rings* trilogy, *The Fellowship of the Ring* and *The Two Towers*, had both become blockbusters and received best-picture nominations, the films had won only in the technical categories. The Academy was not usually fond of fantasy films, none of which had ever been named best picture, but Jackson's achievement was hard to ignore—and the conventional wisdom had long been suggesting that Oscar voters were waiting for the final film, *The Lord of the Rings: The Return of the King*, to reward Jackson for the entire series.

But that movie wouldn't be out until mid-December. In the meantime, members made do with videocassette screeners, and with an accelerated slate of advance screenings that swamped L.A.'s prime screening rooms.

One of the few movies that didn't get caught in the crunch was *Seabiscuit*, director Gary Ross's adaptation of the Laura Hillenbrand best-seller about a legendary racehorse in the 1930s. Released into theaters in July and on video in December, *Seabiscuit* was the only top contender widely available on DVD. Universal spent lavishly to keep *Seabiscuit* fresh in voters' minds, and the studio also made the most of the DVD release by throwing a party at the Beverly Hills Hotel's storied Polo Lounge. The Academy had tried to crack down on parties in which lobbying opportunities were disguised as social occasions, but a soiree to celebrate a DVD release was well within its new, stricter guidelines. Even as members waited to see how the screener wars would play out, DVD copies of *Seabiscuit* were available to any voter with $19.99 or a Blockbuster rental card.

"JUST TO TELL YOU, Michael," Roy Christopher said to Seligman, "we got our first bid in on the Oscar statues."

The veteran production designer grinned. He was used to Seligman pushing him to keep costs down—though for the seventy-fifth Oscar show, with its balky spinning globe, his budget had hit the $1 million mark for the first time. The seventy-sixth show figured to be less expensive, but its futuristic collection of panels and platforms was complicated by the use of forced perspective, which meant that seven Oscar statues ranging in height from ten to twenty-two feet had to be specially made.

"They have to be bent a little bit," Christopher said. "The first bid was a quarter of a million dollars."

Seligman didn't say anything, but the stunned look on his face spoke volumes.

"Do you want to sit down, Michael?" asked Roth.

"We're getting other bids," said Christopher quickly.

"Good," said Seligman.

"It's okay," shrugged Roth. "We'll end up doing them in Manila."

By this point, mid-December, some of Roth's ideas had fallen by the wayside as the producer discovered the limitations of the Oscar format. His plan to move nominees midway through the show, for instance, didn't get far: "It turns out," he said, "that it wouldn't have saved much time after all."

But Roth was still determined to make the show young, fast, and funny. Comedians Jack Black and Will Ferrell were among the earliest bookings, and Roth held out a slim hope that Black, star of the rock 'n' roll comedy *School of Rock*, could sing a medley of all five nominated songs. He'd also been avidly but so far fruitlessly pursuing the likes of Orlando Bloom, Keira Knightley, and Johnny Depp to appear on the show.

The task was complicated by the fact that he didn't know what would be nominated, though the board in his office contained some guesses. The board listed *The Return of the King* as a sure nominee, along with *Mystic River* and Peter Weir's seagoing saga, *Master and Commander*. The fourth slot was held for either Miramax's prime Oscar entry, Anthony Minghella's Civil War drama *Cold Mountain*, or *Seabiscuit*. A slate of contenders for the last spot included *Lost in Translation*, the Tom Cruise movie *The Last Samurai*, and the animated *Finding Nemo*. (Two Revolution movies, *Mona Lisa Smile* and *The Missing*, had once been listed as possibilities, but their cards had since been removed from the board.)

"One way to introduce the best pictures," said Roth as he looked at the board, "is to go very straight. Pacino for *Lost in Translation*, Ian McKellen for *Lord of the Rings*, Oprah for *Cold Mountain* or *Seabiscuit* or *Mystic River*."

"Jim Carrey is so clever, he could do one of them," said Herman. "Last year, he wanted to do a picture clip. Depending on what gets nominated, as long as he didn't make fun of it, he could have fun with *Master and Commander*, or *Last Samurai*, or even *Lord of the Rings*."

"It's a bit of a fine line," agreed Roth. "Where could he goof around?"

"He could goof around within reason on all of them," said Herman. "If we put him on *Master and Commander* or *Last Samurai*, who are the directors?"

"Peter Weir and Ed Zwick," said Roth.

"Do either of them have a sense of humor?"

"No," Roth said quickly. "Neither does Minghella, neither does Gary Ross, neither does Eastwood."

Roth stood up, slipped out of his shoes, and walked around the back of his chair, examining the names of the films in contention. "Universal is spending as much money as everybody else combined to get *Seabiscuit* nominated," he said. "And now *Cold Mountain* will start."

That last film had yet to be released, but Miramax was building up word-of-mouth through advance screenings. "Harvey has once again done a brilliant job of waiting for the field to play out," Roth said with a sigh. "He waited until everything else was out, and then he'll put out *Cold Mountain* and grab the momentum. He didn't show it early, he's putting it out on Christmas Day, and they'll go into January as the hot movie. I still think we're looking at a *Lord of the Rings* sweep—but who knows? Maybe he'll steal it again like he stole it with *Shakespeare in Love*."

IN MOST CATEGORIES, Oscar nominations were made by a vote of the members in the appropriate branch. Things were different for foreign films and documentaries, where committees made the choice. And in three categories—visual effects, makeup, and sound editing—the decision came down to a process popularly known as the bakeoff.

The bakeoffs were held the week of January 18 at the Academy's Samuel Goldwyn Theater. On January 21, the visual effects program was due to start at 7:30, but by 7:00 much of the theater was already full; the dominant gender in the room was male, the primary clothing color black. Each of the seven finalists had five minutes to introduce up to fifteen minutes of persuasive film clips, followed by a short Q&A session. The finalists had been chosen from a field of nineteen contenders by an executive committee, which was made up of thirty-four members from the visual effects branch. One of the entries, though, boasted not only the most realistic computer-generated character ever created, but also as many special effects shots as most of the other finalists combined. "Why don't they just give *Lord of the Rings* a special achievement award, and everybody else can go home?" asked one bemused member.

But that wasn't how a bakeoff worked—and within the Academy, everybody knew about movies that had either hurt or helped their chances with bakeoff presentations. The previous year, for instance, *The Planet of the Apes* had been inexplicably passed over for a makeup nomination in favor of *Frida* and *The Time Machine*, movies that reportedly made snappier presentations.

The Pirates of the Caribbean: The Curse of the Black Pearl was up first, with a reel that zipped through the entire movie, cutting from one effects shot to another: Johnny Depp stepping off the mast of his sinking ship, cannons bombarding a city, a pirate with a skeleton hand, a ship in a storm, more ghostly pirates . . . Afterward, Edlund asked the film's special effects coordinator, Terry Frazee, if he had any interesting stories from the production. "No, Richard, no interesting stories," said Frazee. "Just hard work."

For the next two hours, six more films strutted their stuff. The *Master and Commander* crew did an exceptionally good job of pointing out how difficult it was to make a computer-generated ocean seem real, while *The Return of the King*'s reel was predictably overwhelming. *Peter Pan* had the unenviable task of following that epic with its whimsical small-scale effects, which were immediately overshadowed by a presentation that conclusively proved that *Terminator 3* lost virtually nothing in the transition from a two-hour movie to a fifteen-minute special effects reel. *X-2* and *The Hulk* rounded out the night, and then the voters had to work quickly: the PricewaterhouseCoopers reps on hand only stayed for fifteen minutes before collecting the ballots and leaving.

THE DAY AFTER THE BAKEOFF, police arrested Russell Sprague in the Chicago suburb of Homewood, Illinois. For years, investigators said, Sprague had been receiving Oscar screeners from Carmine Caridi, a sixty-nine-year-old character actor who lived in Los Angeles, and uploading those films to the Internet. Sprague was charged with criminal copyright infringement. At the next meeting of the board of governors, Caridi, who claimed he had no idea his friend was pirating the films, was expelled from the Academy.

JOE ROTH got up from his desk, walked across the room, and stuck his head out the door. "Try Jamie Lee," he said to his assistant, Colleen King. "Then Pat Kingsley, then Sean Penn on his cell phone."

Three and a half hours earlier, nominations had been announced. *The Lord of the Rings: The Return of the King* and *Master and Commander: The Far Side of the World* were the big winners, with eleven and ten nominations, respectively; *Mystic River*, *Lost in Translation*, and *Seabiscuit* rounded out the best-picture category. In what was immediately seen as an anti–Harvey Weinstein vote, *Cold Mountain* received nominations for Jude Law and Renée Zellweger, but was shut out of the best-picture and best-director competitions. Bill Murray got his best-actor nomination for *Lost in Translation*—and in an even bigger surprise, Johnny Depp landed one as well for his outrageous comic turn in *Pirates of the Caribbean*. Tom Cruise, considered a top candidate for *The Last Samurai*, was passed over, as was Russell Crowe, who once figured to be a shoo-in for *Master and Commander*. Sean Penn, who had drawn raves for both *Mystic River* and *21 Grams*, received a nomination for the former.

After speaking with Kingsley about Cruise and Depp, Roth reported to Herman, Seligman, Pierce, and musical director Marc Shaiman. "Pat's instinct is that Tom will skip the whole thing," he said. "But she knows we're offering best director, which is the second most prestigious category, so she'll talk to him. Johnny Depp, she said he's got to be there. But if we want him to present, he did it once before and he had a horrible time and said he'd never do it again."

King stuck her head in the office. "Joe, Sean Penn on line one."

Roth picked up the phone to speak to the four-time nominee, who had never before attended the Oscar ceremony. "Sean, congratulations!" he began. "If you ask me, you should have been nominated for two movies, not one, but I guess they don't do that." He listened for a minute, then continued. "So we're hoping that you'll be there, and I'd love to let people know early that you'll be there. I think it'll be good for you *and* me, frankly." The implication was clear: if they knew the sometimes prickly Penn was coming to the show, Academy members might be more inclined to vote for him.

When he hung up, Roth was smiling. "Sean is coming," he announced.

"Yahoo!" said Herman.

"He wants a seat for his mother, and one for his wife. But he's not presenting. He says he thinks he'll be too nervous to do anything but sit there."

"ACT ONE, it's all comedy and sex," Roth told dozens of Oscar staffers who had filled the Kodak's lower lobby for a production meeting. "Act two, still all comedy and sex."

For about fifteen minutes, Roth laid out his vision of the Oscar show: young, fast, funny . . . and pretty long. "Less than four hours," he promised. "More than three."

While Roth was trying to add new wrinkles to the show, ABC had added a first of its own: the network was putting the show on a five-second delay. The move had been prompted by Janet Jackson flashing a breast during the recent Super Bowl halftime show—a bit of allegedly accidental exposure that turned out to be not just another symptom of the coarsening of pop culture, but the watershed moment at which a cross-section of concerned citizens, moral arbiters, and cultural overlords decided that enough was enough.

The board of governors objected to ABC's decision, but decided not to fight it. Roth tried to lobby Disney CEO Michael Eisner, for whom he'd once run the studio, but he found his old boss preoccupied with a takeover bid and a stockholder revolt. "I tried to talk to Michael Eisner this morning to complain about the five-second delay," Roth said at the meeting, "but he's got other things on his mind."

As distressing as Janet Jackson's breast had apparently been to some Super Bowl viewers, so were many of the advertisements that ran during the game itself. There were numerous ads for products that promised to cure erectile dysfunction; there was a Budweiser ad that featured a dog biting a man's crotch, another that centered around a horse farting. These, however, did not concern the Academy. Budweiser may have been a sponsor of the Oscars, but the Academy prescreened every commercial that ran during its show; if the ad didn't pass muster, it didn't air.

The reasons for this had less to do with good taste than with a long-standing attempt to avoid the appearance of favoritism or impropriety. The Academy had long ago taken control of the show's advertising, largely to ban movie ads or spots that featured any of the night's nominated actors. In 1985, the Academy refused to let Coca-Cola run ads that used the nominated song "Ghostbusters" unless they also produced ads featuring the other four nominated songs. Even Disneyland couldn't advertise on the show, because its name contained the name of a movie studio.

"The feeling is that for one night, we are really trying to be about the art of motion pictures, not about the business of motion pictures," said Bruce Davis. "If you're selling them at the same time that you're honoring the art, it blurs the message. We're a little prim about this stuff, but we do maintain a certain amount of decorum." (They also restricted advertising to about half an hour over the course of a three-and-a-half-hour show, significantly less than most other awards shows.)

After the formal meeting ended, Roth stood at the side of the room while staffers broke into smaller groups to go over their plans. ABC was still on his mind, but it wasn't just the delay that bothered him. "The hardest part of this whole thing is the promos," he said. "They only want to show them on ABC, which has half the audience of NBC and CBS. It's like promoting a movie—if I was putting out *Mona Lisa Smile* and I could only advertise on ABC, I'd be dead."

GIVEN THE LARGE NUMBER OF DEATHS in the film community since the last Oscar show, the final round of cuts for the In Memoriam film had been particularly brutal. But the year had also seen the passing of several people who deserved to be singled out at greater length: eighteen-time Oscar host Bob Hope, four-time winner Katharine Hepburn, and two-time winner and past Academy president Gregory Peck.

In December, Roth had mentioned this to the board of governors as a reason for not bestowing any honorary awards. But like other Oscar producers, Roth had no control over the board, as he learned when its members voted an honorary award to Blake Edwards, the director of the *Pink Panther* movies.

Edwards arrived at the Kodak on the Wednesday of Oscar week. Although the honoree was eighty-three years old, Roth was determined that his segment could still be fast and funny. He approached Edwards about a stunt that would take its cue from Peter Sellers's slapstick physical comedy in *The Pink Panther* and its sequels; although he'd recently injured his foot and was getting around by using a wheelchair and a cane, Edwards agreed. With the help of a pretaped segment, a souped-up wheelchair, a breakaway wall, and a stuntman who looked like Edwards, the director would appear to lose control of his wheelchair, shoot across the stage, and crash through a wall on the far side.

The veteran stuntman Mickey Gilbert would do the dirty work. Edwards would be waiting with Roth behind the wall, ready to emerge when presenter Jim Carrey came to get him. "If I had to guess," said Roth as he stood onstage watching preparations, "I'd say that Jim will drag or fireman-carry Blake onto the stage."

The producer dismissed the idea that it might be inappropriate to drag an octogenarian lifetime-achievement winner onto the stage, or to turn an honorary Oscar presentation into a stunt. The crowd that gathered around Edwards as he sat in the wings, meanwhile, just wanted to see something funny. Among the stagehands and bystanders, Jim Carrey and Billy Crystal jockeyed for position.

The stunt would open with a shot of Edwards sitting in his wheelchair in the wings. When Carrey introduced him, he'd push a control button on the armrest and then act shocked as the chair took off with unexpected force. Horvitz wouldn't be shooting that portion until Friday, but on Wednesday the director needed to work out his shots, and Edwards needed to practice looking shocked.

He did so several times, reacting as a stagehand yanked on a cord to pull the wheelchair out of the camera frame. When one take drew an exaggerated but appropriately horrified look from Edwards, the crowd around him burst out laughing.

"That's great!" laughed Carrey.

"That is *so* funny," added Crystal.

Carrey turned and grinned at his fellow funnyman. "We're looking at our future, you know," he said.

THE NEXT DAY, Steven Spielberg stood on the stage of the Kodak, frowning as he looked at the card he'd just pulled out of a rehearsal envelope. In the truck, Horvitz waited for Spielberg to read the name on the card. In the audience, fourteen stand-ins waited to see which of them would be going onstage to pretend he'd just won the Oscar for best picture.

But Spielberg couldn't do it. "You want me to read this?" he said uneasily. "*Really?*"

He showed the card to stage manager Garry Hood, who was standing nearby. FOR THIS REHEARSAL ONLY, it read, THE OSCAR GOES TO *THE LORD OF THE RINGS: THE RETURN OF THE KING*.

"Yeah, just read it," said Hood, who knew that the name was there completely by chance.

Spielberg, though, just couldn't bring himself to bestow any early kudos on the movie that had become a prohibitive Oscar favorite. "It's obvious it's going to win," he muttered. "Should I really?" Then inspiration struck. "The Oscar goes to *Cat on a Hot Tin Roof*," he said. "Lawrence Weingarten, producer."

In Hollywood, few handicappers would have quarreled with Spielberg's take on the race. Other studios had tried to battle Peter Jackson's monster: for several weeks, TV ads for *Mystic River* featured Clint Eastwood talking about how his movie was "a really fine piece of material for actors, it's not about special effects," which was essentially a quieter way of saying, "Filthy hobbitses, we hates 'em." But Eastwood's film had failed to pick up any momentum through the early rounds of critics' and guild awards. There were still questions in the best-actor category, where Bill Murray was considered a strong bet to knock off front-runner Sean Penn, while Johnny Depp had scored a stunning win at the Screen Actors Guild awards. But aside from the occasional grumble about the twenty minutes of false endings that concluded *The Return of the King*, that movie's preeminence wasn't even threatened by the usual whispering campaigns. *The New York Times* dubbed it "the cleanest, most aboveboard, most decent Oscar race in years," and then added, "and the most boring."

"In a lot of ways, the competition has been a little more gentlemanly this year," agreed Bruce Davis. "Which is good, because the board is in a mood where, if something really underhanded had come up, they were clearly prepared to rule that a picture is not eligible as best picture. And until somebody gets that death penalty, there will be a tendency to push the edges."

The year's most blatant infraction came late in the game from Spielberg's company, DreamWorks. Trade ads on behalf of Shohreh Aghdashloo, a supporting-actress nominee for *House of Sand and Fog*, reprinted features that had run in several magazines, including *Rolling Stone*. "Will win: Renée Zellweger," they read. "Should win: Shohreh Aghdashloo." Miramax, the aggrieved party in an Oscar dispute for once, charged that the ads broke the unwritten rule of never attacking an opposing candidate. DreamWorks immediately apologized and pulled the ads, and the Academy decided not to penalize the company.

Back at the Kodak, Spielberg finished his rehearsal and stood in the wings watching a monitor with Joe Roth. "That's a beautiful set," he said. Then he turned to Roth. "Is there going to be anything on *The Passion of the Christ?*" he asked quietly of the movie that had made a staggering $23.6 million in its first day, while causing an outcry over what some saw as its anti-Semitism.

"Billy might do a couple of jokes," said Roth. "But not much."

Spielberg nodded. "Good," he said. "That's good."

FRIDAY WAS LARGELY devoted to music, which was not necessarily good news for Roth. The nominated songs worried him and put a serious crimp into his plans for nonstop sex and comedy. While the likes of Elton John, Pearl Jam, and Bono had been passed over, the nominees were a largely slow and somber group. Two of them, "The Scarlet Tide" and "You Will Be My Ain True Love," were mournful ballads from *Cold Mountain*. Another, "Into the West," was a stately tune from *The Return of the King*. The fourth song, "A Kiss at the End of the Rainbow," was an intimate, intentionally clichéd love song from the Christopher Guest spoof *A Mighty Wind*; the actors who performed it in the film, Eugene Levy and Catherine O'Hara, planned to do it at the Oscars in character.

The final song was the only up-tempo tune of the bunch, but "Belleville Rendez-Vous" was far from a guaranteed crowd-pleaser. A slight, jazzy ditty from the art-house animated French film *The Triplets of Belleville*, the song had been performed in the movie by a group of unknowns. Roth and Herman tried to interest Destiny's Child in the Andrews Sisters–style tune, then turned to Bette Midler; when those overtures failed, they went with the original performers, songwriter Sylvain Chomet and a French-Canadian chanteuse named Betty (pronounced Be-*tee*.)

If it worked, "Belleville Rendez-Vous" could be fun. More problematic were the *Cold Mountain* songs—old-fashioned ballads written by Sting and by Elvis Costello and T Bone Burnett, and meant to evoke the Civil War music of the South.

Burnett, a highly respected producer and performer who had also produced the best-selling soundtrack to *O Brother, Where Art Thou?*, was arranging and trimming the songs, and he'd recruited both Sting and Costello to perform them along with Alison Krauss, the young bluegrass singer who handled lead vocals on both.

Roth figured the best way to deal with the two songs was to perform them together, along with the similarly yearning song from *The Return of the King*, which was sung by Annie Lennox. The songs were almost agonizingly deliberate and austere; Sting's in particular was little more than a stylish drone. If Roth's goal was to produce a fast, young, and funny Oscar show, a medley of "You Will Be My Ain True Love" and "The Scarlet Tide" was the antithesis of what he wanted: the songs were slow, they were written to sound 150 years old, and they were dead serious. When the numbers were performed back to back, with a surprisingly lengthy break between them to slightly change the instrumentation and replace Sting with Costello, their stillness and glacial pace caused frowns at the production table.

To give the songs an extra kick, Roth had planned to bring all the participants together for an encore on a short, jubilant gospel song, "Liberty," which would be led by the Sacred Harp Singers from *Cold Mountain*. But at the last minute Lennox decided she didn't want to appear in the encore, making it so unwieldy that Roth decided it should be cut from the show.

As Krauss rehearsed her songs one final time, Jack Black and Will Ferrell arrived for their own late-night rehearsal. Oblivious to the fact that Krauss was onstage, the two comics walked down the front row, checking out seat cards and turning to talk to an MTV film crew that trailed Black. It was an instructive tableau: the singer that Roth was forced to book tried to negotiate her intimate, haunting songs one last time, while the comic he would have preferred wandered in front of her, drawing all the attention as he went.

STAR DAY was ordinarily something of a ritual, but Joe Roth didn't put much stead in rituals. He quickly did away with a couple of the day's more ceremonial aspects: he asked the photographer assigned to shoot him with stars to back off ("What am I going to do, put them on my wall?" he asked, entirely rhetorically), and shunned the usual format in which the producer remained in his office while a procession of stars were taken to see him every fifteen minutes.

"It felt like being sent to the principal's office," he said before taking a seat in the wings with writer Jon Macks and a woman who made changes in the TelePrompTer copy. "I've been sent to the principal's office before, and I see no need to do that to Clint Eastwood." He shrugged. "It's a working session. It shouldn't be ceremonial."

It was also a workday for Susan Futterman, who during the show would be controlling a pair of buttons tied to the five-second delay. One would bleep out any offending words; the other would change to a reverse shot of the audience in the case of any untoward exposure.

When Robin Williams showed up at the Kodak, Futterman grew particularly attentive. Backstage, the hyperkinetic comedian kept up a nonstop comedy routine that veered wildly and unpredictably from *The Passion of the Christ* to Janet Jackson's Super Bowl appearance. When he stopped to take a breath, Futterman stepped in.

"Now Robin," she said, "you have to be good."

"I will," he promised.

"No *Jesus*," she said patiently. "No *Christ*."

"No *Jesus*, no *Christ*," he repeated.

"No *goddamn*. No C-word."

"No C-word?" he said, amazed that she'd bring it up. "No shit."

After Williams left, Futterman hung around to see Jamie Lee Curtis, who took the stage and promised the small audience, "I'm going to look *so* hot. I figure that this is my last shot up here, so I am going to look so fabulous. Every single fashion rule I've ever made for myself, I'm breaking in one night."

When Curtis left the stage, Futterman approached her. "What are you going to wear?" Futterman asked anxiously. "Are your nipples covered?"

"Yes, my nipples are covered," Curtis said incredulously. Then she spotted a nearby camera crew from Oprah Winfrey's show. "Get over here!" she yelled to the crew. When they obliged, Curtis turned to Futterman.

"Ask me again," she commanded.

"Are your nipples covered?" Futterman said obediently.

"Yes, my nipples are covered," Curtis announced.

Reassured, Futterman left. Curtis turned to her assistant. "That was actually scary," she said.

AT THE END OF STAR DAY, while most of the crew was eating dinner and recharging for the dress rehearsal, Roth met with Seligman and Herman in his office. They'd spent a couple of days trimming the script and looking for ways to save time—but after a day of revisions made to satisfy the presenters, things weren't looking good.

"Well, we gained about two and a half minutes during today's rewrites," said Seligman. "Basically, everything we'd taken out is back in. The thing with Ben Stiller and Owen Wilson is longer, John Travolta and Sandy Bullock is longer . . ."

"Yeah, but it's funny," said Roth. "And now we're getting lots of pressure to put the gospel thing back in." He sighed. "Harvey's been pressuring us, I've been getting lots of calls."

"If we cut it," said Herman, "we have to cut it tonight. That's not a decision we can postpone."

"I know," said Roth. "Let's see how it goes tonight. T Bone has promised to shorten the other songs and speed them up. So we'll see. We'll look at the timings, and then we'll decide."

"We shouldn't wait for the timings to come in," said Herman. "We should decide as quickly as possible after we see the songs."

"We definitely have a time problem," added Seligman. "We're back up over 3:45, close to 3:50."

"I know your opinion, Michael," said Roth.

"I'm not expressing an opinion," insisted Seligman. "I'm just telling you the facts."

AT DRESS REHEARSAL, "You Will Be My Ain True Love" and "The Scarlet Tide" didn't appear to be appreciably faster than before, despite Burnett's promise to "blow the roof off this place." And with Lennox opting out and the encore requiring a complete reset and a new introduction from Liv Tyler, "Liberty" was spirited but jarring.

A few minutes after the songs were performed, John Hamlin walked into Roth's office with Andrea Wong, ABC's senior vice president of alternative programming and specials. When Wong ducked into Roth's rest room, Hamlin sighed. "I knew she'd be upset," he said to Angela Pierce. "But I guess if you've got to do those two songs, it's best to get them over with early in the show."

In the truck, Roth quickly decided that "Liberty" had to be eliminated. Seligman and Herman spoke to Burnett and Costello in the hallway outside the green room, where Costello fought for the gospel tune.

"I'm just making a case for the heart of the show," he insisted. "You're missing the chance to say something important."

"I understand what you're saying," said Seligman, who felt that Costello wanted to retain the song for the political statement he saw in it. "But we're at the point with this show where we just can't spare the time."

"You say you can't spare that thirty seconds, but I'm saying that thirty seconds will be a burst of energy that will impact the whole show."

"I know what the song means to you," said Seligman, "and I apologize."

"You don't have to apologize," said Burnett. "I understand."

"We all understand," said Costello. "But that song is *important*. You could be cutting thirty of the most important seconds of the show."

When Herman and Seligman left, Burnett shook his head at what he saw as the show's typical failure of nerve. "I think that Oscarosis has taken over," he said. "That's what Errol Morris called it at a party the other night: Oscarosis."

When the rehearsal ended, Garry Hood cleared the house so that Billy Crystal could show his opening movie to an audience of top staffers and Academy officials.

As he waited for the film to begin, Bruce Davis thought about the Academy's decision to move the Oscars from March to February. "Not one member has complained about not having enough time to do the initial screening process, which was our big worry," he said. "Harvey kept saying that nobody's going to be able to see all the movies, that it'll cause big problems." He laughed. "He said it so much that I was beginning to believe him."

BEFORE THE REAL STARS ARRIVED, fans in the bleachers along Hollywood Boulevard had to content themselves with the celebrity press. Just after 3:00 the day of the show, fashion guru Steven Cojocaru strutted down the red carpet, drawing a few screams. Preshow host Maria Menounos got a similar reaction for her cleavage. And E!'s Melissa Rivers drew shrieks when she flung a broken shoe into the crowd. (Immediately, bleacher dwellers began taking photos of the woman who'd caught Rivers's shoe.)

By 4:00, the star quotient was rising and Roth had taken up a position near the center of the red carpet. "Anything to pass the time," he said.

Inside the Kodak, Jamie Lee Curtis and Christopher Guest were the first celebrities to head for their seats. As show time approached, Diane Lane worked the front row. "You look *smashing*," she told Curtis, who was clad in a low-cut, strapless aquamarine gown by Monique Lhuillier. Moving down the row, Lane stopped to show Susan Sarandon how to fasten a strap on her shoe, then congratulated Scarlett Johansson.

At 5:10, announcer Andy Geller tried to get the crowd into their seats by telling them that the show would begin in ten minutes. Backstage, preshow cohost Chris Connelly prepared to conduct some live preshow interviews from his spot outside the greenroom. Roth offered to serve as a celebrity wrangler. "How many names do you need?" he asked.

"Less than five," said Connelly.

"Less than five," repeated Roth, who turned, went into the green room, and began grabbing stars. Tom Hanks was the first; as it turned out, Hanks was the only one the preshow had time to use.

In the front row, Renée Zellweger approached thirteen-year-old best-actress nominee Keisha Castle-Hughes. "You were magnificent," she said. *"Magnificent."*

With ten minutes to go, another preshow host, Billy Bush, began broadcasting from the orchestra section of the Kodak. He parroted David Letterman's unfortunate line of nine years earlier ("Uma, Oprah"), plopped into a seat between Zellweger and Nicole Kidman, then pulled Castle-Hughes out of her chair to meet Johnny Depp, on whom she'd admitted a crush. In the wings of the stage, Billy Crystal paced, got loose, and eyed Bush on the monitor. "That is the most annoying man on TV," he said.

5:30 P.M., PACIFIC STANDARD TIME: *"Live from the Kodak Theatre at Hollywood & Highland, welcome to the 76th annual Academy Awards."*

Crystal cleared his throat and walked toward the back of the stage. Jim Carrey was caught on camera as he walked to his seat in the front row, accompanied by a page.

After an introduction by Sean Connery, Billy Crystal's opening film played. Similar to Crystal's previous movies, it featured the comic inserted into scenes from many of the year's prominent movies, from *Terminator 3* to *Cold Mountain*, *Pirates of the Caribbean*, and *Finding Nemo*. By far the biggest reaction came when Michael Moore suddenly appeared during a battle scene from *The Lord of the Rings: The Return of the King*. "Stop this war!" Moore shouted, video camera in hand. "Shame on you hobbits, shame on you! This is a fictitious war!" When Moore was summarily stepped on and crushed by a huge elephant, the audience roared. In the wings, Catherine Zeta-Jones, who would be presenting the first category, watched on a monitor. "That's *so* great," she said to her escort. For the end of the movie, Crystal had tried desperately to recruit Johnny Carson to play the wise wizard Gandalf, but Carson declined and Jack Nicholson did the cameo instead.

As Crystal went into his "Wonderful Night for Oscar" medley, Zeta-Jones took her place at the rear of the stage. When he'd finished, she presented the best supporting actor award to Tim Robbins for *Mystic River*. Despite fears that his outspoken liberal politics might seep into his speech, Robbins simply thanked the cast and crew, his family, and then pleaded with victims of violence and abuse to seek help. As he walked into the wings with his Oscar, Zeta-Jones screamed with delight and grabbed him around the neck from behind.

Just after 6 p.m., *The Lord of the Rings: The Return of the King* won its first Oscar of the night, for art direction. The win drew resounding applause from the audience at the Kodak.

Robin Williams followed, and stayed away from anything Susan Futterman might have to bleep. But as he tore into the envelope containing the name of the best animated feature winner, *Finding Nemo*, Williams ripped so aggressively that he tore off a chunk of the envelope, which fluttered to the ground. On the way off the stage, Williams kept up a running line of jokes as he congratulated winner Andrew Stanton. "Dude! Dude!" he drawled in his best stoner voice. "That's so righteous!"

During the second commercial Renée Zellweger walked into the wings. A page trailed her, holding up the voluminous train of her dress. Zellweger presented the Oscar for costume design to *The Return of the King*, its second win of the night; immediately afterward, during the best-picture clip for *Master and Commander*, she was hustled back to her front-row seat. The aide followed, still carrying her train. "Oh, thanks," said Zellweger. "I could pick up some interesting things back there."

At the same time, Chris Cooper stood in the wings loosening up. Cooper shook his arms and legs, jerked his elbows, did some quick shadow boxing, rolled his neck, and opened and closed his mouth. He made a variety of guttural noises. Then, suddenly, he stopped, stood bolt upright, buttoned his tuxedo jacket, and waited for his cue.

Seven minutes after handing out an Oscar, Zellweger was back onstage to pick one up, this time as the winner in the best supporting actress category. "I am overwhelmed," she said softly, though she'd been the prohibitive favorite in the category. "I am overwhelmed." When she walked offstage, she spotted *Cold Mountain*'s executive music producer towering over the rest of the staffers in the wings. "T Bone Burnett!" she shouted.

"You did good," Burnett told her quietly, patting her arm. "You did good." Zellweger sighed and leaned into Burnett, who wrapped her in a hug. Nearby, Alison Krauss borrowed her manager's tuxedo jacket to keep warm before going onstage.

At the one-hour mark, Ben Stiller and Owen Wilson handed out the awards for short subjects. The winners for live-action short, Aaron Schneider and Andrew J. Sacks, both brandished sheets of paper as they accepted their Oscars, but only Schneider got to read his. After he'd thanked about three dozen people (including Joe Roth and Marc Shaiman for not interrupting his speech) in a breathless but dull minute and twelve seconds, Horvitz cued conductor Harold Wheeler to start the music. Sacks glared at his partner as they walked away from the microphone. Backstage, Tom Hanks left the Kodak via the loading dock. On his way out, he passed Uma Thurman and John Cusack, the only celebrity occupants of the smoking section outside the green room.

Including the time spent changing sets, the performance of the two *Cold Mountain* songs and "Into the West" took up more than ten minutes; it was, as Roth had feared, austere, ethereal, and *very* slow. In the lower lobby of the Kodak, few people in the bar or lobby paid attention to the monitors. One exception was actress Annette O'Toole, who together with her husband, Michael McKean, had been nominated for writing "A Kiss at the End of the Rainbow." O'Toole stood a few feet from one monitor, eyeing the competition in her category. Sean Penn, who'd gone to acting school with O'Toole, walked by with his wife, Robin Wright Penn. "Do you know Annette O'Toole?" he asked her; when she said she didn't, he brought his wife over to meet his old friend.

After chatting with O'Toole for a few minutes, Robin Wright Penn turned to her husband. "What do you want to do?" she said. "Go back to the seats, or get a smoke?" Penn decided he wanted to go back to his seat, but the doors were closed until the next commercial break, so he joined a large crowd at the end of the hallway that led to the seats.

A few minutes later, Joe Roth joined the crowd as well. During the commercial, he went into the theater to fetch Blake Edwards.

At the end of the break, Catherine Zeta-Jones walked backstage, finding herself behind the mogul who'd pushed her best supporting actress campaign for *Chicago*. "Hi," he said, sticking out his hand. "Harvey Weinstein, Miramax Pictures."

Zeta-Jones laughed. "Nice to meet you," she said.

Then Weinstein shrugged. "Well, at least we bring our girls home," he said. "Catherine one year, Renée the next."

At the hour-and-a-half mark, *The Return of the King* won its third Oscar, this one for visual effects. Jamie Lee Curtis stepped outside the green room, spotted a friend, yanked down the top of her dress, and flashed a breast.

The Blake Edwards stunt went off smoothly. Horvitz ran tape of Edwards sitting in the wings, then cut to Mickey Gilbert speeding across the stage, grabbing the statuette from Carrey, and crashing through the wall. Roth helped Edwards get into place behind the rubble, and the director pretended to be dazed as he followed Carrey to the microphone. "Don't touch my Oscar," he snapped at the comic.

Afterward, Roth approached Edwards and Carrey in the wings. "Great," he said. "Great," he repeated. "Great great great great great great great great great great great great great great."

Edwards smiled, but looked unconvinced.

"You got the only standing ovation of the night so far," Roth told him.

"No," Edwards said.

"Yeah," Roth insisted, "you got the only standing ovation."

Outside the stage door, Bill Murray waited for his cue to come to the stage. Behind him, an elevator door opened. Murray nonchalantly stepped backward, into the elevator. The page assigned to escort him hesitated, then stepped in with him.

"Can we go up?" asked Murray, deadpan.

"Yeah, I guess so," she said. Murray rode the elevator up, then down, then back up, killing a couple of minutes before he was due onstage.

While *The Return of the King* was winning Oscars number four and five, for makeup and sound mixing, Dency Nelson spoke urgently to Horvitz on his headset. "Lou, I'm here with Joe," he said. "Julia does not want to use the stairs center. She wants to use the stage-right ramp."

This was a major change—worse, in a way, than the last-minute rewrite Roberts had insisted upon the year before. It meant the large staircase that dominated one of Roy Christopher's most dramatic sets would go unused, that a key look would never be seen, and that two consecutive star entrances would be made in exactly the same way. If Roberts had suggested as much at rehearsal, a lengthy discussion would have ensued—but since she didn't attend rehearsal, since she made the request just before she was due to take the stage, there was no time to talk about it.

Horvitz wasn't surprised. When Roth had told him about the plans to give Roberts a big, grand entrance down the staircase, the director had been skeptical. "My experience with her," he'd told Roth, "is that she does not like to come down stairs." Roth told him not to worry. "I'll get her to do it," he said.

But Roberts wouldn't do it, not even after the entrance had been adjusted so she'd only have to walk down the last couple of steps. Horvitz immediately acquiesced; like everybody else in the crew, he knew that Roberts was a special priority for Roth. Dency Nelson showed Roberts her new, quick entrance. "Oh, thank you so much," she said. She waited in the wings for her cue, speaking quietly with Roth the whole time.

"It's now official," said Billy Crystal onstage. "There is nobody left in New Zealand to thank." He introduced Roberts, who delivered her tribute to Katharine Hepburn, then returned to the wings and watched the ensuing film package with her arm around the producer's shoulder. When the montage ended, Roberts nodded. "That's so nice," she said. She turned, hugged and kissed Roth, and apologized again for changing the entrance.

When Roberts had left, Roth turned toward the back door. "I'm going to walk," he said. But instead of heading back to the truck, he stepped out the door, lit up a cigarette, and hung around with a dozen stagehands in the smoking section. A couple of the crew members grinned and whispered about the bigwig in their midst. When the producer finally got back to the truck, Horvitz greeted him with a smile. "What a surprise," he said. "Julia didn't want to use the stairs."

Roth shrugged. "I tried," he said.

Early in the show's third hour, the Oscar for best documentary feature went to Errol Morris, the filmmaker who'd been overlooked in the past despite acclaimed films like *The Thin Blue Line* and *A Brief History of Time* (and who, according to Burnett, coined the word *Oscarosis*). After winning for *The Fog of War*, his documentary about the Vietnam War and the former secretary of defense Robert McNamara, he began his speech by saying, "I'd like to thank the Academy for finally recognizing my films." A minute later, he turned political. "Forty years ago this country went down a rabbit hole in Vietnam, and millions died. I fear we're going down a rabbit hole once again, and if people can stop and think and reflect on some of the ideas and issues in this movie, perhaps I've done some damn good here."

As Morris left the stage, Frank Pierson introduced the In Memoriam segment. The three-and-a-half minute film honored thirty men and women, from actors Gregory Peck, Hope Lange, Art Carney, Alan Bates, Gregory Hines, Ann Miller, and Donald O'Connor to controversial directors Elia Kazan and Leni Riefenstahl to experimental filmmaker Stan Brakhage and movie trailer pioneer Andrew Kuehn. In the wings, Sting and Phil Collins stood together, watching on a monitor. When composer Michael Kamen, with whom both men had worked, appeared on-screen, Sting clasped his hands together as if in prayer, and extended them toward the screen. Then he turned to Dency Nelson. "Is this show running on time?" he asked.

"We're actually not doing too bad," said Nelson, who checked the time in his rundown. "We're supposed to be at this point in the show at 7:52, and it's 7:54. So we're only two minutes over." He laughed. "Of course, let's look at the total time." He turned a page. "The show's timed at 3:43, and we're two minutes over that."

Sting and Collins presented the Oscar for best score to Howard Shore; it was the sixth win for *The Return of the King*, followed immediately by number seven when the film won the award for editing. "Did you know that people are moving to New Zealand just to be thanked?" asked Crystal.

As Jamie Lee Curtis introduced the songs from *A Mighty Wind* and *The Triplets of Belleville*, Jim Carrey, Will Ferrell, and Jack Black analyzed Oscar swag in the hallway outside Roth's office. "Dude, did you get the gift basket from this thing?" asked Black.

The giveaway had undergone a physical downsizing; where hard goods once filled mammoth baskets, the new one was an elegant valise that contained a plethora of vouchers. It may have lacked the most astonishing offer of the previous year's basket—free Botox injections—but the new one made up for that with lots of travel, including a week in New Zealand, this time with airfare included.

But the vouchers were strictly nontransferable. "There's a lot of great shit that you can't give away, that's the bummer," Black continues. "There's, like, twelve trips . . ."

"All to Mexico," added Ferrell.

"Yeah," said Black. "Trips to Cabo, and you can't give any of 'em away." He turned to Carrey. "Are you going to the ball?" he asked.

"No," said Carrey, laughing. "I'm blowing that shit off."

A little after eight o'clock, Tom Cruise arrived at the loading dock and headed straight to the green room. In the wings, Charlize Theron and Catherine Zeta-Jones checked out each other's outfits: Theron in beaded Gucci, Zeta-Jones in a red silk-chiffon Atelier Versace. "You could *not* be more beautiful," Theron said.

Zeta-Jones laughed, returned the compliment, and then turned the conversation to acting. "I loved you in *Monster*," she said. "It was wonderful."

"Oh, you're more talented than me," said Theron.

"No," demurred Zeta-Jones.

"No, really," insisted Theron. "You do more things really well. You should hear *me* sing."

Zeta-Jones made it back to her seat in time for Black and Ferrell, who sang what they claimed were the lyrics to the song used to play winners off when their speeches run overtime: "No time to thank your parakeet / You're boring / Look at Catherine Zeta-Jones / She's snoring . . ." As Black and Ferrell read the nominees for best song, Catherine O'Hara and Eugene Levy were led toward the stage, where a camera could catch their reaction in the unlikely event that "A Kiss at the End of the Rainbow" won. It didn't: instead, the award went to "Into the West," number eight for *The Return of the King*.

"Awww, it's that *Lord of the Rings* movie," grumbled O'Hara good-naturedly as she walked through the crowd in the wings. "It's a sweep!"

Behind her, Annie Lennox came offstage accompanied by cowriters Fran Walsh and Howard Shore. "This is one hell of a night," said Lennox, who was beaming from ear to ear.

A few minutes later, *The Return of the King* picked up another award, for best adapted screenplay—its ninth out of nine nominations, in a category in which the competition was tough. With only two categories remaining, best director and best picture, the film was suddenly almost a sure thing for an unprecedented eleven-for-eleven sweep.

First, though, Sofia Coppola won the original screenplay award for *Lost in Translation*. When she walked offstage, she became the first winner to receive a round of applause in the wings—an ovation led by Tom Cruise, who greeted her as soon as she left the stage. A minute later, though, Cruise was even more enthusiastic in handing the best-director Oscar to Peter Jackson.

When Jackson came offstage, stage manager Doug Smith told the director about the ending Roth had envisioned: all the night's winners on the stage, mingling as the credits rolled. Because Jackson was nominated for best picture, he couldn't remain backstage with the rest of the winners—and while it was looking like a sure thing that he'd be onstage with the final award of the night, Smith couldn't take any chances.

"At the end of the night," he told Jackson, "if you're still in your seat, we're going to invite you up onstage as a winner."

"Right," said Jackson. "And I'll bring the other Oscars with me."

In a break with tradition, the best-actor and best-actress awards were presented in between best director and best picture. The decision had been made months earlier, when Roth and his staff were considering the effects of a possible *Rings* sweep: "We didn't want to have the same group come to the stage two or three times in a row," he said. "It felt like it would take all the drama out of the end of the show."

The best-actress award came first; as expected, Charlize Theron won. A minute later, Blake Edwards was led into the wings to wait alongside the night's other winners. "Charlize won for *Monster*," his assistant told him.

"Good," said Edwards.

Slowly, the wings grew crowded with men and women toting Oscar statuettes. Theron asked for a tissue, then congratulated Edwards. Howard Shore walked by with a pair of Oscars. "I'm so happy," he sighed.

The final commercial break took place a few minutes before midnight, East Coast time. "When we return, the Oscar for actor in a leading role," said announcer Andy Geller. "And also coming up, Steven Spielberg and the winner for best picture." For Roth, this was a victory: he'd known for days that his show would be longer than three and a half hours, so his goal had been to make sure that announcer Geller could tease the final two awards before midnight in the East.

To begin the show's last act, Sean Penn won the best-actor award and was greeted with a standing ovation. When he left the stage, Nicole Kidman chased him down, shouting, "Sean! Sean! Take this!" She handed over the envelope bearing his name, a souvenir all winners were given along with their statuettes.

Just past midnight, East Coast time, Steven Spielberg opened the night's final envelope. The name inside was the same as in his rehearsal envelope three days earlier, but this time Spielberg didn't balk. "It's a clean sweep!" he announced. "*The Lord of the Rings: The Return of the King.*"

As Peter Jackson dragged ten cast and crew members onto the stage with him, Geller gave the stats: the eleven Oscars tied with *Titanic* and *Ben-Hur* for the most ever won by a movie. The former film, though, lost in three of the categories in which it was nominated, the latter in one; the previous record for a sweep was *Gigi*'s nine-for-nine in 1959.

"Remember," said Billy Crystal at the end of the night, parroting a TV ad campaign for Las Vegas. "What happens at the Oscars, stays at the Oscars." The night's winners, spread out across the back of the stage, stayed in a long line rather than mingling; it wasn't until Horvitz went to the usual package of show highlights that they began to socialize.

Annie Lennox, still beaming, walked across the stage to say hello to the four diminutive actors who played hobbits in Jackson's epic: Elijah Wood, Sean Astin, Billy Boyd, and Dominic Monaghan. Astin spoke into his cell phone, then handed it to Wood. As the hobbits celebrated, Clint Eastwood remained in the aisle near his seat, speaking quietly to a handful of friends.

Backstage, Susan Futterman was all smiles. "Never used the button," she said. "Isn't that wonderful? We were well prepared, but we never used it. That's the way we like it."

As the last stragglers left the Kodak and headed for the parties, the stage was nearly deserted. Downstage center, stuck to the floor, was a shred of the best animated feature envelope; Robin Williams had torn it off when he ripped open the envelope, and it had been there ever since.

Over in the Renaissance Hollywood Hotel, in a foyer outside the press rooms, Sean Penn stood with his wife and his mother and wiped away a few tears. Tim Robbins and Susan Sarandon passed around a cell phone. And Peter Jackson, waiting his turn in front of the cameras, took off his glasses and wiped his forehead with a tuxedo-clad forearm. "I need a Coke," he sighed.

Standing with Jackson, Steven Spielberg laughed. "Oh, it's not over yet," he said to the new Oscar winner. "You know what gets tired? You think it's your legs that'll get tired, but it's not." He nodded toward the glittering statuette clutched in Jackson's sweaty hand. "It's your arm. Your arm gets tired holding it."

THE DAY AFTER THE OSCAR SHOW, South African president Thabo Mbeki officially congratulated Charlize Theron for winning the country's first Academy Award, calling her life and her victory "a grand metaphor of South Africa's move from agony to achievement." In New Zealand, Prime Minister Helen Clark said the *Lord of the Rings* sweep made it "an incredibly proud day to be a New Zealander."

DreamWorks took out a full-page trade ad congratulating Renée Zellweger on her best supporting actress Oscar. Opinions were divided on whether the ad was a good-faith gesture because Zellweger was providing voiceovers for the studio's upcoming animated film *Shark Tale*, or an apology for the Shohreh Aghdashloo ads that had targeted Zellweger.

Ratings for the show were good, almost one-third higher than the previous year's war-deflated numbers, and slightly better than the 2002 figures. The audience was also younger and more male than for the past few Oscar shows.

Joe Roth pronounced himself pleased. "I enjoyed it very much," he said. "The two big challenges were the music, which worked out as well as it could, and the fact that there was a movie that won eleven awards. So the same music was played and the same people were thanked all night." He laughed. "Halfway through, when *Lord of the Rings* clearly was going to sweep, I felt like the producer of a Super Bowl who had a 61–0 score at halftime, trying to figure out how to keep it going."

The most amusing part of the experience, he said, was finding out how many people thought that Blake Edwards himself had crashed through the wall. (In his *Daily Variety* column the next day, Army Archerd called it "the big scare of the night.") "Ninety percent of the people I talked to thought it was Blake in the chair," Roth said. "Even people in the special effects business, which I thought was kind of wild, didn't realize that we had pulled the old bait and switch."

Andrew Sarris, a critic who Roth said was a hero of his, reviewed the show in *The New York Observer* and called it "the funniest and least tedious in memory." After noting that the show had received a considerable number of what he thought were mysteriously negative reviews, Sarris concluded, "As far as this old critic's concerned, Mr. Roth, you did a fine job."

And yet, despite the fact that Roth had booked young comics, pushed hard on the promotional front, even turned the presentation of an Oscar into a sight gag, the format itself was subject to an unusual amount of scrutiny. In the days after Roth's show, the two leading Hollywood trade papers, *Daily Variety* and *The Hollywood Reporter*, ran articles suggesting that it might be time to revamp the entire Academy Awards presentation. The *Reporter* article was written by Robert Osborne, who had recently published the Academy's official chronicle, *75 Years of the Oscar*. His piece, headlined IT'S TIME TO RETHINK OSCAR'S BIG NIGHT, suggested that the Academy consider handing out the awards at a banquet, the way they'd done until World War II (and, though Osborne didn't point it out, the way the Golden Globes did it). In *Variety*, an unsigned editorial lambasted "the predictability of the kudocast," said it was "hobbled by fundamental limitations of format and protocol," and offered a few suggestions: no more awards for shorts, no clips of the best picture nominees, less shtick from the host.

Roth thought about it a month after the show, and conceded some of the points. "You are constrained somewhat," he said, "by the elements you're given and the things you can't change."

The review committee focused on many of the usual concerns, including the length of the show and the question of whether the In Memoriam segment still made sense at a time when nearly every other awards show also trotted out a similar device. It also focused on the thank-you speeches, always a sore spot. In the past, Pierson had seriously suggested getting thank-you lists from all nominees, and running those lists on a crawl at the bottom of the screen as winners made their way to the stage; this time, he turned his attention to the fact that only about two-thirds of the nominees make it to the nominees' luncheon, and the ones who don't often give the longest speeches. The committee agreed to make a video compiling good and bad acceptance speeches, and send it to all future nominees.

In March, the board of governors voted to stick to the accelerated schedule and hold the 77th Academy Awards on February 27, 2005.

In June, the Academy made public for the first time the roster of those who'd been invited to become new members. Frank Pierson released the list of what he said were 127 "remarkably accomplished" film professionals in an attempt to disprove the widely held view that most Academy members were old and out of touch. The list of actors included recent nominees Shohreh Aghdashloo, Keisha Castle-Hughes, Patricia Clarkson, Scarlett Johansson, Sean Penn, and Ken Watanabe, along with Maggie Gyllenhaal, Viggo Mortensen, and Paul Bettany. Sofia Coppola was invited to join by both the writers' and directors' branches, though Academy rules stipulated that she could only choose one.

The following month, the organization conducted its annual review of the rules governing Oscar campaigning. Citing the relatively genteel nature of the past campaign season, the board introduced only one significant new rule, which prohibited "specific and disparaging references to other pictures or individuals competing in a given category."

Epilogue

The Oscar Gods

"IT'S A STRANGE SHOW," said Frank Pierson slowly. Sitting in his office on the top floor of the Academy headquarters, flanked by framed posters from his films *Cool Hand Luke*, *Cat Ballou*, and *Dog Day Afternoon*, the president of the Academy thought about the three Oscar shows that had taken place during his tenure, and the countless others he'd seen during his forty-six years in the business. "I think that it's gotten better over the years—and if it has, the one who deserves the most credit is Gil because he's really developed the awards show format. But it's strange."

He trailed off, then chuckled. "Mike Nichols and I were going to do the show one year, and we both quit," he said, remembering the forty-second Oscar show, in April 1970, for which he and the noted stage and film director Nichols had originally been hired. "We were still conceptualizing, very early in the process, when we started feeling that we were failing, and that we weren't going to be able to do what we wanted to do."

Pierson grinned. "We couldn't figure out how to do it," he said. "As

Mike said, 'Every time we got a show going, some asshole had to hand out an Oscar.' "

FOR THE THREE AND A HALF DECADES since Pierson and Nichols were stymied by the Oscar assignment, a succession of others have grappled with the same problems. Joe Roth's Academy Awards looked a lot like Laura Ziskin's Academy Awards, which looked a lot like Richard and Lili Zanuck's Academy Awards, which looked a lot like Quincy Jones's Academy Awards. And all of them looked a lot like Gil Cates's Academy Awards. The format, created decades ago and refined by Cates in the early 1990s, was inescapable and to a large degree inalterable: two dozen awards, film clips, five songs no producer can choose.

Certainly, the Oscars do change—but more slowly and more incrementally, perhaps, than the pop culture, the media culture, the corporate culture, in which they reside. To some, particularly some within the Academy, the deliberate pace with which the show accommodates the world around it is a sign of strength, inviolability, and incorruptibility. It would be unseemly, after all, for the august institution to drop awards, chase demographics, ditch the grand old format in pursuit of this year's model. Better to retain the template, as confining as it may be, and let producers tinker with it, sometimes drastically but more often not.

"Complaints about the format raise a deeper philosophical issue," said Pierson. "Is this simply a show we put on to raise the money to do the good work that the Academy does? If that's the case, then you put on the best show that you possibly can, and anything that doesn't entertain the audience is out the window. If you were going to be hardheaded about the whole thing, you'd say that the documentary shorts and short subjects don't belong on the show, and we should give them along with the scientific and technical awards on another night, or during the commercials. Or are the Oscars our annual tribute to the best work for our members and others around the world in the arts and sciences of motion pictures? If that's what they are, then those other awards absolutely belong."

He shrugged. "It's a question the Academy has yet to clearly answer one way or another. So in the meantime, the show remains something of a hybrid. And, of course, another word for *hybrid* is *mongrel*."

The Academy, then, has heard the complaints and knows the limitations of its show. The board might someday eliminate some or all of the three awards for short films; they considered that in the past, and almost did it once. But for years it seemed inconceivable that the Academy would ever move any of the other awards into a pre-show or to a separate ceremony, a step tantamount to admitting that some branches of the Academy are more important than others. Those were moves no producer could expect, though many might have wished for them.

BUT THEN CAME the Academy Awards of February 2005, when suddenly some Oscar certainties started appearing significantly less certain. In the months before the show, odds did not look good for high ratings. None of the nominated movies (*Million Dollar Baby*, *The Aviator*, *Ray*, *Sideways*, *Finding Neverland*) were close to being *Titanic-* or *Lord of the Rings*–scale blockbusters. Ratings for other awards shows in the winter of 2004 and 2005 had been little short of catastrophic: the Grammys, for instance, dropped nearly 30 percent, to its lowest number in ten years. And the nominated songs weren't the kind that'd lure viewers. Passing over Mick Jagger's "Old Habits Die Hard," which had won the Globe and would have given the Oscar show a bona fide rock legend, the music branch nominated a slate that included one tune sung by a boys' choir entirely in French ("Vois Sur Ton Chemin," from *Les Choristes*) and another sung in Spanish by the Uruguayan singer-songwriter Jorge Drexler ("Al Otro Lado Del Río," which had been buried deep in the end credits of *The Motorcycle Diaries*.)

Retaking the reins of the Oscar show, Gil Cates knew that it was a year for drastic steps, a time to attempt the kind of overhaul that other producers may have occasionally had the nerve to envision, but never had the clout to carry out. Well aware that he had to first win over the Academy, he went before the board of governors and posed a simple question: do you want to do things the way they've always been done, or do you want to try to improve the ratings?

The board opted for ratings, so Cates made his moves. He ditched the five best-picture clips, long a staple of Oscar shows but an expendable element when similar clips had already been seen countless times by any viewer remotely interested in the competing movies. He also abandoned the policy of booking the original performers to sing nominated songs, instead asking the biggest mainstream star he could find, Beyonce, to tackle three of the five. (If the choice had made musical sense, he would have liked to have given her all five.)

But the move that attracted the most attention was Cates's choice of comic actor Chris Rock as host. Best known for his uncensored HBO specials and for his gigs hosting shows like the MTV Movie Awards and the Grammys, Rock was not one to hold his tongue. At one awards show, he appeared onstage following a performance by the band Good Charlotte to sniff, "Good Charlotte? Sounds more like mediocre Green Day to me." Clearly, Rock posed something of a risk, and not just because his stand-up routine was usually sprinkled with four-letter words. "People talk about Chris cursing, but that's just a smoke screen," suggested Cates. "They're really worried about Chris saying what he thinks about the performers or the winners."

In the weeks after Rock's appointment, the Drudge Report briefly created a stir by bringing up the new host's comments about how straight black men never watch the Oscars. Other comments of Rock's slipped by almost unnoticed, such as his suggestion that the thing he'd bring to the Oscars that other hosts didn't was "weed," or his explanation of eligibility rules for the Academy: "If you're darker than a paper bag, you can't get in."

Still, Cates and the network figured that the comic was a pro who knew his audience and would behave once the time came. More problematic, at least for some inside the Academy, was Cates's decision to overhaul the way some Oscars would be handed out. He floated some of the same proposals that had been suggested by Quincy Jones and David Salzman almost a decade earlier, though those first-time producers had seen their ideas immediately dismissed by the Oscar vets. Cates, on the other hand, had far too much history and too much clout to be so easily dismissed—so the Academy consented when he announced that he'd like to hand out some awards in the aisles, and in other categories bring all the nominees onstage before the envelope was opened.

The new approach, of course, could have been seen as imposing a hierarchy, making some categories more important than others and denying certain winners that glamorous if lengthy and terrifying walk to the stage. As word spread, Cates received his share of phone calls, along with a memorable letter that read, "On behalf of all the nominees, you're an asshole."

Thursday night, three days before the Oscar show, the producer tried to sell the new approach to the nominees in the three categories who'd receive their Oscars in the aisles, and the seven others in which all the nominees would assemble onstage. All eighty-six nominees had been invited to come to rehearsals at the Kodak, one category at a time; when the first group was assembled, Cates addressed them.

"Congratulations, everybody," he began. "Let me tell you what this is all about, because there's been so much misunderstanding. It's been my hope for the last several years to get more of the nominees on camera. Since I've been doing the show we've gotten the producers on camera, and the cinematographers and the writers. My goal is to be able to show every nominee."

In truth, this was only part of the reason for the new approach. Cates did want to get more nominees onscreen, but the move was also designed to eliminate time-consuming walks to the stage by anonymous filmmakers who'd likely be seated fifteen or twenty rows back. He also simply wanted to shake up the look and feel of the show, to try something unexpected and new.

In front of the nominees, though, Cates emphasized the first reason, and then offered a bonus. "Normally, the limit on speeches is forty-five seconds, and I hope you keep to it," he said, lowering his voice conspiratorially. "But because you're this close to the microphone, you can take another five or six seconds." Cates repeated his sales pitch nine more times over the next couple of hours, and most of the nominees seemed ready to give the experiment a shot. The sound nominees were predictably the prickliest, though Cates made another concession and allowed them to rewrite their own intro.

Chris Rock, meanwhile, used his rehearsal time to run through some of his monologue, which included jokes about how there are only a handful of real movie stars in Hollywood ("Clint Eastwood is a star; Tobey Maguire's just a boy in tights"), how producers who can't get Russell Crowe shouldn't settle for Colin Farrell, and how those who can't get Tom Cruise shouldn't settle for Jude Law. "Who is Jude Law?" he asked. "Why is he in every movie I've seen for the last four years?" For the most part, though, the comic dispensed with his real material and paced the stage, looking into the audience and grinning wickedly as he mocked many of those whose names and faces he spotted on the seat cards.

"Cate Blanchett, everybody," he said, rehearsing his introduction of the nominated actress. "I still don't know who the fuck she is." A minute later: "We couldn't get Daniel Day-Lewis, so here's Jeremy Irons!" Then, to introduce the actress who'd be presenting the foreign language award: "A couple of years ago she won an Oscar, was a big star. What the fuck happened? Ladies and gentlemen, Gwyneth Paltrow!"

Throughout his three rehearsals, Rock's barbs continued to fly, though they were always aimed at stars who weren't yet on the premises. Only one luminary avoided his scorn—the one who was backstage, and whose rehearsals had been among the tensest and most tightly controlled of all. "Beyonce," he said, looking at the diva's card. "I'm not going to say anything bad about her, or she'll come out here and kick my ass."

During his final rehearsal, on the morning of the show, Rock gleefully ripped most of the stars who'd be in attendance, then smiled. "I say this out of love," he insisted. "Like Don Rickles."

That night, Rock toned down his act and lost some of the edge that had made his rehearsals so uncomfortably entertaining. Cate Blanchett became "Academy Award nominee Cate Blanchett," Jeremy Irons was "comedy superstar Jeremy Irons," and Gwyneth Paltrow simply merited a joke about the unusual name she'd given her baby daughter: "Our next presenter is the first woman to ever breastfeed an Apple." Still, some stars were visibly ill-at-ease during Rock's monologue, wary of being caught laughing at their colleagues on camera. And Sean Penn, when he took the stage to present the best actress award late in the evening, felt compelled to defend one of Rock's first targets: Jude Law, he announced, is "one of our finest actors."

Afterward, opinions were divided on the quality of the relatively defanged Rock's act, but ABC was happy: ratings fell over the previous year by less than five percent, a strong showing considering the movies in contention (*Million Dollar Baby* having been the big winner) and the dramatic hits taken by other recent awards shows.

One reason for the better-than-expected ratings may have been the show's timing: at three hours and fourteen minutes, it was the shortest Oscar show in twenty years. "All the stuff that Gil did to speed the show up worked," said ABC consultant John Hamlin afterward. "Doing the awards in the aisles, not doing the best picture clips . . . It all worked."

Still, Hamlin's point of view was not a unanimous one, with opinions widely divided over what *Entertainment Weekly* dubbed the "glitch-filled, vaguely experimental Oscars." Some people liked the awards that were presented in the aisle, where each nominee got a close-up, but felt that grouping everyone onstage as the envelope was opened was awkward and demeaning. Others liked the camaraderie of the onstage presentations, but found the in-audience awards rushed and uncomfortable.

In the aftermath, Cates received kudos from the Academy's review board, but also heard some of the most critical post-show comments he'd ever received. David Geffen, for one, called to tell the producer that he thought it was the worst Academy Awards in years. And Geffen's Dream-Works partner Steven Spielberg weighed in as well, informing Cates that he didn't like the way some winners were denied their walk to the stage. "I don't know why Spielberg was so concerned with those people getting to walk down the aisle," Cates said, "but he was."

IN THE END, then, Cates's grand, nervy overhaul was still an Academy Awards show: big, long (if not judged solely against other Oscar shows), sometimes slow, and reliant on what Cates calls "the Oscar gods."

"As a producer, you're dependent on so much that's beyond your control," says Bruce Davis. "You can script what the presenters are going to say and where the songs are going to go. But what people remember about the evening is what those winners say. And you have no control of how much thought they've given it, whether they're going to say something wonderful or brilliant or funny or heartbreaking. If you get two or three of those moments in the course of that *looong* three-and-a-half-hour epic, people remember it as a great show. If you get just one of those, people say, 'Ah, nothing happened!' And there's nothing the producer can do."

Cates got those moments with Jack Palance and Cuba Gooding, Jr.,

Quincy Jones got them with Kirk Douglas and Christopher Reeve, Laura Ziskin got them with Denzel Washington and Halle Berry. On those nights, the Oscar gods were in attendance. Other years they went to bed early.

It has now been fifteen years since Allan Carr shook up the Academy Awards and took a big fall. The Academy of Motion Picture Arts and Sciences is in the homestretch of its first hundred years, with lots of money in the bank and plans that reach well beyond the dispensing of gold statuettes. Outside, the battle rages over campaigning, positioning, and cashing in on Academy Awards. Inside, the Academy fine-tunes its rules, imposes the occasional penalty, and holds to its position—its naïve, perhaps foolish, but entirely admirable position—that it's all about the artistry. And somewhere, the man who paved the way for the past decade and a half of Oscar shows has to smile as he sees what has come to pass: amped-up promotion, supermodel fashion shows, trophy boys, green rooms sponsored by *Architectural Digest*, and a theater designed like a European opera house sitting at the back of a Hollywood mall. Occasionally, Carr is even remembered along the way—sometimes as the producer who failed, but once in a while, maybe, as a fabulous showman just a little ahead of his time, the unfortunate victim of what might have been a bad rap.

One such moment of remembrance took place on Saturday, March 25, 1995, two days before the sixty-seventh Oscar show. Gil Cates had been in charge of the ceremony for six years; it was midway between Carr's debacle and his death. David Letterman was hosting the show that year, and earlier in the evening he'd rehearsed much of his material. He'd raffled off a car, showed a film with New York City cab drivers, and presented another in which a series of big stars ran variations on the line "Would you like to buy a monkey?" Plus he'd introduced a Stupid Pet Trick.

At about 11 p.m., Bruce Vilanch walked into the production office upstairs in the Shrine Exhibition Hall. The writer, who'd gotten his Oscar start on a certain show six years earlier, sat down at his desk, shook his head, and broke into a beatific smile.

"Did you like the spinning dog?" he asked. "I want to send a tape of it to Allan Carr, along with a note that says, 'And to think, you got in trouble for Snow White. How times have changed.' "

Acknowledgments

"I'D LIKE TO THANK THE ACADEMY"—isn't that how Oscar thank-yous always begin? And in this case, I certainly would like to thank the Academy. But plenty of others also deserve my gratitude, and since there's no flashing TelePrompTer and no stickman to play me off, I'm going to violate protocol by pulling out a long list.

This book began with Howard Karren, an editor at *Premiere* magazine, who in early 1994 asked if I'd be interested in writing about the inner workings of the Academy Awards show. As I recall, the story was assigned to be five thousand words in length, though Howard and I both knew that if we got the access we wanted, it would end up far longer than that. Six months and about thirty thousand words later, Howard found himself staring at a manuscript considerably heftier than he'd expected, or wanted. But he liked it enough to go to bat for it—and to my surprise and great pleasure, Susan Lyne, the founder and editor-in-chief of *Premiere*, wanted not only to run the story relatively intact, but to turn it into an annual feature. I must start by thanking both Howard and Susan. At *Premiere*, thanks also to Chris

Acknowledgments

Connelly, Anne Thompson, James Meigs, Kathy Heintzelman, Leslie Van Buskirk, Sean Smith, Kristin Lootens, Christine Spines, Charlie Holland, Catriona Ni Aolain and Peter Herbst—plus, of course, the many fact-checkers who every year waded through page after page of indecipherable scrawls from dozens of reporter's notebooks.

The photographers who shot the Oscars for *Premiere* put up with far more restriction and interference than I did, and continually produced remarkable work despite the many obstacles. Thanks to Lara Jo Regan, who inaugurated the assignment and shot the first four years; to David Strick and Antonin Kratochvil, each of whom took over for a year; and to Art Streiber, who adroitly handled the gig for the last five years. Additional thanks to Art's assistant, Armando Gonzalez, and to their intrepid Academy escort, Steve Streich. Several others also helped secure the photographs used in this book: Aaron Rath, Lori Reese, Marion Durand, Helene Lagrange, and Gabriela Kratochvil.

My agent, Sarah Lazin, helped focus my thinking and offered invaluable advice on how to turn a batch of magazine articles into a book. Denise Oswald, my wonderfully sympathetic and supportive editor at Faber and Faber, understood what I wanted to do and kept me on track as I tried to figure out how to do it. Thanks also to Sarah Almond at Faber and Faber.

The Academy of Motion Picture Arts and Sciences did not authorize or approve this book. All the same, I could not have written it without the support and cooperation of the Academy. My thanks go to Academy presidents Arthur Hiller, Robert Rehme, Frank Pierson, and Richard Kahn, to executive director Bruce Davis, and to executive administrator Ric Robertson. Particular thanks are due to John Pavlik, a reliable, honest, and effective supporter of the project for more than a decade. Thanks also to Leslie Unger, Toni Thompson, Kim Tamny, Jane La Bonte, Frank Lieberman, and Bob Werden; I know that many times their publicists' instincts argued against giving a writer the kind of access I had, but they did so anyway. At the Academy's archives, thanks to Jeff Gough and Snowden Becker.

Many of the staff and crew who worked on the Oscars were of invaluable assistance, both by sharing stories and by not kicking me out when I got in the way. They include Louis J. Horvitz, Jeff Margolis, Robert Z. Shapiro, Bruce Vilanch, Buz Kohan, Hal Kanter, Carrie Fisher, Roy Christopher,

Acknowledgments

Robert Dickinson, Chuck Workman, Mike Shapiro, and Douglass M. Stewart. Also Don Was, Boyce Miller, Eva Demergian, Mike Thomas, Anat Reichman, Daniel Salzman, Lynn Padilla, Capucine Lyons, Dina Michelle, Julie Kaneko Hall, Angela Pierce, Colleen King, and many others over the years, a few of whom I'm sure I've forgotten. Special thanks to the stage managers, in whose domain I spent a great deal of time: Garry Hood, Dency Nelson, Rita Cossette, Peter Margolis, and particularly Debbie Williams.

Danette Herman is admirably zealous in protecting the stars who trust and depend on her, but she nonetheless granted me access to her terrain with grace and good humor. Michael Seligman likewise made sure I always had what I needed—this despite the fact that he was inexplicably and unfortunately edited out of my first *Premiere* story back in 1995.

This book could not exist without the cooperation and forbearance of the men and women who have produced the Oscar show: Joe Roth, Laura Ziskin, Quincy Jones and David Salzman, and Richard and Lili Fini Zanuck.

The most essential producer to the project, though, was Gilbert Cates. I met Gil in January 1994, when he was in the midst of producing the sixty-sixth Oscars and I had the task of persuading him to give me unfettered access; after we spoke for about fifteen minutes, he shrugged and said, "Okay, let's do this." From that point on, Gil's commitment was as total as it was crucial. He is a man of integrity and class, without whose help this book would have been impossible. I also owe an enormous debt to Gil's press rep, Chuck Warn, who shepherded me through the complexities of the Oscars with an insight and wit I could not have found elsewhere. If my errors of misinterpretation and indiscretion occasionally made things difficult for Gil and Chuck—and I know that there were times when they did—I can only offer my apologies, and offer profound thanks for making this possible.

Final thanks, of course, have to go to the two people who learned many years ago that they wouldn't be seeing me very much come mid-March (later mid-February)—and that when they did see me, likely as not I'd be distracted by production schedules and unreturned phone calls. This is for my wife, Mary, and my son, Adam.

Index

Aaliyah, 175, 183
Abdul, Paula, 10
Academy of Motion Picture Arts
and Sciences, 12–13, 16, 34, 54,
67, 79, 84, 132, 160, 200, 274, 275,
321, 385, 387–89, 390, 394; actors'
branch of, 94; allocation of tickets
by, 55; Awards Presentation Review Committee of, 35, 315–16,
351–52; and anti-Communism,
195–96; and performances of
nominated songs, 205, 267, 330–
31; and theft of Oscar statuettes,
232, 236; board of governors, 25,
35, 221, 281–82, 322, 366; and
budgets for telecasts, 12, 225, 256;
campaign rules of, 72, 108, 352–
53, 384; cinematography branch

of, 294, 346; computer hackers
and, 225–26, 229–30; date
changed for awards ceremony by,
352, 373; directors' branch of, 385;
documentary branch of, 282;
earthquake at headquarters of,
38–39; film archives of, 143; history of, 17–23; hosts and, 28–29,
69, 98–99; and In Memoriam
segment, 166, 252; income of, 12,
23; independent films and, 140;
membership policies of, 22, 30,
135, 385; Motion Picture Association of America and, 52, 358;
music branch of, 29, 99, 221;
nomination process of, 22, 39–41,
73–74, 99–100, 190–91; preshow
produced by, 211; presidents of, 4,